Kindred Strangers

PRINCETON STUDIES IN AMERICAN POLITICS:
HISTORICAL, INTERNATIONAL, AND COMPARATIVE
PERSPECTIVES

SERIES EDITORS

IRA KATZNELSON, MARTIN SHEFTER, THEDA SKOCPOL

Kindred Strangers

THE UNEASY RELATIONSHIP BETWEEN POLITICS AND BUSINESS IN AMERICA

David Vogel

PRINCETON UNIVERSITY PRESS

PRINCETON, NEW JERSEY

Library of Congress Cataloging-in-Publication Data

Vogel, David, 1947–
    Kindred strangers : the uneasy relationship between politics and
business in America / David Vogel.
        p.   cm. — (Princeton studies in American politics)
    Includes bibliographical references and index.
    ISBN 0-691-02746-3 (alk. paper)
    1. Business and politics—United States.   2. Corporations—United
States—Political activity.   3. Industrial policy—United States.
I. Title. II. Series.
JK467.V643   1996
324'.4'0973—dc20   95-42251
                                                                        CIP

This book has been composed in Baskerville

Princeton University Press books are printed on acid-free paper
and meet the guidelines for permanence and durability of the
Committee on Production Guidelines for Book Longevity of the
Council on Library Resources

Printed in the United States of America by Princeton Academic Press

1 3 5 7 9 10 8 6 4 2

For Charlotte Vogel
and in memory of Harry Vogel

CONTENTS

PART THREE: *The Dynamics of Business Power*

ACKNOWLEDGMENTS

I WOULD LIKE to express my appreciation to my editor, Peter Dougherty, for suggesting this project and to my good friends, Theda Skocpol and Martin Shefter, for encouraging me to pursue it. I also want to thank Dennis Quinn, Graham Wilson, and David Yoffie for their constructive comments on the introductory essay.

The chapters in this book are reprinted by permission from the following sources:

Chapter One: *Business Journal of Political Science*, VIII:1 (January 1978).

Chapter Two: *Public Interest*, Summer 1983.

Chapter Three: *California Management Review*, Fall 1992.

Chapter Four: Steven Wills and Maurice Wright (eds.), *Comparative Government-Industry Relations*. Oxford: Clarendon Press, 1987.

Chapter Five: *Political Science Quarterly*, Winter 1980–81.

Chapter Six: *Lobbying the Corporation*, Basic Books 1978.

Chapter Seven: *Business Ethics Quarterly*, January 1991.

Chapter Eight: *Journal of Public Policy*, vol. 10, no. 4, 1991.

Chapter Nine: *British Journal of Political Science*, vol. 17, part 4, 1987.

Chapter Ten: *British Journal of Political Science*, January 1983.

Chapter Twelve: B. Bock et al. (eds.), *The Modern Corporation: Size and Impacts*. New York: Columbia University Press, 1984.

Kindred Strangers

THE STUDY OF BUSINESS AND POLITICS

IN 1959 Robert Dahl wrote that "for all the talk and all the public curiosity about the relations between business and politics, there is a remarkable dearth of studies on the subject."[1] Dahl based his observation on a survey of journal articles and dissertations in political science during the 1920s, 30s, and 50s. Had he examined management research published during this period, he would have reached a similar conclusion: management textbooks and journals all but ignored politics and public policy.

Much has changed in the last thirty-five years. There is now a substantial body of literature on the relationship between business and government in the United States. Social scientists have explored the interaction of business and government in a wide variety of areas. Many business schools have also made the study of business, government, and society an important focus of teaching and research. But although much has been written about business-government-society relations in the United States, the full scholarly potential of this subject has yet to be realized. The study of business has not emerged as a distinctive subfield within political science, while only a handful of political scientists teach at business schools. Nor has the intellectual gap between the study of politics in business schools and the study of business in political science departments been bridged. In this sense, Dahl's paradox remains half-true.

This is particularly unfortunate because the study of the relationship between business and government has never been more important. The contemporary triumph of capitalism has made corporations the most important non-governmental institutions not only in western democracies, but globally. We are now dependent on business and government to address a wide variety of critical issues and problems, ranging from the protection of environmental quality to the provision of medical care and the dissemination of information technology. It has therefore become critical that we better understand how these institutions interact with one another. Business is too important to occupy its present marginal position in political science.

The first part of this essay examines the principle areas of contemporary research on business-government relations. Part two places the pieces in this volume in the context of this literature. These essays demonstrate the importance of placing the politics of business in both a historical and comparative framework and in integrating research on politics and management. The concluding section develops an agenda for future research on the interaction of business and government.

CURRENT RESEARCH

The considerable increase in research on business-government relations over the last quarter-century stems from a number of factors. They include: the ongoing debate over business power, the substantial increase in business political activity itself, the increased availability of data on corporate campaign finance, the expansion of the political agenda to include more policy areas that affect business, the changing pattern of interest-group representation, the globalization of the American economy, and the heightening of public expectations of business.

The Power of Business

One important strain of contemporary research on the politics of business stems from the rather heated debates about the distribution of power in America that began during the late 1960s and early 1970s in both political science and sociology. Business, many critics of American society claimed, was not simply another interest group, competing with other organized and unorganized interests for political access and influence. Rather, they argued that business was unique: its needs and interests dominated those of all other institutions and organizations in American society, including government.

These critics explored the sources and scope of business dominance as part of their more general critique of American democracy and pluralism. Drawing on both Marxism and the tradition of power-elite research inspired by C. Wright Mills, they argued that the close social and ideological ties between economic and political elites, the dependence of the state on "business confidence," and the ability of business to define and thus limit the terms of public debate made a mockery of American pluralism.[2] Their depiction of the political power of business in America was in turn challenged by other scholars on both substantive and methodological grounds.[3]

This debate over the sources and extent of business power in capitalist societies was revitalized in 1977 with the publication of Charles Lindblom's *Politics and Markets*.[4] Undoubtedly the most influential study of business-government relations published in the United

States during the last two decades, Lindblom's work put the analysis of business political dominance back on center stage. It also stimulated a number of other studies on the sources and the extent of business power, most of which have tended to support Lindblom's portrait of the power of business in capitalist democracies.[5] More recently, some scholars have attempted to move beyond generalizations about the nature of business influence in capitalist democracies and have attempted to specify the circumstances under which particular firms, sectors, and business inter-industry coalitions are able to influence political outcomes.[6]

Business Political Activity

The study of business by political scientists has also been affected by the significant changes in business political activity that have occurred since the early 1970s. In their now classic study of corporate lobbying and the American trade policy published nearly thirty years ago, Bauer, Pool, and Dexter were struck by the low level of business participation in national politics.[7] Many of the firms they studied had made no effort to communicate their policy preferences to members of Congress. Indeed, many had difficulty figuring out their preferences in the first place. Business lobbyists, for their part, had few resources and tended to be ill informed. Consequently, business appeared to have little impact on the passage or content of trade legislation.

It is clear in retrospect that one reason for the relative lack of research on business political activity through the 1960s was the paucity of such activity.[8] Not surprisingly, a common critique of pluralism during the 1960s was that the real sources of business political influence were hidden from public view. According to Bachrach and Baratz, business exercised power primarily by defining the terms of political debate and controlling the political agenda; accordingly, the extent of business political activity was neither an important source nor an accurate measure of its political influence.[9] Indeed, business was so influential precisely because the real exercise of its power was hidden.

However, during the 1970s the political activity of American business at the federal level increased substantially. Acting both independently and collectively, corporations became highly visible and sophisticated participants in the political process. Attempting to influence the political agenda and policy outcomes, they hired large numbers of lobbyists and lawyers, opened Washington offices, established and funded political action committees (PACs), expanded the size of their governmental relations staffs, developed sophisticated strategies for influencing public opinion, and learned how to mobilize the "grass roots." This historically unprecedented level of business political activity at the federal level shows no signs of abating. Business political mobilization has become a permanent feature of contemporary American politics.[10]

It remains debatable whether devoting additional resources to influencing public policy and public opinion has made business more powerful; indeed, especially since the early 1980s, much business political activity has been directed at challenging the interests of other firms. But in any case, by making the exercise of its power more overt, business has certainly made it easier for scholars to both describe and measure it. The result has been numerous studies of the patterns of political activity and influence of individual companies, trade associations, and interfirm coalitions and organizations.[11]

Campaign Finance

A related factor that has strongly influenced the study of business-government relations over the last two decades is the increased availability of detailed information on corporate campaign spending. Thanks to changes in federal campaign contribution laws, the 1970s marked the first time in American history that scholars had access to detailed information on business contributions to candidates and political parties. The extent to which the emergence of PACs since the mid 1970s has affected business political influence remains controversial. But there is no question that corporate PACs have transformed both the manner and the extent to which business political activity is studied.

The availability of detailed data on the funds raised and spent by corporate PACs has led to studies not only of the impact of campaign spending on legislation but also on variations in the level of political activity among particular firms and industries. PAC data have also been employed to produce sophisticated quantitative studies on the significance of regional, sectoral, and ideological differences among firms. Indeed, precisely because corporate campaign spending can be so readily quantified, studies of business campaign finances have come to dominate contemporary scholarship on business political activity, organization, and influence.[12] During the past fifteen years, more articles have been published in political science journals on corporate PACs than on any other aspect of business political activity.

The Expansion of the Political Agenda

A fourth development shaping the study of business-government relations has been the expansion of the national political agenda. Thirty years ago most firms were affected by relatively few federal policies. It is not coincidental that two of the most important studies of business and the political process written prior to 1965, *American Business & Public Policy* and *Politics, Pressures and the Tariff*, both deal with the same political issue, namely, trade policy.[13] Throughout much of American history, setting tariff rates has been among the most important—and contentious—federal policies affecting business.

Trade policy remains extremely important and continues to be extensively studied by political scientists.[14] But it now represents only one of many areas of federal policy in which business firms have an important stake. Especially significant has been the major expansion of government regulation, especially in the areas of health, safety, and the environment. Consequently, government regulation of business has emerged as an important area of study within political science, with environmental politics becoming a significant public policy subfield in its own right.[15] In addition, there have been substantial changes in the nature and scope of economic regulation, long one of the more stable areas of public policy. A number of other policy areas which directly affect business, including tax, energy, and technology policy, have also come to occupy a more prominent place on the political agenda. Consequently, political scientists have produced a considerable literature on how these public policies both affect and are affected by business.[16]

Interest Group Representation

Both the increased interaction between business and government as well as the expansion of business political activity that occurred during the 1970s were part of a much broader transformation of American politics. The number of interest groups increased, the political agenda expanded and became more unstable, and interest groups developed new strategies to influence public policy.

Although relatively few students of interest groups and the policy process have addressed business political organization or business-government relations per se, their research has often included a business component. Consequently, studies of the changing role and nature of interest groups in American politics as well as on the dynamics of the political agenda have contributed to our understanding not only of the nature and significance of business political activity but also of broader changes in the dynamics of business-government relations.[17] In addition, the literature on public interest lobbies has illuminated the important role of these organizations in affecting public policies toward business.[18]

Comparative Political Economy

The study of business-government relations in the United States has also been influenced by the revival of the field of political economy. The study of political economy has a long and distinguished intellectual history—indeed, no contemporary scholar has yet produced a work comparable in scope or significance to Shonfield's 1964 *Modern Capitalism*.[19] Due in part to the increasing salience of economic issues within both international and domestic politics, this field expanded significantly during the 1970s.[20] The globalization of the American economy during the last quarter-century, accompanied by periodic concerns about its international "competitiveness," has provoked a lively debate about the relative strengths and weaknesses of the American state in general and the American pattern of business-government relations in particular vis-à-vis other capitalist nations. This in turn has stimulated studies that critically examine American policies toward industry, many by placing it in either a comparative or international context.[21] In addition, it has engendered a number of cross-national studies of the political organization of business which include a focus on the United States.[22]

Changing Public Expectations

A final strain of contemporary research on business and public policy derives from management education. The second half of the 1960s was characterized by significant changes in the social and political environment of business. Large corporations found themselves under intense public criticism: they were accused of promoting or condoning racial discrimination, neglecting the inner cities, supporting repressive regimes from Latin America to South Africa, despoiling the environment, and profiting from the war in Vietnam. Critics of business organized product boycotts, protested at annual meetings, filed shareholder resolutions, and published exposés of corporate policies and practices. At the same time, the newly formed public interest movement began to press for more government regulation.

These developments, coming after more than two decades of substantial public support for business and in the midst of an unprecedented period of national prosperity, caught most managers by surprise. The standards by which the public evaluated the performance of business appeared to have suddenly changed, and managers seemed to be unsure as to how to respond to these new expectations and pressures. What were the practical implications of the revival of public demands for "corporate social responsibility?" Precisely to whom and for what should managers consider themselves responsible? How could companies reconcile the pursuit of their economic objectives with these new social and political demands?

The result was the creation of a new area of management research and teaching: the interdisciplinary field of "business, government, and society" and the related field of business ethics.[23] Both have grown substantially during the last quarter century.[24] Much of this literature describes and critically evaluates the responses of firms to the economic and political pressures of their various constituencies or "stakeholders."[25] It has also explored the meaning of corporate social responsibility and the social and political significance of corporate philanthropy.[26]

APPROACHES TO BUSINESS-GOVERNMENT RELATIONS

The twelve articles and essays in this volume by no means exhaust the contemporary study of business-government relations in the United States. They do, however, illustrate a number of different approaches to this subject. They address three broad topics: the distinctiveness of American business-government relations, the contemporary political and social environment of business, and the nature of business political power. Three important themes underlie these essays. The first is the importance of historical analysis. These essays demonstrate the need to place the analysis of contemporary developments in business-government relations in an appropriate historical context. The second is the value of comparative research. The study of business-government relations in America stands to benefit significantly from the extent to which scholars also examine parallel developments in other capitalist nations.

The third is the importance of interdisciplinary research. While most of these pieces were published in political science journals or in volumes edited by political scientists, one-third were either published in management journals or were written primarily for management audiences. Rather than separate the two, this volume integrates them around a set of common themes, demonstrating the value of forging a link between the study of business by political scientists with the study of business, government, and society by students of management.

America in Comparative Perspective

In 1974 and 1975, *New York Times* business editor Leonard Silk and I undertook a study of the political views of American corporate executives. In the course of listening to several hundred chief executive officers at a series of conferences sponsored by the Conference Board, I was struck by the vehemence with which they denounced the role of government. Some of this hostility was clearly a function of the political and economic environment of the mid 1970s. Not only was the United States in the midst of the most severe economic downturn of the postwar period, but the substantial increase in Democratic representation following the 1974 Congressional elections had led to fears of a "veto-proof" Congress.

However, the views I heard were actually neither unique nor novel. Distrust and suspicion of public authority have been a recurrent feature of American business ideology since at least the 1840s. Nor was this animosity toward government simply rhetorical. Rather, it reflected two distinctive features of the political economy of the United States, namely, the limited role of the federal government in shaping the pattern of American economic development and the relative openness of the American political system to demands from nonbusiness constituencies. Both date from the nineteenth century and in many important respects remain true today.

Chapter 1 can be seen as part of the literature on American "exceptionalism," a large and diverse corpus which includes works ranging from *The Liberal Tradition in America* by Louis Hartz and *Modern Capitalism* by Andrew Shonfield, to *American Politics: The Promise of Disharmony* by Samuel Huntington and *Protecting Soldiers and Mothers* by Theda Skocpol.[27] My essay attempts to describe and explain one particular dimension of American exceptionalism: the persistence of an "adversary relationship" between business and government.

This is not to suggest the absence of important areas of cooperation between business and government in the United States. Nor is it to ignore the existence of conflicts between business and government in other capitalist societies. Rather, it is to argue that *compared to other capitalist nations*, there has been relatively less cooperation and more mistrust between economic and political elites in the United States. Thus Galbraith's popular depiction of the American political economy as a "new industrial state" characterized by close cooperation between "big business" and "big government," continues to describe other capitalist nations, especially those in Asia, more accurately than it does the United States.

On a number of important dimensions, the overall scope of government economic intervention has declined in capitalist societies since the early 1980s, making America's pattern of limited government and reliance on market forces less distinctive than it was two decades ago. Nonetheless, compared to their counterparts in other capitalist nations, firms in America remain less dependent on and consequently more independent of government. In this sense, American business is still "freer" than in any other major industrial nation.

An "adversary culture" characterizes not only significant aspects of the relationship between business and government, but also the political relationships among firms themselves. The organizational structure of the business community or capitalist class has long fascinated many sociologists (though fewer political scientists). The former have produced a steady stream of research that purports to describe various mechanisms of class or intercorporate unity to buttress their portrait of a powerful and unified business elite. These include kinship ties among the members of family controlled firms, corporate interlocks, and common sources of bank financing.[28]

Intriguing as this kind of evidence may be, I argue that the operation of these integrative mechanisms is overshadowed by the strong centrifugal forces that lie at the core of the American business system. The priority that American owners and managers attach to preserving their autonomy extends not only to their relationship to government, but also to each other. Compared to other capitalist nations, the distribution of both political and economic power within the American business community remains highly fragmented; it is a "community" in name only. Both cross industry or "peak" associations, and trade associations are weaker in the United States than in other capitalist societies. Equally important, America's large and efficient capital markets provide multiple sources of access to financing, thus enabling firms to remain relatively autonomous and keeping economic decision-making relatively fragmented.

Probably no other area of public policy so clearly illustrates the strength and persistence of the adversarial relationship between business and government in the United States as environmental regulation. During the last quarter-century the scope of environmental regulation has expanded significantly in all advanced industrial societies. All affluent nations more strictly regulate business decisions that affect the physical environment as well as public health than they did in 1970. For the most part these regulations address relatively similar problems and in many cases impose comparable standards.

But while environmental problems and compliance standards may be similar across national boundaries, chapter 2 argues that the American *style* of regulation—the way protective regulations are made and enforced—remains distinctive. These differences are particularly striking when compared to Great Britain's regulatory style, which is far more typical of other capitalist nations. The British experience suggests that there is nothing inherently legalistic, coercive, or highly conflictive about either the making or enforcement of environmental regulation. That it has taken this form in the United States reflects not only the historical pattern of mistrust between government and business, but the unusual access of American environmental organizations to political institutions, especially the courts.

The defining political feature of contemporary government regulation in the United States is the lack of administrative discretion. Unlike in other capitalist nations, where regulatory bureaucracies enjoy considerable autonomy, their decisions in the United States, whether responsive or detrimental to business interests, are subject to a highly legalistic, often politicized, and usually prolonged system of "review." The periodic efforts to "reform" the regulatory process in the United States have invariably floundered because neither business nor public interest groups are willing to permit any diminution of their ability to challenge agency decision-making. The American style of regulation, like its British counterpart, is deeply rooted in both political culture and political institutions.

The distinctiveness of business-government relations in the United States also emerges from the comparative study of business ethics, the focus of chapter 3. As in the case of environmental regulation, the ethical behavior of business managers has become a focus of increased public concern in nearly every capitalist nation in recent years. In virtually every country this increased visibility has been driven by a number of highly visible and publicized scandals involving prominent business leaders, politicians, or governmental officials.

Yet no capitalist nation approaches the United States in the intensity of public concern with the moral conduct of its business managers. Nor has any other nation undertaken such a vigorous effort to expand the definition of white-collar criminal behavior or to punish white-collar criminals. More laws and regulations affecting managers carry criminal penalties in the United States than in any other capitalist nation. And more American managers have been subject to these penalties, which often include prison terms, than in all other industrial democracies combined.

This particular dimension of American "exceptionalism" is in large measure rooted in America's Protestant heritage—a heritage which believes in the compatibility of ethics and profits and which expects those who have wealth to use it responsibly. Ironically, it may be precisely because Americans have such high expectations of business conduct that they become so outraged when these expectations are not met—as is invariably the case. In any event, the emergence of business ethics onto the American political agenda has exacerbated both public mistrust of business and business mistrust of government.

In the cases of environmental regulation and the definition and prosecution of white-collar crime, there are signs that some of the differences between the United States and other capitalist nations are diminishing. As environmental movements have gained political strength in a number of capitalist nations, primarily in northern Europe, the regulatory process has become more adversarial. And as a result of the increasing role of the European Union in shaping national regulatory policies, European environmental regulation has become more legalistic. At the same time, the prosecution of white-collar crime in Europe has recently increased.

Accordingly, each of these dimensions of American business-government relations—the adversarial relationship, the American style of regulation, and the American approach toward business ethics— are best understood in dynamic rather than static terms. They constitute benchmarks that can be used to trace patterns of convergence and divergence in the relationship between business and government in the United States and other capitalist nations over time. Equally important, they demonstrate the value of studying the experiences of other capitalist nations in order to better understand America.

The distinctive relationship between business and government in the United States has implications not only for business regulation but also the international performance of American firms. During the 1980s a rather heated debate emerged over whether the United States could or should develop an industrial policy, perhaps along the lines of Japan, America's most successful industrial competitor. Many argued that the "weakness" of the American state, specifically its inability to coordinate business investment in critical sectors, represented a source of competitive disadvantage for American firms.[29]

However, chapter 4 argues that the relative weakness of the

American state has been exaggerated. The United States government has managed to pursue a number of sectoral or industrial policies in areas such as defense, agriculture, medical technology, aerospace, and housing. The pattern of growth and development in each of these sectors has been heavily dependent on government support. What distinguishes the United States is not so much the *existence* of government support for industry but rather its unique *structure, extent,* and *purpose.* In contrast to other capitalist nations, government support for business in the United States has been more limited, relatively ad hoc, and relatively decentralized. It also has often been motivated by purposes other than international competitiveness, such as national security or public welfare.

Moreover, during the critical decade of the 1980s the American state proved to be far stronger and more independent of society than many observers had predicted. Notwithstanding strong domestic political pressures, it refused to interfere with the massive reorganization of the American business system brought about by a combination of international competition and the emergence of a market for corporate control. In retrospect this restructuring has substantially strengthened the international competitiveness of important segments of American industry. Chapter 4 thus offers a political explanation for some of the significant improvements in the performance of American industry that became noticeable during the 1990s. We may now be in a better position to appreciate some of the important strengths of America's distinctive approach to government intervention in the economy.

The Political and Social Environment of Business

Arguably, one of the most important changes in the relationship between business and government in the United States during the last twenty-five years has been the emergence of the public interest movement. Through their influence over the political agenda and access to both the courts and the Congress, environmental and consumer organizations have become important sources of countervailing power to business. Their ability to give voice to previously underrepresented interests has, ironically, made American society much more pluralist than it was when "pluralism" enjoyed its greatest influence as a depiction of American politics during the 1950s and 60s.

Chapter 5 places the political strategy of the contemporary public interest movement in a historical context. It argues that this movement can be distinguished from its New Deal predecessor in its attitude toward public authority. While seeking to strengthen the ability of government to control business, the public interest movement also has invested considerable political effort in strengthening its independence from government: hence the emphasis it has placed on the right to sue regulatory agencies in the courts. The importance the public interest movement has attached to promoting political "participation" in the regulatory process can be seen as a reflection of its deep-seated fears of regulatory "capture" by corporate interests.

Political scientists have written extensively on the ideology and organizational structure of public interest organizations and their impact on public policy. But largely because they have tended to reify politics by identifying it with government, they have neglected one of the movement's most important and original contributions to American politics: its efforts to challenge business *directly*. Acting on the assumption that business itself constitutes a system of power or "private government"—one whose power is comparable, if not greater than, that of the "official" government—activists have also frequently lobbied the corporation itself.

For example, they have organized boycotts of companies whose social performance they disliked, researched and published exposés of corporate policies, filed shareholder resolutions to challenge various corporate policies in both the United States and overseas, and pressured institutional investors, primarily churches, foundations, universities, and public sector pension funds, to either vote their shares against management or divest their stock as a form of political protest.

The origins of this tactic, which is described in chapter 6, lay in the civil rights movement in the 1950s and 60s and the antiwar movements of the 1960s and 70s. The contemporary civil rights movement began with the Montgomery bus boycott, while Vietnam War protestors directly attacked Dow Chemical for producing napalm. During the 1970s and 1980s, antiapartheid activists employed a variety of political tactics in their largely successful campaign to pressure American firms to withdraw their investments from South Africa. In recent years, the use of "direct" pressures to injure, or at least embarrass, companies has become increasingly common.

While the economic impact of this politicization of the consumer and shareholder role has been limited, its political impact has not. Consumer boycotts have successfully challenged business decisions ranging from the killing of dolphins by tuna fish processors to the marketing practices of infant formula producers in developing countries. Equally important has been the increasing popularity of social or ethical mutual funds which subject investment decisions to various social or political screens—positive as well as negative. More generally, the "rating" of companies according to their social performance has become a sizable cottage industry, resulting in innumerable lists of corporate heroes and villains.[30]

These initiatives reflect an increase in public sophistication about the social performance of large companies. Instead of regarding "big business" as one amorphous or undifferentiated mass, critics of business are increasingly distinguishing among companies, critically evaluating and comparing various aspects of their social performance with that of other firms. And many companies, in turn, have attempted to differentiate themselves from their competitors or deflect public criticism by emphasizing their social commitment to protecting the environment, promoting women and minorities, and improving the communities in which they do business.

These developments are related to a much broader phenomenon, namely, the revival of both public and academic interest in the subject of business ethics. Both academic and popular writing on business ethics, and the related subject of corporate social responsibility, has expanded enormously over the last decade.[31] Much of this literature has little or no political content; it consists of either condemnations of business behavior or exhortations to managers to behave better on the (usually mistaken) grounds that "good ethics is good business."

But chapter 7 suggests that the reemergence of public debate about the social role and ethical behavior of business has also raised a number of important issues that touch at the very core of capitalism as an ethical system. For example, what is the actual relationship between ethics and profits? At what point does profit-seeking become profiteering? Should we care about the motivations of business managers or only the social consequences of their decisions? Each of these issues has become the subject of lively and often heated debates both within the business community and between business and other constituencies. And the way these debates have been resolved has often had important political implications, as Congressional approval of a "windfall" tax on oil company profits during the 1970s demonstrates.

At the same time, the politics of government regulation have become increasingly complex. It is no longer possible—if it ever was—to understand the politics of health, safety, and environmental regulation as pitting virtuous representatives of the *public* interest against self-interested companies motivated only by profit. The notion that companies often attempt, and frequently succeed, in using the regulatory process to collect rents from the public or maximize their profits at the expense of their competitors has long been widely recognized by students of regulation.[32] What has been less widely observed is that the obverse is true as well: not only do companies sometimes support the expansion of social regulation, but, on occasion, consumers oppose it.

Chapter 8 describes four occasions in which consumers successfully mobilized to repeal or weaken regulations designed to protect them. Their efforts were often supported by business and opposed by consumer organizations. This particular constellation of political forces remains rather unusual; numerous other protective regulations, many of which provide far fewer benefits to consumers than these, have been challenged primarily by business. Nevertheless, these four cases do illustrate the unpredictability and growing complexity of the regulatory process. They also suggest the emergence of an important political gap between public interest groups and those citizens whose interests they purport to represent—one which is likely to expand as protective regulations increasingly come to regulate the behavior of individuals as well as companies. To the extent that consumer and environmental regulations are weakened this is likely to be due not only to the political influence of large firms but also to the political mobilization of consumers, property owners, and small businessmen.

The Dynamics of Business Power

As suggested at the outset of this essay, the degree of power exercised by business has long been a subject of intense and frequently polemical debate among social scientists. The four concluding essays in this volume seek to contribute to this debate by challenging the view that business dominates the political process in the United States.

The way political scientists write about business power has changed substantially since the late 1960s and early 1970s. Since the mid 1970s, most writers on business political influence have either assumed or argued that business firms exercise disproportionate influence over the governmental process. Of particular importance has been the highly visible "conversion" of two of the discipline's most influential pluralists, namely, Robert Dahl and Charles Lindblom. Chapter 9 criticizes the "new" views of business power of both these scholars.

Ironically, the academic popularity of the "privileged position" school coincided with the most sustained and effective challenge to the political power of business in America during the postwar period. The argument of chapter 10 is that it is misleading to view corporate power as stable or static. What is more important is to examine how much and why its political effectiveness varies over time.

Chapter 11 employs this approach to compare the power of business in different capitalist societies during the last three decades. It does so by examining the extent to which it has fluctuated over time. It concludes that, by this measurement, American business has actually fared *worse* than its counterparts in most other major capitalist nations.

If, according to Lindblom, the political position of business is "privileged" in America, one is left wondering what language would be appropriate to describe the political influence of business in Japan, a nation with much weaker sources of countervailing power to business and in which a political party closely identified with business faced no serious electoral opposition for more than three decades. My point is not that business does not enjoy substantial political influence in every capitalist society; it is rather that the *variations* in its influence—both over time and across different countries—are equally important. Accordingly, the portrait of the dynamics of business influence that underlies the "structural dependence" argument is simplistic.[33]

Chapter 12 approaches the study of business power from a longitudinal perspective: it presents case studies of four "rounds" of federal clean air legislation. This essay demonstrates that numerous factors affect the ability of business firms to get what they want from Congress, not just their economic importance or degree of political activity. Moreover, the interests of business itself are frequently divided, thus significantly diluting the political effectiveness of its lobbying and grass-roots organizing. Understanding the dynamics of coalition-building, both among firms and industries and between business and nonbusiness constituencies, is essential to any analysis of the extent and scope of business power. Business power cannot simply be studied as an abstraction; its influence needs to be empirically demonstrated.

FUTURE RESEARCH AGENDA

We have clearly learned much about the relationship between business and government in the United States during the last three decades. However, the intellectual fragmentation of this field has prevented it from realizing its full intellectual potential. This fragmentation has two dimensions, one within political science and one between political science and schools of management.

Notwithstanding all that has been written during the last quarter-century on various aspects of business-government relations, the subject itself has not become a distinctive subfield within political science. There are no institutional or organizational vehicles that bring together American scholars with a common interest in this topic. The study of business-government relations has not developed a distinctive research agenda, one capable of capturing the imagination or inspiring the work of each generation of political scientists. Not surprisingly, over the last two decades, only a handful of political scientists have specialized in this area, and their number shows little sign of growing.

To be sure, many political scientists have written about various aspects of the politics of business. But they have done so primarily in the context of other intellectual agendas or disciplinary subfields. And precisely because they do not see themselves as engaging in a common intellectual enterprise, these scholars rarely draw or build upon each other's work. Thus students of environmental or policy or economic deregulation are unlikely to be familiar with recent scholarship on business campaign spending. Nor are scholars who write about American trade or technology policy familiar with research on the sources of business power or the changing patterns of interest-group mobilization. As a result, we have made relatively little progress in developing a more sophisticated theoretical understanding of business-government relations.[34]

The study of business-government relations has also suffered from the lack of communication between political scientists interested in business and students of management interested in politics. In contrast to the situation in political science, the study of business, government, and society—and the related area of business ethics—*has* developed into a distinctive subfield within business schools.[35] Business school faculty have produced a considerable body of research on how companies manage (or, as is frequently the case, mismanage) their political and social environment. Their work describes how companies have responded to continual changes in their political and social environment and how they have attempted to use the political process as a source of competitive advantage. They examine how investment, production, and marketing decisions both shape and are shaped by political and social pressures, how companies have reacted to consumer boycotts and public and media criticism, and how they have attempted to use public and community relations and corporate philanthropy to enhance their political effectiveness and market performance. This literature draws upon the fields of corporate strategy, business ethics, and business and society to fill in the critical "black box" of how business manages a variety of aspects of its "nonmarket" or "external" environment—an environment which includes, but is not limited to, its relationship with government. It thus takes seriously the notion of the corporation as a political and social, as well as an economic institution.

Unfortunately, much of this research has taken the form of cases or case studies written for the purpose of classroom instruction, published either separately or in textbooks. It tends to be descriptive or proscriptive, rather than analytical. While political scientists have generated a number of theories about the role of business in the political process and the importance of business to government, only a few management scholars have attempted to theorize about the role of politics in managerial decision-making or the importance of politics to business.[36] Their work, moreover, is not well known outside of business schools.

The literature produced by business school faculty contains a wealth of information and a number of useful concepts which political scientists could profitably use to better understand the sources, purposes, and results of business political activities. At the same time, the study of business, government, and society could benefit considerably from the intellectual rigor that characterizes much of the political science literature on business. Students of management need to become familiar with the research of political scientists on how governmental decisions affecting business are made, while political scientists need to draw upon the work of management scholars on how business decisions affecting political participation are made.

Ultimately what is needed is an analysis that links both perspectives, one that shows the interrelationship between the role of politics in shaping management decision-making and the role of business in influencing governmental decision-making. At the same time, those political scientists who study various aspects of business need to define their research in terms of an intellectual agenda that cuts across disciplinary subfields. The result will be a much needed and long overdue intellectual synthesis of this critically important subject—one which should contribute to a better understanding of the political and social role of the corporation in modern capitalist societies.

Notes

1. Robert Dahl, "Business and Politics: A Critical Appraisal of Political Science," in *Social Science Research on Business: Product and Potential* (New York: Columbia University Press, 1959), p. 3.
2. The best-known work in the power-elite tradition is G. William Dom-

hoff, *Who Rules America?* (Englewood Cliffs: Prentice-Hall, 1976). The most influential Marxist study of business power is Ralph Miliband, *The State in Capitalist Society* (New York: Basic Books, 1969). For a more popular version of this general argument, see Morton Mintz and Jerry Cohen, *America, Inc.* (New York: The Dial Press, 1991). For a summary and empirical assessment, see Harold Kerbo and L. Richard Della Fave, "The Empirical Side of the Power Elites Debate: An Assessment and Critique of Recent Research," *The Sociological Quarterly*, vol. 20, no. 1, Winter 1979, pp. 5–22. See also Michael Reagan, *The Managed Economy* (London: Oxford University Press, 1963).

3. For a defense of pluralism that focuses on the political role and influence of business, see Edwin Epstein, *The Corporation in American Politics* (Englewood Cliffs: Prentice-Hall, 1969).

4. Charles Lindblom, *Politics and Markets* (New York: Basic Books, 1977).

5. See for example, Edward Greenberg, *Capitalism and the American Political Ideal* (Armonk: M. E. Sharpe, 1985); *The Structure of Power in America*, edited by Michael Schwartz (New York: Holmes and Meier, 1987); and Dan Clawson, Allan Neustadtl, and Denise Scott, *Money Talks* (New York: Basic Books, 1992). For a list of scholarly articles, see footnote 2 for chapter 9. For critical assessments of Lindblom, see Dennis P. Quinn, "Investment Incentives: A Five Country Test of the Lindblom Hypothesis," in *Research in Corporate Social Performance and Policy* (JAI Press, 1988), vol. 10, pp. 87–111 and David Marsh "Interest Group Activity and Structural Power: Lindblom's Politics and Markets," *Western European Politics*, vol. 6, no. 2, April 1983, pp. 2–13. For analyses that place Lindblom in the context of the debate over corporate power, see Lawrence B. Joseph, "Corporate Political Power & Liberal Democratic Theory," *Polity*, vol. 15, 1982–83, pp. 246–67; L. G. Bykerk, "Business Power in Washington: The Insurance Exception," *Policy Studies Review* 1992, vol. 11, no. 3/4, pp. 259–79 and David Jacobs, "Radical Models of the Business-Government Relationship," *Research in Corporate Social Performance and Policy* 1985, vol. 7 (Greenwich: JAI Press), pp. 1–23. For an important theoretical analysis of some of the implications of Lindblom's work for American democracy, see Stephen L. Elkin, "The Political Theory of American Business," *Business in the Contemporary World*, vol. I, no.3, Spring 1989, pp. 25–37.

6. See, for example, Dennis Quinn and Robert Shapiro, "Business Political Power: The Case of Taxation," *American Political Science Review*, September 1991, vol. 85, no. 3, pp. 851–74; Duane Swank, "Politics and the Structural Dependence of the State in Democratic Capitalist Nations," *American Political Science Review* March 1992, vol. 86, no. 1, pp. 38–55; and David Jacobs, "Corporate Economic Power and the State: A Longitudinal Assessment of Two Explanations," *American Journal of Sociology*, vol. 83, no. 4, January 1988, pp. 852–81. For an earlier effort, see Lester Salamon and John Siegfried, "Economic Power and Political Influence: The Impact of Industry Structure on Public Policy," *American Political Science Review*, December 1977, vol. 71, pp. 1026–43.

7. Raymond Bauer, Ithiel De Sola Pool, and Lewis Dexter, *American Business and Public Policy* (Chicago: Aldine Atherton, 1963, 1972).

8. Two of the most important studies of business political activity published prior to 1970 are Epstein, *The Corporation in American Politics* and Karl Schriftgiesser, *Business and Public Policy: The Role of the Committee for Economic Development: 1942–1967* (Englewood Cliffs: Prentice-Hall, 1976).

9. Peter Bachrach and Morton Baratz, *Power and Poverty: Theory and Practice* (New York: Oxford University Press, 1970).

10. For research on the timing, causes, and significance of this mobilization, see Cathie Jo Martin, "Business and the New Economic Activism," *Polity*, Fall, 1994, pp. 49–76; and Patrick Akard, "Corporate Mobilization and Political Power: The Transformation of U.S. Economic Policy in the 1970s," *American Sociological Review*, vol. 57, October, 192, pp. 597–615.

11. See, for example, *Business Strategy and Public Policy*, edited by Alfred Marcus, Allen Kaufman, and David Beam (Westport, Conn: Quorum Books, 1987); Robert Miles, *Coffin Nails and Corporate Strategies* (Englewood Cliffs: Prentice-Hall, 1982); Mike Ryan, Carl Swanson, and Rogene Buchholz, *Corporate Strategy, Public Policy and the Fortune 500* (Oxford: Basil Blackwell, 1987); Sar Levitan and Martha Cooper, *Business Lobbies* (Baltimore: The Johns Hopkins University Press, 1984); Graham Wilson, *Business and Politics* (Chatham: Chatham House, 1985); and Michael Useem, *The Inner Circle: Large Corporations and the Rise of Business Political Activity in the U.S. and the U.K.* (New York: Oxford University Press, 1984).

12. Books on business and PACs include Clawson, Neustadtl, and Scott, *Money Talks*; Edward Handler and John Mulkern, *Business in Politics: Campaign Strategies of Corporate Political Action Committees* (Lexington: Lexington Books, 1982); Theodore Eismeier and Philip Pollock III, *Business, Money and the Rise of Corporate PACs in American Elections* (New York: Quorum Books, 1988); and Mark Mizruchi, *The Structure of Corporate Political Action* (Cambridge: Harvard University Press, 1992). During the past fifteen years, more articles have been published in political science journals on PACs than on any other aspect of business political activity. See Dinna Evans, "Oil PACs and Aggressive Contribution Strategies," *Journal of Politics*, November 1988, vol. 50, pp. 1047–56; David Gopoian, "What Makes PACs Tick? An Analysis of the Allocation Pattern of Economic Interest Groups," *American Journal of Political Science*, May 1984, vol. 28, pp. 181–259; Kevin Grier, Michael Munger, and Brian Roberts, "The Determinants of Industry Political Activity, 1978–1986, *American Political Science Review*, vol. 88, no. 4, December, 1994, pp. 911–26; Richard Hall and Frank Wayman, "Buying Time: Money Interests and the Mobilization of Bias in Congressional Committees, *American Political Science Review*, September 1990, vol. 84, pp. 797–820; Craig Humphries, "Corporations, PACS and the Strategic Link between Contributions and Lobbying Activities," *Western Political Quarterly*, June 1991, vol. 44, pp. 353–72; Laura Langbein, "Money and Access: Some Empirical Evidence," *Journal of Politics*, November 1986, vol. 48, pp. 1052–62; Marick Masters and Gerald Keim, "Determinants of PAC Participation among Large Corporations," *Journal of Politics*, November 1985, vol. 47, pp. 1158–73; John Wright, "PACs, Contributions, and Roll Calls: An Organizational Perspective," *American Political Science Review*, 1985, vol. 79, pp. 400–414;

John Wright, "PAC Contributions, Lobbying, and Representation," *Journal of Politics*, August 1984, vol. 51, pp. 713–29; John Wright, "Contributions, Lobbying, and Committee Voting in the U.S. House of Representatives," *American Political Science Review*, June 1990, vol. 84, pp. 417–38; Craig Humphries, "Corporations, PACS and the Strategic Link Between Corporations and Lobbying Activities," *Western Political Quarterly*, vol. 44, no. 2, June 1991, pp. 353–72.

For articles on corporate PACs by sociologists, see Val Burris, "The Political Partisanship of American Business: A Study of Corporate Political Action Committees," *American Sociological Review*, vol. 52, December 1987, pp. 732–44; Alan Neutstadl and Dan Clawson, "Corporate Political Groupings: Does Ideology Unify Business Political Behavior?" *American Sociological Review*, vol. 53, April 1988, pp. 172–90; Dan Clawson and Alan Neustadtl, "Interlocks, PACs, and Corporate Conservatism," *American Journal of Sociology*, vol. 94, January 1989, pp. 749–73; John Boies, "Money, Business and the State: Material Interests, Fortune 500 Corporations, and the Size of Political Action Committees," *American Sociological Review*, vol. 54, October 1989, pp. 821–33.

13. Bauer, Pool, and Dexter, *American Business and Public Policy*; E. E. Schattachneider, *Politics, Pressure and the Tariff* (Englewood Cliffs: Prentice-Hall, 1935).

14. See, for example, Judith Goldstein, *Ideas, Interests and American Trade Policy* (Ithaca: Cornell University Press, 1993); and Helen V. Milner, *Resisting Protectionism: Global Industries and the Politics of International Trade* (Princeton: Princeton University Press, 1988).

15. See, for example, James Q. Wilson, ed., *The Politics of Regulation* (New York: Basic Books, 1980), and Richard Harris and Sidney Milkis, *The Politics of Regulatory Change* (New York: Oxford University Press, 1989). On environmental policy, see James Lester, ed., *Environmental Politics and Policy* (Durham: Duke University Press, 1989); Charles O. Jones, *Clean Air* (Pittsburgh: University of Pittsburgh Press, 1975); and Walter Rosenbaum, *Environmental Politics and Policy* (Washington, D.C.: Brookings Institution, 1994).

16. On economic (de)regulation, see Martha Derthick and Paul Quirk, *The Politics of Deregulation* (Washington, D.C.: Brookings Institution, 1985). On tax policy, see John Witte, *The Politics and Development of the Federal Income Tax* (Madison: University of Wisconsin Press, 1985); and Cathie Jo Martin, *Shifting the Burden* (Chicago: University of Chicago Press, 1991). On energy policy, see Richard Vietor, *Energy Policy in America Since 1945* (Cambridge: Cambridge University Press, 1984); and M. Elizabeth Sanders, *The Regulation of Natural Gas* (Philadelphia: Temple University Press, 1981).

17. On the dynamics of the political agenda, see John Kingdon, *Agendas, Alternatives, and Public Policies* (New York: Harper Collins, 1984) and Frank Baumgartner and Bryan Jones, *Agendas and Instability in American Politics* (Chicago: University of Chicago Press, 1993). On interest groups, see Jack Walker, *Mobilizing Interest Groups in America: Patrons, Professions, and Social Movements* (Ann Arbor: University Press, 1991); Robert Salisbury, *Interests and Institutions: Substance and Structure in American Politics* (Pittsburgh: Uni-

versity of Pittsburgh, 1992); Kay Scholzman and Mark Petracca, ed., *The Politics of Interests: Interest Groups Transformed* (Boulder: Westview Press, 1992); Graham Wilson, *Interest Groups in the United States* (New York: Oxford University Press, 1981). For articles on this subject, see Kay Lehman Schlozman and John T. Tierney, "More of the Same: Washington Pressure Group Activity in a Decade of Change," *Journal of Politics*, vol. 45, 1983, pp. 351–77; Kay Lehman Schlozman, "What Accent the Heavenly Chorus? Political Equality and the American Pressure System," *Journal of Politics*, vol. 46, no. 4, November 1984, pp. 1006–32.

18. See Jeffrey Berry, *Lobbying for the People* (Princeton: Princeton University Press, 1977) and Andrew McFarland, *Public Interest Lobbies* (Washington, D.C. American Enterprise Institute, 1977). See also Walker, *Mobilizing Interest Groups*.

19. Andrew Shonfield, *Modern Capitalism: The Changing Balance of Public and Private Power* (New York: Oxford University Press, 1965).

20. See, for example, Peter Katzenstein, ed., *Between Power and Plenty* (Madison: University of Wisconsin Press, 1978), and John Zysman, *Governments, Markets and Growth: Financial Systems and the Politics of Industrial Change* (Ithaca: Cornell University Press, 1983).

21. See, for example, *The State and American Foreign Economic Policy*, edited by John Ikenberry, David Lake, and Michael Mastanduno (Ithaca: Cornell University Press, 1988); John Ikenberry, *Reasons Of State: Oil Politics and the Capacities of American Government* (Ithaca: Cornell University Press, 1988); Chalmers Johnson, ed., *The Industrial Policy Debate* (San Francisco: ICS Press, 1984); and Otis Graham, *Losing Time: The Industrial Policy Debate* (Cambridge: Harvard University Press, 1992); and Stephen Wilks and Maurice Wright, eds., *Comparative Government-Industry Relations: Western Europe, the United States, and Japan* (Oxford: Clarendon Press, 1987).

22. See Graham Wilson, *Business and Politics* (Chatham: Chatham House Publishers, 1985); Tom Bottomore and Robert J. Brym, *The Capitalist Class: An International Study* (New York: New York University Press, 1989); and Mark S. Mirzuchi and Michael Schwartz, eds., *Intercorporate Relations: The Structural Analysis of Business* (Cambridge: Cambridge University Press, 1987). For an excellent cross-national survey of business political activity which does not include the United States, see *The Politicisation of Business in Western Europe*, edited by M.P.C.M Van Schendelen and R. J. Jackson (London: Croom Helm, 1987).

23. See *The Business Establishment*, Earl Cheit, ed. (New York: John Wiley, 1964); R. Edward Freeman, *Strategic Management: A Stakeholder Approach* (Marshfield, Mass.: Pitman, 1984); Dow Votaw and S. Prakash Sethi, *The Corporate Dilemma: Traditional Values Versus Contemporary Problems* (Englewood Cliffs: Prentice-Hall, 1973) and William Frederick, "From CSR1 to CSR2: The Maturing of Business and Society Thought," *Business and Society*, vol. 33, no. 2, August 1994, pp. 150–64.

24. For one of the classics of this field, which predates the social turbulence of the late 1960s, see *The Corporation in Modern Society*, Edward S. Mason, ed. (Cambridge: Harvard University Press, 1959).

25. For an excellent collection of case studies of corporate responses to nonmarket pressures, see the various editions of S. Prakash Sethi, *Up Against the Corporate Wall* (Englewood Cliffs: Prentice-Hall, 1971, 1974, 1982).

26. For one of the few contributions to this literature by a political scientist, see Neil Mitchell, "Corporate Power, Legitimacy, and Social Power," *Western Political Quarterly*, vol. 39, no. 2, June 1986, pp. 198–212, and Neil Mitchell, *The Generous Corporation* (New Haven: Yale University Press, 1989).

27. Louis Hartz, *The Liberal Tradition in America: An Interpretation of American Political Thought Since the Revolution* (New York: Harcourt, Brace, 1955); Shonfield, *Modern Capitalism*; Samuel Huntington, *American Politics and The Politics of Disharmony* (Cambridge, Mass.: Harvard University Press, 1981); Theda Skocpol, *Protecting Soldiers and Mothers: The Political Origins of Social Policy in the United States* (Cambridge, Mass.: Harvard University Press, 1992).

28. See, for example, Betz Mintz, "United States," in Tom Bottomore and Robert S. Brym, *The Capitalist Class: An International Study*, pp. 207–37; Micheal Schwartz, *The Structure of Power in America: The Corporate Elite As a Ruling Class* (New York: Holmes and Meier, 1987); and Michael Soref and Maurice Zeitlin, "Finance Capital and the Internal Structure of the Capitalist Class in the United States," in Mark S. Mizruchi and Michael Schwartz, eds., *Intercorporate Relations: The Structural Analysis of Business* (Cambridge: Cambridge University Press, 1987), pp. 56–84; Michael Useem, *The Inner Circle*; and Mark S. Mizruchi, "Similarity of Political Behavior among Large American Corporations," *American Journal of Sociology*, vol. 95, no. 2, September 1989, pp. 401–24.

29. See, for example, Lester Thurow, *Head to Head: The Coming Economic Battle Among Japan, Europe, and America* (New York: William Morrow and Company, 1992); Otis L. Graham, Jr., *Losing Time: The Industrial Policy Debate* (Cambridge: Harvard University Press, 1992).

30. See, for example, Steven D. Lydenberg, Alice Tepper Marlin, Sean O'Brien Strub, and the Council On Economic Priorities, *Rating America's Corporate Conscience* (Reading, Mass.: Addison-Wesley, 1986); Mary Scott and Howard Rothman, *Companies With a Conscience: Intimate Portraits of Twelve Firms That Make a Difference* (New York: Citadel Press, 1992); and Peter Kinder, Steven Lydenberg, and Amy Domini, *Investing for Good: Making Money While Being Socially Responsible* (New York: Harper Business, 1993).

31. In addition to more than fifty monographs, popular books, and texts, there are two academic journals devoted entirely to this subject: *The Journal of Business Ethics* and *Business Ethics Quarterly*. For representative collections of cases and essays, see Joseph C. Badaracco, Jr., *Business Ethics: Roles & Responsibilities* (Chicago: Irwin, 1995); and W. Michael Hoffman and Robert E. Frederick, *Business Ethics: Readings and Cases in Corporate Morality* (New York: McGraw Hill, 1984, 1990, 1995).

32. See, for example, George J. Stigler, "The Theory of Economic Regulation," in *The Citizen and the State*, George J. Stigler, ed. (Chicago: University of Chicago Press), pp. 114–44.

33. For an important statement of the structuralist position, see Fred L.

Block, *Revising State Theory: Essays in Politics & Postindustrialism* (Philadelphia: Temple University Press, 1987).

34. For some preliminary efforts, see V. V. Murray, ed., *Theories of Business-Government* (Toronto: Trans-Canada Press, 1985) and Barry M. Mitnick, ed., *Corporate Political Agency: The Construction of Competition in Public Affairs* (Newbury Park: Sage Publications, 1993).

35. For an excellent overview of the research generated by the former, see the annual editions of *Research in Corporate Social Performance and Policy* (Greenwich: JAI Press, 1978–1995). The number of management faculty who specialize in this field has grown significantly during the last decade. There are two scholarly organizations: the Social Issues Division of the Academy of Management and the International Association of Business and Society, both of whom hold well-attended annual meetings. The latter organization also has its own journal, *Business and Society*.

36. See David Yoffie and Sigrid Bergenstein, "Corporate Political Entrepreneurship," *California Management Review*, vol. XXVIII, no. 1., Fall 1985, pp. 124–39; David Baron, "Integrating Market and Nonmarket Strategies," *California Management Review*, Winter 1995, pp. 47–65; and David Baron, *Business and Its Environment* (Englewood Cliffs: Prentice-Hall, 1993). For a creative attempt to link corporate strategy with public policy, see Robert H. Miles, *Coffin Nails and Corporate Strategies* (Englewood Cliffs: Prentice-Hall, 1982). See also the essays in Alfred Marcus, Allen M. Kaufman, and David R. Beam, eds., *Business Strategy and Public Policy: Perspective from Industry and Academia* (New York: Quorum Books, 1987).

PART ONE

America in Comparative Perspective

Chapter One

WHY BUSINESSMEN DISTRUST THEIR STATE: THE POLITICAL CONSCIOUSNESS OF AMERICAN CORPORATE EXECUTIVES

THE most characteristic, distinctive, and persistent belief of American corporate executives is an underlying suspicion and mistrust of government. It distinguishes the American business community not only from every other bourgeoisie, but also from every other legitimate organization of political interests in American society. The scope of direct and indirect government support for corporate growth and profits does not belie this contention; on the contrary, it makes it all the more paradoxical. Why should the group in American society that has disproportionately benefited from governmental policies continue to remain distrustful of political intervention in the economy?

It is of course possible to attribute at least some of the public distrust of government by members of the business community to political posturing; continually to denounce government is a way of assuring that the policies of government reflect corporate priorities. Wilbert E. Moore suggests:

> When businessmen did, and do, make extreme, ideologically oriented pronouncements on freedom from political interference, it is surely fair to say that they do not mean to be taken with total seriousness. . . . Often, in fact, the sayers and the doers are not the same people. . . . [T]he extreme spokesmen of business ideology are more often lawyers and public relations men than they are practicing executives. . . . These are generally men, who like professors and Congressmen, 'have never met a payroll'.[1]

Yet this explanation is unsatisfying. In fact, the gap between what executives or their spokesmen say in public and in private is far less than most students of business appreciate. Neither the public nor the private views of executives are formed in a vacuum; executives tend to believe their own propaganda, if for no other reason than that much of it is actually directed at themselves. A study based on extensive private interviews with chief executives during 1974 and 1975 suggests that, if anything, the private views of corporate executives are more critical of government than their public pronouncements.[2] The lack of acceptance of a large and powerful state is also not confined to small businessmen or reactionary sunbelt capitalists. It also dominates the political and social outlook of the top managers of 'Fortune 500' firms.[3] As Clifford Geertz argues, 'the function of ideology is to make an autonomous politics possible by providing the authoritative concepts that render it meaningful, the suasive images by means of which it can be sensibly grasped.[4] For virtually all American businessmen, including corporate executives, a critical authoritative concept in terms of which they make sense of the world is the notion of governmental involvement as inimical to a sound economy and incompatible with a free society.

Even if the hostility of businessmen expressed toward their government is considered a rhetorical device designed 'to establish and maintain the subservience of governmental units to business constituencies to which they are actually held responsible',[5] as McConnell argues, we still must explain why this particular line has enjoyed such widespread popularity among American corporate executives—in sharp contrast, for example, to the public pronouncements of their counterparts in most other capitalist nations. What is so striking about American business ideology is the remarkable consistency of business attitudes toward government over the last one hundred and twenty-five years. A sense of suspicion toward the state has managed to survive the most impressive and decisive political triumphs. Indeed, the level of public hostility toward government appears to have been particularly high during the 'twenties and the 'fifties—the two decades in this century when corporate political hegemony was most secure.

The dominance of the ideology of Social Darwinism among American businessmen during the latter half of the nineteenth century has been amply documented, and James Prothro's *Dollar Decade* offers a vivid documentation of the anti-governmental nature of corporate thinking during the 'twenties.[6] Studies of executive opinions from the Great Depression through the mid-'sixties present a portrait both of business resentment toward the New Deal and of the unwillingness of executives in the post-war period to abandon the ideal of the self-regulating market. In their extensive and thorough study of corporate attitudes, based on material published between 1935 and 1948, Sutton and his co-authors write in *The American Business Creed*: 'Business comments on government are rarely complimentary; that the government should have only limited powers and be restrained in their use is a fundamental and ever-recurring proposition in the business creed. The breech of these principles is viewed as a grave threat to the integrity of the economic system.' They conclude:

But it is the substance of the business creed which provides the most striking evidence of the influence of American traditions. For various reasons, the ideas of the political economists of the nineteenth century have gained more enduring acceptance in America than in Europe. It is these ideas—of Adam Smith, Ricardo, Malthus, the Mills and their popularizers—which form the preponderant classical strand in the business creed, and give it its most distinctive character in the modern world. . . . It is in its vigorous cries against *government interference* and *socialism* and in its persisting faith in the workability of a vaguely defined free economy that the business creed is genuinely distinctive. The Western world has not swung over to totalitarian collectivism but outside America it no longer nourishes a Spencerian distrust of the state and a goal of maximal freedom for private enterprise.[7]

After studying the image of government in a large number of selected business journals published between September 1951 and February 1952, Marver Bernstein states:

The journals selected for analysis generally share a common approach to the role of government and the nature of the economy. Their views may be summarized as follows:

1. The state is intrinsically evil. State intervention in economic affairs is dangerous.
2. Freedom is defined as freedom *from* governmental intervention in economic affairs. Freedom exists naturally as long as government does not destroy it by interfering with economic affairs.
3. There is an exclusive identification of *free enterprise*, i.e., an economy which is unhampered and uncoerced by governmental controls, with freedom, morality, and economic opportunity.
4. All good things flow from the free, unfettered operations of the free enterprise economy. Bad results are attributed to the predicted, inevitable consequences of governmental interference.[8]

In his presidential address delivered to the annual meeting of the American Economic Association in 1962, Edward S. Mason noted:

The relationship between government and business in the United States can only be described as one of latent hostility which occasionally, as in the past year, breaks out into rather more open hostility . . .

It is clear to the most obtuse observer that there is a much more distant relationship between business and government leadership in the United States, than, say, in Britain, France or the Netherlands.

Much more important, in my opinion, is the fact that the really revolutionary changes in the role of government and in the relation of var-

ious groups to government produced by the great depression and the
war have not yet been fully accepted in this country. Where counter-
revolution is still considered to be a possibility no one is quite prepared
to lay down his arms.[9]

The most recent book-length study of contemporary corporate
ideology arrives at a similar conclusion:

> The dominant attitude of corporate executives toward government offi-
> cials—whether elected or appointed—is one of hostility, distrust, and
> not infrequently, contempt. (One executive noted: 'we do our job and
> the government messes things up.')
>   Businessmen share a deep skepticism about the ability of government
> to do anything efficiently, and they believe that the achievement of soci-
> ety's objectives whenever possible is best left in their hands. The reason
> for government inefficiency, businessmen invariably insist, is that public
> decisions are made without the discipline of the marketplace.[10]

The attitude toward international government regulation of
American-based multinational corporations provides the most recent
illustration of the almost instinctive anti-statist bias integral to American corporate culture. Since multinational corporations are a relatively new phenomenon, the attitude of their executives toward controls by states in the international arena furnishes almost a
laboratory setting for recording their true values. Their vision, not
surprisingly, involves a world in which business corporations have
replaced the nation-state as the effective unit of economic policy and
resource allocation. There is nothing particularly international or
global about the chairman of Dow Chemical's dream of establishing
the world headquarters of the Dow company on the truly neutral
ground of . . . an island (owned by no nation), beholden to no nation
or society'.[11] For all their global-spanning capacities and pretensions
to a new world international order free from the strife of nation-
states, the ideology of the executives of multinational corporations
are as American as free enterprise; they have simply projected
American corporate ideology on to the international scene. Visions
of a world economy without the intrusion of governments emanate
almost exclusively from the executives of American owned and managed multinational corporations. They have become confused with
the multinational corporation itself only because multinational corporations are disproportionately American owned and managed.[12]

Throughout the twentieth century, executives have periodically
appeared to be on the verge of accepting the legitimacy of governmental participation in economic affairs. The contention that corpo-

rate executives have at last come to recognize that government has a critical and legitimate role to play in a modern industrial society is made about both the Progressive period and the mid-'sixties. A number of radical, liberal and populist critics of business wrote in the 'sixties that the emergence of the 'managed economy' or the 'new industrial state' signified the obsolescence of business's traditional hostility to an activist state.[13]

On the other hand, observers more sympathetic to business took virtually the identical development as a cause for celebration. In a seminal article in the January 1966 issue of *Fortune*, Max Ways, the magazine's senior editor, suggested that there was no longer any tension between rising government expenditures and the preservation of corporate autonomy; under the new arrangement, which he labeled 'creative federalism', both would be achieved.[14] A year later, Theodore Levitt, in an article in *Harvard Business Review*, enthusiastically heralded the results of this new sense of partnership:

> Whether they know it or not, the leaders of the economically most significant sector of the American business community—the top executives of the larger corporations—are just completing what may turn out to be the most remarkable ideological transformation of the century, perhaps since the beginning of the corporate economy.
>
> It may seem the height of grandiloquence to say so, but there is abundant evidence that the American business community has finally and with unexpected suddenness actively embraced the idea of the interventionist state.[15]

Not coincidently, the revisionist literature published during this same period makes a similar analysis of business-state relations during the Progressive Era. Both Kolko and Weinstein report the ascendancy of the doctrine of 'corporate liberalism' among businessmen during the century's first decade. Sharply departing from the *laissez-faire* ideology of the 1890s, this doctrine accepted a strong national government as critical to political stability and economic growth.[16]

The similarities between the two periods (1965–71, 1902–12) are indeed striking. Both are characterized by the relative absence of industrial strife and general economic prosperity. Both periods also witness the popularity of the doctrine of corporate social responsibility among business leaders, indicating both their optimism about the future of the economy and their willingness to co-operate with government to solve various social problems (largely the assimilation of immigrants in the earlier decade and blacks in the later).[17]

Yet what is noteworthy is how little impact each of these more 'enlightened' conceptions of the role of government in the society had upon subsequent business thinking. The First World War, far from marking the beginning of a new stage of political capitalism, instead signified its climax. Cuff's study of the War Industries Board demonstrates what little lasting impact its structure had on the business conception of government's proper role. It would be hard to distinguish Prothro's portrait of the beliefs of businessmen in the 'twenties from descriptions of business views during the 1880s.[18] The early and mid-1970s witness almost an identical backlash to the 'twenties: the revival of fears of too much government regulation, the demand that corporate taxes be reduced and the concern that corporate social responsibility has gotten out of hand. The progressivism of corporate liberalism and the promises of creative federalism, with their more tolerant views of the role of government, were both short-lived. Indeed, it is questionable to what extent they ever actually dominated business thinking.

The Hostility of Business to Government

While granting both the sincerity and the persistence of executive beliefs, one can still be skeptical about the degree to which they reflect corporate behavior. This argument has been made by many writers on business-government relations. Thus, V. O. Key, Jr., contends: 'Despite the extraordinary diversity of their political actions, business spokesmen expound more or less uniformly a philosophy of *laissez-faire*; free competition, free enterprise, and the "American way." But this is an orthodoxy of ritual rather than of practice. In their actions businessmen pragmatically advocate state intervention today and nonintervention tomorrow.'[19] McConnell writes: 'A conclusion that must be drawn from the examination of business politics is that the noisy denunciations of government heard from business spokesmen are not to be taken at face value. It has been seen repeatedly that in day-to-day affairs, business and government are not only hostile but so closely meshed as to be indistinguishable.'[20] And from Wilbert Moore: 'Business interests have generally sought governmental intervention of some kind while generally opposing intervention of other kinds. The examples are so well known as to need no more than bare mention.'[21] This contention obviously has a great deal of plausibility. Executives do, in fact, support governmental policies that they perceive to be in their interest and oppose those that they do not; to do otherwise would be rather bizarre. Yet by collapsing the distinction between the interests of business executives and their perception of the impact of governmental policies, this statement begs the real issue, which is: *in terms of what criterion do executives decide whether governmental policies are in their interest?*

The business community has been remarkably consistent in its opposition to the enactment of any government policies that would centralize economic decision making or strengthen the authority of government over the direction of the business system as a whole. It is only with respect to policies that have their impact on a particular firm or industry that its much heralded pragmatism at times comes into play. The criterion by which business evaluates government policy has remained quite firm: does the proposed intervention strengthen or weaken the autonomy of management? There is certainly an element of hypocrisy in businessmen's denunciations of government intervention in the economy; their hostility to government appears to vanish whenever their profits are at stake. Corporate executives tend to resolve their apparent contradiction between their beliefs and their practices by denying that government policies that assist private capital accumulation—either directly or indirectly—actually represent government intervention. This perception should be taken seriously: for the most part, government policies that merit business approval do not interfere with management prerogatives. They do not strengthen the power of government. The patterns of interest-group liberalism or small constituencies, which define much of government subsidy and regulatory activity, represent the usually successful attempts of business to receive the benefits of public support without sacrificing autonomy. For all practical purposes, they *do not involve the extension of public authority or power.*[22] McConnell's 'large constituencies' or Lowi's 'redistributive issues' refer to government policies in which the relevant unit affected by a decision is larger than a particular firm or industry—most likely the entire business system—and it is these politically meaningful extensions of public authority that the overwhelming majority of American corporate executives have, at least initially, opposed. Thus the business community virtually unanimously bitterly opposed government protection of the rights of workers to organize into unions—as well as virtually every extension of the welfare state. Executives did not take the principles of Keynesian economics seriously until the mid-'sixties, nearly thirty years after Keynes first articulated them, and soon before they became obsolete. The principal elements of American post-war foreign policy, namely permanent peacetime military mobilization and foreign aid, were initially greeted with considerable skepticism by executives; they were reluctantly supported only because of the effectiveness of the Truman administration's red scare. The development of the political and military machinery necessary to define and defend the American empire in the post-war period was decisive for U.S. corporate growth. Initially, however, most businessmen opposed the United States government's assumption of an international role because of their hostility to large government expenditures.[23] With the exception of the First World War, American businessmen have not encouraged any of the four major wars fought by the United States in this century; indeed American involvement in the war that proved the most beneficial to the business system—namely, the Second World War—was strongly opposed by substantial segments of the business community. Currently, all but a handful of executives are firmly opposed to any form of governmental planning, an incomes policy or, indeed, any measures that would reduce private control over investment or pricing decisions.

To be sure, an administration very closely linked to business did enact wage-price controls. Yet what is striking is not so much that the controls were enacted—a decision in any event made because of pressure from foreign governments concerned about the dollar—or that they were initially greeted with approval. It is rather how, in spite of the obvious benefits they provided business in its negotiations with labor, corporate executives so quickly turned against them. Three years later, in 1976, the experience with controls was frequently cited by executives as an argument against the bureaucratic inefficiencies and economic distortions similarly deemed to be inherent in planning. The parallel between the reaction of business to wage-price controls and the other even more ambitious peacetime flirtation with public management of wages and prices, namely the National Recovery Act, are rather remarkable considering the forty-year interval between them. In both cases a sense of patriotism led to initial enthusiastic support followed rather quickly by disillusionment and then bitter hostility. Whatever their impact on the viability of American capitalism, they were perceived by businessmen as too great an interference with the autonomy of management.

In examining the position of executives with respect to economic policies, it is important to distinguish between policies that in retrospect appear to have been in the interests of business—and thus have elicited relative support from the business community with the passage of time—and the position of executives at the time when the proposals were first debated and enacted. One must be careful about reading back the contemporary attitudes of the business community into the past.[24] While some regulatory legislation was clearly initiated by segments of the business community—the laws establishing the Federal Communications Commission and the Civil Aeronautics Board are the most notable examples—their more typical response was one of vehement opposition. While it is always possible to find quotations from various businessmen in support of any proposal, the opinions of all businessmen do not count equally in assessing business opinion. (Indeed, as we will subsequently explore in more detail, many executives whose views appear relatively 'enlightened' are generally regarded as deviants by their peers.) Moreover, it is important not to confuse regulations supported by executives because the alternatives appeared more disadvantageous—state workman's compensation and federal environmental protection are examples a half-century apart—with corporate support for government intervention. On balance, the preponderance of corporate opinion has been opposed to the overwhelming majority of governmental regulations that attempt to interfere with business. Pension reform, the FDA, CPSC, OSHA, SEC and the FTC—the list is endless—all were initially regarded with considerable suspicion by the mainstream of corporate opinion.[25]

Studies of American business have suffered from a marked ethnocentric bias. The degree of current business-government integration is remarkable only by contrast with the previous history of government intervention in the economy. The popularity (or to be more precise, notoriety) of Galbraith's notion of a 'new industrial state' reveals more about the pattern of American industrialism than it does about the contemporary state of American capitalism. Only in the United States would Galbraith's description of business-government planning and co-ordination seem remarkable or objectionable—to either the left or the right. When all the myriad instances of governmental support of business have been accounted for, the American state remains, by virtually every conceivable qualitative and quantitative criteria, the least interventionist in the advanced industrial world. By focusing on the level of subsidies and regulation—what Lowi terms 'distributive' and 'regulatory' issues—writers on the American corporation have overlooked the extraordinary passive role of the American state with respect to the direction of economic development.[26] The United States is virtually the only capitalist nation which engages neither in an incomes policy, wage-price controls, nor in national planning; and the degree of state participation in production is smaller in the United States than in virtually any other nation in the world—industrial or nonindustrial. To the extent that the United States has moved toward establishing institutions or mechanisms that make some sort of public economic policy possible—i.e., the enactment of the Federal Reserve System to supervise private banking or the establishment of the Council of Economic Advisors to legitimate fiscal policy—it has done so far later than any other industrial system. The American state still lacks essential information about the basic functioning of the economy and even if that information were available the fragmentation of authority and power within the federal bureaucracy would make any coordinated government policy extremely problematic.

It is revealing that the term American executives use most frequently to describe their system is 'free enterprise': one that is hardly in use anywhere outside the borders of the United States. By labeling their system a 'free enterprise' system, American businessmen are, however crudely, attempting to distinguish the American corporate system from that of every other capitalist nation. Indeed, with all the interaction between American executives and those of other nations, it is striking what little impact other national patterns of industrial organization have had upon the opinions of American businessmen. Save for a brief flirtaton with corporatism in the 1920s and 1930s, the American bourgeoisie has been remarkably immune from the influence of foreign ideologies. On the contrary, it has tended to view the relatively high degree of public and private integration in other capitalist nations—to say nothing of socialist ones—with considerable distaste. The attitude of American businessmen has been far from pragmatic, for by any objective economic criteria the least free economies, those of Japan, France and Sweden, have had a far superior economic performance for most of the postwar period. Their distaste for other systems—all of which are invariably characterized by more extensive government participation in economic decisions—is really one of principle: what is precious about the American system is not so much its superior performance but rather the relative autonomy that its managers enjoy. All of the executives' rhetoric about the links between a free society and a free enterprise system really confuses their position: the true meaning of freedom for the American bourgeoisie is the ability of those who own or control economic resources to allocate or appropriate them as they see fit—without interference from either labor unions or government officials. And, in terms of this criterion, by any comparative standard, they have been remarkably successful in preserving the integrity of the American enterprise. The fundamental direction of the American economy remains more decentralized than in any other industrial nation. The fact that the American state in the 1970s had the weakest control in the capitalist world over corporate investment decisions is in no small measure a reflection of political preferences of its business community: America remains the world's freest economy.

In sum, the anti-statist ideology that characterizes the American bourgeoisie should not be dismissed as rhetoric. Not only is it sincerely held, but it does have an impact on the political positions and postures of corporate executives. It is, in short, a political phenomenon that merits analysis.

THE NATURE OF AMERICAN ECONOMIC DEVELOPMENT

The relatively extreme value placed by the American bourgeoisie on the principle and practice of autonomy—with its attendant mistrust of government—is a function of the history of American industrialization. The critical period to examine is not the first six or seven decades of the nation's development but rather the period of industrial take-off that began in the 1840s and 1850s and climaxed in the creation of the warfare-welfare state of the 1930s and 1940s. If we define industrial capitalism as a system in which the majority of the work force does not own any means of production but are rather paid industrial employees, then the United States only becomes capitalist sometime around the middle of the nineteenth century.[27]

If we are interested in understanding the consciousness of American capitalists, then it is to the period immediately before the Civil War that we must turn. For this is the period when the role in the economic system that contemporary corporate executives play was created; this is the period of the formation of the American industrial capitalist class and thus the impressionable years of its birth and childhood. The extraordinary lack of impact of the corporate-state co-operation of the pre-Civil War period on the consciousness of American businessmen over the next 125 years surely represents one of the most vivid examples of collective amnesia in American history.[28] It is readily explicable, however, as belonging quite literally to the pre-history of American industrial capitalism. The 1840s and 1850s are the critical period in the history of the American business system; these years witness the formation of the contemporary legal structure of the modern corporation as well as the ideology of its managers and owners.

Students of class consciousness have successfully attempted to explain the varying degrees of class or revolutionary consciousness among the working class in terms of the varying national patterns of industrialization. Presented most vividly by Hartz in *The Liberal Tradition in America* and more systematically documented by Giddens in *The Class Structure of the Advanced Societies*, the argument is a simple one. Giddens writes: 'the labor movement tends to be socialist in orientation where it is formed in a society in which there was fairly important post-feudal elements, and will be closely integrated with a political movement to the degree that the active incorporation of the working class within the citizenship state is resisted.'[29] Hartz's formulation can be summarized even more tersely: the prior existence of feudalism in capitalist societies is a necessary condition for the emergence of socialism. This framework can be used to understand the variation in political consciousness among the bourgeoisie as well as among the working class. As Giddens suggests, the conditions under which a nation industrializes leave a permanent legacy to its political and economic institutions and to the relationship between them. The pattern of industrialization not only affects a society's subsequent institutional arrangements, as Gerschenkron argues; it also shapes the ideology of those who industrialize it.[30]

The distrust of the state that characterizes the consciousness of the American bourgeoisie is built into the structure of American capitalism; it is as much a characteristic of the American political order as is the absence of an effective and viable socialist tradition. The relationship between institutional structure and ideology is one of interdependency: the institutional structure of a nation's period of industrialization stamps an indelible mark upon the consciousness of its industrializing elites. Their consciousness—in this case, that of the suspicion of government—is created by these structures and in turn influences them.

In the two decades prior to the Civil War, the transformation of the relationship between business corporations and the American states set the institutional framework for the subsequent development of the American capitalist system. As the basis of economic growth moved from trade and agricultural exports to industry, the emerging industrial elites began to outgrow the need for governmental participation in economic development. The panic of 1837 contributed significantly to a deterioration of public confidence in public regulation and administration. By the mid-1840s private capital was strong enough to demand successfully that the states significantly reduce their intervention in business matters. Whereas a decade earlier the relative inexperience of native entrepreneurs and their inability to raise capital without public backing fostered a dependence on state and local authorities, by the 'forties their growing self-confidence and ability to attract foreign investment made them look upon government as less unnecessary. Once the construction of the infrastructure was completed and the Indians banished to west of the Mississippi, American capitalists faced none of the obstacles that in most European nations made a strong state critical to industrialization. There was no aristocracy to overthrow, no foreign armies to mobilize against and, most importantly, only one nation that had previously industrialized with which to compete. After the Civil War the federal government did play a vital role in American industrial growth: it subsidized railroad construction, enacted tariffs to protect domestic industry and physically subdued both strikers and Indians. Yet what distinguishes each of these actions, as well as the subsidies that the states continued to offer throughout the nineteenth century, is that they resulted in little interference with managerial autonomy.

As in the case of the First World War, the Civil War had no significant impact on the development of public administration in the United States. Temporarily strengthening its scope and size to defeat the most critical domestic opposition to capitalist growth, the federal bureaucracy rapidly atrophied once its task was completed. The spoils of war and the economic growth it generated were given away to the private sector.

After the 1840s governmental assistance continued but governmental authority declined. Wallace Farnham's essay on the relationship between the federal government and the Union Pacific Railroad demonstrates the pattern quite clearly.[31] 'Government giveaway' to 'private profit seeking enterprises may be our economic history', as one critic argues, but the critical word is 'giveaway'.[32] It denotes a fundamentally passive role, in marked contrast to the more pioneering and active efforts of the state in shaping industrial development in most other capitalist—and all socialist—nations. While most other states in capitalist societies increased their role and power as industrialization proceeded, the authority of the American state declined and its size remained relatively small. When seen in comparative terms, it simply had a less necessary role to play. With the defeat of the South, the American bourgeoisie's triumph in civil society was virtually complete. While complaints against the business corporation surface periodically through the latter half of the nineteenth century, they do not present any serious challenge to the growth of national markets or the creation or disciplining of an industrial working class—problems that made a strong state imperative in much of Europe. In sum, to a far greater extent than in any other capitalist nation (with the partial exception of England) the American bourgeoisie succeeded in creating the industrial system by its own initiative. Throughout the period of industrialization the critical decisions about the direction of economic development were in private hands. Compared to that of other capitalist nations, the American state's role was more supportive than directive. The result is that the structure of the American government tends to resemble that of civil society—the precise opposite of the relationship in Japan or France.

The alleged economic incompetence of the American government, so heralded throughout the business community, is also a function of the peculiarities of American industrial development. From the inauguration of the spoils system by Andrew Jackson in the 1830s through the New Deal one hundred years later, the federal government was a stepchild of American society. The kind of talent, ability and energies that went into the creation and initial development of the republic in the late eighteenth and nineteenth centuries—a period of political and governmental competence that is a universally venerated feature of our national heritage—were channeled into the business sector after the nation's first half-century. De Tocqueville wrote: 'When public employments are few in number, ill-paid and precarious, whilst the different lines of business are numerous and lucrative, it is to business, and not to official duties, that the new and eager desires engendered by the principle of equality turn from every side.'[33]

It was the pursuit of economic gain and material growth that occupied the nation's most talented individuals and consumed most of their political and administrative energies for a little over half the history of the republic. Ironically, it was precisely the widespread acceptance of the principles of democracy in the antebellum period that contributed to the deterioration of the quality of public administration: 'democratic ideals of the competence of the common man and rotation of office. . . lessened the chance of the states developing able and prestigious administrative bureaucracies.' Hartz concludes:

> Political thought, not inexplicably in light of the general triumph of democratic ideals, was gradually overwhelmed by an exaggerated belief in rotation and the joyous acceptance of inexperience . . . Business thought . . . was never overwhelmed in such a way despite the mass faith in opportunities for sudden wealth . . . In the halcyon world of the fifties, it may have been believed that anyone could win a fortune by investing in railroad securities, but it was not believed that the mandates of natural law required the annual election of locomotive engineers.[34]

The relative retardation of the development of national political institutions in the United States has no parallels in any other capitalist nation. By 1910 the critical features of a modern corporate structure were firmly established in the United States: these included large-scale bureaucratic industrial organizations, relatively large concentrations of wealth in the hands of corporate shareholders, and oligopolistic market structures. A surprisingly large number of the current '*Fortune* 500' also dominated the American economy in 1909: American Tobacco, Armour and Co., Standard Oil (now Exxon), United Fruit (now United Brands), U.S. Rubber, Dupont, Singer, U.S. Steel, Westinghouse, General Electric, American Can.[35] By contrast, the modern American bureaucratic state—professionally administered and collecting and distributing a significant share of national wealth—really dates from the presidency of FDR. Not until the late 'thirties did the annual revenues of the federal government rival those of the assets of the largest industrial corporation. In an almost literal sense, public bureaucracy in the United States is only half as old as its counterpart in the private sector; most corporations are far older than the government agencies of comparable importance. If one dates the emergence of the first national bureaucratic institution in American society from the development of the railroads in the 1870s and 1880s, the contrast becomes even more dramatic: the public sector does not become equally organized for another half-century.[36]

In every other capitalist nation, a strong bureaucratic state either precedes or emerges alongside the multidivisional firm; in the United States the pattern is reversed. The impact of this fact on the attitude of the bourgeoisie toward the state is decisive. In the United States the professionally managed, oligopolistic, multidivisional firm literally exists for a generation without the modern equivalent of the state. Whatever may be the interdependence of the corporation and the government that has developed over the last generation, the former existed for a significant amount of time without the latter: executives perceive the modern warfare-welfare state as an upstart. Just as the aristocracy in Europe looked down upon the bourgeoisie as *nouveau*—and indeed, after centuries of intermarriage and extensive political and economic ties, continues to do so—so the American bourgeoisie regards state officials with a sort of contempt; they are newcomers to American institutional life whose later arrival testifies to their inexperience and irrelevance to economic development. Witness the following statement of Rawleigh Warner, Jr., Chairman of the Board of Mobil, an unusually articulate and well-educated executive:

> We have been through a period of everybody talking about the shortcomings of our system. But if you go back before the last 30 or 40 years—before the day of increasing government controls—our system, in spite of some obvious inequities, had produced more wealth and spread it over more people than any other system ever devised. We need to criticize our system, but we need to keep some basic, positive facts in mind.[37]

BUSINESS AND DEMOCRACY IN AMERICA

The attitude of American businessmen toward government cannot be fully explained with reference to the relatively passive and limited role of the state in American industrial development; it is also critically linked to the legitimacy of democratic traditions in America. In no nation have the principles and practices of democracy and of the free market been as intricately connected as in the United States. The Jacksonian Revolution was a democratic revolution which prefigured a capitalist one. The movement for general incorporation that would transform state mercantilism into competitive capitalism effectively mobilized the nascent capitalist class as well as small farmers and urban workers. They were united around the principle of equality of economic opportunity—a convergence of the concepts of economic and political liberty expressed in Henry Clay's phrase 'the self-made man'.[38]

As the pace of American industrialization accelerated in the latter third of the nineteenth century, however, the principles of democracy and capitalism came into conflict. By 1880 the number of Americans who were self-employed was reduced to barely one-third of the work force. Of these a significant proportion were small farmers and merchants, without effective market power against the industrial enterprises that produced a steadily growing share of national wealth. The occupational and economic structure of industrial America has effectively undermined the identity of business and popular interests: the Civil War was the last domestic political struggle in which all the interest groups of the market economy—from small farmer to wage earner to industrialist (outside the South)—were united. From the perspective of those who did not own or manage large-scale economic institutions—most notably the farmer, industrial worker and self-employed professional—the successful industrialists and financiers of the 1880s no longer reflected democratic economic and political aspirations. They were now regarded as an obstacle to their realization.

In the late nineteenth century self-employed farmers became the first of many groups excluded from the corporate umbrella to equate an increase in state control over business with democratic aspirations. This development coincides with and parallels a significant increase in anti-state rhetoric on the part of businessmen—even as the federal government begins to play a supportive role in industrialization. The two are closely linked: the American business community's mistrust of the state is significantly a function of its perception of the state as democratic—and thus, after 1850 in principle and after 1880 in fact, open to popular pressures hostile to industrial elites. McCloskey writes:

> With respect to program, the most obvious example of such alteration is to be found in the shifting conservative attitude toward government

intervention in business affairs. Hamilton, of course, had proposed the active cooperation of business and government for the greater glory of both the commonwealth and the propertied interests; and this Hamiltonian ideal, while never unanimously approved, was an element in conservative doctrine throughout the first seventy-five years of the Republic. After the Civil War, however, it became clear that capitalism was now strong enough to get along without more active assistance from government than it already enjoyed. Equally important, it began to appear that in a partnership between government and business the danger of gratuitous political interference was becoming too serious to justify the risk. The idea of a positive relationship between government and economic life thus fell out of favor among those who underwrote the conservative program.

. . . The advantage of the propertied interests was the aim of both the Hamiltonian and the post-bellum programs, and the difference was only in the choice of means. *The change had been impelled partly by a broadening of government's popular base, which aggravated the threat of encroaching legislation,* and partly by an unexampled increase in the independence and vitality of the business community.[39] [Emphasis added.]

Regardless of the actual distribution of political power in the United States, the USA has from the beginning of its history been one of the world's most thoroughly democratic societies. In no other society have democratic aspirations and ideals so thoroughly permeated the political culture. Critical to the hegemony of the liberal tradition in American society is popular acceptance of the state as an effectively neutral mechanism, beholden not to privileged interests but to the will of the people; it is not a coincidence that the doctrine of pluralism has enjoyed its greatest vogue among social scientists in the United States. Similarly, one of the most characteristic and recurrent political doctrines in American history, populism, both requires and celebrates popular participation in the governmental process.

Efforts from both the left and the right to disentangle the government from the democratic process in the United States are unconvincing. It is impossible to understand the meaning of government to American citizens—including to corporate executives—without appreciating its thoroughly democratic associations; in the United States to be antistatist is also to be antidemocratic. The opposite is also true; to favor a positive state role in society is to be prodemocratic. Other combinations certainly can and do exist. Fascism, for example, is prostatist and antidemocratic while anarchism reflects precisely the opposite relationship. Neither ideology, however, has had an important impact on the American political consciousness.

It is the relatively democratic nature of the American state—embedded in popular ideals and in legal institutions prior to the development of industrial capitalism—that is in large measure responsible for the particular vehemence of the American bourgeoisie's antagonism toward an expansion of governmental authority. During the latter half of the nineteenth century, this relationship was acknowledged frankly by businessmen and their spokesmen; Social Darwinism was both antigovernmental and antidemocratic. This attitude persists, though it is expressed a bit less crudely and openly, in the twentieth century. Describing the business ideology of the 1920s, Prothro writes:

> Despite the high enthusiasm with which business viewed the increasing exaltation of economic superiority during the 1920s, the[y were] permeated by a nagging and persistent fear of the capacity of government to subvert this natural development . . . *The conspicuous antigovernmental orientation of business organizations is itself an incident of the more basic fear that popular control will, through the device of universal suffrage, come to dominate the governmental process.* Although economic success is perfectly geared to the nature of man, political power is dependent upon an artificial arrangement which runs directly counter to the laws of nature and which gives full play to the corruptibility of the masses. The unconscionable attempt of the masses, misguided by parasitic politicians, to better their lot through political processes constitutes the most unnerving of all the violations of fair play. Government is capable of meritorious service in the cause of *right*, but politics as it is practiced in the twentieth century offers the constant threat of intruding the mass man's delusions into the social order.[40] [Emphasis added.]

The following quotations, recorded at a series of private meetings of corporate executives half a century later, suggest both the continuity and the consistency of an antidemocratic ethos within the business community:

> The normal end of the democratic process gives unequal people equal rights to pursue happiness in their own terms. There is a difference between the free enterprise system and a democracy which we also espouse.
>
> We are dinosaurs, at the end of an era. There is a shift of power base from industry and commerce to masses who cannot cope with the complexities of the modern world. Dolls have taken over the power structure.
>
> One-man-one-vote will result in the eventual failure of democracy as we know it.

In this good, democratic country where every man is allowed to vote, the intelligence and property of this country is at the mercy of the ignorant, idle and vicious. [This last statement was actually made in 1868.][41]

The fears of executives about the dangers that the democratic process poses for capital accumulation seem to bear only the most casual relationship to political reality: the periods when the political hegemony of business was at its height, namely the 1870s, 1920s and 1950s, reveal no reduction in business suspicion of the governmental process. The nagging sense of political insecurity that has been so characteristic of American businessmen since the Civil War reflects the fact that, perhaps more than any other faction in the history of American society, business executives have never doubted the persuasiveness of the high-school civics textbooks' description of the American political process. Accepting their nation's most powerful legitimating ideology, they remain concerned that governmental policy will indeed come to reflect popular preferences. Their hostility to both the ideal and the idea of government involvement in the economy is significantly due to their lack of confidence in their ability to dominate the political process. Unlike France, Germany, and Japan, we have no tradition of a strong and autocratic state or of a bureaucracy independent of popular pressures.[42]

In the last decades of the nineteenth century, movements of agrarian discontent were relatively successful in using the political process, particularly at the state level, to curb at least some of the more flagrant abuses of corporate power. The establishment of the Interstate Commerce Commission and the passage of the Sherman Act partially reflected these antibusiness political pressures. Yet for a period of thirty-six years, between 1896 and 1932, corporate interests were relatively immune from effective popular control. Many of the reforms of the Progressive Era significantly reduced anti- or noncorporate political participation. Samuel Hays documents this process at the municipal level while Walter Dean Burnham's study, *Critical Elections and the Mainsprings of American Politics*, demonstrates the role of Bryan's nomination and subsequent defeat in 1896 in effectively depriving the United States of a two-party system for over a generation.[43] Whatever the origin or effectiveness of its reforms, the Progressive Era produced no institutional force or political faction capable of challenging effectively corporate interests and goals. On the contrary, the 'twenties illustrate vividly how quickly executives were able to forget the lessons of Progressive reform. The left, including the Socialist party and the Industrial Workers of the World, was destroyed, the intelligentsia was intimidated, the farmers were rendered impotent, the trade-union movement was broken. Equally important, the Supreme Court effectively struck down popular efforts to control business. The 'twenties remain the golden age of corporate capitalism.

It is in this context that the full significance of the New Deal, and the subsequent history of American politics, must be appreciated. For most of the history of capitalism, the large business corporation in the United States effectively enjoyed a monopoly of the political and institutional power without parallel in the capitalist world in the twentieth century. The history of the last forty years, however, has witnessed the mobilization, organization and institutionalization of a wide diversity of nonbusiness and anticorporate interests. What is critical about the business perception of these institutions—which include the welfare-state and regulatory state bureaucracies, organized labor, the welfare-rights movement, the consumer movement and the environmental movement—is that the existence and purpose of each of them is critically connected with an activist state. Not only is virtually every institution or organization that contemporary businessmen consider opposed or indifferent to their needs and values a product of the last forty years; each of them can date its origin to periods of an expanding and increasingly powerful state whose expansion and strength can in turn be traced to the political mobilization of nonbusiness constituencies. To focus on the economic impact of the New Deal and the Great Society really misses the essential drama of these reform periods for business executives: they spawned institutional and organizational sources of power outside direct corporate purview.

The critical key to understanding why businessmen are more antistatist than virtually any other major interest in American society lies in the unique role of the state at their institution's birth. Business—both large and small—developed during a period when the state was relatively weak and small: in the case of virtually all other major national institutions, the state and the political process played a critical role in their formation.

The relationship between organized labor and the Wagner Act, between welfare rights and social welfare organizations and the Great Society, and between the environmental movement and the government legislation of the early 'seventies is symbiotic. For nonbusiness institutions and organizations, their very political existence is closely bound up with governmental decisions and with the extension of the power and size of the federal government. Whatever the disappointments of these factions in achieving their policy goals—and obviously they are greater than that of business—they rarely succumb to the kind of antistatist hysteria that has been a staple of corporate ideology since the 1840s. Their occasional flights of radical rhetoric notwithstanding, their leadership as well as their rank and file essentially identify their political welfare with that of a large, strong government. Relatively powerless within civil society, they rely upon the political process to provide them with whatever protection they can secure against the interests and power of corporate capital.

The relative hostility of executives toward the government and the democratic process thus reflects a broader intolerance toward all nonbusiness institutions and nonmarket roles. American corporate executives have been spoiled. Capitalism in America did not grow out of a heritage of feudalism. The American business community has not had the historical experience of coexisting or competing with a plurality of other institutions, such as an established military, established clergy, established state, established universities or, more importantly, an established aristocracy. From the Civil War through the New Deal, American business really confronted no effective economic or political competitors to its expansion and prestige. The victory of the North in the Civil War eliminated the most important alternative mode of production to industrial capitalism, and a generation later financial and industrial concentration reduced the second—independent commodity production—to a secondary role. From the 1870s through the early 1930s, the only national institution in American society (with the exception of the church) was the large business corporation. (The percentage of the gross national product produced by small businesses in the United States is among the lowest in the capitalist world.[44] And the United States was one of the last industrial nations to unionize.)

The New Deal can thus be seen as the major discontinuity in the development of American capitalism. Whatever the merits of the revisionist arguments with respect to the Progressive Era, they are fundamentally misleading as an analysis of the New Deal. Unlike the Progressive Era, the New Deal did not simply enact reforms which could then be ignored when the political pendulum shifted to the right; it created three central institutions in American life that survived it: trade unions, a federal bureaucracy and, indirectly, a number of relatively independent universities. (In this context it is significant that the New Deal marks the entrance of academics to positions of prominence in American public life; the reform agencies of the Progressive Era were staffed largely by businessmen.) A conservative counter-offensive was waged by business after both world wars. What prevented 1946 from being a repetition of 1919 was largely the institutional innovations of the New Deal, not the relative enlightenment of the post-Second World War business community. In sharp contrast to those of the Progressive Era, the reforms of the New Deal were the result of a relative politicization of American public life; they were largely inspired by popular pressures.

In this sense, the New Deal confirms the corporate perception that in America the intervention of the state is linked to its democratic nature: the major expansion of the authority and the size of government in the history of American capitalism occurred precisely during the period when direct corporate political influence was weakest and popular antibusiness pressures strongest. It is not surprising that the reforms of the second Roosevelt met with far more extensive hostility from business than those of the first. The former were less under their control and thus resulted in a relative strengthening of the authority of government.

CORPORATE CLASS CONSCIOUSNESS

Ideologies appear wherever systematic factual assertions about society contain (usually by implication) evaluations of the distributions of power in the societies in which these assertions are developed and propagated. We may suppose that a group generally accepts a view of society consonant with its interests; we need not think that ideologies are consciously fashioned to serve these interests or that groups are incapable of acting upon beliefs which appear to contradict these interests. [Norman Birnbaum[45]]

The attitudes of business toward government and the democratic process can also be understood in more theoretical terms. Giddens makes a useful distinction between 'class awareness' and 'class consciousness'. Class awareness exists in any structurally differentiated society. It is characterized by 'a common awareness and acceptance of similar attitudes and beliefs, linked by a common style of life, among members of [a] class'. It does not require recognition that there may exist other classes; indeed, in the case of the middle class, 'it may take the form of a denial of the existence or reality of classes'.[46] Class consciousness, on the other hand, involves at a minimum, a conception of class identity and therefore of class differentiation. It may also involve a conception of class conflict when, Giddens continues, 'perception of class unity is linked to a recognition of opposition of interest with another class or classes'.[47] Another sociologist, Morris Rosenberg defines class consciousness in similar terms:

Class consciousness . . . refers to the individual's psychological *perception* of his own position in the class structure. It contains a number of minimum elements: the individual must identify himself with the class to which he belongs according to the objective definition; he must feel

united with others in the same objective position; and he must feel sepa-
rated from, or must disidentify with, people in a different objective class
position. These cognitive actors represent sentiments of awareness. They
are often viewed as overlaid with affect, leading to characteristics such as
intra-class friendship and inter-class antagonism and resentment.[48]

The particular conditions of American industrialization have fostered class awareness, not class consciousness, among businessmen.
The American business community, unlike its counterparts in most
other capitalist nations, did not have to engage in a political and
military struggle to break down barriers to the development of a
market economy. Unlike the French or the British bourgeoisie who
had to organize themselves as a class to struggle against a restrictive
and repressive feudal system, American businessmen confronted
no such obstacle: from the very beginning of our nation's history,
American businessmen confronted a climate extraordinarily sympathetic to individual enterprise and economic development. Never
having confronted a systemic obstacle to their ownership of the
forces of economic production, businessmen in America have no
revolutionary tradition. Their sense of themselves as a coherent political and social entity was not forged in a baptism of fire. On the
contrary, American capitalist ideology traces its intellectual origins to
the age of Jackson. The suspicion of governmental authority that
characterizes the Jacksonian hostility to corporate charters was profoundly individualistic in orientation: government was seen as inhib-
iting individual opportunity. While businessmen remained committed to this negative view of government long after it had been
stripped of its democratic associations—and implications—the Jacksonian classless imagery of the people versus the money power remains central to business thinking. American corporate executives
are Jacksonian populists: they remain committed to the ideal of individual liberty and enterprise.[49]

The extent to which capitalism has been ideologically unchanged
in America—either by an aristocracy or by a socialist working-class
movement—has also inhibited American businessmen from developing a stronger sense of internal unity. The sense of classlessness that
pervades American society, cited so frequently by both defenders
and critics of America's unique political tradition, not only made
American unions relatively indifferent to socialist ideology; the individualistic ethic that is so critical a component of the liberal tradition
also inhibits a sense of solidarity within the bourgeoisie. Nearly one
hundred and fifty years ago, de Tocqueville remarked:

> To tell the truth, though there are rich men, the class of rich men does
> not exist; for these individuals have no feelings or purposes, no tradi-

tions or hopes, in common; there are individuals, therefore, but no definitive class. . . . The rich are not compactly united among themselves.
. . . In their intense and exclusive anxiety to make a fortune, they lose
sight of the close connection which exists between the private fortune of
each of them and the prosperity of all. . . . The discharge of political
duties appears to them to be a troublesome annoyance, which diverts
them from their occupations and business. . . . These people think that
they are following the principle of self-interest, but the idea they entertain of that principle is a very rude one; and the better to look after
what they call their business, they neglect their chief business, which is
to remain their own masters.[50]

The member of the bourgeoisie occupies two roles simultaneously,
that of businessman and that of capitalist. In the former role he
relates to other firms and industries as competitors, while in the latter he is concerned about the relationship of the business system to
the rest of society. One relationship emphasizes his individuality and
independence: the other stresses the dependence of his economic
position upon the maintenance of the socioeconomic system of capitalism. Tension between these roles is built into the nature of a market society. The interests of business as a whole are quite distinct
from the sum of the objectives of each firm or industry and are
often incompatible with the goals of any particular enterprise.

Examples of this contradiction are numerous. Polanyi demonstrates that capitalism itself was made possible only when the central
authority of the state, placing the long-term interests of the emerging system above that of individual craftsmen, merchants and
farmers, severely curtailed local monopolistic restrictions on the
free flow of land, labor, and capital.[51] More recently, a number of
executives have been distressed by the habit of firms in financial
trouble of going to the government for subsidies and bailouts—at
the very time when the overwhelming majority of executives are
campaigning for a reduction of government interference in the
economy.[52] Corporate corruption can also be understood in similar
terms: it is the process by which individual corporations place their
immediate economic welfare ahead of the public reputation of the
business community and the public's confidence in the integrity of
government officials. The process by which executives advance their
common or class interests is thus by no means an automatic one: the
discipline of the market so heralded by Adam Smith clearly has no
counterpart when it comes to a wide variety of critical public policy
issues.

The lack of systemic challenges to corporate expansion during the nineteenth century meant that executives were free, to a far greater extent than during the comparable period of industrialization in any other capitalist nation, to pay disproportionate attention to their roles as businessmen. Business did require governmental assistance, but mostly on an *ad hoc* basis. Because its role was largely passive, the lack of uniform and consistent public policies did not retard industrial development; the anarchy of the marketplace could easily be transplanted to the public realm. The contemporary result is predictable: the American bourgeoisie has become the most fragmented in the capitalist world. The business community is largely a community in name only; its internal structures of authority remain remarkably decentralized: investment decisions are made by firms or industries relatively independently of each other. The largest important unit of political activity in the United States is the trade association, although for those industries dominated by large firms even industry-wide organizations are not particularly important.

It is not only that American executives, by virtue of their fiercely competitive spirit, at times behave irresponsibly toward the society as a whole: they often behave irresponsibly toward each other. American businessmen, for example, are far more likely than their counterparts in most other capitalist nations to drive their competitors into bankruptcy. These tensions within the business community are naturally exacerbated by adversity. The last few years have witnessed a growing readiness to name competitors' products in advertisements and an astonishing increase in private antitrust suits—developments suggesting that the mores of the marketplace are not conducive to a sense of community. As one executive recently put it, 'We don't have a business community. Just a bunch of self-interested people.'[53]

Their lack of solidarity is relatively less important for American businessmen. As long as a consciousness of class interests—and thus class conflict—is absent from virtually all other political groups in American society, then its lack among businessmen is not a particular handicap; each executive can blindly pursue his narrow self-interest, both inside and outside the marketplace, in the belief that all other Americans, however some social scientists might like to divide them into owners and workers, are doing the same. Moreover, to the extent that businessmen both believe and act as if America were a classless society, they also inhibit the emergence of class consciousness among their employees; both the bourgeoisie and the working class can openly and honestly share the belief that their life-chances are a function of their individual efforts.

Even in a society whose major political participants are oblivious of their class roles, issues periodically emerge that do affect the interests of business as a whole. It is with respect to some of these kinds of issues that American businessmen tend to act irrationally from the point of view of the economic and political viability of the business system. The liberal tradition, with its focus on the self-sufficiency and autonomy of the individual, inhibits American businessmen from appreciating and making political judgements on the basis of their common or class interests; their unit of analysis remains rooted in the enterprise. They remain the victims of ideas over which they have no control and which are often obsolete. A classic example of this systemic irrationality is the thirty-year struggle of American businessmen against Keynesian economics. It was only with extreme reluctance that the majority of top executives in the 1960s and 'seventies began to recognize that what was rational from the perspective of the individual firm was irrational from the perspective of the economic interests of business as a whole.

American businessmen appear to behave quite rationally toward government when the interests of their firm or industry are at stake, yet their understanding of the American business system remains remarkably shortsighted and provincial: they confuse their role as businessmen with their interests as capitalists. It is in terms of this dichotomy that the American businessman's distrust of government and the democratic process can be more fully explained. From the point of view of the individual enterprise, the governmental process is indeed fraught with uncertainty; on balance, governmental intervention in the economy does indeed undermine entrepreneurial autonomy, and noncorporate interests have in fact benefited from the increasing size and scope of governmental authority. Yet, when measured not against the individualistic ideal of 1830 but rather in the light of the realities of political life in advanced capitalist societies, both a relatively strong government and a relatively responsive political system have proven extremely functional for the development of American capitalism. It is not that businessmen fail to recognize specific acts of public assistance; most executives have nothing but kind words to say about those particular agencies or programs that play a constructive role in the life of their companies. Industries may be embarrassed by protective regulations or subsidies, but they are not opposed to them. It is rather that they see these policies as exceptional. They do not understand that the American capitalist system requires a large degree of state intervention for its very survival; they only want to support those policies and agencies that directly benefit their firm or industry. To analyze governmental activities on a case-by-case basis thus loses the forest for the trees: it does not understand that the steady expansion of business-government inter-action—whether inspired by businessmen or their critics—repre-sents part of a broader dynamic that can be observed in every single industrial society. It is a dynamic that, at least up to the present, has not only proven compatible with private accumulation but may well be essential to it.[54]

A similar confusion informs the attitude of American businessmen toward democracy. The pre-eminent position of the principles and processes of democracy in the American political system has proved particularly compatible with corporate profits and growth. Whatever may be inconveniences of a relatively open and responsive govern-mental system to the achievement of specific corporate objectives—and they are often considerable—they are clearly the price the American bourgeoisie pays for a luxury enjoyed by no other busi-ness community in the advanced capitalist nations—the absence of a socialist opposition. American executives continually complain about the large number of organizations and interest groups that routinely turn to the state to redress their grievances against the corporation, but this state of affairs is certainly preferable to one in which these non or antibusiness factions did not use the political process because they perceived it as fixed against them. The latter would seriously undermine the political stability upon which a sound economic sys-tem depends. Judging all governmental decisions in terms of their economic impact on their own firms, American executives remain insensitive to the interdependency of the legitimacy of both institu-tions.

THE CONTEMPORARY DYNAMIC

What are the political implications of the relative lack of class con-sciousness of American corporate executives? The first challenges that business confronted, which required a positive rather than a passive state role, took place at the turn of the century. The transi-tion from competitive or *laissez-faire* to corporate or monopoly cap-italism generated social and economic tensions that required a con-ception of both corporate and governmental responsibilities that transcended an entrepreneurial or individualistic ethos. Co-ordina-tion and co-operation, both among firms and between corporations and the government, was required. If executives were to meet these challenges successfully, the business community had to become somewhat more conscious of its class or common interests.

The Progressive Era represents American businessmen's finest hour. While the revisionists exaggerate the extent to which most executives actually endorsed the reforms enacted during this period, Kolko's *The Triumph of Conservatism* does document that in the case of the most important reforms—the Clayton Antitrust Act, the Federal Trade Commission and the Federal Reserve Act—at least a handful of particularly powerful and prominent executives were capable of looking beyond the interests of their own firms to that of the business system as a whole. The doctrine of corporate liberalism, described in Weinstein's *The Corporate Ideal in the Liberal State*, was a class-conscious ideology: it accepted a more powerful state role and was thus contrary to the judgement of most businessmen who remained classical conservatives.[55] Those socially conscious executives who accepted its tenets were able to play a leadership role in enacting reforms that contributed to the stability of the business system for a generation.

It is a mistake, however, to generalize the conclusions of the revisionists to political reforms after the Progressive period. The enlightened business leadership of the Progressive Era was made possible by an unusual centralization of authority within the business community during this period. Not only were most major industries dominated by a single entrepreneur, but at the apex of the system stood a few individuals whose personal stature and economic power fully enabled them to understand and represent the interests of business as a whole. It is thus not surprising that the first attempt at corporate public relations was initiated by John D. Rockefeller after the Colorado mine massacre. At the height of his power, J. P. Morgan dominated the American business community to a greater extent than any individual previously or subsequently. The most delicate negotiations, regarding the boundaries of government intervention in the economy could be resolved by private conversations between President Theodore Roosevelt and J. P. Morgan— with each individual confident that he had the power to dominate his respective constituencies. In addition, during this period—and neither before nor after—the markets of the largest firms were coextensive with that of the nation as a whole, and thus the interests of the largest firms tended to merge with those of the national economy. The result was that its relative lack of class consciousness was not a handicap to business during the Progressive Era: the individual interests of many of the most powerful capitalists were themselves coincidental with that of the larger industrial system.

Since the 1920s four developments have markedly reduced the ability of corporate executives to generate their own political leadership: the decline of the dominance of the Morgan financial interests; the reduction in market control of many of the turn-of-the-century monopolies, e.g., Standard Oil, U.S. Steel, International Harvester; the displacement of entrepreneurs by professional managers; and the internationalization of U.S. corporations. The impact of the first two developments is obvious: they significantly decentralized authority within the corporate system, making it less likely that the position of any one firm could provide a point of departure for understanding the needs of business as a whole. Most of the voluminous literature on the separation of ownership and control is concerned with its impact on corporate economic behavior; what has been overlooked is its impact on corporate political consciousness.[56] This is serious: the managerial revolution severely undermined the formation of corporate class consciousness and business solidarity.

Unlike entrepreneurs, the views of managers tend to be relatively unoriginal and predictable. Their selection process encourages a bureaucratic mentality. While a handful do go on to distinguished careers in public or university life, most develop perspectives that are peculiarly and uniquely suited to the preservation and growth of the specific enterprise to which they have devoted most of their adult lives; there is nothing in their training or selection process that encourages a broader political sophistication or the ability to exercise political leadership.[57] While most of them commonly hold equity interests in the firms they administer, these interests are only rarely sufficient for control: the managers remain fundamentally trustees for the firm's owners and are indeed legally required to act according to their best judgement of the owner's interests. Unlike the owner-manager, the professional manager thus cannot even unequivocally speak for the firm he represents; his shareholders— whether individual or institutional—constantly look over his shoulder and make his role analogous to that of a paid employee. In sum, corporate executives are not a bourgeoisie in the nineteenth century sense of the term. They are united neither by kinship ties nor a unique class-generated ethos. Hacker concludes: 'Even though their paths undoubtedly cross in the course of business, our top managers are not linked together in ways that make them a cohesive culture. Nor do they have the kind of self confidence that characterizes a bourgeoisie. Balzac would find nothing to write about here.'[58]

The growing anonymity of corporate executives since the 1930s, has been compounded by recent increases in the rate of turnover of occupants of executive suites. Due to the political and economic pressures that have beset business over the last few years, the average tenure of a chief executive officer has declined from five to seven years to between three and five. Four years is barely time enough to master the operations of an international, multidivisional enterprise, let alone to develop an appreciation of the problems faced by the capitalist system. High rates of management turnover are simply not conducive to the development of class consciousness. On the contrary, they encourage an ever greater focus on short-run profit maximization.

A critical factor that underlies the defensiveness of American corporate executives since the New Deal is that they have been incapable of generating their own political leadership. They have been forced to confront systemic challenges at least as serious as during the Progressive Era with an internal structure of leadership and authority that in many ways is as fragmented as that of the late nineteenth century. The growing role of government in the American economy since the 'thirties can be understood as a structural response to the inability of American businessmen to look after their own interests and those of American capitalism. The New Deal not only saved the business system, it saved it in spite of the virtually unanimous opposition of businessmen themselves. That the business system has functioned comparatively well during the last four decades is in no small measure due to the important political defeats that business has experienced; the success of many of the liberal challenges to business has proven functional to American economic growth and political stability. To some extent business wins when it loses: liberal political constituencies—often critical of specific business policies though sympathetic to the capitalist system—have played an important role in balancing the too-rigid antistatist outlook of the business community. The state, guided to an important extent by the pressures and power of noncorporate constituencies, most notably the liberal intelligentsia and the trade union movement, has taken upon itself the responsibility for articulating and implementing the needs of the business system as a whole. The governmental process mediates between the subjective preferences of businessmen and the long-term interests of the business system. Elected and appointed government officials are usually more sophisticated and enlightened than mainstream Dallas Country Club opinion and it is they who represent the objective interests of the American bourgeoisie. Moreover, it is service in critical policy-making positions in government that gives many businessmen a more informed sense of the realities of American political life and an understanding of the political and social environment of the business system. This frequently distances them from their fellow executives whose world view remains more narrowly economic.

The importance of government to business is not adequately measured by the number of former or future executives holding public positions. For the most part these officials simply reproduce the competitive divisions of the marketplace in the public sector. Their influence on government policies is by no means inconsequential, but their decisions most directly affect the interests and preoccupations of relatively narrow, and often competing, business constituencies. The class or systemic interests of business actually preoccupy a relatively small group of government officials and institutions, most notably the Office of the President, the Council of Economic Advisors, the Federal Reserve Board, the Office of Management and Budget, the National Security Council and the holders of the top positions in the Departments of State, Treasury and Defense. It is the prominent role of businessmen in these positions—people such as Charlie Wilson, Douglass Dillon, Robert McNamara, David Packard, Roy Ash, John Connally, Dean Acheson, Averell Harriman—that has given rise to an extensive literature on the cohesion and interpenetration of business and government elites.[59] The conclusions of much of this literature oversimplify the dynamics of business-government relations in the post New Deal era. These higher level policy-makers do not serve the critical and long-term interests of American business by using their public positions to advance their interests as businessmen. On the contrary, they perform a constructive role in their context precisely to the extent to which they are able to transcend their role as businessmen and formulate a broader strategy for defining and coping with the interests of the American capitalist system—interests that include a legitimate role for public authority and thus are often contrary to the preferences of most businessmen. The growing importance of government over the last four decades has thus made the lack of corporate class consciousness a manageable problem for the American business system; the political system has provided business with the leadership that it is incapable of generating on its own.

A similar analysis clarifies the role of private research organizations, such as the Conference Board, the Council on Foreign Relations, the Brookings Institution and the Committee for Economic Development. These organizations have frequently been referred to as conduits between the two sectors; they allegedly provide a vehicle through which corporate interests can be articulated and transformed into public policy. To the extent that they help the American political and economic system function more effectively, however, they do so by not mirroring the views and opinions of their business membership. On the contrary, their role is an educational one. They provide a forum through which political leaders, relatively sophisticated executives and, most importantly, their own highly professional staffs (frequently supplemented by outside consultants) can enlighten businessmen as to the political and economic realities of their domestic and international environment. The public reports of these organizations are invariably more sophisticated than the executives whose corporations provide much of their funding; they do not so much reflect corporate preferences as shape them. By contrast, the Chamber of Commerce of the United States, the National Association of Manufacturers and almost all trade associations have minimal impact on the broader issues of government involvement in society largely because their staffs too closely echo the views of their membership. A similar analysis can be made of the numerous, well-publicized conferences at which executives allegedly use the informal social atmosphere to increase their access to public decision making. In fact, the exchange of influence is probably reversed: they provide the opportunity for government officials and other business leaders to raise the consciousness of the majority of business participants.

The businessmen who occupy positions of leadership within the business community and society—either by virtue of their public stature or their position as head of powerful non-profit institutions, including government, universities, foundations, research organizations, etc.—are not typical businessmen; public roles and settings, except perhaps at a local level, make most corporate executives uncomfortable. Rather, business leadership tends to be disproportionately drawn from the legal profession (McCoy, Dulles) and investment banking (Simon, Dillon). To the extent that corporate executives do play a prominent public role, they tend to be either bankers (Champion, Lundborg) or sons of successful entrepreneurs (David Rockefeller, Edgar Kaiser, Irwin Miller, Thomas Watson Jr., Henry Ford, II). Those in the first three categories are by nature positioned to promote an understanding of business problems as a whole while those in the latter are members of an authentic bourgeoisie. It may be more than coincidence that American business was saved during the 1930s under the leadership of a member of one of the nation's most aristocratic families.

CONCLUSION

Our argument is that American businessmen, throughout most of their history and particularly over the last forty years, have proven incapable of understanding adequately the economic and political requirements of the socioeconomic system upon whose political stability and economic growth their own social existence rests. Not only is there nothing automatic about the process by which members of the bourgeoisie become aware of their class interests but, on the contrary, the process is highly problematic. Although our discussion of this issue has been confined to the United States, our conclusion raises a much broader issue: to what extent have students of capitalism systematically exaggerated the political capacities of the business community? Should Marx's description of the political immobilization of the French bourgeoisie in *The Eighteenth Brumaire of Louis Bonaparte* be seen as prototypical rather than unusual?[60] Ironically, did Marx himself, in his attempt to use the French and British bourgeois revolutions of the seventeenth and eighteenth centuries as a model for the impending proletarian revolutions, contribute to an overestimation of the ability of the bourgeoisie to identify their common interests and effectively mobilize around them?

Indeed, a recent study by Saboul of the French Revolution[61]—traditionally viewed by both non-Marxist and Marxists as the classic bourgeois revolution—argues that the political, economic and social reforms that destroyed the aristocratic, quasi-feudal order and established the foundation for capitalism were neither initiated nor supported by the bourgeoisie; they were achieved in spite of them. Similarly, both Joseph Schumpeter's *Capitalism, Socialism, and Democracy* and Barrington Moore's *Social Origins of Dictatorship and Democracy*, in their seminal comparative analysis of the dynamics of modern capitalism, place relatively little emphasis on the historical role of business communities.[62] Moore accounts for the development of both democracy and fascism largely in terms of the relationship between the landed aristocracy and the peasants; the preferences of the bourgeoisie play a passive role. Schumpeter contends that in Europe it is the aristocracy that has provided the political leadership in capitalist societies. Reaching conclusions remarkably similar to those of de Tocqueville, he writes:

> Of the industrialist and merchant the opposite is true. There is surely no trace of any mystic glamour about him which is what counts in the ruling of men. The stock exchange is a poor substitute for the Holy Grail. We have seen that the industrialist and merchant, as far as they are entrepreneurs, also fill a function of leadership. But economic leadership of this type does not readily expand, like the medieval lord's military leadership, into the leadership of nations. On the contrary, the ledger and the cost calculation absorb and confine.
>
> I have called the bourgeois rationalist and unheroic. He can only use rationalist and unheroic means to defend his position or to bend a nation to his will. Nor are his experiences and habits of life of the kind

that develop personal fascination. A genius in the business office may be, and often is, utterly unable outside of it to say boo to a goose—both in the drawing room and on the platform. Knowing this he wants to be left alone and to leave politics alone.

· · ·

The inference is obvious: barring such exceptional conditions, the bourgeois class is ill equipped to face the problems, both domestic and international, that have normally to be faced by a country of any importance . . . But without protection by some non-bourgeois group, the bourgeoisie is politically helpless and unable not only to lead its nation but even to take care of its particular class interest.[63]

If the above analysis is correct, we would expect that the economic system will perform better when business plays a less direct role in the formation of public policy. In fact, since the 1930s, corporate profits have been consistently higher under Democratic than under Republican administrations; yet the latter are more likely to reflect the political preferences of the business community.

Our analysis generates the following working hypotheses about the political consciousness of businessmen in advanced industrial societies. Since our data are largely confined to the American experience, they should be regarded as tentative.

(1) The mistrust of the state by businessmen is a function of the state's previous role in industrial development: the greater the state's leadership and direction, the greater the cohesiveness between present business and governmental elites.[64] Put differently, the weaker the authority of the state with respect to industrial policy, the greater the likelihood that contemporary businessmen will oppose extensions of the state's authority.

(2) The ideological hostility of businessmen toward their state is a function of their state's democratic heritage: the greater the responsiveness of the state to popular or interest-group pressures, the more likely it is that businessmen will find increased state authority over economic decisions threatening.

(3) The smaller the state's previous role in industrial development, the greater the fragmentation of authority within the business community.

Our essay stresses the uniqueness of the American business system in order to underline the usefulness of understanding the nature of American capitalism in comparative terms. In terms of the above hypotheses, France, Germany, and Japan would represent cases at the opposite ends of the continuum. In each nation the state played a leadership role in industrialization, virtually creating the business community. In addition, each state (Prussia in the case of Germany) had strong autocratic traditions that in France and Japan continue into the present. There is in fact relatively little principled opposition toward strong government by French, German, or Japanese businessmen. In addition, economic decision making is relatively concentrated in the banks in Germany and in the state in Japan and France.

Britain falls somewhere in the middle of the continuum, though its experience more closely resembles the United States than that of the nations on the continent. The British state played a supportive role in the early stages of capitalist development but its participation was far less than in those nations that industrialized after it. Non-business institutions, including the government, were not allowed to atrophy as in the United States; throughout the period of industrial development they continued to attract competent leadership and were accorded relatively high prestige. The British government was certainly more closely identified with democratic traditions and more responsive to mass pressures than the French, German, or Japanese, but clearly less closely than the American. In fact, businessmen in Britain have felt relatively less comfortable with their government than in most capitalist nations: at least some of the antistatist ideology of the executives of multinational corporations can be traced to British-based firms. (Britain is the second largest home of multinational corporations). On the other hand, economic and political elites are far closer than they are in the United States, and British businessmen express far less mistrust of their government than their American counterparts; indeed, if anything, the contempt flows in the opposite direction. Finally, the fragmentation of economic and political decision making is second only to the United States.[65]

Having begun with ideology, we conclude with social structure. The perception of the American state that is shared by American corporate executives is a function of its particular role in the development of American capitalism. The social and economic conditions of nineteenth century America, as well as the international economic environment, made the emergence of a strong national state less critical to industrial growth. The relative conservatism of the American working class meant that the American bourgeoisie did not need a powerful central authority to preserve industrial order while, on the other hand, the relative openness of the American governmental system meant that business could not trust public authorities to safeguard their immediate interests.

The weakness of the American state is a function of the strength of American capitalism—both politically and economically. Domestically in the latter half of the nineteenth century and internationally since the Second World War, the American state could largely confine its role to that of an umpire because the private sector was strong enough to compete successfully. American multinational-corporation managers could transfer the suspicion of government of their forefathers to the international arena because their power *vis-à-vis* foreign firms was roughly analogous to their strength with respect to noncapitalist forces in late nineteenth century America: for a generation after the Second World War, all the world had become like pre-New Deal industrial America. While American businessmen occasionally complain that the American government gives its nationals far less direct political and economic assistance than do those of the other capitalist governments, the relative distance between business and the U.S. government abroad is characteristic of the United States' role as a hegemonic power; it projects the historic structure of American business-state relations on an international scale. *In this sense, an antistatist ideology is a luxury that can only be enjoyed by a relatively powerful and successful bourgeoisie.* Because its structure of authority is particularly fragmented, i.e., investment decisions are relatively decentralized and the American business community lacks the authority to discipline its own members, corporate executives find it difficult to act collectively. Their individualistic ideology both reflects and reinforces this objective reality. To the extent that the challenges that confront American business are best handled by a relatively decentralized, competitive business structure, the American model will remain viable and the lack of solidarity and institutional cohesion within the American business community will prove functional for the business system. This state of affairs has clearly characterized the greater part of American economic development until the present.

On the other hand, American business currently faces a number of difficulties, including a relatively unstable business cycle, 'stagflation' and problems of international resource scarcity and foreign competition that may now make a collective or disciplined response more appropriate. If this is true, then American businessmen will face far greater difficulty than their counterparts in other capitalist nations whose pattern of economic development renders the principle and practice of strong state authority, or at least extensive private-public co-ordination, more acceptable. One can predict that, if domestic political or international economic pressures force the American state significantly to increase its authority over business decisions, American executives will find the adjustment a painful one. Having enjoyed a relatively high degree of freedom from out-side interference, they will find its diminution particularly difficult to accept.

NOTES

1. Wilbert Moore, *The Conduct of the Corporation* (New York: Vintage Books, 1962), pp. 278–79.

2. Leonard Silk and David Vogel, *Ethics and Profits: The Crisis of Confidence in American Business* (New York: Simon and Schuster, 1976). For survey data that confirm the book's portrait of business attitudes toward government, see William Martin and George Cabot Lodge, 'Our Society in 1985: Business May Not Like It', *Harvard Business Review*, LIII (1975), 143–52.

3. A recent poll of *Fortune* 500 chief executives conducted by the maga-zine reported that when asked to identify the biggest 'problem faced by business in general' 35.2 per cent named 'government' (Charles Burck, 'A Group Profile of the Fortune 500 Chief Executives', *Fortune*, 93 [May 1976], 172–77.

4. Clifford Geertz, 'Ideology as a Cultural System', in David E. Apter, ed., *Ideology and Discontent* (New York: Free Press, 1964), pp. 47–76, at p. 63.

5. Grant McConnell, *Private Power and American Democracy* (New York: Vintage Books, 1966), p. 294.

6. The most important studies are: Richard Hofstadter, *Social Darwinism in American Thought* (Boston, Mass.: Beacon Press, 1944); Robert Green Mc-Closkey, *American Conservatism in the Age of Enterprise 1865–1910* (New York: Harper and Row, 1951); James Prothro, *Dollar Decade: Business Ideas in the 1920s* (Baton Rouge: Louisiana State University Press, 1954).

7. Francis X. Sutton, Seymour Harris, Carl Naysen, and James Tobin, *The American Business Creed* (New York: Schocken Books, 1956), pp. 185, 280–81.

8. Marver Bernstein, 'Political Ideas of Selected American Business Jour-nals', *Public Opinion Quarterly*, XVII (1953), 258–67.

9. Edward Mason, 'Interests, Ideologies and the Problem of Stability and Growth', *American Economic Review*, LIII (1963), 1–18. See also Andrew Shonfield, *Modern Capitalism* (New York: Oxford University Press, 1965). For a comprehensive review of recent literature in this area, see Thomas DiBacco, 'The Political Ideas of American Business: Recent Interpretations', *Review of Politics*, XXX (1968), 51–58.

10. Silk and Vogel, *Ethics and Profits*, p. 46.

11. Quoted in Robert Gilpin, *U.S. Power and the Multinational Corporation* (New York: Basic Books, 1975), p. 136.

12. The notion that multinational corporations are essentially a function of United States' hegemony forms the essential thrust of Gilpin's analysis.

13. See, for example, Michael Reagan, *The Management Economy* (New York: Oxford University Press, 1963); John Kenneth Galbraith, *The New Industrial State* (Boston: Houghton-Mifflin, 1967); Charles Reich, *The Green-*

ing of America (New York: Random House, 1970); Morton Minz and Jerry Cohen, *America Inc.* (New York: Dial Press, 1971).

14. Max Ways, 'Creative Federalism', *Fortune*, 73 (January 1966), pp. 120–22 *et seq.*

15. Theodore Levitt, 'The Johnson Treatment', *Harvard Business Review*, XLV (1967), 114–28.

16. Gabriel Kolko, *The Triumph of Conservatism* (Chicago: Quadrangle Books, 1963); James Weinstein, *The Corporate Ideal in the Liberal State* (Boston, Mass.: Beacon Press, 1968).

17. Morrell Heald, *The Social Responsibilities of Business: Company and Community, 1900–1960* (Cleveland, Ohio: The Press of Case Western Reserve University, 1970).

18. Robert Cuff, *The War Industries Board* (Baltimore: Johns Hopkins University Press, 1973); Prothro, *Dollar Decade*. For business thinking during the latter part of the nineteenth century, see also Edward Kirkland, *Dream and Thought in the Business Community* (Chicago: Quadrangle Books, 1956).

19. V. O. Key, Jr., *Politics, Parties and Pressure Groups* (New York: Thomas Crowell, 1964), p. 77.

20. McConnell, *Private Power and American Democracy*, p. 293.

21. Moore, *Conduct of the Corporation*, p. 279.

22. This is the thrust of McConnell's book as well as of Theodore Lowi's *The End of Liberalism* (New York: W. W. Norton, 1969). Lowi writes: 'the pluralist's embrace of government turned out to be, in its own way, as anti-governmental as capitalism', p. 47. What weakens both the studies—a weakness made apparent by the contrast between the radicalism of their critique of private-public relations and the innocence of their solutions (McConnell advocates large constituencies, while Lowi calls for the rule of law and judicial democracy) is that the authors confine their analysis of the problem of public control of private power to one case study: the United States. It is this defect, so prevalent among students of American politics, that this essay attempts to overcome.

23. For a detailed discussion of the deep reluctance with which American businessmen acquiesced in the creation of a strong state in the post-war period in order to conduct foreign policy, see David S. McLellan and Charles E. Woodhouse, 'The Business Elite and Foreign Policy', *Western Political Science Quarterly*, XIII (1960), 172–90; Thomas DiBacco, 'American Business and Foreign Aid: The Eisenhower Years', *Business History Review*, XLI (1967), 21–35; also see a doctoral dissertation in preparation for the Department of Sociology at the University of California, Berkeley, by Clarence Lo, 'The Home Front Quagmire: The Organization of Dissent and Economic Policy During the Korean War'. Franz Schurmann describes a similar gap between political and business elites after the Second World War. He writes: 'But imperialism would cost a lot of money, and business was expected to pay a large share of it. Why should a business sacrifice present earnings earmarked for its own corporate expansion to a federal budget which would give them to foreign governments to generate economic recovery abroad, which would benefit America generally but not necessarily the

particular business that had poured its huge corporate taxes into government.' *The Logic of World Power* (New York: Pantheon, 1974), p. 27.

24. Thus Robert Lane contends that with the passage of time businessmen become more reconciled to regulation: 'the period of impact yields insensibly to a more relaxed period of continuation.' See 'Law and Opinion in the Business Community', *Public Opinion Quarterly*, XVII (1953), 239–57.

25. Though his view is somewhat exaggerated, Theodore Levitt's litany contains much truth. He argues:

It is not necessary to recount in detail the dismal record of American business's endless series of lost causes. Whether we talk about the Sherman Antitrust Act or the Federal Reserve Act, or the Federal Trade Commission Act or the National Park Service Acts, or the Child Labor Acts or the Securities Exchange Act, or the Wagner Act or the Fair Labor Standards Act of 1938, or the Old Age and Survivors Insurance Benefits Act or the Federal Housing Acts, or the Marshall Plan or Aid to Dependent Children Act, or the Federal Education Act, the Poverty Program, or Medicare—business as a rule fought these programs and lost. Often it fought them with such gruesome predictions of awful consequences to our private enterprise system that one wonders how the foretellers of such doom can now face themselves in the mirror each morning and still believe themselves competent to make important decisions on major matters in their own companies.

('Why Business Always Loses', *Harvard Business Review*, XLVI (1968), 81–89.)

26. In a seminal article, 'American Business Public Policy, Case-Studies and Political Theory', *World Politics*, XVI (1964), 677–715, Theodore Lowi distinguishes among distributive policies—those that affect the revenues of an individual corporation, i.e., contracts, subsidies; regulatory policies—those that affect group interests, i.e., consumer protection laws; and redistributive policies—those that affect the distribution of resources among social classes, i.e., tax policy.

27. It is difficult to document the birth of American capitalism with precision, but the 1850s appear the most reasonable date. According to George Taylor, the 1850s witnessed 'the emergence of the wage earner'—a permanent working class. David Montgomery estimates that 60 per cent of the American labor force was employed by 1860. The above are cited in Eric Foner, *Free Soil, Free Labor, Free Men* (New York: Oxford University Press, 1970), p. 32. Both Stuart Bruchey in the *Roots of American Economic Growth, 1607–1861* (New York: Harper and Row, 1965) and Norman Ware, *The Industrial Worker 1840–1860* (New York: Quadrangle Books, 1964), suggest that by mid-century the fluidity of antebellum American life had become somewhat reduced and that a more rigid industrial class structure was emerging.

28. See for example, Louis Hartz, *Economic Policy and Democratic Thought* (Chicago: Quadrangle Books, 1968); Oscar Handlin and Mary Handlin, *Commonwealth: A Study of the Role of Government in the American Economy, Mas-*

sachusetts, 1774–1861 (Cambridge, Mass.: Harvard University Press, 1969); for a more comprehensive summary of this period, see Robert Lively, 'The American System: A Review Article', *Business History Review*, March 1955, 81–96. What was distinctive about the pattern of business-government cooperation in pre-Civil War America was that it was largely carried out at the local level. The federal structure thus made the development of national political institutions to construct an infrastructure less necessary; by the 1840s, however, state authorities had become rather weak. It is the nature of the national government's role that is critical to an understanding of the political economy of American industrialism and the attitude of business toward government.

29. Louis Hartz, *The Liberal Tradition in America* (New York: Harcourt, Brace and World, 1955); Anthony Giddens, *The Class Structure of Advanced Societies* (New York: Harper and Row, 1975), p. 207.

30. Alexander Gerschenkron, 'Economic Backwardness in Historical Perspective,' in David Landes, ed., *The Rise of Capitalism* (New York: Macmillan, 1966).

31. Wallace Farnham, 'The Weakened Spring of Government: A Study in Nineteenth Century American History', *American Historical Review*, LXVIII (1963), 662–80.

32. David Bazelon, *The Paper Economy* (New York: Vintage Books, 1959), p. 179.

33. Alexis de Tocqueville, *Democracy in America*, Vol. II (New York: Schocken Books, 1961), p. 298. For over one hundred years—from the inauguration of the spoils system in 1829 to the arrival of FDR's 'Brain Trust' in the 1930s—the best and the brightest devoted their energies almost exclusively to the private sector.

34. Thomas Cochran, *Business in American Life: A History* (New York: McGraw-Hill, 1972), p. 124; Hartz, *Economic Policy*, p. 31.

35. Alfred D. Chandler, Jr., 'The Beginnings of Big Business in American Industry', *Business History Review*, XXXIII (1959), 1–31.

36. Chandler, *Strategy and Structure* (Cambridge, Mass.: MIT Press, 1962).

37. Rawleigh Warner, Jr., 'On Business and Education', *Princeton Alumni Weekly*, 76: 12 (26 January 1976), 8–12.

38. Quoted in John William Ward, 'The Ideal of Individualism and the Reality of Organization', in Earl Cheit, ed., *The Business Establishment* (New York: Wiley, 1964), p. 51. See also James Willard Hurst, *Law and the Conditions of Freedom* (Madison: The University of Wisconsin Press, 1956). On p. 16 Hurst writes:

Thus the grant of corporate status became a notable issue in the years of Jacksonian Democracy. This did, indeed, involve serious issues concerning the power structure of the society; the Jacksonian polemics on this score forecast the issues in the background of the Granger movement and the Sherman Act. But, aside from the sensitive matter of banks, currency, and credit, the demand for freer incorporation, deep down, fitted the dominant temper of the times, Jacksonian as well as Whig.

39. McCloskey, *American Conservatism in the Age of Enterprise*, pp. 23–24.

40. Prothro, *Dollar Decade*, pp. 53–54.

41. These quotations are from Silk and Vogel, *Ethics and Profits*, pp. 188, 194.

42. Contrast, for example, Lowi's pattern of interest-group liberalism with Ezra Suleiman's study of the French bureaucracy in *Politics, Power, and Bureaucracy in France* (Princeton, N.J.: Princeton University Press, 1974).

43. Samuel Hays, 'The Politics of Reform in Municipal Government in the Progressive Era', *Pacific Northwest Quarterly*, LV (1964), 157–69; Walter Dean Burnham, *Critical Elections and the Mainsprings of American Politics* (New York: W. W. Norton, 1970).

44. Note by contrast Suzanne Berger's study of the importance of small-scale enterprise to the Italian economy in 'The Uses of the Traditional Sector: Why the Declining Classes Survive,' unpublished paper. Although this paper focuses on the attitudes of the executives of relatively large firms, the contrast in the attitude of American small businessmen toward government with that of their economic counterparts in France and Italy is even more striking. American small businessmen are fierce individualists, bitterly resentful of government interference in their affairs. On the other hand, the traditional sectors in France and Italy are utterly dependent on government assistance and protection and much of their energy is directed toward securing public benefits. See John H. Bunzel, *The American Small Businessman* (New York: Knopf, 1962).

45. Norman Birnbaum, 'The Sociological Study of Ideology', *Current Sociology*, IX (1960), 91–117.

46. Giddens, *Class Structure*, p. 111.

47. Ibid., p. 112.

48. Morris Rosenberg, 'Perceptual Obstacles to Class Consciousness', *Social Forces*, XXXII (1953), 22–27.

49. The literature on the individualistic strain in American business ideology is extensive. See Ward, 'The Ideal of Individualism', p. 51. Also see Irvin Wyllie, *The Self-Made Man in America* (New Brunswick, N.J.: Rutgers University Press, 1954); John Cawelti, *Apostles of the Self-Made Man* (Chicago: University of Chicago Press, 1965).

50. De Tocqueville, *Democracy in America*, pp. 167, 193.

51. Karl Polanyi, *The Great Transformation* (Boston, Mass.: Beacon, 1944), p. 19. See especially Chaps. 3–10.

52. Treasury Secretary Simon notes:

> If you believe in a free marketplace and in the right to succeed in business, you also must accept the other side of the coin, the right to go out of business . . . I believe that if companies fail to adapt to changes in competitive conditions . . . they have no claim to public support . . . [T]he public should not be fleeced of taxes to keep any business alive that, like the dinosaur, has outlived its usefulness.

Quoted in John Minahan, 'Is Free Market A Dirty Word?' *Saturday Review*, II: 21 (12 July 1975), 18–19.

53. Silk and Vogel, *Ethics and Profits*, p. 179.

54. See, for example, James O'Connor, *The Fiscal Crisis of the State* (New York: St. Martin's Press, 1973), p. 197. Also see Galbraith, *The New Industrial State*. This point is admittedly a controversial one. An observer more sympathetic to business writes:

> The thoughtful and fair-minded reader will grant the difficulty of proving that the legislation business opposed has in any way seriously damaged our economy.
>
> . . . [W]ith all his calculating pragmatism, all his unsentimental zeal to junk what is old and decaying, and all his eagerness to find and adopt new things for his business, the modern executive acts in a contradictory manner when it comes to new ideas about social reform and relations between business and government. He welcomes new things in his business, but not in the relationship of his business to his government and his society.

(Theodore Levitt, 'Why Business Always Loses', pp. 84–84.)

55. Kolko, *Triumph and Conservatism*, and Weinstein, *The Corporate Ideal*.

56. For the most recent and thorough review of this debate and its significance, see Maurice Zeitlin, 'Corporate Ownership and Control: The Large Corporation and the Capitalist Class', *American Journal of Sociology*, LXXIX (1974), 1073–1119.

57. Most studies of top management emphasize the insularity of the typical chief executive. Thus, Levitt writes:

> One of the most distressing facts about so many highly intelligent business leaders I know—men whom I respect and admire—is how poorly informed they are about matters on which they have strong views. A weekly inside-dope newsletter from Washington, speeches by like-minded sycophants at association meetings and luncheon clubs, and the business press are generally very inadequate for a man's continued education about the realities of our world . . .
>
> It is no surprise therefore that the usual executive is a poor pragmatist when it comes to the externals. He simply lacks the equipment. Preoccupied with internal change and uncertainty, he generally denounces any external changes being proposed.

(Levitt, 'Why Business Always Loses,' pp. 83–84.)

Similarly, Andrew Hacker notes:

> The difficulty, when all is said and done, is that corporation executives are not very interesting people. And not the least reason for their blandness is the sort of individuals they have to become in order to get where they do. . . . There is not much point, then, in musing about how nice it would be if our corporate managers underwent more instruction in moral philosophy or modern sociology. The simple fact is that they are busy men, on the way up during most of their formative years, and the exigencies of the climb compel them to think of themselves rather than for themselves.

Andrew Hacker, 'The Making of a [Corporation] President', in Harry Treb-
ing, ed., *The Corporation in the American Economy* (Chicago: Quadrangle
Books, 1970), pp. 74–75. See also Clarence Randall, 'Business Too Has Its
Ivory Towers', in Trebing, *The Corporation*. For similar appraisals, see C.
Wright Mills, *The Power Elite* (New York: Oxford University Press, 1957),
Chap. 6, 'The Chief Executives'; and David Finn, *The Corporate Oligarch*
(New York: Clarion, 1969).

58. Andrew Hacker, 'Is There a Ruling Class?' *New York Review of Books*,
22: 7 (1 May 1975), 9–13.

59. Literature in this tradition includes G. William Domhoff, *Who Rules
America?* (Englewood Cliffs, N.J.: Prentice-Hall, 1967); David Horowitz, ed.,
Corporations and the Cold War (New York and London: Monthly Review Press,
1969); Wright Mills, *The Power Elite*; Ralph Miliband, *The State in Capitalist
Society* (New York: Basic Books, 1969).

60. An important school of contemporary Marxist thought, structuralism,
argues roughly this position. See Nicos Poulantzas, *Political Power and Social
Classes* (London: New Left Books, 1973). Structuralism argues that the 'only
way [the long-term interests of the capitalist system] can be protected . . . is
through the relative autonomy of the state, through a state structure which
is capable of transcending the parochial, individualized interests of specific
capitalists and capitalist class fractions.' David Gold, Clarence Lo, Erik Olin
Wright, 'Recent Developments in Marxist Theories of the Capitalist State',
Monthly Review, 27:5 (October 1975), 29–41. Not surprisingly, Poulantzas
draws heavily on *The Eighteenth Brumaire* for his argument. An interesting
sidelight about this issue is presented in Anthony Sampson's study of the
multinational oil corporations, *The Seven Sisters* (New York: Viking, 1975), p.
310: 'Dr. Kissinger, after one meeting with the oilmen (during the negotiations with OPEC), was heard to complain that they were a living disproof of
the maxim of Marx, that the captains of industry always know in the end
where their true political interests lie.' The Secretary is evidently unfamiliar
with recent developments in the Marxist theory of the state.

61. Albert Soboul, *The French Revolution*, translated from French by Allen
Forrest and Colin Young (London: New Left Books, 1974).

62. Joseph A. Schumpeter, *Capitalism, Socialism, and Democracy* (New York:
Harper Torchbooks, 1942); Barrington Moore, Jr., *Social Origins of Dictatorship and Democracy* (Boston, Mass.: Beacon Press, 1966).

63. Schumpeter, *Capitalism, Socialism, and Democracy*, pp. 137–38.

64. John Zysman advances a similar hypothesis:

One could hypothesize, for example, that where institutional structures
for state leadership in industry already exist, conservative groups will
use these structures to maintain stability and thus preserve their power.
Where such structures are absent, not having emerged naturally as a
part of the nation's industrial development, conservative groups will resist their creation and often see the state as a potential weapon in the
hands of their political enemies not a potential ally. Changing the structure of industrial power and the instruments for exercising it is likely to

be viewed as an attack on the position, privileges, and power of existing elites not simply a technical rearrangement for more effective industrial management.

(John Zysman, 'Financial Markets and Industrial Policy: The Structural Basis of Domestic and International Economic Strategies', unpublished paper, p. 15.)

65. The above paragraph draws upon Edwin M. Epstein, 'The Social Role of Business Enterprise in Britain: American Perspective', *Journal of Management Studies* (forthcoming). Epstein writes: 'It will be recalled that the first British Factories Acts were passed nearly a half-century before their American analogues. While a restless or over-energetic state is still instinctively the object of suspicion, post-World War II Britain is unquestionably a mixed economy and is accepted as properly so by all but the most reactionary elements of the political and business communities.' In addition, British economic and political elites are far more socially cohesive than in the United States.

Chapter Two

COOPERATIVE REGULATION: ENVIRONMENTAL PROTECTION IN GREAT BRITAIN

A GROWING NUMBER of politicians, editorial writers, academics, and business leaders have been urging that the public and private sectors work together more closely in order to improve the performance of the American economy. Much attention has naturally focused on Japan, whose system of business-government cooperation has become widely admired in the United States. Yet while Japanese institutions function extremely well in many respects, Japan hardly provides a model of effective government regulation, the one arena in which the aims of American business and government most conflict.

If one examines Japanese environmental protection policies, for example, the shortcomings of the close ties between business and government emerge clearly. The singleminded commitment of both institutions to rapid industrial development in the post-war period has exposed the Japanese public to considerable discomfort and injury; by the late 1960s Japan was literally the most polluted nation in the world. It was only after a series of widely-publicized outbreaks of a number of particularly horrible pollution-related diseases that the Japanese government first attempted to balance its commitment to economic expansion with the protection of public health and amenity. While the Japanese have devoted considerable resources to improving their physical environment since the special "Pollution Diet" of 1970, controversy continues: There have been violent demonstrations, the public humiliation of corporate executives, and a series of protracted, expensive, and extremely bitter lawsuits. The Japanese economy has been able to absorb considerable expenditures on pollution control without impairing its international competitiveness, but the Japanese still find it difficult to integrate environmental concerns into their political system.

LOOKING TO BRITAIN

If we are searching for an alternative model of effective business-goverment cooperation in the area of social regulation, we should look to Great Britain. The British government does many things very poorly—particularly in areas affecting the economy—but regulating industrial emissions and controlling land use are not among them. Britain has the oldest system of environmental controls of any industrial society: The basic legal and administrative framework of its system of air pollution control dates from the 1860s. In the decades following World War II, Britain has made considerable progress in improving the quality of its air and water and has preserved much of the character and beauty of its countryside and coastal areas. It has done so, moreover, without measurably impairing the economic performance of British industry; Britain's economic difficulties over the last half-century do not stem from its system of environmental regulations. On the contrary, British regulatory authorities have pursued a consistent policy of close cooperation with industry. They continue to rely more on persuasion and voluntary agreements and less on legal coercion than any other industrial democracy.

When compared to the other OECD nations, Britain's environmental policy must be judged a considerable success. It has led to far less antagonism between industry and government than we find in the United States, the Netherlands, or Sweden, and has been far more effective than the policies of France and Italy. In addition, the British have been more successful in integrating environmental pressure groups into their existing political institutions than either the Germans or the Japanese. According to a recent survey conducted throughout the European Economic Community (EEC), the British public is significantly less dissatisfied with the efforts of its government to protect the environment than are the Italians, French, Danes, Belgians, Dutch, or West Germans.[1] The contrast with America is particularly striking: In no other industrial country have environmental regulations created as much antagonism on the part of business or produced as much conflict between government and environmental organizations.

The British experience demonstrates that there is indeed a sensible alternative to the American adversarial style of regulation. It is in fact possible for a pluralist democracy to regulate business reasonably well without making the regulatory process into an ideological, political, and legal battleground. Moreover, in view of the similar political and cultural traditions of the United States and Great Britain, particularly when compared to those of Japan, the British regulatory system might well have some lessons to teach us about how to improve our own regulatory practices. These lessons will have very significant limitations—no regulatory scheme can be transplanted entirely—but are important nonetheless.

As one would expect, there are a number of similarities between the politics of environmental protection in Britain and the U.S. Both nations have a long tradition of public interest in environmental matters; the "countryside" in British political culture has historically occupied a position analogous to the "wilderness" in the United States. Beginning in the mid-1960s, public concern with the quality of the environment increased in both countries. The membership of existing environmental organizations increased considerably—for example, the number of local Amenity Societies in Britain grew from 550 in 1966 to 1250 in 1975—while a number of new, more activist pressure groups, including a chapter of Friends of the Earth, and the Conservation Society was formed. The environmental movements in each are relatively non-partisan, non-violent, and moderate in political outlook. In addition, many of the environmental conflicts that have recently surfaced in Britain—such as those over the siting of a third London airport, the construction of roadways in rural and urban areas, the legal limits on size of trucks, the lead content of gasoline, toxic waste disposal practices, the protection of endangered species, and the appropriateness of nuclear power—are quite similar to those in the United States.

A permanent Royal Commission on Environmental Pollution was established within a few months of the U.S. Council on Environmental Quality, while the organization of a Department of the Environment in Britain closely followed the establishment of the Environmental Protection Agency. Between 1969 and 1974 each nation enacted a number of important environmental statutes. Four major environmental laws were enacted by the American government—the National Environmental Policy Act (1969), the Clean Air Act Amendments (1970), the Federal Water Pollution Control Act (1972), and the Noise Pollution and Control Act (1972)—while three were approved by Parliament—the Deposit of Poisonous Waste Act (1972), the Water Pollution Act (1974), and the Control of Pollution Act (1974). All were enacted with substantial bipartisan support.

Systematic Informality

These comparisons, however, are deceptive. In spite of the common roots of their legal systems, the administration of environmental controls in the United Kingdom and the United States could not differ more sharply. The contrasts in the public policies of the nations are most dramatically revealed in the area of pollution control.

The regulation of most industrial sources of air pollution in Great Britain is under the jurisdiction of Her Majesty's Alkali and Clean

Air Inspectorate. Originally established in 1863 to regulate the hydrochloric acid produced by the manufacture of alkali, the responsibilities of the Inspectorate have since expanded steadily. At present they encompass 60 separate industrial processes, or approximately 2,200 plants. These include virtually all major industrial sources of air pollution, including those of nationalized industry. Other stationary sources of air pollution, such as those from individual households, are regulated by local authorities, while vehicle emissions are the responsibility of the Department of Transport. The Water Act of 1973 established ten regional water authorities throughout England and Wales, each roughly corresponding to a major river system. In addition to controlling industrial emissions, they are also responsible for sewage disposal, flood control, and water supply. A National Water Council acts as a coordinating body and establishes national guidelines for water quality. Overall responsibility for pollution control policy in Great Britain rests with the Central Unit on Environmental Pollution of the Department of the Environment, while the coordination of environmental policy for Scotland, Wales, and Northern Ireland is the responsibility of their respective Departmental Secretaries.

In contrast to the United States, both the courts and the national legislature play a relatively minor role in shaping British environmental regulations. In unusual cases, regulatory issues may be referred to the High Court for adjudication, but only with the consent of the minister whose department is responsible for enforcing the statute in question. The decisions of both the Alkali Inspectorate and the Regional Water Authorities may be appealed to the appropriate minister, usually the Secretary of State for the Environment. At his discretion he may choose to hold a formal hearing, but he is not bound to follow the recommendations of the hearing officer. This, however, occurs relatively infrequently; firms rarely challenge regulatory authorities in the courts. Individuals do have the right to sue polluters under various common-law doctrines, but these are limited in scope and have become less important in recent years. The environmental statutes approved by Parliament have been primarily administrative in nature, essentially establishing a framework for policies that are then implemented by civil servants.

The distinctive hallmark of the British system of pollution control is its flexibility. According to an official government document, "authorities, both central and local, are expected to operate on the philosophy that standards should be reasonably practicable." This principle was made explicit in the Alkali Act of 1874, which specified that polluters should use the "best practicable means" (BPM) of "preventing the discharge into the atmosphere of noxious gases." The Alkali Inspectorate defines "practicable" in three dimensions: local physical conditions and circumstances, corporate financial resources, and the current state of technological knowledge. "Means" refers not only to the installation of pollution control equipment, but also to its maintenance and design, as well as to the operation of the plant itself. Each "scheduled" plant is assigned its own emission limits by the Alkali Inspectorate, which is then responsible for monitoring their enforcement. All sources of effluent discharged into inland water, estuaries, and inshore seas must first be granted a "consent" by a Regional Water Authority. These are individually negotiated with each polluter and are established to reflect the nature of the substances being discharged, the capacity of the river system to absorb them, and the ultimate disposition of the water supply. They may be either unconditional, or subject to such factors as the duration of the discharge, its rate, quantity, and composition. Unlike in the United States, where the discretion of regulators has been severely circumscribed by the courts and the legislature, inspectors in Great Britain continue to have plenty of flexibility to take into account local circumstances and make suitable decisions. They are given plenty of autonomy and are trained to be decision makers with as much responsibility as possible.

FINDING THE "BEST PRACTICABLE MEANS"

The principle of BPM means that the costs of compliance are an important factor in establishing emission requirements. Even when improved pollution technology is available, plants are not required to install it if doing so would impair their economic viability. Only new plants are required to install improved abatement technology; older facilities are generally given additional time to comply, depending on the projected life of their existing pollution control equipment or that of the plant itself. Field inspectors consider financial hardship a legitimate justification for delayed or reduced compliance, and are extremely reluctant to enforce regulations that will create additional unemployment. As a result, the actual enforcement of emission controls varies with the economic health of particular industries and regions, and with the state of the economy as a whole. In contrast to the United States, the British government does not use environmental standards as a device to force companies to develop new techniques of pollution control; instead BPM is regarded, in the words of one of the first Chief Alkali Inspectors, as an "elastic band," tightening "as . . . science develops and places greater facilities in the hands of the manufacturers." He added:

> When necessary it could be shown that this phrase ["best practicable means"] would give greater security to the public than would the adoption of any fixed standards, at the same time pressing with less severity on some of the manufacturers, but more equally on all.[2]

The principle of BPM also means that industry-wide emission requirements can be modified to meet local environmental conditions. Thus, if there are relatively few other local sources of a particular pollutant, or if the prevailing winds or river conditions allow emissions to disperse naturally, requirements are accordingly less severe.

Lord Ashby, the first chairman of the Royal Commission on Environmental Pollution, recently observed:

> There is a striking contrast between the style of environmental legislation in Britain and in the USA. British lawmaking is piecemeal, reluctant, never wanting to pass statutes which promise more than could be performed. Some American lawmaking is unlike this; for example the US Water Pollution Control Amendment Act, 1972, which aspired to make all rivers fishable and swimmable by 1985.[3]

British environmental legislation contains no statutory deadlines and does not require that emission standards be based solely on either technical or health criteria, as is true in the United States. In general, the British make less use of both emissions standards and general environmental quality standards. The Annual Report of the Alkali Inspectorate does include a series of appendices that list "presumptive standards" for most classes of measurable emissions from plants under its jurisdiction. These standards, which are established after extensive consultation with the industries that have to adhere to them, serve as guides to individual companies and field inspectors; a firm is "presumed" to be in compliance if it meets them. However, they can be and are exceeded without a firm necessarily being in violation of the law. While the British have recently been making greater use of both emissions and general environmental quality standards, this is primarily a response to pressures from the EEC. The latter's efforts to harmonize environmental regulations among its member states have met with considerable resistance from the British, who contend that their more pragmatic and piecemeal approach is, in the long run, both more efficient and more effective. As the Secretary of State for the Environment wrote in 1977:

Except in clearly defined cases, we believe that it is better to maintain gradual progress in improving the environment in light of local circumstances and needs than to operate through the formulation of rigid national emission standards which may in particular circumstances be either unnecessarily harsh or insufficiently restrictive.[4]

Britain's reluctance to establish strict legal requirements for pollution control reflects the preference of its regulatory officials for securing compliance through persuasion and negotiation. British pollution control agencies are extremely reluctant to prosecute companies or publicly criticize them. As long as companies are making "reasonable" efforts to reduce emissions, they are considered law-abiding. Prosecution is thought to reflect badly on the image of regulatory authorities and is viewed as a last resort, to be used only when companies appear to be acting in "bad faith." This outlook was first expressed by Robert Angus Smith, the first Chief Inspectorate under the Alkali Act. He noted in 1872 that:

Some of the public would have preferred to see [us] frequently in court with cases of complaint, but I knew well that . . . habits must grow, and that to torment men into doing what required much time to learn was to return to the old system of teaching by the cane, instead of the intellect.[5]

One of his successors wrote nearly a century later: "Experience has convinced me that a spirit of mutual confidence and goodwill between inspectors and industrialists is essential to progress." His successor in turn argued in his annual report that:

Abating air pollution is a technological problem—a matter for scientists and engineers, operating in an atmosphere of cooperative officialdom. Great care has to be exercised by all to prevent the development of adversary attitudes.[6]

Not surprisingly, while self-regulation has fallen into disrepute in the United States in recent years, the British continue to make extensive use of it. Companies are often expected to monitor each other's adherence to standards that have been negotiated by their trade associations and to report violators to the government.

THE USES OF TRUST

Crucial to the effectiveness of the British regulatory system is the mutual respect that exists between industrialists and regulatory officials. The former display a remarkable degree of confidence in both the technical competence and good judgment of pollution control inspectors. With rare exceptions, they regard the pollution abatement measures required of their firms as "reasonable"; indeed, company engineers frequently seek out the advice of their counterparts in government in order to improve their pollution-control performance. Each inspector employed by the Alkali Inspectorate has a degree either in chemistry or chemical engineering, and is required to have had at least five years of experience working in industry. Officials in turn believe that most plant managers and company engineers are genuinely interested in curtailing emissions as much as possible. As one student of British air pollution control policy put it, the Alkali Inspectorate's "relation to the manufacturer is more like that of a doctor getting the patient's cooperation in treating a disease than of a policeman apprehending a culprit." One official summarized the contrasts between the British and the American approaches to enforcement in the following terms:

> We look upon our job as educating industry, persuading it. We achieve more this way. The Americans take a big stick and threaten, "solve your problem." We say to industry, "Look, lads, *we've* got a problem." In this way we've got industry well and truly tamed.[7]

The 1974 report of the Royal Commission on Environmental Pollution put the alternative confronting British pollution control authorities this way:

> either we have, as now, an authority which because of its close relationship with industry and consequent understanding of the problems is able to assess the technical possibilities for improvement in detail and press for their adoption; or an authority which sees its job as one of imposing demands on industry and which, because of the sense of opposition this approach would create, could not obtain the same co-operation by industry in assessing the problems and devising solutions.[8]

The contrast in the approaches of the British and American governments toward regulating industry is similar to the contrast in the division of national and local authority in each country. Local governmental units in Britain are not allowed to enforce stricter pollution control standards than those deemed appropriate by national authorities; however, on occasion the national government will allow standards to be relaxed in response to community pressures. In the United States, it is precisely the opposite. In some specific areas, state and local governments can impose requirements on industry that are stricter than those of the federal government, but if a particular state or community wishes to relax national environmental standards in order to maintain or attract industry, they may find it difficult. Paradoxically, while the United States has both a federal system and encompasses a much larger and more diverse geographic area, air and water pollution-control policy is actually far more centralized than in Great Britain. Since the late 1960s, the authority of state and local governments to control air and water pollution has been substantially reduced, even as the federal government's authority has increased significantly. In Great Britain, on the other hand, local governmental units continue to play a relatively important role both in setting standards and in their enforcement.

IS BRITISH REGULATION LESS STRICT?

It is obviously difficult to compare the severity of environmental regulations in the two countries—if for no other reason than that the British system operates more informally. It is striking, however, that while the appropriateness of using cost-benefit analysis to evaluate government regulation of industry is bitterly debated in the United States, it has failed to arouse much controversy in Great Britain. The explanation is a simple one: Its use would be superfluous. American corporate executives, and academics sympathetic to them, urge the use of cost-benefit analysis precisely because so much of American environmental regulation is written and enforced without reference to the costs of complying with it. In a sense, the use of cost-benefit analysis represents a surrogate for the inability of American industry to have its interests taken more seriously. The British business community has less need to urge the establishment of a formal system of cost-benefit analysis precisely because economic considerations are already integrated into its regulatory procedures. As a British government official noted in 1970:

> If money were unlimited there would be few . . . problems of . . . pollution control that could not be solved fairly quickly. We have the technical knowledge to absorb gases, etc. The only reason why we still permit the escape of these pollutants is because economics are an important part of the word "practicable."[9]

There is in fact one area in which a direct comparison of the effects of regulation is possible: energy development. The contrasts are dramatic. Although oil was discovered in Alaska before it was discovered in the North Sea, the latter area went into production well before the former—even though it presented far greater technical difficulties. (In fact, the same company—British Petroleum— was involved in both developments.) The development of Alaska's oil and natural gas reserves was delayed for a considerable period of time as a result of objections by environmentalists, even though rapid development was strongly favored by the government and residents of Alaska. While some of the residents of Scotland were concerned about the impact of energy development on their local communities, the development of North Sea oil proceeded as rapidly as was technically and economically feasible. It did so, moreover, without adversely affecting the physical beauty of the Scottish countryside and coastal areas.

Unlike the situation in the United States, permission to engage in off-shore drilling was never an issue in Britain, since the oil-bearing waters off the coasts are controlled by the central government. However, both nations have had to establish environmental standards for the establishment of on-shore facilities for the importation of energy from off-shore. Michael Thompson's account of the contrast between British and American regulatory requirements is worth quoting at length.

> Recently California and the United Kingdom have approved sites for Liquid Energy Gas (LEG) terminals. In this, and perhaps this alone, they are the same. After a long drawn-out process in which it proved impossible to approve any of the proposed sites California finally, with the help of a new statute passed expressly for the purpose, was able to give approval for an LEG facility at the remotest of all the sites on the list of possibles—Point Conception.
>
> Scotland has a longer coastline than California and most of the country is very sparsely populated (less than 25 persons to the square mile) and yet the approved site, at Mossmorran and Braefoot Bay on the Firth of Forth, lies within the most densely populated part of the entire country (with a population density of between 250 and 500 persons per square mile). Moreover, laden tankers will pass within a mile or so of Burntisland (an industrial town) and sometimes within 4 miles of Edinburgh—the capital city of Scotland! If the California siting criteria (explicit in Statute 1081) were to be applied to the Scottish case it would be quite impossible to approve the Mossmorran/Braefoot Bay site and, if the United Kingdom criteria (implicit in the Mossmorran/Braefoot Bay approval) were to be applied to the California case, any of the suggested sites could be approved which means that the terminal would go to the first site to be suggested—Los Angeles harbour.[10]

The counterpart of the "family-like" cooperation that exists between industry and government in Britain is the relative absence of effective opportunities for participation by other political constituencies. The Trade Union Council is consulted by the Alkali Inspectorate in the setting of presumptive standards and both the regional water councils and local air pollution authorities are responsive to elected local officials. In addition, individual citizens, community organizations, and amenity groups do use the hearing procedures established under the Town and Country Planning Act of 1947 to press for improvements in pollution control as a condition for granting a firm permission to expand or relocate. But while British officials are more accessible than their counterparts in most European countries, compared to the United States their system of pollution control is a remarkably closed one. The information that officials may disclose to the public is severely circumscribed by law and limited even further by custom: With rare exceptions both the air and water emissions authorized for each individual factory, as well as the extent to which firms have complied with them, remain secret. Even the names of companies that have been prosecuted are not made public. Moreover, the negotiations between industry representatives and government officials usually take place in private, with little or no opportunity for public participation.

It can be argued that companies in Britain cooperate with regulatory authorities because the latter are too lax. This point has often been made by many of the newer British environmental organizations established over the last 15 years. They especially resent the extraordinary secrecy that surrounds the relationship between industry and the regulatory authorities. As one journalist put it in *The New Scientist*, "In Britain today, data on individual emissions are guarded more closely than military blueprints." Yet it is striking that even many of the bitterest critics of this secrecy are nevertheless prepared to concede that pollution control officials are in fact conscientious and dedicated, and that it would be unfair to describe them as "captives" of the companies whose pollution they are responsible for controlling.

FINAL RESULT: A CLEANER ENVIRONMENT

The available evidence suggests that the British commitment to pollution control is in fact a serious one. While Britain, like every other industrial society, continues to have a number of serious local pollution problems, the overall quality of its physical environment has improved considerably in recent years. According to the periodic surveys conducted by the National Water Council, the water quality in England and Wales has steadily improved throughout the postwar period. As of 1980, nearly three-quarters of the lengths of English and Welsh rivers were unpolluted and less than 5 percent were considered "poor" or "grossly polluted." These figures represent an improvement over 1970 and also compare favorably with those for

other members of the EEC.[11] Twenty years ago there were no fish in
the lower Thames and the river emitted a disgusting smell; as of
1977, the river contained more than one hundred species of fish and
was largely odorless. In the early 1950s London was an extremely
dirty city, with high levels of smoke and sulphur dioxide; today, although London remains an important manufacturing center, its air
is as clear as that over East Anglia.

Since 1960, national emissions of smoke have fallen about 80 percent, and over the last decade emissions of sulphur dioxide, nitrogen
oxides, and hydrocarbons have all recorded declines.[12] Between 1973
and 1976 lead emissions from plants regulated by the Alkali Inspectorate were halved, arsenious oxide emissions were reduced by
nearly two-thirds, and emissions of vinyl chloride monomer from
PVC plants declined by more than three-quarters. Moreover, the
cost involved in all these efforts was not trivial, especially considering
the undistinguished performance of the British economy. According
to the most recent available figures, total expenditures on pollution
control in Britain were estimated at 2.5 billion pounds per year, or
between 1.5 and 2 percent of GDP at factor cost.[13] For the 1977–78
fiscal year, the total annual cost of water pollution controls for all
private industry in the U.K. was estimated at 200 million pounds,
and of air pollution, 560 million pounds. While direct comparisons
are difficult, according to data gathered by OECD for 1975, the percentage of British private investment in pollution control was less
than that of the U.S. and Japan, roughly comparable to that of Germany and the Netherlands, and greater than that of France, Finland, Denmark, Norway, and Sweden.

Thus, in many respects, the British approach toward environmental protection might be viewed as a model for regulatory reformers
in the United States. It enjoys a relatively high degree of legitimacy
among the diverse constituencies affected by it, while at the same
time it manages to avoid the time-consuming and expensive lobbying
and legal wrangling that exists in the United States. While Britain
has devoted fewer resources than the United States to reducing air
and water pollution over the last decade, what it has committed appears to have been allocated much more efficiently. Environmental
policy in the U.K. has also been free of the unpredictability and
abrupt changes in direction that have taken place in the United
States. Thus, just as Japan might have something to teach us about
how government and business can work together to promote industrial growth, so Britain might be in a position to instruct us in the
virtues of cooperation between business and government in the area
of government regulation.

REGULATION AND POLITICAL CULTURE

Unfortunately, neither happens to be the case. Environmental regulation, like public policy in general, does not take place in a vacuum. Each nation's approach to regulating industry, like its policies for promoting industrial growth, is the product of distinctive political traditions and institutions. We could no more establish the Alkali Inspectorate as a unit of the Environmental Protection Agency than we could transplant MITI to the Department of Commerce. *For in many important ways, each nation controls industrial emissions in much the same manner that it regulates everything else.* Thus Britain is a nation of remarkably few laws, rules, and regulations, while the United States, as the most casual glance at the Federal Register reveals, relies heavily on formal rules and procedures to control governmental and corporate behavior. If one compares the British and American approaches to insurance regulation, equal employment, banking regulation, consumer protection, occupational health and safety, or securities regulation, a clear pattern emerges: In each case Americans rely heavily on formal rules, often enforced in the face of strong opposition from the institutions affected by them, while the British continue to rely on flexible standards and voluntary compliance—including, in many cases, self-regulation.

How can we account for these significant differences in regulatory styles between two nations whose political traditions are in many respects so similar? Both the effectiveness and the legitimacy of British environmental policy appear to rest on three elements, none of which exists in the United States to the extent each does in Britain: a highly respected civil service, a business community that places a high value on acting "responsibly," and a public that is not unduly suspicious of business-government cooperation.

As numerous scholars have noted, Britain in the last quarter of the nineteenth century witnessed an important cultural backlash against the values of industrialization. Just as England neared the pinnacle of her industrial strength, the British business community suffered an erosion of its competitive spirit. Instead of seeking to expand its political and cultural influence, it was coopted by a resurgent aristocracy; rather than continuing industrial growth and expansion, it sought economic stability and social acceptability. As Martin Weiner writes in *English Culture and the Decline of the Industrial Spirit, 1850–1980*, "More and more in the twentieth century, the higher echelons of the larger businesses were dominated by men whose standards had been formed in the gentlemanly mode." Weiner quotes one writer of the 1930s: "A gentleman, we must realize, never strives too much; it is not considered the thing." The erosion of the market ethos within the industrial sector was accompanied by a corresponding increase in the prestige of the civil service, particularly as the latter became dominated by aristocratic personnel and values.

The British system of pollution control was initially developed during this same period. It would certainly be an exaggeration to suggest that "a gentleman does not pollute his neighbor's rivers"; certainly firms in Britain over the last century have treated their surrounding environment as irresponsibly as those in any industrial society. But one important consequence of the desire for social respectability on the part of British industrialists in the latter part of the nineteenth century was their willingness to accept a variety of constraints on their pursuit of profits. To the extent that they assimilated non-market values, they became subject to a set of informal social controls that reduced the necessity for strict legal ones. Thus, the British regulatory system not only continues to assume "good faith" on the part of corporate managers; it remains absolutely dependent on it. The Alkali Inspectorate, for example, has no independent means to assess the ability of companies to invest in improved methods of pollution control; it must rely on the cooperation of the companies it regulates. Were managers in Britain less amenable to persuasion or less willing to compromise, the British government's approach to controlling pollution would not work.

Similar pressures do exist in some American communities, but not on a national or industry-wide scale. Trade associations in America are generally incapable of exerting any control over the conduct of their members, while a refusal to cooperate with regulatory officials or follow the example set by industry leaders does not carry the social stigma it does in Britain. While businessmen in America who "stand up" to regulatory agencies—even to the extent of violating the law—are often regarded as heros by other members of their industry, the opposite is true in Great Britain. For companies in Great Britain, a prosecution is considered a "black mark." A few years ago, a director of a chemical firm was pressured to resign from the governing body of the Chemical Industries Association because his firm had violated industry standards regarding the disposal of toxic wastes. America has remained very much a business culture. Unlike in Britain, the civil service reforms of the late-ninteenth and early-twentieth centuries did not diminish the power or prestige of industry. While in Britain the professions and the civil service constitute an attractive alternative to employment in industry—and are thus capable of attracting first-rate talent—in America the pursuit of wealth through economic activity has remained the dominant interest of the nation's upper classes. Not only did business in America never develop an attitude of deference to public officials, but within the business community itself, executives continued to judge both their own performance and that of their peers almost exclusively by economic criteria: In a society without a Queen's Honors List, the only socially recognized measure of achievement in business is "the bottom line." Business executives in America continue to view government officials in much the same terms that they view their competitors: The challenges to profitability posed by each should be met as aggressively as possible. British businessmen are both less competitive with each other and more willing to cooperate with government officials.

THE POPULIST FACTOR

The third critical factor affecting the context of regulation in the United States and Great Britain is the public's perception of business. In part because of the great success of the American corporation over the last century, the American public periodically expressed antagonism toward the economic and political power of large companies. On the other hand, in part because British firms have generally performed less well for several decades, the British public appears to worry less about the misuse of their power. The British may be less willing to work for large corporations, but they do not seem particularly to fear and distrust those who manage them. Britain lacks a strong populist tradition: Outside of segments of the trade union movement—whose concerns are narrow and do not include most areas of government regulation—the British public is far less hostile to "big business" than is the American. And in contrast to the American middle class, the British middle class does not appear to be as concerned about the "capture" of government by business; it also seems not to regard the pursuit of profits by large corporations as an intrinsic threat to its health and safety. Moreover, like the British business community, it shares a degree of confidence and trust in public officials that is generally lacking among both the American public and the American business community.

There are those in Britain who would prefer the same administrative "safeguards" that exist in environmental regulation in the United States. They urge increased disclosure, less cooperation with business, more prosecution, and greater opportunities for public participation in shaping of pollution control policy.

Their impact on public policy has, however, been rather limited.

The lack of stronger public support for these changes—even among many of those active in the environmental movement—is part of the general deference toward administrative officials still exhibited by the British public; the latter have not been convinced that radical changes are necessary in order for their government to regulate corporate conduct effectively. In large measure, they are right: The British public receives significantly greater environmental protection than the rather limited political strength and access of the British environmental movement would suggest. And this is due in large measure to both the integrity and competence of British public officials and the willingness of British industry to cooperate with them.

American environmentalists and their supporters have been highly suspicious of any cooperation between business and government. Among the first preoccupations of the resurgent American environmental movement of the 1960s was countering the perceived threat to the environment posed by the political influence of business. Virtually every aspect of contemporary American environmental policy that distinguishes it from British policy—its frequent use of prosecution, its insensitivity to the costs of compliance, its centralization in Washington, its reliance on fixed rules and rigid deadlines, its limitations on administrative discretion—was originally proposed by pro-environmental groups little more than a decade ago. They successfully argued that unless an elaborate set of legal restrictions was placed on the decisions of both the newly-established regulatory agencies as well as on business, the latter would soon "capture" the former just as they appeared to have done so many times in the past. For American environmentalists, "cooperation" was equivalent to "cooptation"; the effectiveness of the "new" regulation was to be measured by the extent to which it met with resistance from industry. Making government and business into adversaries was not an unfortunate by-product of effective environmental regulation; for many it was considered the very definition of "effectiveness."

It is difficult to judge how realistic this fear of "cooptation" was. In all likelihood, had there been more cooperation from the outset, at least some of the inefficiencies and inanities of U.S. environmental regulations might have been avoided. But we also might have made less substantial progress in improving air and water quality over the last decade. In view of the absence of a tradition of effective business-government cooperation in this area, particularly at the federal level, as well as the historic pattern of business resistance to expansions of governmental authority, the case for a policy of "coercing" industry and restricting administrative discretion was not an unreasonable one. Since 1970, American companies have certainly spent considerably more on pollution control than those in Britain. For all its heavy-handedness, the American pattern of regulation *does* have two distinct advantages: It is capable of bringing about substantial changes in corporate practices in a relatively short period of time, and its effectiveness does not depend on the consent of the regulated.

OUR COMPETITIVE CULTURE

To a certain extent, each society does have something to teach the other. The British would probably benefit from more clearly defined standards, a greater willingness on the part of government to prosecute, and increased opportunities for public participation in the policy process. For America, on the other hand, more flexible regulations and closer consultation with business might well result both in more sensible rules and more reasonable enforcement policies. In fact, there are some signs that the two systems are converging. Pressures from the EEC, whose approach toward regulating industry has been strongly influenced by the example of the United States, is forcing British authorities to adopt more rigid standards, while in the United States the changes in regulatory policy brought about by the Reagan administration clearly bring our regulations closer to those of the British.

But these changes only make sense at the margin. Were the British to attempt to enforce environmental standards that industry regarded as unreasonable, or conduct their negotiations with industry more publicly, the cooperation of business would be undermined. Similarly, to the extent that the American government attempts to consult more with business, or diminishes the public's ability to participate in the policy process, the legitimacy and possibly the effectiveness of American environmental policy become impaired. In a sense, our approach to regulating industry requires conflict between business and government in much the same way that the British approach depends upon cooperation.

Proposals to improve regulation, like those to transform the way we make economic policy, cannot be evaluated in isolation. For all the obvious advantages of a regulatory system based on "good faith" rather than mutual mistrust, the former may simply be incompatible with our commitment to both interest group and economic competition. Companies might like more reasonable regulations and more competent regulators, but would they be willing to surrender their right to challenge agency decision-making in the courts? Environmentalists might prefer industry to be more cooperative and law-abiding, but would they be willing to allow industry and government to sit down privately and negotiate pollution control standards? Equally important, our adversarial regulatory system is the counterpart of a highly competitive economic system: The conflict-ridden relationship between business and government in the United States is the political counterpart of the highly competitive relationships that exist within the American business community. To the extent that the British experience is any guide, a more cooperative and responsible business community might also be a less competitive one. Instead of constantly bemoaning the lack of cooperation between business and government, we should occasionally reflect on some of its virtues.

NOTES

1. David Handley, "L'Ecologie et Les Attitudes Politiques des Frances," unpublished paper, University of Geneva.

2. Quoted in Timothy O'Riordan, "The Role of Environmental Quality Objectives in the Politics of Pollution Control in Progress," in *Resource Management and Environmental Planning*, ed. Timothy O'Riordan and R. Kerny Turner (New York: John Wiley & Sons, 1980), p. 225.

3. Lord Ashby, "The Politics of Pollution: Reflections on the Evolution of Environmental Policy in Britain, 1800–1980" (Paper presented at Cornell University), p. 11.

4. Quoted in O'Riordan, "Environmental Quality Objectives," p. 239.

5. Quoted in Maurice Frankel, "The Alkali Inspectorate," *Social Audit* (Special Report, Spring 1974): 5.

6. Gerald Rhodes, *Inspectorates in British Government* (London: George Allen and Unwin, 1981), p. 145.

7. Timothy O'Riordan, *Environmentalism* (London: Pion Ltd., 1981), p. 237.

8. Rhodes, *Inspectorates*, p. 149.

9. Frankel, "Alkali Inspectorate," p. 9.

10. Michael Thompson, "Postscript," unpublished paper (Luxemburg, Austria: Institute for Applied Systems Analysis, 1982).

11. Great Britain, "Pollution Control in Great Britain: How it Works," Department of the Environment, Central Unit on Environmental Pollution (London: Her Majesty's Stationary Office, 1976), p. 27.

12. Great Britain, "The United Kingdom Environment 1979: Progress of Pollution Control" (London: Her Majesty's Stationary Office), pp. 3–6.

13. Great Britain, "Digests of Environmental Pollution with Statistics: Pollution Control Costs," No. 4, Department of the Environment (London: Her Majesty's Stationary Office, 1981).

Chapter Three

THE GLOBALIZATION OF BUSINESS ETHICS: WHY AMERICA REMAINS DISTINCTIVE

IN A NUMBER of important respects, the increased globalization of the economies of the United States, Western Europe, and Japan is making business practices more uniform. The structure and organization of firms, manufacturing technologies, the social organization of production, customer relations, product development, and marketing— are all becoming increasingly similar throughout the advanced industrial economies. One might logically think that a similar trend would be taking place with respect to the principles and practices of business ethics.

This is occurring, but only very slowly. Business ethics has not yet globalized; the norms of ethical behavior continue to vary widely in different capitalist nations. During the last decade, highly publicized incidents of misconduct on the part of business managers have occurred in virtually every major industrial economy. These scandals have played an important role in increasing public, business, and academic awareness of issues of business ethics in the United States, Western Europe, and Japan. Yet the extent of both public and academic interest in business ethics remains substantially greater in the United States than in other advanced capitalist nations. While interest in business ethics has substantially increased in a number of countries in Europe, and to a lesser extent in Japan, no other capitalist nation approaches the United States in the persistence and intensity of public concern with the morality of business conduct.

The unusual visibility of issues of business ethics in the United States lies in the distinctive institutional, legal, social, and cultural context of the American business system. Moreover, the American approach to business ethics is also unique: it is more individualistic, legalistic, and universalistic than in other capitalist societies.

RECENT BUSINESS SCANDALS

Much of the current surge in public, business, and academic interest in business ethics in the United States can be traced to the scandals associated with Wall Street during the 1980s. Characterized by one journalist as "the most serious corporate crime wave since the foreign bribery cases of the mid-1970s," these abuses began with money-laundering by the Bank of Boston in 1986 and check-kiting by E. F. Hutton in 1987. They went on to include: violations of insider-trading regulations by Paul Thayer, who received a five-year jail term; Dennis Levine and the so-called "yuppie Five"; and Ivan Boesky, who was fined $100 million and sentenced to prison for three years. Half of all the cases brought by the SEC alleging illegal use of stock market information since 1949 were filed during a five-year period in the middle of the 1980s.

In 1988, "junk-bond king" Michael Milken and his firm, Drexel Burnham, were indicted for violating federal securities laws and regulations. Both subsequently paid large fines and Milken was sentenced to prison for ten years, subsequently reduced to two. At about the same time, the public became aware of widespread evidence of fraud in the savings and loan industry. A number of bankers were indicted and convicted, including Charles Keating Jr., head of one of the nation's largest savings and loan associations. In 1991, Salomon Brothers admitted that it had committed, "irregularities and rule violations in connection with its submission of bids in certain auctions of Treasury securities."[1] Two managing directors were suspended and the investment bank's Chairman and Chief Executive, John Gutfreund, was forced to resign after admitting that he had known of the firm's misconduct, but had neglected to report it.

Much of the recent increase in interest in business ethics outside the United States can also be attributed to various business scandals that came to light in Europe and Japan during roughly the same time-period. In 1982, an American company that had acquired a leading British member of Lloyd's found "undisclosed financial commitments and funds missing from the firm's reinsurance subsidiaries."[2] In 1985, another major scandal struck London's insurance market: 450 individual members of Lloyd's lost $180 million underwriting policies organized by agents who were alleged to have stolen some of the funds. At about the same time in London, "a wave of suspicious price movements in advance of takeover bids ... prompted concern that insider trading is spreading."[3] In 1987, Geoffrey Collier, a top trader at Morgan Grenfell Group PLC, was indicted for illegally earning more than $20,000 on two mergers involving his prestigious investment banking firm.

The same year, Ernest Saunders, the chief executive of Guinness, a major British-based alcohol beverages company, was accused of attempting to illegally prop up the price of his company's shares in order to help support its bid for the Distillers beverages group. Saunders was arrested and spent a night in jail. He was subsequently forced to sell many of his possessions, including his spacious home in Buckinghamshire, to meet legal costs, and all of his remaining assets were frozen. Saunders' trial did not begin for another three and half years, making the "Guinness Affair," the most prolonged financial scandal in the history of the City of London. In 1990, Saunders was found guilty of having helped engineer the stock's "fortuitous rise" and was sentenced to five years in prison. Three other prominent executives were also found guilty in what has been described as the "financial trial of the century."[4] *The Guardian* noted, "The six-month trial has lifted the lid on the seamy side of the City, exposing a sordid story of greed, manipulation and total disregard for takeover regulations."[5]

In 1991, another prominent British businessman, Robert Maxwell, was implicated in a number of wide-ranging abuses, including the looting of a large pension fund and deceptive record-keeping designed to conceal the insolvency of various firms that he controlled. Maxwell died under mysterious circumstances shortly before his "massive international confidence game"—involving large numbers of respectable British and American banks and accounting firms— became public.[6] It was subsequently revealed that Maxwell had plundered a total of £450 million from various pension funds he controlled.

In the fall of 1991, the Irish press reported that "four times in the [space of] 16 months, major Irish companies have been hit by crises over secret deals, alleged cover-ups and hidden conflicts of interest."[7] These "crises" included the falsification of company records by Aer Lingus Holidays and Goodman International, the purchase by Irish Sugar of a firm in which the company's chief executive was a part owner, and the "questionable purchase" of a piece of property by Telecom Eireann which had been previously owned by the firm's chairman, Michael Smurfit. Smurfit, the wealthiest businessman in Ireland, was forced to resign his position following press disclosure of this apparent conflict of interest.

In 1989, the French stock market experienced two "blockbuster scandals" that "hinted of insider trading before takeovers."[8] In the most celebrated case, investors in France, Luxembourg and Switzerland bought more than 200,000 shares in the Triangle Corporation, shortly before the firm was acquired by Pechiney, the state-owned aluminum company. The stock purchases had been made in the United States and had been brought to the French Governments' attention by the Securities and Exchange Commission. While the accusations were "modest by American standards," they "ballooned into a huge scandal" that dominated the front pages of the French press for more than a week.[9]

In 1990, an official at Deutsche Bank, Germany's largest commercial bank and a major participant in Frankfurt's bank-dominated securities market, was implicated in tax evasion linked to insider trading.[10] By the summer of 1991, "the number of people under investigation in Germany for insider trading and/or related tax evasion [had] . . . risen to 25."[11] The following year, billionaire financier Carlo De Beneditti, Olivetti's Chief Executive Officer, was sentenced to six years in prison for having been an accessory to the 1982 collapse of Banco Ambrosiano. Thirty-two co-defendants were also convicted.[12]

Japan, too, has recently experienced a considerable number of business-related scandals. In the spring of 1987, one of the subsidiaries of the Toshiba Corporation was discovered to have sold advanced milling equipment to the Soviet navy to be used for making submarine propellers, in violation of both Japanese law and an international treaty restricting the export of military-related technology to Communist-bloc countries. Both the Chairman and President of the company were forced to resign. Shortly thereafter numerous cases of influence-peddling by the Recruit Company become public: a press report revealed that the firm had given shares at below-market prices to a number of prominent politicians in the ruling Liberal Democratic Party in exchange for various political favors. A number of politicians were forced to resign and the chairman of Recruit, Hisashi Shinto, along with several of his fellow executives, were indicted on bribery charges. On October 9, 1990, Shinto was convicted: he was fined $170,000 and given a two-year prison term, which was suspended due to his age.

In 1991, another major scandal surfaced in Japan. Nomura Securities and Nikko Securities, two of Japan's major brokerage firms, admitted to having lent more than $250 million to a well-known underworld organization. Tax authorities revealed that the same two firms had been secretly reimbursing large clients for stock market loses; other firms were subsequently implicated in this practice as well. In addition, the Sumitomo Bank, Japan's second largest, had lent more than $1 billion to an Osaka trading company headed by a former official of the bank, who then squandered nearly $2 billion in "shady deals." In another major banking scandal, a number of Japan's most prestigious financial institutions, including the Industrial Bank of Japan Ltd., were linked to a scheme involving $2.5 billion in fraudulently obtained loans. In the Spring of 1992, former Chisan Co. Chairman Hirotomo Takai was sentenced to four years in prison and fined $3.8 million dollars for evading $25.6 million in taxes, "the largest-ever tax fraud by an individual."[13] And in 1992, Sagawa Kyubin, a mob-related company, was revealed to have donated more than $17 million to a number of prominent Japanese politicians, including three former prime ministers and two current cabinet members.

Three important business-related scandals have also occurred in Australia. In July 1989, five prominent businessmen, including Ian Johns, the former managing director of an Australian merchant bank, were arrested and charged with insider trading. The following month, Laurie Connell, a prominent Perth financier, was charged with making statements in the annual report of Rothwells, the merchant bank that collapsed in 1988. In 1990, George Herscu, the bankrupt Australian property magnate, was sentenced to five years in jail for bribing a state government minister. Two years later, Alan Bond, one of Australia's most successful entrepreneurs—his fortune is estimated at $7.6 billion—was sentenced to two and one-half years in prison for fraud.

THE RESPONSE

As a response, in part, to these numerous cases of business misconduct, the level of public, business, and academic interest in issues of business ethics increased throughout much of the industrialized world. While interest in this subject was largely confined to the United States during the 1970s, during the 1980s it spread to a number of other capitalist nations as well. In 1983, the first chair in business ethics was established in Europe at the Netherlands School of Business; a second was established at another Dutch university three years later and four more have been founded subsequently in other European countries. In 1986, the Lord Mayor of London organized a formal conference on company philosophy and codes of business ethics for 100 representatives from industry and the professions. The following year, a group of 75 European business managers and academics established the European Business Ethics Network (EBEN); its first conference was held in 1987, and four more have been held since, most recently in Paris in 1992. In 1987, the first European business ethics journal, *Ethica Degli Affari*, was published, in Italy.

Since the mid-1980s, two ethics research centers have been established in Great Britain, in addition to one each in Belgium, Spain, Germany, and Switzerland. A survey of developments in European business ethics published in 1990 reported that, "since three or four years ago the stream of publications (on business ethics) has been rapidly growing," with a disproportionate amount coming from Great Britain, Germany, Austria, and Switzerland.[14] In addition to the EBEN, business ethics networks have been established and national conferences held in Italy (1988), France (1989), and the Netherlands (1990).

Three leading European business schools—INSEAD in France, the London Business School, and Italy's Bocconni—have established elective courses in business ethics and several others have held public conferences on this topic; some have also begun to include sessions on ethics in their executive educational programs. The first European business ethics casebook was published in 1991 and the first issue of a management-oriented publication, *Business Ethics: A European Review*, appeared in the winter of 1992.[15] Interest in business ethics is also increasing in Japan, though on a much smaller scale. In 1989 and 1991, the Institute of Moralogy sponsored international ethics conferences in Kashiwa City, Chiba Ken, Japan.

THE "ETHICS GAP"

Notwithstanding these initiatives, the "ethics gap" between the United States and the rest of the developed world remains substantial. By any available measure, the level of public, business, and academic interest in issues of business ethics in the United States far exceeds that in any other capitalist country. Nor does this gap show any sign of diminishing: while interest in the subject in Europe has increased in recent years, its visibility in America has increased even more.

In America, each new disclosure of business misconduct prompts a new wave of public indignation, accompanied by numerous articles in the business and popular press which bemoan the general decline in the ethical conduct of managers and seek to explain "what went wrong" in the most recent case. This is frequently followed by Congressional hearings featuring politicians demanding more vigilant prosecution of white-collar criminals; shortly thereafter, regulatory standards are tightened, penalties are increased, and enforcement efforts are strengthened. Executives, in turn, make speeches emphasizing the importance of good ethical behavior for business success, using the most recent round of indictments and associated business failures to demonstrate the "wages of sin." Business educators then re-emphasize the need for additional instruction in ethics, often receiving substantial sums of money from various businessmen to support new educational programs. The most recent scandal then becomes the subject of a case, to be taught in an ever increasing number of business ethics courses designed to assist the next generation of managers in avoiding the pitfalls of their predecessors. When a new scandal occurs—as it invariably does—the cycle begins anew.

No comparable dynamic has occurred in other capitalist nations, where public interest in business ethics tends to be episodic rather than cumulative: thus, only in America are the 1980s referred to as a "decade of greed." As the *Financial Times* noted in the summer of 1992, "Despite the all-pervasive scandals of the 1980s, there is a tendency in Europe to regard the study of business ethics as faddish."[16] To be sure, the level of public concern with the morality of business does vary in other capitalist nations. For example, it has been much higher in Great Britain and the Netherlands than in Japan. But no other nation has approached the United States in the intensity and duration of public interest in business misconduct. Why? Why are Americans so outraged? How can one account for the distinctive importance of issues of business ethics in American society?

The most obvious explanation is that the conduct of American business has in fact been less ethical. Thus, Americans may be more preoccupied with the ethics of business because there is more misconduct to worry about. Not surprisingly, this explanation is favored by many European managers. However it is not persuasive. Certainly Japan has experienced at least as many major business scandals, and yet there is less interest in business ethics in Japan than in any other major capitalist nation. Moreover, when one compares the relative size of the American economy to that of other capitalist nations, it is not true that either more, or more important, cases of misconduct by businessmen have surfaced in the United States during the last decade.

Rather the importance of issues of business ethics in the United States lies in the distinctive institutional, legal, social, and cultural context of the American business system. In brief, Americans are more concerned with the ethics of business because they have higher expectations of business conduct. Not only is more business conduct considered unethical in the United States, but unethical behavior is more likely to be exposed, punished, and therefore become a "scandal" in America than in other capitalist nations.

MORE REGULATION

The most important reason why there appears to be so much more white-collar crime in the United States is that there are so many more laws regulating business in the United States to be broken.

Moreover, regulations governing business tend to be more strictly enforced in the United States than in other capitalist nations. In addition, thanks to more aggressive journalism, as well as to government disclosure requirements, business misdeeds are more likely to be exposed in the United States.

One British journalist commented following the "Maxwell mess," that, "unlike in America, there is no vigorous probing process that names and uncovers embarrassments. Regulators here are invariably shy about using their powers and often are unable to do so."[17] The situation in Britain is in striking contrast to the resources the American federal government devoted to investigating and prosecuting Michael Milken. Moreover, British libel laws also make it more difficult for journalists to disclose the abuses they do uncover. Some observers have suggested that the French insider-trading scandal of 1989 would have been buried, "as previous French governments . . . have buried previous scandals, were it not for the SEC's involvement."[18] One Japanese journalist recently observed, "In Japan today, if you have the word 'Inc.' attached to your name you can commit crimes with little risk and only minor penalties."[19] In fact, the only reason why the "dubious behavior" of Japan's brokerage firms in reimbursing clients for losses became a major financial scandal in 1991 was due to the involvement of organized crime; otherwise the government would have been unlikely to investigate.

By contrast, with the active help of an unrestricted and uninhibited media that places a high priority on investigative reporting, Congressional committees with substantial resources to conduct investigations, and ninety-five entrepreneurial United States Attorneys, America appears to have developed a "great . . . scandal machine [that is] running with ferocious momentum."[20] The chances that business misdeeds will escape exposure and prosecution are fewer in the United States than in any other capitalist nation.

Moreover, many activities for which American managers and corporations have pleaded guilty or have been convicted—most notably making campaign contributions from company funds and providing gifts to foreign government officials to secure contracts—are not illegal in other capitalist nations. This is also the case with respect to the violations of American securities laws to which Michael Milken pleaded guilty, as well as for Salomon Brothers' violations of the Treasury Department's bond trading rules (in fact, the rule that Salomon broke only came into existence in the United States some months earlier). With the exception of France, insider trading was legal throughout Europe until the early 1980s. It is still not against the law in Germany—although there is a voluntary code prohibiting it—and was only banned in Japan in 1989.

The issue of sexual harassment also illustrates the contrast between the standard of business conduct in America and other capitalist nations. Americans in general and American women in particular have higher standards for the conduct of male managers and more reason to expect that their complaints will be taken seriously by both the press and by government officials than in most other capitalist nations. While sexual harassment has been considered a form of sex discrimination in the United States since 1979, it only become illegal in France in 1992, while the concept itself was translated into Japanese for the first time in 1989. The first successful legal action against sexual harassment in Japan took place in April 1992. Moreover, American laws and regulations governing workplace discrimination on the basis of sex are both stricter—and better enforced—than in most other capitalist nations.

Legal Vulnerability

Another distinctive feature of the contemporary legal environment of business in the United States is the relatively large exposure of both individual executives and corporations to legal prosecution. As recently as two decades ago, the prosecution of individuals for white-collar crime in the United States was relatively rare. On occasion, high-status individuals were sentenced to prison; for example, in 1938, Richard Whitney, who had been president of the New York Stock Exchange, was found guilty of embezzlement and sentenced to five years in federal prison. In the early 1960s, a handful of senior managers from General Electric and Westinghouse received light prison sentences after they were found guilty of price-fixing.

However, this began to change in the early 1970s when, in connection with Watergate, a number of high-status individuals were sentenced to prison. By the end of the decade, what began as a trickle had become a flood: "Businessmen spent more time in jail for price-fixing in 1978 than in all the 89 years since the passage of the Sherman Antitrust Act."[21] Sixty-five percent of the individuals convicted of security law violations during the 1980s received jail sentences.

While the Federal Corrupt Practices Act made senior managers personally liable for monitoring its enforcement, the most important increase in the exposure of individual managers for corporate compliance took place in the area of environmental law. As recently as 1983, "jail sentences for polluters were unheard of."[22] In 1984, Federal courts handed out prison terms totaling two years and individual fines totaling $198,000. But five years later they handed out prison terms totaling 37 years and fines totaling $11.1 million. The number of individuals indicted increased from 40 in 1983 to 134 in

1990. Between 1986 and 1991, a total of 90 individuals were jailed for Federal environmental crimes. Of those sentenced to prison for environmental violations through 1988, one-third were corporate presidents while less than one-quarter were workers who had actually released the pollution.

During the 1980s Congress added tougher criminal penalties to a number of environmental statutes while federal sentencing guidelines issued in 1987 increased penalties for a number of environmental violations, putting them on a par with drug-related felonies. "As a result, jail has become much more likely for defendants in environmental cases, even for first-time offenders."[23] The Clean Air Act Amendments of 1990 not only expanded the number of violations that can be treated as criminal, but subjected to criminal prosecution any executive who had knowledge that a particular violation had taken place. According to a government official, now senior executives "realize that there is a real risk" of a prison term when environmental damage can be traced specifically to a company's acts. He added, "the word has really gotten out because of the increased level of enforcement." A corporate lawyer commented, "[Prosecutors] don't have much flexibility. If [the company] make[s] a mistake, the guy's going to jail."[24]

The *Economist* observed, "Polluters . . . have replaced drug-money launderers as the favorite target of government prosecutors out to make a name for themselves."[25] The number of lawyers employed by the environmental crimes section of the Justice Department increased from 3 in 1982 to 25 in 1991, while the criminal enforcement program of the Environmental Protection Agency grew from 23 investigators in 1982 to 60 in 1991. Similar expansions took place in a number of states.

A growing number of executives also have been indicted on criminal charges for violations of workplace health and safety regulations. In one "landmark" case, Film Recovery Inc., three corporate officials were, for the first time in American history, found guilty of murder in connection with the death of an employee. The owner and executives were jailed for 25 years each and fined for murder, involuntary manslaughter, and reckless conduct for knowingly exposing their employees to workplace hazards. Nearly one-half of American states now have legislation providing for corporate criminal liability for the death of employees. "Los Angeles County law-enforcement officers have been requested to treat every workplace fatality as a potential homicide."[26]

Not only has there been a steady increase in the number of corporate law violations classified as criminal, but the federal government also has become much more aggressive in seeking large financial penalties against corporations. The average corporate fine increased eight-fold between 1988 and 1990. Prominent corporations fined substantial sums from the mid-1980s to 1992 include the Bank of Boston ($500,000 for violating the Bank Secrecy Act of 1970); Exxon ($100 million for the *Exxon Valdez* disaster); Chrysler ($7.5 million for rolling back odometers in more than 60,000 vehicles); General Electric ($10 million for overbilling the government for computers); Northrop ($17 million for weapons test fraud); Salomon Inc. ($200 million in penalties); and Drexel Burnham ($650 million in fines and restitution for violations of federal securities laws). The penalty imposed on Drexel was the largest in the history of capitalism and helped force the firm into bankruptcy—a fate that has not befallen any large firm subject to government prosecution in either Europe or Japan.

One important reason why so many American corporations have established ethics codes and training programs has to do with federal sentencing guidelines that went in effect on November 1, 1991, but which had been made public much earlier. These guidelines not only double the median fine for corporations found guilty of crimes such as fraud, but state that companies convicted of various crimes will receive more lenient treatment if they have previously demonstrated good faith efforts to "be a good corporate citizen." For example, "a fine of $1 million to $2 million could be knocked down to as low as $50,000 for a company with a comprehensive program, including a code of conduct, an ombudsman, a hotline, and mandatory training programs for executives."[27]

ENFORCEMENT IN EUROPE AND JAPAN

It is true that regulation has been strengthened and penalties increased in other capitalist nations as well. For example, in response to the deregulation of London's capital markets that took place in the mid-1980s, the British Government moved to better protect the interest of investors. Britain now has unlimited fines and up to two years of imprisonment for insider-trading violations. However, the British have emphasized the streamlining of industry self-regulation, not the establishment of a government oversight body similar to the American Securities and Exchange Commission. Notwithstanding the Saunders case, enforcement, while it has increased, still "remains infrequent" in Britain.[28]

In response to the insider-trading scandals that occurred in France during the late 1980s, the French Government expanded the size and power of the Commission des Operations de Bourse, its principal stock market oversight agency. Previously known as a "small and toothless watchdog," its budget was increased fourfold and its staff size doubled—making it comparable in resources to the S.E.C.[29] It also was empowered to impose fines of up to 10 million francs (approximately $2 million) or up to ten times the illegal profits in cases involving insider trading. Insider trading in France is also punishable by up to two years in prison. However, France's regulatory agency has yet to use its new authority to impose civil fines for insider trading, although through the summer of 1991, it had conducted 79 investigations and turned 15 of them over to prosecutors.

Following a highly publicized number of financial scandals in Japan, four prominent businessmen—the president and chairman of Nomura, the chairman of Sumitomo Bank, and the president of Nikko Securities—were forced to resign in the fall of 1991. But only one individual was arrested. The Ministry of Finance subsequently imposed suspensions of up to six weeks on Japan's four leading stockbrokers. Although this represented "some of the stiffest sentences ever meted out by ministerial order," unlike in the case of Drexel, the penalty did not affect the four companies' dominance of Japanese stock trading. Nor has the Ministry of Finance made a serious effort to strengthen its regulation of Japan's financial markets. The maximum fine for violating the recently enacted ban on brokers for paying compensation for losses is only ¥500,000 (approximately $3,760). There has been only one prosecution for insider trading, and only one for share-price manipulation, "even though market professionals consider this to be a chronic problem."[30]

The prosecution of violators of environmental regulations has increased in a number of European countries. For example, the German penal code was recently amended to provide for the increased use of criminal penalties. "The German criminal law system is considered to be one of the best legal systems for the protection of the environment."[31] The number of criminal proceedings nearly doubled between 1980 and 1985, while the rate of conviction is among the highest in Europe.

Criminal law has also begun to be used to enforce environmental regulations in Spain, Sweden, Holland, and Finland. However, criminal penalties are still not imposed on polluters in France, Italy, and Britain. Historically, the British have been reluctant to impose any form of judicial penalties against violators of environmental regulations. This has recently begun to change; for example, the number of successful civil prosecutions against companies and individuals initiated by the newly established National Rivers Authority increased from 334 in 1989 to 574 in 1990. But fines remain modest: only two have been for more than £200,000, with the average less than £10,000. Moreover, the individuals who have been prosecuted have been small businessmen and farmers, not corporate executives. Even in Germany, it remains highly unusual for senior managers to be held personally responsible for environmental violations committed by their subordinates.

On balance during the last 15 years, more corporate officers and prominent businessmen have been jailed or fined in the United States than in all other capitalist nations combined. Likewise, the fines imposed on corporations in the United States have been substantially greater than in other capitalist nations. While the penalties for white-collar crime also have increased outside the United States, over the last decade the magnitude of the difference between the legal vulnerability of corporations and individual managers in the United States and those in other capitalist nations has increased. This development both reflects the high standards that exist for corporate conduct in the United States and also serves to reinforce the perception that business misconduct is more pervasive in the United States.

Public Expectations

The high expectations of business conduct in the United States are not confined to the legal system. They also are reflected in the ways many Americans invest and consume. For example, "ethical investment" funds in the United States enable individuals and institutions to make their investment strategy consistent with their political/social values either by avoiding investments in firms they judge to be behaving irresponsibly or by increasing their holdings of the stocks and bonds of firms that are acting "socially responsibly." While such funds exist in a number of European countries—including Britain and the Netherlands—they both originated and remain much larger in the United States. The same is true of the use of various social criteria to screen investments by institutional investors. For example, in no other capitalist nation have so many institutional investors divested themselves of shares of firms with investments in South Africa.

The American penchant for evaluating and comparing corporate social and ethical performance extends beyond capital markets; it also informs consumer judgments of business. Various private nonprofit organizations in America regularly "rank" corporations in terms of their behavior on such dimensions as women and minority employment, military contracting, concern about the environment, and animal testing; one such guide, published by the Council on Economic Priorities, has sold more than 350,000 copies.[32] Such rankings are virtually unknown outside the United States, as are awards for "excellence in ethics." The Japanese may be obsessed with ranking corporations, but they appear to have overlooked this particular dimension of corporate performance.

Similarly, the number of companies that have been subject to consumer boycotts on the basis of their social policies has increased substantially in the United States in recent years. By contrast, consumer boycotts are much less common in Europe and virtually unknown in Japan (the most recent took place in the early 1970s and it involved the prices of televisions). A number of consumer boycotts have taken place in Great Britain, but far fewer than in the United States—even after taking into account the relative sizes of the two economies.

Once again, the contrast in public expectations of business behavior in the United States and other capitalist nations is marked: relatively few consumers or investors outside the United States appear to pay much attention to the political and social behavior of the firms whose products they consume or whose stocks and bonds they purchase. Indeed, what is striking is how little writing on business ethics in continental Europe actually mentions individual corporations at all; rather, it tends to focus on more abstract concerns having to do with the relationship between ethics and economics. This is also true of the numerous statements of the Papacy on the "moral philosophy of business," which focus on the justice or lack thereof of the economic system, not on the ethics of particular corporations.[33] More generally, the debate over the role of business in Europe has focused on how to organize the economy, while in the United States it has emphasized standards of conduct for companies whose private ownership is assumed.

This in turn may be due to another distinctive characteristic of American society, namely, the considerable emphasis that has historically been placed on the social obligations of business. Because business corporations played a critical role in the development of cities and the shaping of communities in the United States, they have long been perceived as social institutions with substantial responsibility for the moral and physical character of the communities in which they have invested. Both the doctrine of corporate social responsibility and the practice of corporate philanthropy date back more than a century in the United States. By contrast, in both Europe and Japan, the responsibility of business has historically been defined more narrowly. Since all these economies, with the exception of Britain, industrialized later, it was government rather than corporations that both set the terms of economic development and assumed responsibility for various civic functions. Even today, corporate philanthropy remains primarily an American phenomena.

BUSINESS VALUES

Ironically, it may be precisely because the values of "business civilization" are so deeply ingrained in American society that Americans tend to become so upset when the institutions and individuals whom they have looked up to—and whose values and success they have identified with—betray their trust. More generally: "In the United States . . . the single all-pervasive 'ought' rampages widely beyond the control of the 'is.' The result is a unique and ever-present challenge . . . posed by the gap between the ideals by which the society lives and the institutions by which it functions."[34] Because the public's expectations of business conduct are so high, the invariable result is a consistently high level of public dissatisfaction with the actual ethical performance of business.

An important key to understanding the unique interest of Americans in the subject of business ethics lies in America's Protestant heritage: "The United States is the only country in the world in which a majority of the population has belonged to dissenting Protestant sects."[35] This has important implications for the way in which Americans approach the subject of business ethics. By arguing that one can and should do "God's work" by creating wealth, Protestantism raised the public's expectations of the moral behavior of business managers. Thus, thanks in part to the role played by Reformed Protestantism in defining American values, America remains a highly moralistic society. Compared to the citizens of other capitalist nations, Americans are more likely to believe that business and morality are, and should be, related to each other, that good ethics is good business, and that business activity both can and should be consistent with high personal moral values.

While the high expectations of business conduct shared by Americans have a strong populist dimension, this particular understanding of the proper relationship between business and morality is not in any sense anti-business. It is also shared by much of the American business community. Indeed, the latter appear as concerned about the ethical lapses of their colleagues as is the American public. A survey of key business leaders conducted by Touche Ross in 1987 reported that more than two-thirds believe "that the issue of ethics in business has not been overblown in the current public debate."[36] Admittedly, some of these expressions of concern about business ethics amount to little more than public relations. But it is impossible to read through the reports on business ethics in the United States issued by such organizations as the Business Roundtable, Touche Ross, or the Conference Board without being struck by the sincerity of the concerns of the executives whose views they report.

Where else but in the United States would a group of nationally prominent executives establish and fund an organization such as the Business Enterprise Trust in order to offer annual awards for outstanding ethical behavior by corporations and individual managers?[37] While the belief that good ethics and high profits go hand in hand is certainly not confined to American businessmen, they seem to articulate it more frequently than do their counterparts in other capitalist nations. One senses that many of the latter are a bit more cynical about this relationship. For example, in Germany, "Insider trading doesn't have much of a stigma. Tax evasion is a gentleman's sport."[38]

Because the moral status of capitalism in Europe has traditionally been problematic, there appears to be much more cynicism about the ethics of business in Europe and Japan. Europeans, in part due to the legacy of aristocratic and pre-capitalist values, have always tended to view the pursuit of profit and wealth as somewhat morally dubious, making them less likely to be surprised—let alone outraged—when companies and managers are discovered to have been "greedy." For their part, the "Japanese seem almost inured to the kind of under-the-table favors whose disclosure sparked the [1991] scandal." As one Japanese investor put it, "It's so much a part of Japanese culture and tradition that the people don't think they're doing anything wrong."[39]

One Japanese political consultant recently mused: "I wonder sometimes when the Japanese people will rise up and say, 'We've had enough.' But the only answer I can give for sure is 'Not in this century, at least.'"[40]

Not surprisingly, many Europeans regard the current level of interest of Americans in the ethics and morality of business conduct—to say nothing of other aspects of American society—as somewhat excessive. Corporate codes of conduct, ethics training programs, lists of "ethical" and "unethical" firms—are all seen as signs of an "unusually moralizing society," one that "people in old and cynical Europe often find difficult to take . . . seriously."[41] The extent of moral scrutiny and self-criticism that pervades contemporary American society prompted the *Economist* to publish an editorial entitled, "Hey, America, Lighten Up a Little."[42]

KEY DIFFERENCES IN BUSINESS ETHICS

The United States is distinctive not only in the intensity of public concern with the ethical behavior of business, but also in the way in which business ethics are defined. Americans tend to emphasize the role of the individual as the most critical source of ethical values, while in other capitalist nations relatively more emphasis is placed on the corporation as the locus of ethical guidance. Second, business ethics tends to be much more legalistic and rule-oriented in the United States. Finally, Americans are more likely to consider their own ethical rules and standards to be universally applicable.

Business ethics in the United States have been strongly affected by the "tradition of liberal individualism that . . . is typical of American culture."[43] Not surprisingly, a frequent characteristic of business ethics cases developed in the United States is that they require the individual to decide what is right on the basis of his or her own values. While the company's goals and objectives or the views of the individual's fellow employees are not irrelevant, in the final analysis they are not intended to be decisive. Indeed, they may often be in conflict.

By contrast, "in European circumstances it is not at all evident that managers, when facing a moral dilemma, will navigate first and foremost on their personal moral compass."[44] Rather, managers are more likely to make decisions based on their shared understanding of the nature and scope of the company's responsibilities. The legitimate moral expectations of a company are shaped by the norms of the community, not the personal values or reflections of the individual. The latter has been labeled "communicative" or "consensual" business ethics."[45]

One possible outcome of the tension between the interests and values of the company and those of the individual employee is whistle-blowing. Critics of business in the United States have urged increased legal protection for whistle-blowers—and, in fact, some regulatory statutes in the United States explicitly protect those who publicly expose violations of various company policies.

By contrast, the idea that there could even be such a tension between the individual and the organization is thoroughly alien to Japanese business culture, where whistle-blowers would be regarded more as traitors than heroes. Only a handful of European countries have laws protecting whistle-blowers. And few non-American firms have established formal mechanisms, such as the appointment of ombudsmen, to enable employees to voice their moral concerns about particular corporate policies. Workers in many other capitalist nations may well feel a greater sense of loyalty toward the firms for which they work, and a greater respect for those in authority.

A second critical difference between business ethics in America and other capitalist countries has to do with the role of law and formal rules. Notwithstanding—or perhaps because of—its traditions of individualism, Americans tend to define business ethics in terms of rules; the writing on business ethics by Americans is replete with checklists, principles, and guidelines for individual managers to follow in distinguishing right from wrong.

Americans' tendency to think of ethics in terms of rules is reflected in the widespread use of corporate codes among U.S.-based companies. Such codes are much less common in Europe, although their use has recently increased in Britain. One French observer notes:

> The popularity of codes of ethics in the United States meets with little response in Europe. America's individualism does not correspond to the social traditions of Europe. These large differences make fruitless all desire to imitate the other's steps.[46]

One French manager, whose firm had recently been acquired by an American company, stated:

> I resent having notions of right and wrong boiled down to a checklist. I come from a nation whose ethical traditions date back hundreds of years. Its values have been transmitted to me by my church and through my family. I don't need to be told by some American lawyers how I should conduct myself in my business activities.[47]

Henri-Claude de Bettignies, who teaches business ethics at INSEAD, adds:

> Some European leaders perceive corporate codes of conduct as a device which deresponsibilizes the individual, i.e., he does not have to think for himself, he just needs to apply the codes of conduct which he has learnt and which—through training—have programmed him to respond in a certain "corporate" way.[48]

By contrast, European firms appear to place greater emphasis on informal mechanisms of social control within the firm. Indeed, European managers frequently profess astonishment at the apparent belief of many American executives, as well as government officials, that a company's adoption of a code can actually alter the behavior of its employees.

There is a third critical difference between business ethics in the United States and other capitalist nations. Americans not only tend to define business ethics in terms of rules and procedures; they also tend to believe that American rules and procedures should be applied universally. For example, no other nation requires the foreign subsidiaries of its multinational corporations to follow the laws of their home country as frequently as does the United States. Thus the United States is the only nation that restricts its firms from making payments to secure contracts or other benefits outside its borders. A survey of European executives reported that "nearly 40 percent would never complain about bribery by a business rival—or answer charges of bribery against themselves."[49] Similarly, in no other nation have corporations been so frequently criticized for exporting products that do not conform to the health and safety standards of their "home" country.

Universalism also has a second dimension having to do with the importance of the distinction between "us" and "them." American business culture—and American society—attaches considerable importance to treating everyone in the same arm's-length manner. By contrast, the Japanese—and, to a lesser extent, the citizens of Latin Europe—define their responsibilities in more particularistic terms: managers, as well as government officials, in these countries place less value on treating everyone equally and attach much more importance to fulfilling their obligations to those individuals and institutions with whom they have developed long-standing and long-term relationships. (Significantly, it is very difficult to translate the phrases "equal opportunity" and "level playing field" into Japanese.) On this dimension, Britain and much of northern Europe is much closer to the United States.

All these dimensions are, in fact, inter-related. To summarize the American approach: business ethics is about individuals making moral judgments based on general rules that treat everyone the same. By contrast, business ethics in Europe and Japan have more to do with managers arriving at decisions based on shared values, often rooted in a particular corporate culture, applied according to specific circumstances and strongly affected by the nature of one's social ties and obligations.

CONCLUSION

Regulatory rules and standards, especially within the European Community and between the United States and Western Europe, are certainly becoming more similar. For example, a strengthening of environmental regulation has occurred in virtually all capitalist nations, while legal restrictions on insider trading—a decade ago, largely confined to the United States—are now the norm in Europe. Similarly, a number of European nations have recently enacted legislation banning sexual harassment. The prosecution of white-collar criminals has also recently increased in Europe. In 1989, the first Swede to be found guilty of insider trading was sentenced to five years in prison. Not only are many American legal norms and standards of corporate conduct being adopted in other capitalist nations, but as globalization proceeds and world commerce is increasingly driven by multinational firms, these firms may well come to adopt common ethical standards. These developments are important. But they continue to be overshadowed by the persistence of fundamental national differences in the ways in which business ethics are defined, debated, and judged.

While much has been written on differences in the laws and business norms of developed and less-developed nations, the equally important contrasts in the way in which ethical issues are discussed and defined *among* the developed nations has been all but ignored.[50] Significantly, among the hundreds of ethics cases developed for use in management education in the United States and Europe, only *one*— Toshiba Machine Company—contrasts differences in ethical norms between two advanced industrial nations.[51] We need a better appreciation of the differences in the legal and cultural context of business ethics between the United States and other capitalist nations, and between Western and Asian economies as well, if managers are to work effectively in an increasingly integrated global economy.

NOTES

1. "The Salomon Shocker: How Bad Will It Get?" *Business Week*, August 26, 1991, p. 36.

2. Barnaby Feder, "Overseeing Insurance Reform at London's Venerable Mart," *New York Times*, January 8, 1984, p. 6.

3. Gary Putka, "British Face Finance-Industry Scandals Just as They Move to Deregulate Markets," *Wall Street Journal*, August 12, 1985, p. 20.

4. Robert Rice and Richard Waters, "Fraud Office Drops Charges in Third Guinness Case," *Financial Times*, February 9, 1992, p. 1.

5. *The Guardian*, August 28, 1990, p. 1.

6. "An Honor System Without Honor," *Economist*, December 14, 1991, p. 81.

7. Mike Milotte and David Nally, "A Season of Scandals," *The Sunday Tribune*, September 22, 1991, p. 6; see also Peter Clarke and Elizabeth Tierney, "Business Troubles in the Republic of Ireland," *Business Ethics; A European Review* (April 1992), pp. 134–38.

8. Steven Greenhouse, "An Old Club Transformed," *New York Times*, July 23, 1991, p. C6.

9. Steven Greenhouse, "Modest Insider-Trading Stir Is a Huge Scandal in France," *New York Times*, January 30, 1989, p. D1.

10. Ferdinand Protzman, "Insider Trading Scandal Grows," *New York Times*, July 23, 1991, p. C6.

11. "Sweeping out the Stables," *Economist*, August 31, 1991, p. 15.

12. Alan Riding, "Olivetti's Chairman Is Convicted in Bank Fraud that Shocks Italy," *New York Times*, April 17, 1992.

13. "Top Tax-Evader Gets Four-Year Sentence," *Japan Times Weekly International Edition*, May 11–, 1992, p. 2.

14. Henk J. L. van Luijk, "Recent Developments in European Business Ethics," *Journal of Business Ethics*, 9: 538.

15. John Donaldson, *Ethics in European Business—A Casebook* (London: Academic Press Ltd., 1991).

16. "Ethics and Worse," *Financial Times*, July 3, 1992, p. 12.

17. Paul Farhi and Glenn Frankel, "Pardon Me, Old Bean, But Aren't Your Pants on Fire?" *Washington Post National Weekly Edition*, December 23–29, 1991, p. 20.

18. Greenhouse (1989), op. cit., p. D9.

19. James Sterngold, "Japan's Rigged Casino," *New York Times Magazine*, April 26, 1992, p. 48.

20. The quotation is from *Scandal* by Suzanne Garment. Quoted in Jonathan Yardley, "The Truly Corrupt vs. the Merely Sleazy," *Washington Post National Weekly Edition*, October 7–23, 1991, p. 35. While Garment's book is about political scandals, her analysis can be applied to scandals involving the private sector as well.

21. Nick Galluccio, "The Boss in the Slammer," *Forbes*, February 5, 1979, p. 61.

22. Steven Ferrey, "Hard Time," *The Amicus Journal* (Fall 1988), p. 12.

23. Allen Gold, "Increasingly, A Prison Term Is the Price Paid by Polluters," *New York Times*, February 15, 1991, p. B10.

24. Ibid.

25. "Dishing the Dirt," *Economist*, February 9, 1991, p. 70.

26. Joseph Kahn, "When Bad Management Becomes Criminal," *INC.* (March 1987), p. 48.

27. Ibid.

28. "Investors Beware: Stock Market Rules Vary Considerably," *New York Times*, July 23, 1991, p. C7.

29. Greenhouse (1991), op. cit., p. C9.

30. James Sterngold, "Informal Code Rules Markets," *New York Times*, July 23, 1991, C6.

31. Antonio Vercher, "The Use of Criminal Law for the Protection of the Environment in Europe: Council of Europe Resolution (77)28," *Northwestern Journal of International Law and Business*, 10 (1990), p. 448.

32. Ben Corson et al., *Shopping for A Better World* (New York, NY: Ballantine Books, 1989).

33. Philippe de Woot, "The Ethical Challenge To The Corporations: Meaningful Progress and Individual Development," in George Enderle et al., eds., *People in Corporations* (Boston, MA: Kluwer Academic Publishers, 1990), p. 79.

34. Samuel P. Huntington, *American Politics: The Promise of Disharmony* (Cambridge, MA: Harvard University Press, 1981), p. 60.

35. Ibid., p. 15.

36. *Ethics in American Business*, Touche Ross, December 1987, p. 2.

37. See James O'Toole "Doing Good by Doing Well," *California Management Review*, 33/3 (Spring 1991): 9–24.

38. "The Insider-Trading Dragnet Is Stretching Across the Globe," *Business Week*, March 23, 1987, p. 51.

39. "Hidden Japan," *Business Week*, August 26, 1991, p. 18.

40. T. R. Reid, "In Japan, Too, Money Is The Mother's Milk of Politics," *Washington Post National Weekly Edition*, September 14–29, 1991, p. 18.

41. Ibid.

42. "Hey, America, Lighten Up a Little," *Economist*, July 28, 1990.

43. Van Luijk, op. cit., p. 542.

44. Ibid.

45. Ibid., pp. 543–44.

46. Antoine Kerhuel, "De Part et D'Autre De L'Atlantique" [David Vogel translation].

47. This statement was made at an executive training session at IMD in the fall of 1991 that the author taught.

48. Henri-Claude de Bettignies, "Ethics and International Business: A European Perspective," paper presented at the Tokyo Conference on the Ethics of Business in a Global Economy, Kashiwa-shi, Japan, September 10–12, 1991, p. 11.

49. Paul Lewis, "European Businessmen Don't Take Their Morality So Seriously," *New York Times*, March 3, 1978, Section 4, p. 2.

50. The handful of exceptions includes: Catherine Langlois and Bodo Schegelmilch, "Do Corporate Codes of Ethics Reflect National Character? Evidence from Europe and the United States," *Journal of International Business Studies* (Fourth Quarter 1990), pp. 519–39; van Luijk, op. cit., pp. 537–44; Ernest Gundling, "Ethics and Working with the Japanese: The Entrepreneur and the 'Elite Course,'" *California Management Review*, 33/3 (Spring 1991): 25–39; Joanne Ciulla, "Why Is Business Talking about Ethics?" *California Management Review*, 34/1 (Fall 1991): 67–86.

51. Toshiba Machine Company, Harvard Business School #388–197.

Chapter Four

GOVERNMENT-INDUSTRY RELATIONS IN THE UNITED STATES: AN OVERVIEW

INTRODUCTION

Over the last five years, a lively debate has been waged in the United States over what role—if any—the American government should play in improving the international competitiveness of American industry. Much of this debate has revolved around the issue of industrial policy.[1] Those who favour the adoption of such a policy want the American government to play a more active role in channelling resources into industries in which the United States can create and maintain a comparative advantage.[2] They commonly cite Japan as an example of a nation in which close business-government co-operation at a sectoral level has enabled a number of its industries to improve dramatically their global market share. Critics of such a strategy, on the other hand, contend that the vulnerability of the American government to interest group pressures makes the adoption of a coherent and consistent set of policies toward industry impossible.[3] Not coincidentally, they attribute Japan's economic success to the soundness of its macro-economic policies and argue that the United States can most effectively assist its industry by improving its policies in this area and letting the market-place do the rest.

In spite of their different policy prescriptions, both perspectives share similar assumptions about the nature of business-government relations in the United States. Both assume that the American government has not had a coherent set of policies toward industry; instead they view American economic policy as a series of inconsistent and shortsighted responses to the demands and pressures of particular firms, industries, and regions. Both therefore conclude that the American government lacks the institutional capacity to define and implement policies that can improve the ability of particular industries to adjust to changes in the international economy. One perspective regards this inability as inherent in the American political system, while the other advocates the adoption of new institutions to enable the government to make its sectoral policies more like those of America's major competitors.

The purpose of this chapter is to challenge this accepted understanding of business-government relations in the United States. Specifically, I want to argue that the role of the American government in promoting the development of American industry has been far more extensive—and far more important—than has been commonly assumed. As a result, much of the debate over whether the United States should develop an industrial policy is beside the point. The United States does have a relatively extensive set of policies towards industry: it does, in fact, target 'winners' and encourage the movement of capital and labour away from 'losers'. Contemporary America certainly does not resemble Japan in the latter's single-minded commitment to economic development; American public policy since the New Deal has had a far broader range of objectives. But, over the last half-century, America has pursued sectoral policies no less vigorously—or less successfully—than its major industrial competitors.

If one defines industrial policy exclusively in terms of explicit governmental efforts to promote the international competitiveness of particular industries, then America has had relatively few industrial policies. But then, by like token, neither has much of Europe. Many of the sectoral policies pursued by the French government, for example, have been informed by a variety of objectives, ranging from national prestige to energy independence. Even in the case of Japan, many of the industries promoted by MITI in the 1950s and 1960s were not originally intended to become leading exporters. America is not unique in having its sectoral policies motivated by objectives other than that of international competitiveness. Moreover, many of America's indirect forms of support for industry have been as successful as the more explicit interventions of the governments of other nations. While the intentions of policy-makers do matter, there is little to be gained by deciding whether or not a particular set of sectoral policies qualify as an 'industrial' policy solely on the basis of the objectives of those who formulated it.

The implication of this argument is that both the weakness of the American government and the strength of the 'adversary relationship' between business and government in the United States have been exaggerated.[4] While many policies affecting business have been made in a relatively adversarial setting, their implementation has usually been highly sensitive to the long-term interest of American industry. Due to the importance policy-makers have attached to economic growth, the thrust of America's foreign and domestic policies has been no less supportive of the interests of industry than those of other capitalist states. On the other hand, the American state is much less weak than most students of comparative business-govern-

ment relations have argued. It has demonstrated an impressive capacity both for resisting the demands of declining sectors and regions for assistance and for taking the initiative in defining and redirecting the focus of corporate research and investment. In brief, the
differences between the pattern of business-government relations in
the United States and those of other capitalist polities are less important than has been commonly assumed.

But why, then, has the idea of industrial policy provoked such
contention in the United States? And why has the extent of government assistance to industry in the United States been overlooked by
students of both comparative and American politics? There are a
number of reasons. First, the range of policy instruments available to
the American government to shape the structure of the American
economy are different than in other capitalist polities. For example,
in contrast to all other capitalist nations, the United States has made
extremely limited use of government ownership as a strategy to
shape industrial development. (Both for this reason and because of
the limited scope of America's welfare state, government expenditures as a percentage of GNP are relatively low in the United States.)
In addition, because of the strength of private capital markets in the
United States and the autonomy of America's financial institutions,
America lacks an institutional mechanism for allocating capital to
particular firms and industries as in other capitalist nations, most
notably France and Japan. Thirdly, many of the most important efforts of the American government to promote industrial development have taken place not at the federal level, but at the state and
local one, making them somewhat less visible to students of comparative politics.

On the other hand, the United States makes more extensive use of
private-public partnerships, both at the local and federal level, than
other capitalist nations. And American defence contractors, in spite
of being privately owned, function as much as an instrument of state
policy as any nationalized firm in either Western Europe or Japan.
The United States also relies far more heavily on the tax code as a
means of shaping the direction of private sector investment than any
other nation except Japan. And instead of nationalization, America
has traditionally employed government regulation as a means of directing the development of particular sectors.

Finally, America's industrial policies have tended to be implicit
rather than explicit. American political culture frowns upon close
ties between government and any interest group—including business. Given Americans' historical mistrust of corporate power and
suspicion of business-government co-operation, government officials

have understandably been reluctant to justify particular policies on the grounds of their benefits to a particular industry. Instead, they have defended them on other grounds, such as national security or regional development. Moreover, in many cases, these alternative explanations were, in fact, quite genuine: it is a peculiarity of governmental assistance to industry in the United States that it has frequently been both the unintended and unanticipated consequence of policies designed to achieve other objectives.

American history is replete with examples of this phenomenon. The purpose of the anti-trust laws enacted in the late nineteenth and early twentieth centuries was to prevent monopoly. Yet because of the way they were enforced by the courts, their *result* was to make American firms both larger and more efficient than their counterparts in Europe, since in America, unlike in Europe, companies were forbidden to form cartels as a means of reducing competition.[5] Similarly, the purpose of American agricultural policy since the New Deal has been to stabilize the income of farmers; in this sense American agricultural policy is indistinguishable from that of the European Community or Japan. But the *result* has been to make American farmers more efficient than in any advanced industrial society. The most important and striking example is, of course, American defence spending. The purpose of the Department of Defense is to maintain and promote the nation's security. Yet the *result* of America's large military budget has been to give American firms important competitive advantages in a wide variety of high-technology sectors. Likewise, the American space programme was promoted for reasons of both national prestige and military security, yet its commercial impact has been substantial.

A third reason why the extensiveness of American assistance to industry has been obscured is an ideological one. America exhibits in an extreme form a syndrome in which a nation's ideology of business-government relations bears virtually no relationship to its practices. Unlike on the Continent and in Japan, economics in America is dominated by a neoclassical faith in the efficacy and effectiveness of market-based mechanisms of capital allocation.[6] The conventional wisdom of American economists—shared across the political spectrum from Charles Schultze to Milton Friedman—is that, except in highly unusual circumstances, comparative advantage can only be created by the market. It therefore follows that the government cannot pick 'winners'; it can only retard the movement of capital and labour away from 'losers'.

Yet, not only can American neoclassical economics not account for Japan's successes; it cannot even account for many of those of the

United States. In fact, the Department of Defense, the National Aeronautics and Space Administration, the National Institutes of Health, and the Department of Agriculture have proven no less—or more—capable of picking winners than has MITI. Moreover, the gap between rhetoric and practice has widened considerably under the Reagan Administration. No Administration in recent times has been so committed to the rhetoric of limited government and market-place allocation, yet none has acted more aggressively to reshape the structure of the American economy. To understand business-government relations in America, we need to pay less attention to what American economists and politicians contend government can and cannot do, and examine more closely what the American government has actually done. That is the primary purpose of this chapter.

HISTORICAL BACKGROUND

The rejection of Alexander Hamilton's 'Report on Manufacturing', which recommended that the federal government actively commit itself to a policy of promoting manufacturing, is often viewed as having signalled the unwillingness of the new nation actively to support economic development. In fact, however, it merely reflected the decision of the nation's political leadership to place priority on agricultural rather than industrial development.[7] During the first six decades of the nineteenth century, both the state and federal governments actively intervened to increase the volume and lower the costs of agricultural output; indeed, this constituted the major focus of the nation's foreign and domestic policies in the ante-bellum period.

While the American government played a decisive role in making the United States into the world's most important exporter of agricultural products during the first half of the nineteenth century, from the 1870s through to the 1930s the importance of sectoral policies in the United States diminished considerably. On balance, the *industrial* development of the United States was managed, directed, and financed primarily by the private sector. For example, the level of direct government subsidy for railroad construction significantly declined after 1873, after only one-third of the nation's ultimate railroad capacity had been completed. The main contribution of the federal government to the growth of industry during the industrial revolution was a negative one: high tariffs protected American industry from foreign competition, while the federal courts severely restricted the ability of those adversely affected by the rise of big business from having their grievances redressed. However, the federal government played little direct role in the development of the nation's major industries through the 1930s. Compared with those of other capitalist nations, America's steel, electric, textile, food processing, automobile, and chemical industries grew with relatively little direct government assistance. Only in the area of agriculture did the federal government pursue a relatively active sectoral policy during the last third of the nineteenth century and into the first third of the twentieth.

As I have argued elsewhere, this half-century was critical in shaping the social and political outlook of the American business community.[8] Precisely because the American government played a relatively passive role in shaping American industrial development, America's industrial elite developed an ideology that was highly critical of government intervention. Yet, ironically, for all the adversarial rhetoric that surrounded business-government relations during the industrial revolution, the political and economic triumph of large-scale industry took place more easily in America than in any other capitalist nation. America's farmers, workers, and small businessmen may have been extremely vocal in their denunciations of 'big business', but, unlike their counterparts in virtually every other capitalist nation, their efforts to restrict or to curtail the development of industrial capitalism were noticeably unsuccessful. No other nation made so few efforts to protect its traditional sectors during its period of rapid industrial growth.[9]

The New Deal is commonly and correctly viewed as a major discontinuity in the history of business-governmental relations in the United States. Most accounts of the expansion of the role of government in the economy during the 1930s have tended to emphasize its macroeconomic dimensions, including the significant expansion of the welfare state, the introduction of Keynesian policy, and the recognition of the right of workers to join unions. Each of these policy initiatives was extremely controversial and was strongly—and unsuccessfully—opposed by the majority of the nation's business community. Their enactment made the relationship between business and government during the 1930s relatively adversarial.

Yet there is another dimension of the relationship between industry and government during the 1930s that also needs to be emphasized. The New Deal played a critical role in promoting the re-emergence of sectoral policies in the United States. Notwithstanding the demise of the National Recovery Administration, contemporary American industrial policy essentially dates from the 1930s. The Tennessee Valley Authority represents America's most ambitious effort at government-sponsored regional economic development in progress. In a large variety of sectors, including energy, shipping, trucking, communication, banking, power generation, housing, airlines, and agriculture, the New Deal significantly—and in most cases permanently—expanded the scope for government intervention. With a handful of exceptions, the New Deal's sectoral policies—in contrast to its macro policies—tended to be strongly supportive of and supported by the industries directly affected by them. And this pattern of business-government co-operation was significantly enhanced during the Second World War, when the basis was laid for the government's post-war support of the defence and aerospace sectors of the economy.

CONTEMPORARY AMERICAN INDUSTRIAL POLICIES

Agriculture

Agriculture provides virtually a textbook case of American industrial policy.[10] The primary thrust of the New Deal's agricultural policy was to improve the living standards of America's farmers—then the most impoverished group in American society. It established an elaborate system of price-supports and output-controls through the Agricultural Stabilization and Conservation Service and a system of subsidized credits through the Farmers Home Administration. It also subsidized the costs of providing electricity to farmers via the Rural Electrification Administration and significantly expanded the construction of public works designed to supply both power and water to farmers in the Tennessee Valley and the West. These efforts were expanded during the 1950s, when the Foreign Agricultural Service of the Department of Agriculture was established to help domestic producers respond to overseas market opportunities.[11]

Lawrence and Dyer write:

> For some time . . . our largest and most successful industry in terms of employment, assets, sales, and export value has been agriculture. Yet America was not always 'the bread basket of the world'. Fifty years ago farming was a big business, but a highly fragmented and uncertain one that kept most of its practitioners at or near a subsistence income and made only a handful of them rich. How the United States became the most reliable and productive supplier of food is not widely understood.[12]

The role played by the American government in this transformation was a decisive one. By shielding farmers from the instability of fluctuating prices, the government made it possible for them to invest in expensive farm machinery, fertilizers, and pesticides. In addition, scientists from the USDA and land-grant institutions developed new fertilizers, pesticides, herbicides, and crops; the results of their research were then rapidly and effectively disseminated to individual farmers through agricultural extension services. The result was an astonishing improvement in agricultural productivity: between 1949 and 1959, agricultural output per farm worker per hour increased 85 per cent, between 1959 and 1969 by 77 per cent, and between 1969 and 1979 by 92 per cent—a rate of productivity improvement far in excess of the nation's industrial sector. These advances were made possible by, and, in turn, stimulated demands for, various industrial products: it is not coincidental that agricultural chemicals represent the only high-technology export in which American producers gained world market share betwen 1965 and 1980,[13] or that until recently America was the world's major exporter of agricultural machinery. As *The Economist* recently noted, 'When their combine makers, fertilizer suppliers, rail freighters and so on are counted, farmers are America's biggest business.'[14]

Housing

The pattern of government assistance to industry in the United States is often characterized as an irrational array of subsidies, tax expenditures, and loan guarantees, bearing no relationship to any coherent set of objectives. But this assessment is inaccurate. For one sector has received more direct and indirect assistance from the federal government than all others, namely housing.[15] Loans and loan guarantees to the housing industry totalled nearly $160 billion in 1980 while the housing industry has been the recipient of more tax subsidies than the rest of the economy combined. Housing is not normally regarded as an example of industrial policy, since it does not produce anything that is internationally traded. But it certainly provides another demonstration of the ability of the American government to develop a coherent sectoral policy.

Government assistance to the nation's housing sector began during the New Deal. In order to prevent foreclosures on existing mortgages and restore the health of the nation's banks, the New Deal established three institutions: the Home Owners Loan Corporation, which purchased defaulted home mortgages and then replaced them by new loans; the Federal Housing Administration, which insured mortgages issued by banks, thus enabling banks to issue mortgages with lower down-payments and interest rates; and the Federal

National Mortgage Association, which established a secondary mortgage market, thus increasing the number of banks willing to issue mortgages. Each of these programmes was significantly expanded following the Second World War and in addition, a special subsidized loan programme was established for veterans.

During the 1950s, the federal government began to provide massive support for highway construction, thus making additional land available for housing construction, while state and local governments co-operated by providing funds for community infrastructures. The combination of subsidized mortgages and subsidized highway construction led to a sixfold increase in the rate of new housing construction. Moreover, the substantial increase in the demand for new housing enabled builders to produce homes in much greater volume: the result was that output per employee grew at an annual rate of 2.3 per cent between 1947 and 1965.[16] As in the case of agriculture, American sectoral intervention in this industry has been highly successful: one-third of US gross domestic fixed investment has gone into housing since 1970 and a higher proportion of Americans own their own homes than in any other industrial nation.

Defense and Space

The most important focus of sectoral intervention by the American government over the last forty years has been in the area of defence and space. While there is considerable disagreement about the aggregate impact of the substantial funds dispersed by the Department of Defense and the National Aeronautics and Space Administration in the post-war period, there is little question that they have played a decisive role in creating a comparative advantage for the United States in a wide variety of sectors. The most obvious impact of DoD on America's industrial competitiveness has been to make the United States the world's major producer and exporter of weaponry. Between 1970 and 1985, America's share of world arms transfers more than doubled; currently, 840,000 jobs in the United States are generated by foreign military sales.[17] As with agriculture, government support for this industry has been accompanied by government protection of it: the pronounced bias of American defence procurement towards firms both owned and located in the United States constitutes America's most important non-tariff barrier to trade.

The federal government has also played a critical role in developing the American aerospace industry—the only high-technology sector in which America's share of world exports remains as high as 50 per cent. Prior to World War II, the National Advisory Committee on Aeronautics, NASA's predecessor, built facilities where companies could test new designs, while the Post Office was the airlines' first important customer. The Civil Aeronautics Board established a legally sanctioned cartel for the airline industry, thus providing an important civilian market for commercial aircraft. As late as 1950, military purchases still accounted for 92 per cent of aerospace sales, while during the 1950s and 1960s, the Defense Department underwrote the research and development costs of each new generation of civilian aircraft. Between 1925 and 1975 the federal government channelled more direct support for technological research to aviation than to any other industry. In 1977, 70 per cent of its R & D was funded by the federal government.[18]

The Defense Department also played a central role in the development of both the computer and semiconductor industries.[19] While the transistor was invented in 1947 by Bell Laboratories, independently of military procurement, until 1955 virtually all computer-related research was government funded. IBM made two breakthroughs in the late 1950s that were responsible for making it into the world's leading manufacturer of computers—namely, the random access magnetic-core memory and transistorized computers. Both were federally funded; indeed, until 1960, the government was the major purchaser of computers. In addition, NASA's willingness to pay for the developmental costs of semi-conductors played a critical role in the development of this industry, helping to reduce the costs of an integrated circuit twenty-five fold between 1962 and 1968 and encouraging a number of new firms to enter this market. NASA and DoD accounted for more than one-third of semi-conductor sales in 1967 and for over 70 per cent of annual sales during the first four years of integrated circuit production.

Robert Reich concludes:

> The U.S. government has responded to emerging industries primarily through its national defense and aerospace programs. Notwithstanding that the goal of economic adjustment has not been an objective of these programs, they have contributed to U.S. leadership in world sales of aircraft, communication satellite technology, hard plastics, synthetic rubber, computers, semi-conductors, lasers, fiber optics, radio and television communication equipment, robotics, optical instruments, scientific instruments and many other products.[20]

Under the Reagan Administration, the role of the Defense Department in promoting industrial development increased substantially.[21] Defence spending on research and development doubled between 1980 and 1985. DoD's 1985 budget allocates $35 billion for research and development in new technologies—roughly one-third of all anticipated research and development expenditures in the United States—while DoD procurement of electronics components and systems is scheduled to triple between 1982 and 1987. In 1979 the Defense Department initiated a joint development programme with nine computer and semiconductor manufacturers to develop large-scale integrated circuits: nearly one billion dollars has been budgeted for this programme over the next decade. The Reagan Administration has also established a $1 billion programme to develop a 'super-computer' over the next five years, DoD is also becoming more heavily involved in funding research for advanced lasers, advanced computer software, and fiber optics; it is also currently the major purchaser of these products. The Administration's Strategic Defense Initiative, with a projected budget of $26 billion, will fund basic research in a number of technologies with important commercial applications; hence the considerable eagerness of a number of European high-technology companies to participate in it.[22] Indeed, SDI has been described as an industrial 'martial' plan.[23] As one government official put it, 'Defense research presses the limits of science and technology.'[24] And in his 1986 State of the Union address, the President announced a programme of government support for the development of a transatmospheric vehicle, or 'space plane'. This vehicle, dubbed the 'Orient Express', would have important military applications, and is intended to help restore the pre-eminence of the United States in aerospace technology. NASA and Pentagon funding is scheduled to total more than $350 million by 1988.

Perhaps even more importantly, the Pentagon has begun to play a more active role in improving the efficiency of American manufacturing.[25] Man Tech, as it is called, has promoted laser welding, and the development of photogrammetry, an optical system for measuring the precision of machine cuts. The Pentagon is currently working with Westinghouse Electric to develop robotic assembly systems, and is supporting the development of software that will link computer-aided design and computer-aided manufacturing into integrated, factory-wide systems; the latter represents an effort to develop an automated 'factory of the future'. DoD is also providing financial incentives for American defence manufacturers to develop sophisticated manufacturing systems which hold the promise of dramatically improving productivity in the manufacture of high-technology products with relatively short production runs.

The Reagan Administration's most explicit effort to use public resources to improve the comparative advantage of American industry involves space.[26] In announcing a national policy to accelerate the commercial development of space, the President stated that 'the benefits our people can receive from the commercial use of space literally dazzle the imagination.'[27] Indeed, the Administration's programme in this area has frequently been compared to the role played by the federal government in developing the nation's railway system more than a century earlier. As one observer noted: 'Anyone who was sitting around in 1840 thinking about this railroad thing couldn't begin to imagine a fraction of the economic potential that would eventually be realized by opening up the West.'[28]

The government's space programme has already produced its first industry, satellite communications, whose annual sales volume is currently $3 billion. A second industry, based on the information provided by remote sensing satellites, has begun to emerge; already one firm provides daily crop-supply predictions that have proved valuable to both farmers and the Department of Agriculture. Each year NASA publishes a list of the products produced by its researchers that are in commercial use. The list already includes robotic systems, high-temperature lubricants, and, most importantly, solar technology. However, the really ultimate commercial potential of space lies in manufacturing. There are a considerable number of products, including various drugs, devices for measuring microscopic electronic components, and semiconductors made from gallium arsenide crystals, that can be manufactured far more cheaply and accurately in space than they can on earth. The Center for Space Policy predicts that space-related activities may involve sales of $855 billion per year by the year 2000—not including the resources spent by NASA or the military.

Given the considerable expense and risk involved in space manufacturing, virtually all the initial development costs have been financed by the federal government. NASA has already spent $200 million to create the infrastructure needed to exploit space and continues to charge companies far below the marginal costs of each shuttle flight. NASA has already turned over both rocket launching services and remote sensing to the private sector and hopes that eventually the shuttle programme will be privately owned and managed as well. Initially, private firms were hesitant to become involved in space manufacturing and experiments; the first twenty shuttle flights included only ten experiments for American companies. But this is beginning to change: already five business-university research centers have been established to design programmes in this area and corporate interest is increasing.[29]

Nor are America's current initiatives in industrial policy exclusively defence and space-related. America's biotechnology industry, now beginning to become commercially viable, was literally created by the federal government. While universities, venture capitalists, scientists, and entrepreneurs have all played a role, the support of the National Institutes of Health for basic research has been decisive. One source notes:

> NIH created the knowledge and personnel base, actively worked to transfer a technology from the laboratory to the market and invented a quasi-regulatory oversight system that encouraged research. Together, these elements have amounted to a national industrial policy for biotechnology, even if NIH did not deliberately set out to create the industry that exists today.[30]

Likewise, the American pharmaceutical industry significantly benefited from military spending during the Second World War and, more recently, federal spending has played a major role in the development of new medical technologies in the United States: the government is the major purchaser of medical technology through its multibillion subsidy of medical treatment, and has also funded the development of specific innovations, such as the artificial heart. In short, it is not coincidental that virtually all of the sectors in which American industry continues to enjoy a competitive advantage have been the beneficiaries of direct and substantial governmental assistance.

IMPLICATIONS

This brief survey of American industrial policies requires us to reassess some of the arguments that have been advanced to explain why the development of strategies designed to improve the competitiveness of particular sectors is beyond the capacity of the American government. For example, it has been suggested that American Civil Servants lack both the technical capacity and political authority necessary to engage in sectoral planning. Yet officials in both the Department of Agriculture and the Department of Defense are both highly knowledgeable and enjoy considerable political autonomy. Their ties with their counterparts in the private sector are every bit as extensive and co-operative as those between MITI and Japanese individuals, and French Civil Servants and big business in France. It has also been argued that the vulnerability of government officials in the United States to interest group pressures makes them incapable of exercising authority over the private sector. Yet neither the space nor the defence programme was initially established as a response to industry pressures; on the contrary, it was the government which

was responsible for channelling substantial private and public sector
resources into these sectors in the first place. If anything, the DoD
has displayed far more initiative in its dealings with industry than
MITI, with whom it is frequently compared: its needs have been the
driving force behind the research and development programmes of
the private sector.

In the case of agriculture, defence, and space, American industrial
policies benefit a relatively small proportion of the nation's business
firms—and, indeed, impose considerable short-term costs on the rest
of the economy. And yet the privileged position enjoyed by these
sectors has not been subject to serious political challenge for nearly
forty years, thus suggesting a relatively high degree of consistency in
public sector resource allocation in the United States in the post-war
period. Moreover, American agricultural policy clearly demonstrates
that American government intervention need not degenerate into
pork-barrel politics. Undoubtedly, some agricultural policies make
little economic sense and serve mainly to transfer wealth from consumers to agricultural producers. This is certainly true of dairy price
supports and of various import restrictions. But they are hardly typical of the broad thrust of government intervention in this sector.
And the notion that the federal government cannot make choices
among industries or regions is difficult to square with the observation that agricultural assistance goes to less than five per cent of the
population. It is Europe and Japan, not the United States, that illustrate the 'pork-barrel' nature of government support for farmers.

Finally, it has been argued that the ability of American firms to
secure funds through private capital markets deprives the American
government of an important source of leverage over capital allocation by the private sector.[31] Yet, by manipulating the tax code, providing special loan guarantee programmes, and—in the case of agriculture and housing—establishing a special set of financial
institutions, the American government has demonstrated an impressive capacity to redirect the flow of capital in the United States.

What of the capacity of the American government to resist the
demands of declining or non-competitive sectors for assistance?
Here again, the American government has proved far stronger and
more independent than has commonly been assumed. Direct government subsidy to noncompetitive firms or industries is less common in the United States than in Europe. The number of firms that
have been bailed out by the American government over the last decade can be counted on the fingers of one hand, and, to date, most
of these bail-outs have been costless to the taxpayer. Compared to
the governments of other capitalist nations, the United States has

provided much less protection to its small business sector. Thanks to the weakness of its trade union movement, America has made relatively few efforts to protect its workers from job losses due to international competition. For example, the United States is the only capitalist democracy that does not have legislation limiting plant closures. Ironically, France and Japan, the two nations whose states are considered the 'strongest' of any capitalist democracy have played a much more active role in protecting their small business and agricultural sectors from domestic and international market forces than has the United States.

Certainly the American government has yielded to the demands of a number of non-competitive sectors for protection from foreign producers. But the significance of the American retreat from free trade must be placed in perspective. Most obviously, America in the post-war period has been and remains less protectionist than any other major industrial economy. Moreover, in sharp contrast to the Europeans, who have provided an extensive array of subsidies to workers in sectors such as steel, shipbuilding, automobiles, and textiles—often via nationalization—for the most part, the intervention of the American government has been limited to restricting imports. But while these policies have raised prices for American consumers, they have not interfered with the adjustment of these sectors to international competition. In spite of import restrictions, both employment and investment in domestic steel, automobile production, and textiles have continued to decline. Moreover, although the United States is the only nation whose legislature is primarily elected on a regional basis, America's assistance to its declining and depressed regions has been considerably less than in Britain, France, Sweden, and Italy. In addition, the deregulation of financial markets, telecommunications, and transportation has been more extensive in the United States than in any other capitalist nation, thus demonstrating the ability of the American state to overcome the political pressures of the firms in those sectors that were committed to the regulatory status quo.

Finally, those who classify the American government as 'a weak state' would do well to consider the course of business-government relations under the Reagan Administration. Thanks in large measure to the strong dollar, substantial segments of the American economy, particularly midwestern agriculture and eastern and mid-western heavy industry, were literally decimated during the first half of the 1980s. And yet the Administration was remarkably unresponsive to their demands for assistance. Whether intended or not, the Administration's fiscal and monetary policies have an important sectoral component. By making the dollar overvalued, they rapidly shifted capital and labour away from those so-called 'sunset' industries in which America does not appear to be able to maintain a comparative advantage. More recently, the Administration's efforts to reduce the level of government support for agriculture and housing, on the one hand, and increase expenditures for space and defence programmes, on the other, are clearly intended to help shift resources away from the former two sectors and expand the size of the latter two—thus engineering precisely the kind of politically directed sectoral adjustment that we usually associated with the Japanese.

THE DISTINCTIVENESS OF THE UNITED STATES

The relationship between the American government and American business—particularly big business—has been generally regarded as an adversarial one, in sharp contrast to the more co-operative relationships that appear to be more common in other capitalist societies. Yet it is by no means clear that the relationship between business and government in the United States is as distinctive as most scholars have assumed. Certainly popular antagonisms toward large firms is not a uniquely American phenomenon; it has also characterized domestic politics in other capitalist societies, including Germany, France, and Britain. Compared with other capitalist nations, the relationship between workers, farmers, and small businessmen, on the one hand, and big business, on the other, have not been noticeably conflictual in the United States. American unions have been relatively weak and moderate, American farmers have accommodated themselves to the imperatives of large-scale industrial development since the 1920s, and, except in a limited number of policy areas, American small businessmen have not been an important factor in American politics for nearly a century. Only middle-class reform groups have been more influential in America than in other capitalist nations. On balance, it would be hard to make a case that large firms in America enjoy less political influence vis-à-vis other sectors of the economy than their counterparts in other capitalist polities.

What, then, is distinctive about business-government relations in the United States? America does remain unique in the scope and complexity of its laws and regulations that restrict management prerogatives in a wide variety of areas. The most obvious example is anti-trust policy: no other capitalist nation has sought to establish such a wide variety of legal controls over the terms of competition. As a former chairman of the board of Du Pont put it, 'Why is it that my American colleagues and I are being constantly taken to court—made to stand trial—for activities that our counterparts in Britain and other parts of Europe are knighted or given peerages and comparable honors for?[32] Likewise, no other capitalist nation has established so many rules that restrict exports of goods and services. These range from the Foreign Corrupt Practices Act to a variety of trade embargoes and restrictions on the sale of particular products to specific countries.

Yet, while these restrictions may be annoying to particular firms, their aggregate impact on the competitive position of American industry is rather modest. The enforcement of America's anti-trust laws has been highly selective and has not resulted in levels of market concentration significantly different from those of other capitalist nations. In recent years, the American government has not hesitated to encourage mergers on the part of marginal firms or permit co-operation among firms in the more dynamic sectors of the economy. And while some rules and regulations have certainly restricted exports, on balance, American foreign policy over the last half-century has been highly supportive of American foreign trade and investment.

It is true that over the last two decades, the level of conflict between government officials and corporate managers over the making and implementation of policy in areas such as occupational health and safety, environmental and consumer protection, and equal employment has been substantially greater in the United States than in any other capitalist nation.[33] No other capitalist nation has provided middle-class reform groups with such extensive opportunities to participate in the policy process nor erected so many legal and procedural obstacles to prevent business-government co-operation in the making and enforcement of regulatory policies. As a result, the politics of government regulation of corporate social conduct in the United States have been relatively adversarial.

Yet, at the same time, if one compares the actual implementation of regulatory policy in the United States with that of other capitalist nations, it does not appear that, in the final analysis, American officials have been any less sensitive to the costs of compliance than their counterparts in other capitalist nations. As in the case of anti-trust policy, American controls over corporate social conduct may be far stricter than in other capitalist polities, but their enforcement has been highly selective. For all the numerous, and well-documented, 'horror stories' about the effects of particular regulatory policies on various firms and industries, the burden they have placed on the American economy does not appear to differ significantly from those imposed on firms in other capitalist nations; indeed the United States spends a smaller proportion of its GNP on pollution control than does Japan. It is the way American regulatory policies are made, not the costs of complying with them, that distinguishes government regulation in America from other capitalist nations.

Moreover, it is important to keep the nature of conflict between business and government in America in perspective. Government regulation represents one of the relatively few areas in which there has been considerable antagonism between business and government in the United States. But, even in this policy area, conflict has been the exception, not the rule. Most important, economic regulation in the United States has only rarely challenged management prerogatives; in most cases the initiative for regulation came from the regulated industries themselves. America's current efforts at economic deregulation primarily involve conflicts *among* particular firms and industries, not *between* business and government. Prior to the mid-1960s, the regulation of corporate social conduct was handled primarily at the state level and for the most part it was relatively cooperative. It only became relatively adversarial in the mid-1960s, and the level of conflict has diminished considerably since the late 1970s. The close quasi-corporatist ties between defence contractors and the Department of Defense, farmers and the Department of Agriculture, real estate developers and builders and the Department of Housing, and bio-engineering firms and NIH are the norm, not the exception, of business-government relations in the United States.[34]

Moreover, business-government relations in America have always been relatively co-operative at the state level. During the first half of the nineteenth century, state and local governments played a critical role in promoting the expansion of American agriculture, primarily through financing and organizing the development of the nation's infrastructure: more than two-thirds of the 4,000 miles of canals constructed in the United States prior to the Civil War were financed by state governments. From the outset of the industrial revolution, states competed actively with each other in seeking to attract new investments, while, over the last century, creating a good 'business climate' has been a major priority of most state governments. Although a few states did pursue anti-growth policies during the 1970s, more recently virtually all state governments have become much more active in seeking to improve the performance of their economies.[35] The emergence of Silicon Valley in northern California has created a model of government-business-university cooperation which other states are now trying to duplicate. Every state now has some form of an economic development agency; in thirty of the fifty states, this agency has cabinet-level status and in several states its budget exceeds $100 million. Such agencies typically employ a variety of means of attracting investment, including direct financial assistance, tax incentives, training assistance, and special programmes, such as the establishment of low-cost industrial sites.

CORPORATE POLITICAL PARTICIPATION

What also makes the pattern of business-government relations in the United States distinctive is the nature of corporate political participation. Unlike in other capitalist nations, where there exists a wide array of official and quasi-official channels through which business can regularly communicate its views to public officials, in America corporate political participation tends to be much more *ad hoc* in nature. While in other capitalist nations the consultation of industry by government is assumed, in America it must constantly be asserted; business enjoys few privileges not enjoyed by other interest groups. Business may be no less influential in the United States than in other capitalist nations, but in America its influence comes at a price: companies must invest substantial resources if they are to affect public sector decisions.

For example, if a company or trade association wants to affect a government regulatory policy, it must prepare expert testimony for both congressional committee hearings and agency rule-making proceedings, hire lawyers who can then take an appeal against an agency decision to the federal courts, and then, if necessary, entrust its lobbyists to seek to have the regulatory statute amended in the legislature. The latter strategy may require the company to enter into alliances with other interest groups, mobilize its shareholders and employees to write to or visit their representatives in Washington, and mount a nation-wide public relations campaign designed to influence press coverage of the issue. Each of these efforts involves a considerable expenditure of corporate resources.

By any index, the scope of government intervention in the economy has increased enormously over the last two decades. The American government has become more active in both regulating and promoting business than at any time in its history. As a function of the deregulation of banking and telecommunications, the increase in government spending as a proportion of GNP since 1965, the expansion of social regulation, the growing internationalization of the American economy, and the significant expansion of the Defense budget, the corporate strategy of American firms has become increasingly dependent on government decisions. From this perspective, Reagan has not so much reversed the direction of the New Deal as accelerated it.

The result has been an unprecedented expansion in the amount of resources business firms devote to the political process.[36] For example, in 1961 only 130 firms were represented by registered lobbyists in Washington, D.C., and of these only 50 had their own Washington staffs. By 1979, 650 firms had their own registered lobbyists and 247 had full-time employees in the nation's capital. While only a small minority of *Fortune* 500 companies had public affairs offices in 1970, a decade later more than 80 per cent had established such units. In 1974 there were 89 corporate political action committees; by 1982 there were 1,555. Corporate public relations programmes and efforts to build 'grass roots' support among employees, stockholders, and community groups were relatively rare prior to 1970; they have now become an important component of virtually every effort on the part of the business community to influence public policy. In addition, the American business community has devoted enormous resources toward influencing the climate of intellectual opinion, through its sponsorship of conferences, publications, and academic research.[37] These efforts have, on balance, proved extremely effective. The relative degree of political power exercised by business at both the federal and state levels increased significantly between 1977 and 1985. Business became much more successful both at shaping the political agenda and in influencing the outcomes of a variety of particular public policies, particularly in the areas of tax policy and government regulation.

America continues to differ from other capitalist nations, not only in the resources companies devote to affecting public policy, but also in the decentralized nature of that participation. In spite of its heightened politicization, the American business community, like all other interest groups in American society, remains politically fragmented: there is no peak organization capable of representing the views and interests of American business as a whole.

Over the last century, a number of organizations, including the Chamber of Commerce during the Progressive Era, the National Association of Manufacturers during the 1930s, the Committee for Economic Development during the 1960s and the Business Roundtable during the 1970s, have sought to play such a role. But their efforts have invariably floundered. Even trade associations in America have been far less important than in Europe or Japan; their role atrophied still further during the 1970s as companies became more diversified. In fact, over the last fifteen years, the nature of corporate political participation has become even more fragmented, with individual firms themselves becoming the most important political units. Yoffie and Badaracco write:

A company with a politically active senior executive, a corporate public affairs staff, a PAC, its own media identity, a Washington law firm, and a Washington office or lobbyist has an independent apparatus for political action. It has its own information, contacts, and bargaining chips. It can lobby in Congress, negotiate with executive agencies, and take court action. Such a company can still work, in the traditional ways, through its industry association or through umbrella groups like the Chamber of Commerce. But it can also act on its own.[38]

Finally, compared to other capitalist nations, business-government relations in America have also been less stable. Over the last century the United States has experienced three major changes in the role of government in the economy. The first, associated with the Progressive Era, occurred between the turn of the century and the First World War. The second was the New Deal, which dominated American politics during the 1930s. The third, which still lacks a convenient label, took place between the middle of the 1960s and the middle of the 1970s; it was associated with a major increase in the scope of federal controls over corporate decisions in the areas of personnel policy, environmental and consumer protection, and occupational health and safety. The political turbulence associated with the reforms instituted during each period served to reinforce the long-standing belief of American corporate executives that the American political process is both unpredictable and potentially threatening to their prerogatives. As one executive put it at a business meeting in 1975, at the height of the most recent reform period,[39] 'My industry is regulated up to its neck. You are regulated up to your knees. And the tide is coming in.' Since then, of course, the influence of business over public policy has significantly increased, yet the perception of vulnerability expressed in this quotation remains a permanent feature of American business culture.

CONCLUSION

This chapter has argued that business-government relations in America have been less distinctive than has been commonly assumed. It has primarily focused on the area of industrial policy, since students of business-government relations have frequently argued that it is precisely the inability of America to develop a coherent set of sectoral policies that reveals the distinctiveness of the American political system. We have suggested that America does have a highly developed set of industrial policies, which, on balance, appear to be no more or less coherent, consistent, or successful than those of its major industrial competitors. It now appears that the period *laissez-faire* capitalism, far from establishing the future course of business-government relations in America, may instead come to be seen as a historical anomaly. In many respects we have come full circle: American business-government relations over the last half-century increasingly resemble the pattern of 'state mercantilism' of the first half of the nineteenth century. The only difference is that the former period of co-operation took place primarily at the state level, while, in recent years, the federal role has become much more important. Yet, in a sense, the fundamental dynamics are similar: just as the states financed the construction of canals and roadways in order to enable their citizens to compete more effectively with those of other states, so can many of the recent promotional policies of NASA and the Department of Defense be viewed as an effort to enable American industry to become more internationally competitive.

What does continue to make America distinctive is not so much the effect of its public policies on business as the way in which they are made. Precisely because American politics are highly pluralist and fragmented, companies have been forced to devote substantially greater resources to public affairs than in other capitalist nations. While some firms have cut back on their political activity since Reagan's election, the overall level of political involvement of American business remains extremely high by historical standards. And it is likely to remain so in the foreseeable future—particularly as issues surrounding the international competitiveness of American industry continue to occupy a prominent place on the nation's political agenda. The increased politicization of business represents one of the most significant changes in business-government relations in America over the last two decades.

NOTES

1. See, for example, Chalmers Johnson (ed.), *The Industrial Policy Debate* (San Francisco: Institute for Contemporary Studies, 1984).

2. See Robert Reich, 'Making Industrial Policy', *Foreign Affairs*, September 1982, pp. 852–97; Robert Reich, 'An Industrial Policy of the Right', *Public Interest*, Fall 1983, pp. 3–17.

3. See Charles Schultze, 'Industrial Policy: A Dissent', *Brookings Review*, Fall 1983; J. L. Badaracco, jun. and D. B. Yoffie, 'Industrial Policy: It Can't

Happen Here', *Harvard Business Review*, November-December 1982, pp. 96–175.

4. For the argument that the American state is weak, see Andrew Shonfield, *Modern Capitalism* (New York: Oxford University Press, 1965). For a formal classification of states in terms of their relative strengths and weaknesses, see Peter Katzenstein, 'Domestic Structures and Strategies of Foreign Economic Policy' in *Between Power and Plenty*, edited by Peter Katzenstein (Madison: University of Wisconsin Press, 1978). For more on the adversarial relationship, see Thomas McCraw, 'Business and Government: The Origins of the Adversary Relationship', *California Management Review*, Winter 1984, pp. 33–52.

5. This argument is made by Thomas McCraw in 'Mercantilism and the Market: Antecedents of American Industrial Policy' in Claude Barfield and William Schambra (eds.), *The Politics of Industrial Policy* (Washington, DC: American Enterprise Institute for Public Policy Research, 1986), pp. 33–62.

6. For both an eloquent summary and extensive critique of this position, see Bruce Scott, 'National Strategies: Key to International Competition' in Bruce Scott and George Lodge (eds.), *U.S. Competitiveness in the World Economy* (Boston: Harvard Business School Press, 1985), pp. 71–143.

7. The one notable exception was in the area of military procurement. Eli Whitney, whose development of a system of manufacturing on interchangeable parts was critical to the development of the 'American system of manufacturing', attributed his innovation to government contracts and financing. The Springfield Arsenal was described as 'the most respectable private establishment . . . in the United States': William Diebold, Jr., 'Past and Future Industrial Policy in the United States' in John Pinder (ed.), *National Industrial Strategies and the World Economy* (London: Allanheld, Osmun & Co., 1980), p. 163.

8. David Vogel, 'Why Businessmen Distrust their State: The Political Consciousness of American Corporate Executives', *British Journal of Political Science*, January 1978, pp. 45–78.

9. For the rather different European experience, see Suzanne Berger, 'Regime and Interest Representation in the French Traditional Middle Classes' in Suzanne Berger (ed.), *Organizing Interests in Western Europe* (Cambridge: University Press, 1981).

10. This section is based on Paul Lawrence and Davis Dyer, *Renewing American Industry* (New York: The Free Press, 1983), Chapter 5: 'Agriculture: The American Miracle'.

11. See also Ezra Vogel, *Comeback* (New York: Simon and Schuster, 1985), Chapter 5: 'Agriculture: Export Promotion'; Lawrence and Dyer, op. cit., p. 119.

12. Lawrence and Dyer, op. cit. (n. 10), p. 119.

13. John Young, 'Global Competition: The New Reality', *California Management Review*, Spring 1985, p. 16.

14. 'Elephant-High Farm Debts', *The Economist*, 14 September 1985, p. 17.

15. See Scott, 'National Strategies' (n. 6), pp. 133–4.

16. Ezra Vogel, op. cit. (n. 11), p. 212.

17. Ann Markusen, 'Defense Spending as Industrial Policy'; in Sharon Zuken (ed.), *Industrial Policy* (New York: Praeger, 1985), p. 76.

18. See Reich, 'Making Industrial Policy', (n. 2), p. 864.

19. Ibid. p. 865; also Thomas Egan, 'The Case of Semiconductors' in Margaret Dewar (ed.), *Industry Vitalization* (New York: Pergamon Press, 1982), pp. 121–44; and Ezra Vogel, op. cit., (n. 11), p. 196.

20. Reich, 'Making Industrial Policy', p. 864. And Ezra Vogel adds: 'One survey of private scientists and engineers conducted in the mid-1970s put the commercial value of NASA's contributions up to that time in four fields—integrated circuits, gas turbines, multilayer insulation, and computer simulation—at between $2.3 billion and $7.6 billion in 1974 dollars.' Ezra Vogel, op. cit. (n. 11), p. 196. Michael Schrange notes: '[The Defense Department] was responsible for much of the funding for the most important work in computer graphics, computer networking, artificial intelligence and man-machine interfaces. The Defense Department was the driving force behind the development of numerically controlled machine tools. And Pentagon research is woven throughout the technological advances in the domestic airline industry': Michael Schrange, 'America's Ministry of International Trade and Technology', *The Washington Post National Weekly Edition*, 27 August 1984, p. 31.

21. This section draws upon Reich, 'An Industrial Policy of the Right' op. cit. (n. 2). See also Schrange, op. cit. (n. 20).

22. 'The Selling of Star Wars to Businesses Abroad', *Business Week*, 15 July 1985, pp. 68, 72.

23. Robert Kuttner, 'Blind Faith in Free Trade Doesn't Pay', *Business Week*, 14 October 1985, p. 22.

24. Bruce Steinberg, 'The Military Boost to Industry', *Fortune*, 30 April 1984, p. 45.

25. See Steinberg, op. cit.

26. This section is based on David Osborne, 'Business in Space', *The Atlantic*, March 1985, pp. 45–58.

27. Ibid., p. 45.

28. Ibid., p. 52.

29. Ibid., p. 45.

30. Neil Henderson and Michael Schrange, 'Our Biotech Industrial Policy: Will NIH's Baby have to Walk More on Its Own Now?' *The Washington Post National Weekly Edition*, 31 December 1984, p. 6. See Also Susan Bartlett Foote, 'Coping with Conflict: Public Policies toward the Medical Product Industry', University of California, Berkeley: Center for Research in Management Working Paper, September 1985.

31. This argument is made by John Zysman in *Governments, Markets and Growth* (Ithaca: Cornell University Press, 1983).

32. Quoted in Diebold, op. cit. (n. 7), p. 165.

33. The next two paragraphs are based on David Vogel, *National Styles of Regulation: Environmental Policy in Great Britain and the United States* (Ithaca: Cornell University Press, 1986).

34. This argument is also made by Theodore J. Lowi, *The End of Liberalism*

(New York: W. W. Norton, 1969, 1979) and Grant McConnell, *Private Power and American Democracy* (New York: Random House, 1966), although the conclusions they draw differ from mine.

35. See Mel Dubnick and Lynne Holt, 'Industrial Policy and the States', *Publics*, Winter 1985, pp. 113–29.

36. This section draws upon David Yoffie and Joseph Badaracco, Jr., 'A Rational Model of Corporate Political Strategies', A Working Paper, Division of Research, Harvard Business School, 1984. See also David Vogel, 'The Power of Business in America: A Re-Appraisal', *British Journal of Political Science*, January 1983, pp. 19–44.

37. See Thomas Byrne Edsell, *The New Politics of Inequality* (New York: W. W. Norton, 1984).

38. Yoffie and Badaracco, op. cit. (n. 36), pp. 3, 4.

39. Leonard Silk and David Vogel, *Ethics and Profits* (New York: Simon & Schuster, 1976), p. 52. For a detailed analysis of the changes in the pattern of political influence of business in American politics since 1965, see David Vogel, ibid.

PART TWO

The Political and Social Environment of Business

Chapter Five

THE PUBLIC-INTEREST MOVEMENT AND THE AMERICAN REFORM TRADITION

BEGINNING in the late sixties, a new force emerged in American politics: the public-interest movement. An important part of this movement consisted of a wide variety of law firms, research centers, lobbying groups, membership associations, and community organizations committed to public policies that attempted to reduce the power and privileges of business. By any measure, their impact has been impressive: throughout most of the 1970s, the relationship between regulatory and corporate officials was more strained than at any time since the 1930s. In sharp contrast to the quarter-century following World War II, the most vocal criticisms of government regulation since the late sixties have come from businessmen—not their critics.[1] Public-interest activism succeeded in significantly narrowing the boundaries of managerial discretion; many corporate abuses were reduced and those that continue are now less likely to go unchallenged.[2] In sum, public-interest groups are to the last decade what the trade-union movement was to the thirties and the muckrakers were to the Progressive era: the driving force behind increased restrictions on corporate prerogatives.

At first glance, this political phenomenon appears to represent another example of American interest-group pluralism. Pluralists never argued that self-interest was the only motivation for political participation. While denying that there actually existed such a notion as the "public interest," pluralist theory would appear to have little difficulty appreciating that various groups and individuals might seek to cloak themselves in its mantle in order to achieve ends that corresponded to their own particular conception of the common good. Not surprisingly, recent studies of public-interest politics appear to accept the pluralist interest-group model of American politics; they read like updated versions of David Truman's *The Governmental Process*.[3] We learn of the aims, tactics, political resources, and organizational structures of these new lobbies and are offered case studies of their successes and failures in influencing public policy. While their conclusions might be slightly less sanguine than those expressed in *Who Governs?*, their methodology is quite similar to

Dahl's. Far from challenging the pluralist view of American politics, they in fact confirm it: their studies provide empirical proof that potential political resources are widely distributed in the United States and that the system does contain a considerable amount of "slack." They reinforce Dahl's contention that in the "normal" American political process "there is a high probability that an active and legitimate group in the population can make itself heard effectively at some crucial stage in the process of decision."[4]

If this approach illustrates some of the vitality left in pluralist theory, it also demonstrates its persistent shortcomings. What is still lacking is an adequate appreciation of the place of the public-interest movement in the history of corporate capitalism in America. Like labor, the public-interest movement is not simply another interest group. It represents a historically conditioned response to the problems posed for American politics by the rise of the large business corporation in the latter third of the nineteenth century. More generally, the political ideology that informs public-interest activism needs to be understood in the context of the American political tradition.[5]

This chapter examines public-interest groups from the perspective of some of these broader concerns. It is interested less in their substantive demands—which have been amply treated elsewhere—than in their political philosophy: what is the vision of politics that underlies their political strategy? And what are the limitations of that vision?

The Strategy of the Public-Interest Movement

Public-interest activism is based on a mistrust of both business and government. Its supporters believe that the regulatory agencies responsible for disciplining corporations have been no more successful than the marketplace in assuring that corporations behave responsibly: instead of regulating business, the government has more often been regulated by it.[6] In contrast to those both on its right and its left, public-interest advocates do not believe that business domination of the administrative process is the inevitable consequence of a capitalist or market system.[7] Rather, they attribute the shortcomings of government regulation of business to the limited number of political interests that participate in the formulation and implementation of regulatory policies. Public-interest advocates contend that the American political system is deficient because only a small portion of those interests affected by public policies have effective political and legal representation.[8] Moreover, these unrepresented interests are not a random group of interests; they tend to be those which the masses of individuals have in common. The public-interest movement often refers to itself as a "citizen's movement," a "consumer's movement," or "people's movement," precisely because it is the interests of individuals in these relatively "public" roles that it believes lack sufficient access to the policy process.

If the reason why public policies are biased in favor of business is that corporations are both able to participate fully in the formulation of regulatory policy and to secure redress for improper government action, then the program for reform is self-evident: the public-interest movement wants current unorganized interests to have the same privileges and prerogatives of organized ones. Thus corporations, although they seek the appointment and election of officials sympathetic to their concerns, do not rely upon the good will of public officials to represent adequately their interests; their lobbyists actively participate in the deliberations of regulatory agencies, and if a decision is made that they regard as legally improper, their attorneys appeal it in the courts. The public-interest movement wants citizens and the representatives of citizen interests to enjoy precisely these same rights and resources. Its central contention is that public policy can only reflect the public interest to the extent that those who pressure the state are an accurate reflection of those who are affected by it.

But how are citizens to acquire the ability to compete effectively with corporate lawyers and lobbyists? How can the political system be made genuinely pluralist? Somewhat paradoxically, the public-interest movement argues that the promotion of pluralism is the responsibility of government. They want the state to change the rules of the game so as to reduce the political representation of business and increase the representation of those affected by business decisions. The passage of laws regulating particular areas of corporate conduct are thus necessary but not sufficient; if the power of business is to be effectively countered, government must also make sure that public-interest groups are also able to participate in their interpretation and enforcement.

Just as the previous generation of reformers demanded that government enact policies that compensated for the deficiencies of the marketplace, so do public-interest activists seek the adoption of policies that reflect the shortcomings of government regulation. They argue that the most effective way the government can increase public control over business is by enacting policies that increase the power of the public-interest movement over government. The movement no more trusts the government to make decisions in the public interest than does business: what it wants are the same opportunities to influence public policy that business has historically monopolized.[9]

What are the policy implications of this perspective? How can government put the interests of citizens on a par with those of business? The most important concrete proposals of the public-interest movement involve procedural issues, public subsidy, and agency representation.

Procedural issues fall into roughly three parts. First, consumer and environmental groups want to be able to use the judicial system to challenge agency and corporate decisions that they regard as violations of the public interest. They want the judicial requirements of standing to be sufficiently liberalized so that public-interest organizations can use the lawsuit to advance a wide variety of environmental, aesthetic, and other noneconomic values.[10] Their goal is to have the courts consider public rights, such as clean air, water, open space, the seashore, on a par with traditional private-property rights.[11] Since the courts have broad discretion to determine under what circumstances citizen groups may sue on behalf of the "public interests" when no personal economic injury is alleged, public-interest organizations also advocate the passage of regulatory statutes containing provisions that explicitly recognize the right of citizens to sue if regulations are not being adequately enforced.[12] More importantly, public-interest advocates have strongly supported the passage of regulatory laws that severely limit the discretion of the agencies responsible for enforcing them, thus making it easier for public-interest lawyers to challenge the agency's decisions in the courts.[13]

There is also an additional category of rights that the public-interest movement is interested in expanding: the right to information.[14] The right of privacy, like that of private property, is a major legal prop of corporate power. The public-interest movement wants the public's right to information about a variety of dimensions of corporate conduct to receive the same protection from the courts, administrative agencies, and the legislature that these bodies have historically accorded to the corporation's right to privacy. The Freedom of Information Act and the amendments to it represent a first step in this direction; the public-interest movement would like to see its principles apply to the deliberations of the private sector as well. Similarly, public-interest lawyers want disclosure requirements to reflect not simply the interests of shareholders, but of all the corporation's constituencies.

Finally, public-interest advocates want legislation that guarantees due process for "whistle-blowers," in both the private and public sectors.[15] Since many abuses are first known to individuals who work within a corporate or public bureaucracy, encouraging these employees to "go public" with their stories provides an additional mechanism by which the effectiveness of regulation can be monitored by the public.

Increased public disclosure, liberalized standing requirements, and due process for "whistle-blowers" are each informed by an attempt to put the rights of those affected by corporate decisions on a par with those who make corporate decisions. By expanding public rights, public-interest advocates aspire to reduce private ones; they attempt to reduce the rights of property owners by increasing the rights of citizens.

The expansion of public or citizen rights is, however, only the first stage of the public-interest movement's program for disciplining business. The disproportionate impact of business on the political process is due not simply to the protection accorded to private-property rights; public-interest spokesmen argue that it is also the enormous financial and organizational resources of corporations—particularly when contrasted with the representatives of the public—that enable them to distort the intent of regulations. It logically follows that formal equality of opportunity is insufficient: if those affected by corporations are to be able to have their interests effectively represented, they require resources as well as rights. In essence, the public-interest movement wants the federal government to engage in a kind of political affirmative action program for those lacking sufficient resources to participate adequately in the American interest-group process. They justify federal subsidy not only on the grounds that it is necessary for pluralist democracy to actually work, but on the grounds that the government already subsidizes the political participation of corporations via the tax code: what they want is at least equal treatment.

The most common form of indirect public subsidy of the public-interest movement's legal fees has taken place through the private attorney general concept. Under this concept, courts have the discretion to award attorney's fees to prevailing plaintiffs if the plaintiffs had conferred a substantial public benefit by enforcing a federal statute through their lawsuit. The rationale for this doctrine is quite consistent with the major thrust of the public-interest movement's political philosophy: the government is officially recognizing that citizens have a critical role to play in the enforcement of the letter and spirit of public law and accordingly deserve compensation. In 1975 the Supreme Court delivered a major blow to the practice of public-interest law by restricting the authorization of attorney's fees to suits brought to enforce only those statutes that provided for the compensation of attorney's fees (as of 1976, forty-six federal laws fell into this category). Congressional action to overturn the effect of this decision has rapidly become a major political priority of the public-interest movement.[16] Public-interest advocates also would like the awarding of interim attorneys' fees in protracted cases and, in addition, would like the courts to calculate attorney's fee awards in public-interest cases at marketplace rates.[17] Moreover, the public-interest movement has strongly supported the use of what amount to public-spirited "bounty hunting" provisions in various federal regulatory statutes. These give citizens a financial incentive to assist the government in enforcing its own laws.[18]

Judicial review gives citizens the opportunity to redress grievances after a government agency has acted improperly; it does not speak to the issue of participation in the original deliberations of the agency, an issue that has become a major preoccupation of public-interest lawyers.[19] Specifically, they want federal regulatory agencies to subsidize directly the participation of representatives of currently unrepresented interests. This might take several forms, including the waiving of transcript and copying fees, regularly informing public-interest groups about impending agency activities in which they might be interested, paying the attorney's fees of public-interest groups, defraying the costs of expert witnesses, and subsidizing the travel and other out-of-pocket expenses of public-interest advocates. Since 1975, Congress has passed legislation authorizing four regulatory agencies to provide grants to defray the costs of participation by parties that would otherwise be unable to represent their interests in rule-making proceedings. Public-interest organizations argue that unless this practice becomes the norm, rights of participation are meaningless.[20]

The movement strongly supports legislation that not only authorizes the reimbursement of the various costs of citizen participation in a broad range of administrative proceedings (this is the substance of a bill proposed by Senator Kennedy), but also clearly specifies the circumstances under which departments and agencies must provide for adequate public representation—thus making public-interest representatives as independent as possible from the regulatory bureaucracies.[21]

Public-interest advocates have also strongly pressured for a liberalization of the tax laws restricting lobbying by tax-exempt organizations.[22] In 1970, fifteen public-interest organizations formed a coalition to challenge pending IRS restrictions on their efforts. A provision of the Tax Reform Act of 1976—lobbied for intensively by public-interest organizations—allows public-interest groups to spend up to 20 percent of their budgets on lobbying without forfeiting their tax-exempt status under Section 510(c)(3). Public-interest activists obviously would like the law to be liberalized still further, preferably removing all restrictions on lobbying by public-interest groups and thus enabling them to protect in Congress the victories they have won in the courts.

There is also a third means by which the federal government can increase the resources available to citizen groups; they can help defray some of the costs of mobilizing large numbers of consumers—thus helping the public-interest movement to overcome some of the barriers to collective action analyzed by Olson in *The Logic of Collective Action*.[23] The most frequently advanced proposals for organizational subsidy involve class-action suits and utility consumers. The former represent a major vehicle by which relatively diffuse, that is, public, interests can bargain with corporations on a basis of rough equality, and much of the movement's political energies have been devoted to liberalizing the conditions under which consumers can sue as a class.[24]

Perhaps the most imaginative form of public subsidy advocated by public-interest spokesmen would affect the consumers of utility services.[25] Dissatisfied with the performance of state public-utility commissions, Nader and his associates have proposed that utility companies be required to include in their monthly statements to their consumers a form inviting customers voluntarily to tax themselves a few extra dollars per year. These monies would be collected by the utility company and turned over to a residential utility consumer action group (RUCAG). RUCAG would hire a professional staff to monitor the performance of both the utility and the regulatory agency. Its directors would be elected by those consumers who agreed to fund it, and each consumer would retain the right to withhold his contribution if the organization did not effectively serve his interests. Under the provisions of legislation currently pending in over twenty state legislatures, RUCAG would have semiofficial status to represent formally the interests of utility consumers before agency proceedings. The RUCAG concept is readily generalizable to a wide variety of goods and services: public-interest advocates have envisioned check-off or voluntary contribution schemes for the consumers of automobiles, major appliances, airline tickets, and insurance, among others.[26]

While each of these proposals addresses the strengthening of the capacity of representatives of presently unrepresented interests to pressure the government, none of them involves any changes in the governmental structure itself. There is, however, a third set of policy proposals advocated by the public-interest movement that does focus directly on the structure of the bureaucracy. These proposals differ only in form, not in substance, from those designed to increase the political effectiveness of nongovernmental representatives of public interests. Their purpose is to increase the public-interest movement's political impact by giving it a foothold within the regulatory bureaucracy. The new administrative units that they would create do not have any direct regulatory responsibilities over business. Rather their role is to help the public-interest movement monitor those government officials that do.

The best-known and most controversial example of this kind of policy innovation is the proposal to create an independent consumer agency.[27] The consumer protection agency (CPA) would be unique among government regulatory agencies in that it would have no direct authority over the private sector. Rather, its responsibility would be to represent the interests of consumers before existing regulatory agencies; in this sense it can be considered as a kind of in-house public-interest law firm, its efforts paralleling and assisting those of the consumer movement itself.

The CPA, however, can also be understood in terms of the theory of "civic balance." The public-interest movement regards a substantial section of the bureaucracy—including much of the regulatory machinery—as under the direct control of the profit sector. These captured departments and agencies are considered a critical factor in explaining the extraordinary success of business in influencing the direction of public policy: not only do they protect the profit sector from effective public supervision, but they constitute a lobby within the government, attempting to secure for their "clients" additional largess. Accordingly, if the public-interest movement is to counter effectively the political influence of business, it too requires a captive agency—one that identifies with its interests in much the same way that the Defense Department identifies with defense contractors. And just as a revolving door has traditionally existed between various governmental units and corporations, so does the public-interest movement aspire to be able to shuttle its activists back and forth between regulatory agencies and public-interest organizations with equal ease and predictability.[28]

THE AMERICAN POLITICAL TRADITION

The public-interest movement's mistrust of regulatory officials is in part due to the control of the executive branch by Republican presidents between 1969 and 1976—the very years of the movement's development. Its suspicion of bureaucratic authority is also linked to the traumas of the Vietnam War and Watergate—which helped undermine the liberals' faith in a strong executive. But these developments do not adequately account for the movement's political orientation. Most obviously, many of the themes underlying the procedural reform proposals of the public-interest movement were developed prior to the Vietnam War. For example, the notion of participation was an important part of New Left ideology. Similarly, the idea that the federal government should use its power to give the powerless the financial, organizational, and legal resources they needed to advance their political interests was an integral part of Johnson's "War on Poverty." Moreover, the election of a president relatively sympathetic to the concerns of consumer and environmental organizations in 1976 did not diminish the movement's concern with procedural issues. Quite the reverse: it gave their demands considerable impetus. Carter's election was promptly viewed as providing the movement with an opportunity to make procedural reforms its major legislative priority.

In fact, the political perspective that informs the public-interest movement is not at all peculiar to the last decade; it is deeply rooted in the American political tradition. Its key elements—the importance of individual initiative, the fear of public authority, the value of increased political competition, an uneasiness with majoritarian democracy, the fascination with law and legal procedures, the emphasis on voluntary organizations—all can be found in both Hartz and Tocqueville. The central preoccupation of the public-interest movement is identical to that which concerns Madison and Dahl, namely, what are the conditions that are necessary for pluralist democracy to function properly? The emphasis of the public-interest activists, like that of the political actors described in Boorstin's *The Genius of American Politics*, is on means rather than ends.[29] Their vision of the good society is defined less by what that society decides than by how it decides. Public-interest activists are fundamentally engaged in that most American of occupations, namely, constitution making and revising.

The public-interest movement is largely concerned with one of the central problems of Anglo-American political thought, namely, the relationship between private and public authority. What links the approach of the movement to this problem with the mainstream of the Anglo-American political tradition is the movement's emphasis on preserving and enhancing private rather than public power. The procedural reforms advocated by the public-interest movement attempt to shift responsibility for the control of business from public officials to private citizens; these reforms aim to reduce the dependency of the citizenry upon the state. The reforms are an attempt to transfer the initiative for the making and implementation of public policy from the public sector to civil society. As Ralph Nader has noted:

> A number of . . . procedural rights are characterized as rights that are enforceable by individual citizens themselves. That's a very important distinction in the framework of law. . . . Which laws can only be enforced by government and which are primarily enforced by citizens? How can we extend the latter, which permit broad, decentralized access for advocates throughout the country? These laws don't rely so exclusively on who happens to be appointed to what agency or department of government, and they also permit diversity of initiative throughout the country.[30]

The attraction the courts hold for the public-interest movement—aside from the obvious fact that its ranks are disproportionately populated by lawyers—is the opportunity they provide for citizens to redress directly their grievances. The judicial system represents the public-interest movement's version of direct democracy; it enables individuals and organizations to take the enforcement of the law into their own hands. The movement's emphasis on the courts is not simply a short-term political tactic; rather, the judicial system is its model of democracy in action. Public-interest activists not only want to subject virtually all agency decisions to judicial review; they want agencies themselves to make decisions according to a judicial model.[31] Their goal is to make administrative law "a surrogate political process designed to ensure the fair representation of a wide range of affected interests in the process of administrative decisions."[32]

The common-law system, like the market system to which it is historically related, emphasizes the virtue of competition: both systems assume that the interests of all are best served when relatively equal forces are engaged in an adversary relationship. More critically, both emphasize the role of the state in providing the arena of conflict, not in determining how it should be resolved. This judicial model of state authority has deep historic roots. While consumer and environmental groups are unique in that they have explicitly emphasized the use of the courts to resolve their disputes with business, "the containment of interest conflict within diverse forums of adjudication is an observable pattern of American politics."[33] Both corporations and labor unions during the first half of the twentieth century sought to protect their interests by pressuring the state to establish quasi-judicial mechanisms, namely, the regulatory agencies for business and the National Labor Relations Board (NLRB) for labor. The public-interest movement is essentially following this pattern: like business and labor, it wants the state to provide it with the opportunity to define and defend its own interests in an adversary setting.

Quasi-judicial modes of intervention reflect a particular American conception of the state. Historically, Americans have made two sets of contradictory demands on their government. On the one hand, they have wanted public assistance and support. At the same time, they have wanted the locus of power in the society to remain within civil society. In brief, they have wanted public assistance, but not public control. They have wanted a state powerful enough to give them the rights and resources necessary to advance their economic and social objectives, yet weak enough not to encroach on their autonomy. The result is the pattern of "interest-group liberalism" and "small constituencies" described by Lowi and McConnell; as such, it is a pattern in which the public-interest movement fits perfectly.[34]

Like both labor and business, the public-interest movement wants the state to give it the financial resources and legal authority it needs to pursue its quarrels with its "adversaries." Indeed, the public-interest movement in large measure owes its very existence to the federal tax laws that exempt various activities from federal taxation. Just as the NLRB in effect represents a massive government subsidy to the legal costs of organizing trade unions, so would offices of consumer advocacy within the regulatory commissions and the establishment of a consumer protection agency in effect represent a legal subsidy to the public-interest law movement: their establishment would reduce the number of lawsuits that private plaintiffs would have to initiate.

Just as unions want public assistance to help insure that the power of every employer is countered by an organization of employees, so does the public-interest movement want the state to help it form an organization of consumers to monitor the activities of each regulatory agency. In effect, it wants the state to help create and sponsor a series of "shadow governments." The liberalization of consumer class-action suits and authorization of check-off provisions in utility bills are roughly modeled on the union shop, though they lack the latter's element of compulsion. Similarly, the private attorney general provision that the public-interest movement wants to append all federal regulatory laws does not differ in principle from the myriad services that the government supplies to the private sector as a matter of course—ranging from the statistical data gathered by the Department of Commerce to the funding of highways and dams: both business and the public-interest movement want the state to underwrite as large a share of their costs of "doing business" as they possibly can.

Without doubt, the public-interest movement is attempting to increase the power of the state in American society. But like business in the nineteenth century, it wants that authority to be used exclusively against its adversaries. A parallel can be drawn: the public-interest movement wants to use the courts in precisely the same way that business used them in the late nineteenth and early twentieth centuries. Both want activist judiciaries dedicated to reducing the autonomy and power of those they oppose. Equally important, the public-interest movement wants the federal government to assist it in a way that does not interfere with it. Each of the procedural reforms it advocates is designed to insure that the initiative for government intervention remains with the private—nonprofit—sector, namely, itself. The desire of nonprofit organizations for public assistance is essentially no different from Lockheed's. One suspects that few in the audience were shocked when a congressional committee staffer told the first national meeting of public-interest advocates: "All of you know about your needs for funds in order to participate effectively in a federal proceeding, or to go to court to challenge an agency's decisions. So I think we can begin from that standpoint: You need the money and what better place is there to look than the source of all money, the federal government."[35]

But from the perspective of American history, there is nothing especially bizarre about the federal government being asked to subsidize directly or indirectly the bringing of lawsuits against its own agencies. The defense industry—which was created by government spending—then turns around and devotes a considerable portion of its energies to lobbying for a high level of military expenditures while the trade-union movement, which would not exist in its present form without the Wagner Act, represents an important source of political pressure on the federal government to increase social-welfare expenditures. The public-interest movement is part of this tradition.

THE BREAK WITH NEW DEAL LIBERALISM

The solution offered by the public-interest movement to the problem of disciplining the power of the corporation, on the other hand, does run directly counter to the principles that have dominated left-liberal thinking in the United States since the thirties. Rather than being innovative, in a number of critical respects the public-interest movement represents a throwback to the pre-New Deal tradition of American reform.

The defining feature of the left-liberal New Deal tradition is its embrace of public authority. Regarding the state as the agent of the public interest, it holds that the first and only alternative to the power of big business is that of big government. As Galbraith argued, "It takes a large public bureaucracy to police a powerful private bureaucracy."[36] Writers working in this tradition have a remarkably uniform explanation for the evident inadequacies of government control of business, namely, that public authority has become excessively weak and fragmented. Their alternative is not simply to strengthen the authority of the government over business—a solution to which the public-interest movement is sympathetic—but, more critically, both to increase the concentration of power within the federal government and to strengthen the authority of the state over society as a whole. This strain of reform can be labeled "bureaucratic statism." It includes planners such as Rexford Tugwell, Michael Harrington, and Michael Reagan; critics of pluralism such as Grant McConnell and Theodore Lowi; and most notably John Kenneth Galbraith.[37] Its politics range from left-liberal to democratic socialist. Bureaucratic statists have dominated much of the criticism of business-government relations in America in the generation since the New Deal.

The public-interest movement, however, represents a decisive break with this aspect of the New Deal legacy. The procedural reforms advocated by the public-interest movement are specifically meant to be antibureaucratic; they are an attempt to strengthen the regulatory process through participatory rather than bureaucratic mechanisms.

Unlike bureaucratic statists, the public-interest movement does not believe that the more centralized bureaucratic decision making becomes, the more likely it is to reflect the public interest. Like all other private groups, public-interest organizations are extremely jealous of whatever footholds they have been able to establish in the bureaucracy. They are extremely wary of the periodic efforts of the presidency to make public policymaking more coordinated and coherent—efforts that New Deal liberals have tended to support. Thus, environmental groups were unenthusiastic about the Carter administration's desire to create a Department of Energy—fearing that environmental considerations might be shortchanged. Similarly, the agency for consumer advocacy would clearly decentralize the making of regulatory policy. In *Taming the Giant Corporation*, Nader and his associates insist that the funding of the agency entrusted with responsibility for enforcing the provisions of the Federal Corporate Chartering Act *not* go through the Office of Management and Budget, an office whose fiscal controls over the federal bureaucracy New Deal liberals have traditionally looked on with sympathy. More recently, the public-interest movement has strongly opposed administration efforts to require that new government regulations of business be cleared by administrative units under the control of the White House, fearing a loss of autonomy for the various regulatory agencies to whom it has access.[38]

Without doubt the judiciary is the public-interest movement's favorite branch of government. It epitomizes their ideal of public authority without public bureaucracy. This same branch of government was the arch villain of the New Dealers because it threatened to undermine the autonomy of their administrative agencies. The Administrative Procedure Act, which increases the opportunity for judicial scrutiny of regulatory commission decisions, was enacted over strong liberal opposition in 1946. In a striking reversal, the public-interest movement has advocated that its provisions be considerably strengthened. Similarly, a major concern of those working with the tradition of bureaucratic statism has been to strengthen the independence and autonomy of bureaucratic officials. Nader, by contrast, has precisely the opposite notion of civil service reform. He wants to increase the vulnerability of federal employees to pressures from those outside the government who feel that their complaints are receiving inadequate attention.

If the principles of bureaucratic statism trace their political origin primarily to the New Deal, then participatory statism more closely harkens back to the Progressive era. Nader himself has stated that he has modeled his efforts on that of Lincoln Steffens, and in *The Genteel Populists*, Lazarus makes the parallel explicit.[39] In fact, there are a number of obvious similarities between the public-interest activists and the reformers of the Progressive era. Both are drawn heavily from the upper middle class, are primarily concerned with the social impact of economic activity (as contrasted with the level of economic activity itself), and rely heavily upon the media for their impact. In addition, both are concerned with revitalizing the role of the citizen and are committed to increasing direct public participation in the political process. Both also put a great deal of faith in the efficacy of disclosure as a mechanism for disciplining both business and government. But most fundamentally, both are uncomfortable with public bureaucratic authority; the Progressives sought to exercise this authority in the name of "efficiency"; the equivalent buzzword for the public-interest movement is "participation."[40]

The perspectives of the public-interest movement contrast strikingly with those of the two major critiques of public policy published during the sixties, McConnell's *Private Power and American De-*

mocracy and Lowi's *The End of Liberalism*.[41] These writers attacked the reforms of the Progressive era and the New Deal on the grounds that they had actually weakened public power. Not only had decision making within the public sector become too fragmented, but the boundaries between what was private and what was public had become blurred. What was left was a sort of American version of corporatism, with public policy made by small private and public groups lacking any central direction. But the direction in which the public-interest movement wants to move is precisely the opposite of that advocated by Lowi and McConnell: the reforms advocated by the public-interest movement provide almost a textbook illustration of what Lowi and McConnell are criticizing.

For example, McConnell argues that the dominance by private interests of the governmental process can be reduced to the extent that the size of the political constituencies involved in public policymaking are increased. The public-interest movement, however, has little faith in majoritarian democracy; like the interest groups McConnell describes, they want the public policy decisions affecting business to be parceled out among a large number of small constituencies—albeit including public-interest organizations—with each public-interest organization focusing on a particular dimension of government policy.

While it is true that Lowi's plea for judicial democracy, that is, clear legislative standards, is reflected in the Clean Air and Water Acts, Lowi also severely criticizes the effective delegation of the making of public policy to private organizations. But clearly public-interest groups want nothing so much as to receive "official" recognition from the government; their demands for subsidy are essentially corporatist. Paradoxically, the public-interest movement believes that the public interest can only be adequately represented through the efforts of private interests. The collapse of the distinction between public and private does not trouble public-interest activists. On the contrary, they welcome it; they want to enjoy the same relationship with the state and its agencies that they perceive business interests to be enjoying. In sum, their own quarrel with interest-group liberalism is simply that its principles have not been extended far enough.

A Critique of the Public-Interest Movement

The central political mission of the public-interest movement is to enable those affected by corporate decisions in their roles as citizens, consumers, and taxpayers to have the same influence over public policy as business. The objective, however, mistakenly assumes that genuine political pluralism is possible within the framework of a market system. The power of the corporation in American society, however, is not based on the rights of private property, its extensive participation in the regulatory process, its ability to exchange personnel with various regulatory agencies, or its extensive legal resources. The public-interest movement could counter all these rights and resources, and business would still enjoy a disproportionate influence over the political process. The more important reason public officials display so much deference to the preferences of corporate executives is that the economic viability of particular communities, regions, and the nation as a whole are largely dependent on the rate and location of corporate investment.[42]

The public-interest movement simply has no resource that can match the power of capital. Unlike both business and labor, the public-interest movement has nothing that it can withhold from civil society in order to make credible its political demands. Corporations can refuse to invest, and workers can refuse to work. But what can public-interest organizations refuse to do? Public-interest activists have no activity in society outside of their role as pressure groups; they have no source of power independent of the political process. Press conferences, consumer boycotts, and demonstrations are certainly not without impact.[43] But in the long run they cannot match the power to halt or curtail economic production. Paradoxically, like the Federal Aviation Administration which demands increased appropriations every time there is an airplane crash, the public-interest movement uses every administrative, judicial, legal, and legislative defeat of its views as an argument for the necessity of increasing the political and legal resources available to citizens and reducing those available to business groups. They argue, in effect, if only we had just one more limitation on corporate political activity or additional amounts of funds for public-interest lobbyists or lawyers, then our views would triumph.[44] But the movement is simply chasing a mirage.

The lack of parallels between the social position of business and the public-interest movement is, however, more than simply a cause of perpetual frustration for public-interest activists. It creates a far more serious problem. Precisely because public-interest activism has a far weaker base than does both business and labor, it is much more dependent on public assistance if it is to compete effectively in the political process. Public policy may have significantly contributed to the growth of both big business and organized labor, but these institutions also have extensive histories that cannot be attributed exclusively to government support. This is not the case with the public-interest movement. Not only its effectiveness, but its very existence has been fundamentally dependent on decisions made by the political process.

In one sense, the public-interest movement is highly aware of these realities: that is why it devotes considerably more attention to pressuring for subsidized political participation than does either business or labor. Moreover, the movement has put forth considerable effort to devise mechanisms of financial support that are as independent as possible from political pressures. But at the same time, the movement does not appear sufficiently sensitive to the potential perils of public subsidy. For with the possible exception of direct mail solicitations—and even here the granting of privileged postal rates creates a potential vulnerability[45]—there is virtually no way for the public-interest movement to acquire the funds it needs to counterbalance more adequately corporate resources that are not dependent on the decisions made either by some public agency, the courts, or the legislature.

The movement insufficiently appreciates the extent to which public subsidy is not, and indeed cannot be, free. To paraphrase Justice Marshall, the power to grant tax-exempt status is the power to destroy. Each new direct or indirect subsidy that the movement receives from the state not only increases its power vis-à-vis business, it also increases its vulnerability to the political process—and thus indirectly to business. The price the movement has paid for reducing the dependence of a variety of regulatory agencies on business has been to increase dramatically its own dependency on government. Seen from this perspective, the Supreme Court, the Internal Revenue Service, and Congress have emerged as the primary governmental institutions responsible for "regulating" the public-interest movement.[46]

Moreover, the public-interest movement is so obsessed with reducing the power of the corporation over the government that it overlooks the variety of circumstances under which the autonomy of the corporation cannot be reduced without simultaneously reducing the independence of all institutions—including the public-interest movement itself. This concern is not simply academic. During a recent session of Congress, public-interest and corporate lobbyists found themselves allies for the first time: both strongly opposed the lobbying disclosure requirements advocated by Common Cause on the grounds that such disclosures would handicap their legitimate political activities.[47] Ironically, the more closely the political power of public-interest groups approaches that of business, the greater is the likelihood that they will find themselves subject to the same restrictions on the representation of special interests—a category that the public-interest movement formerly thought was exclusively occupied by the profit sector.

The public-interest movement's most distinctive contribution to the American reform tradition is the emphasis it places on public participation in government. Increasing the participation in the regulatory and judicial processes by those affected by corporate decisions is not simply the central political strategy of the public-interest movement; it is also the linchpin of its legitimacy. Public-interest advocates take considerable pains to emphasize that the preferences of the interests they represent are not themselves identical with the public interest. Instead, advocates tend to define the public interest in procedural terms, arguing that public policies are capable of reflecting the interests of the public only to the extent that all affected parties participate in the policies' formulation.[48]

Ironically, although the movement's defenders want to increase citizen participation in order to reduce the privileges associated with the ownership of private property, the public-interest movement's defense of citizen participation is remarkably similar to the bourgeoisie's historic justification of private-property rights. Just as spokesmen for business in the eighteenth century argued that the protection of private-property rights advanced everyone's long-term interest, not simply those who happened currently to own property, so does the public-interest movement contend that extension of the rights of citizen participation is in the public interest, not simple in the interests of those groups that currently employ the public-interest mantle. Moreover, if business argued that everyone, in principle, could become a property holder, so does the legitimacy of the public-interest movement rest on its promise that the opportunities for increased participation for which it struggles are meant to be available to every citizen.

Both property rights and the right to participation are thus defended less in terms of the substantive merits of the demands of those who happen to be either property owners or public-interest activists at any given time, and more because the granting of these rights by the state makes it more likely that government policy will reflect the interests of the citizenry as a whole. Clearly, at least some of the success the public-interest movement has had in winning support for its rights of access from those who do not necessarily share the movement's substantive goals can be traced to its ability to distinguish between the particular political objectives of its constituencies and the broader procedural values with which the movement publicly identifies.[49]

But like the bourgeoisie, public-interest advocates are not really

interested in expanding opportunities for participation for the sake
of some vague procedural notion of the public interest; their emphasis on procedural rights is essentially a tactic designed to advance
their substantive goals. Public-interest groups do not want participation for its own sake; they want it for the sake of the concrete victories over business that it promises to bring. They do not really want
to participate; what they actually want is to win. In reality, public-
interest activists have no independent measure of the extent to
which the political or legal systems are indeed accessible to all those
affected by them, save the extent to which they are actually able to
triumph over business. For example, while public-interest lawyers
have waged protracted battles over the right to standing, or over
financial subsidy for representation before regulatory commissions,
on the grounds that the interests they represent deserve to be heard,
the achievement of those goals are only intermediate ones: after all,
what is the value of being "heard" if the decision goes against you
anyway? In fact, neither business nor the public-interest movement
actually favors genuine pluralism: instead both believe that the particular interests they represent are themselves the public interest.
From this perspective, the public-interest movement's goal of achieving the same relationship to the political process that business has
historically enjoyed should be taken literally: the public-interest
movement actually wants to dominate the policy process just as business has traditionally done. It bases its claim on the principle of balance; what it really wants is hegemony.

But ironically, the rights for citizen participation for which the
movement has struggled in order to better advance the substantive
goals of its constituencies have turned out, in fact, to be value-neu-
tral. Thus, the majority of the requests for information filed under
the Freedom of Information Act have come from businesses seeking
to acquire information about their competitors.[50] In addition, the requirement that adequate environmental impact statements be filed
before new construction projects receive governmental approval is
increasingly being used by various local political and civic interests to
prevent construction projects that they dislike for reasons having
nothing to do with the protection of the environment.[51] And most
dramatically, there is the emergence of various conservative "public-
interest" law firms that evidently have taken quite literally the public-
interest movement's public commitment to make the judicial process
open to everyone.[52] The movement thus finds itself trapped by its
own ideology: it cannot oppose these efforts without undermining
the basis of its own legitimacy.

Moreover, just as bourgeois ideology assumed that everyone was,
or could be, a property owner, so does the ideology of the public-

interest movement assume that everyone is, or could be, a politically committed citizen. But both views are false and for the same reason: they fail to recognize the extent to which life in a market economy may undermine the ideals of liberal democracy. They mistake the rhetoric of liberal democracy for the reality of capitalism. For the increased access to the state for which the public-interest movement has so painstakingly fought, which, like property ownership, is available in principle to everyone, in reality is open to only a few.

In reality, the only way that one can really live as a "public citizen" is to make a living at it; the public-interest movement has succeeded so well, in part because it has been able to make defense of the "public interest" into a source of private, economic gain, however modest. But precisely because it has succeeded in making opposing business into a business—albeit an unprofitable one—the public-interest movement finds itself facing the same legitimacy crisis as does business. Like business it is criticized as elitist.[53] Only a relatively small number of people have actually taken advantage of the increased opportunities to participate in the policy process that the public-interest movement has made possible—and most of these are public-interest professionals rather than typical citizens. It is almost as difficult to become a professional public-interest advocate as it is to become a capitalist.

In sum, the more successful the public-interest movement has been in accomplishing and realizing both its substantive and procedural demands, the more powerful and pervasive has become the role of government. But the greater the intervention of government in American society, the more the exercise of governmental authority is perceived by the citizenry as an illegitimate interference with their lives. Thus while the public-interest movement promises increased public participation, what it actually delivers to most institutions and individuals is increased regulation. It promises to make public bureaucracies more accountable, but what it has actually done is to increase their number and size. As a result, increased citizen participation has failed to accomplish one of its most important stated objectives, namely, that of increasing the legitimacy of government regulation of business.[54]

NOTES

1. See, for example, Leonard Silk and David Vogel, *Ethics and Profits: The Crisis of Confidence in American Business* (New York: Simon and Schuster, 1976), chap. 2.

2. See Joan Claybrook, "Crying Wolf," *Regulation* (November–December

1978): 14–16; John Tirman, "Business Wars on the Regulators," *Nation*, 30 December 1978, pp. 730–33; and Steven Kelman, "Regulation that Works," *New Republic*, 25 November 1978, pp. 16–20.

3. See, for example, Mark Nadel, *The Politics of Consumer Protection* (Indianapolis, Ind.: Bobbs-Merrill, 1971); Walter Rosenbaum, *The Politics of Environmental Concern* (New York: Praeger Publishers, 1973); Richard S. Lewis, *The Nuclear Power Rebellion* (New York: Viking Press, 1972); Jeffrey M. Berry, *Lobbying for the People* (Princeton, N.J.: Princeton University Press, 1977); David Truman, *The Governmental Process* (New York: Alfred Knopf, 1951).

4. Robert A. Dahl, *A Preface to Democratic Theory* (Chicago, Ill.: University of Chicago Press, 1956), p. 145.

5. The first major gathering of "public-interest advocates," held in 1976 in Washington, D.C., under the auspices of Public Citizen, Inc. (an organization sponsored by Ralph Nader), included representatives of more than 100 citizen organizations—most of which had either been established or significantly revitalized since the mid-sixties. See *Public Interest Perspectives: The Next Four Years* (Washington, D.C.: Public Citizen, 1977). See also John Holcomb, "Public Interest Lobbies," *Enterprise* (December 1977); 3–5, and Gerald R. Rosen, "The Growing Clout of 'Do Good' Lobbies," *Dun's Review* (April 1977): 44–51.

6. This point is stressed repeatedly in Burton A. Weisbrod, Joel F. Handler, and Neil K. Komesar, eds., *Public Interest Law* (Berkeley: University of California Press, 1978).

7. See, for example, Marver Bernstein, *Regulating Business by Independent Commission* (Princeton, N.J.: Princeton University Press, 1955); Gabriel Kolko, *The Triumph of Conservatism* (Chicago: Quadrangle, 1963); Edward Greenberg, *Serving the Few* (New York: John Wiley and Sons, 1974); George Stigler, *The Citizen and the State* (Chicago, Ill.: University of Chicago Press, 1975).

8. "Government, like all other institutions, rarely responds to interests not represented in its deliberations" (Ernest Gellhorn, "Public Participation in Administrative Proceedings," *Yale Law Journal* 81 [January 1972]: 403).

9. Richard A. Frank, Joseph N. Onek, and James B. Steinberg, "Public Participation in the Policy Formulation Process" (Washington, D.C.: Center for Law and Social Policy, January 1977), pp. 1–2.

Joseph Sax makes a similar point in *Defending the Environment: A Handbook of Citizen Action* (New York: Vintage Books, 1970), pp. 57, 60.

10. This discussion of the political strategy of the public-interest movement is based primarily on the following sources: Frank, Onek, and Steinberg, "Public Participation"; Simon Lazarus and Joseph N. Onek, "The Regulators and the People," *Virginia Law Review* 57(1973): 1069–1108; *Balancing the Scales of Justice: Financing Public Interest Law in America* (Washington, D.C.: Council for Public Interest Law, 1976); Charles R. Halpern and John M. Cunningham, "Reflections on the New Public Interest Law: Theory and Practice at the Center for Law and Social Policy," *Georgetown Law Journal* 59 (May 1971): 1095; and Andrew S. McFarland, *Public Interest*

Lobbies (Washington, D.C.: American Enterprise Institute for Policy Research, 1976), chaps. 1 and 2.

11. The notion of standing advocated by the public-interest movement was clearly expressed by the Court's decision in *Environmental Defense Fund Inc. v. Hardin*. See Lazarus and Onek, "The Regulators," p. 1101. The classic statement of the public-interest position is Christopher D. Stone, *Should Trees Have Standing?* (Los Altos, Calif.: William Kaufman, Inc., 1974). The adoption of Stone's position would represent a 180 degree turn from the nineteenth century when, as Morton J. Horowitz documents in *The Transformation of American Law 1780–1860* (Cambridge: Harvard University Press, 1977), the courts often ran roughshod over injuries to the rights of real property owners in order to further economic development.

12. The best-known examples of regulatory legislation containing this proviso are the 1974 amendments to the Freedom of Information Act. Ideally, public-interest advocates would like legislation that enables citizens and citizen organizations to appeal to the courts *all* the decisions of regulatory agencies that they believe violate the intent of the Congress.

13. The National Environmental Policy Act of 1969 required all administrative agencies to establish procedures that consider "environmental amenities and values in their decision-making and to include an environment impact statement [EIS] with every recommendation" (quoted in Karen Orren, "Standing to Sue," *American Political Science Review* 70 [September 1976] 724). "There can be no doubt that a major effect of the EIS requirement has been to give environmental groups a legal and political instrument to cancel, delay, or modify development projects that they oppose" (Eugene Bardach and Lucian Pugliaresi, "The Environmental Impact Statement versus the Real World," *Public Interest* 49 [Fall 1977]: 23).

14. See Thomas Schoenbaum, "The Relationship Between Corporate Disclosure and Corporate Responsibility," *Fordham Law Review* 40 (1972): 588.

15. See Charles Peters and Taylor Branch, *Blowing the Whistle: Dissent in the Public Interest* (New York: Praeger Publishers, 1972). Also see David E. Ewing, "Protecting 'Whistle-Blowers,'" *New York Times*, 1 September 1977.

16. A study of public-interest law noted: "Establishing the authority of courts to award attorneys' fees is of the greatest importance for the institutionalization of public interest law in this country. . . . There are few funding mechanisms for public interest law that offer so many potential benefits and few that are of comparable importance (*Balancing the Scales*, pp. 318–19).

17. Ibid., p. 349.

18. See, for example, William Brown, *How to Stop the Corporate Polluters and Make Money Doing it* (San Francisco, Calif.: Bellorophon Books, 1972).

19. See, for example, Ernest Gellhorn, "Public Participation in Administrative Proceedings," p. 359; Roger C. Cramton, "The Why, Where and How of Broadened Public Participation in the Administrative Process," *Georgetown Law Journal* 60 (February 1972): 525; and U.S., Congress, Senate, Committee on Governmental Affairs, *Public Participation in Regulatory Proceedings*, 95th Cong., 1st sess., July 1977.

20. See Lazarus and Onek, "The Regulators," pp. 1096–97.

21. See Edward M. Kennedy, "The Case for Public Financing of Citizen Participation in Agency Proceedings," *Citizen Participation* 1 (September–October 1979): 3–4, 16.

22. See Richard Corrigan, "Tax Report/Public Interest Law Firms Win Battle with IRS Over Exemptions, Deductions," *National Journal*, 21 November 1970, pp. 2541–49; Charles Goetz and Gordon Brady, "Environmental Policy Formation and the Tax Treatment of Citizen Interest Groups," *Law and Contemporary Problems* 39 (Autumn 1975): 211–31; and Richard E. Cohen, "Public Interest Lawyers Looking Out for Their Own Interests," *National Journal*, 19 June 1976, pp. 860–64.

23. Mancur Olson, *The Logic of Collective Action* (New York: Schochen Books, 1965).

24. "The advantage of class actions is that they allow many small claims to be aggregated in one economically feasible lawsuit" (Ralph Nader and Cirardeau A. Spann, "The Justices Slam the Door," *Nation*, 12 November 1977, p. 496). See also, Philip Schrag and Michael Multsner, "Class Action: A Way to Beat the Bureaucracies without Increasing Them" *Washington Monthly*, November 1972, p. 57.

25. See Robert B. LeFlar and Martin H. Rogol, "Consumer Participation in the Regulation of Public Utilities: A Model Act," *Harvard Journal of Legislation* 13 (February 1976): 235–97.

26. For example, Marty Rogol, director of the Public Interest Research Group, has suggested that "it would be worthwhile to explore the idea of trying to build into a federal funding package a requirement that, for every $100,000 paid to nursing homes . . . a certain amount has to be set aside for resident advocacy and similar programs" (*Public Interest Perspectives*, p. 73). Clearly this principle could be readily extended to a wide variety of federal programs.

27. For a historical background of this proposal, see Richard Leighton, "Consumer Protection Agency Proposition: The Origin of the Species," *Administrative Law Review* 25 (Summer 1973): 269–311.

28. There remains, however, one critical distinction: unlike employees in the profit sector, individuals who move to government from the nonprofit sector generally tend to increase their salaries. Indeed, the sixty-odd individuals from the public-interest movement who received jobs in the Carter administration may be the first group of people in nearly 100 years to increase their income by transferring from the private to the public sector. See Linda Charlton, "Government Service Is No Financial Sacrifice," *New York Times*, 12 February 1978.

29. See, for example, *The Federalist Papers*, ed. Roy P. Fairfield (Garden City, N.Y.: Doubleday and Co., 1961): Robert Dahl, *Who Governs?* (New Haven, Conn.: Yale University Press, 1961); Daniel Boorstin, *The Genius of American Politics* (Chicago, Ill.: University of Chicago Press, 1953).

30. *Public Interest Perspectives*, p. 2. See also, Sax, *Defending the Environment*, pp. 57, 60.

31. For a sophisticated defense of this position, see Abram Chayes, "The

Role of the Judge in Public Law Litigation," *Harvard Law Review* 89 (May 1976): 1281–1316.

32. Richard B. Stewart, "The Reformation of American Administrative Law," *Harvard Law Review* 88 (June 1975): 1670.

33. Orren, "Standing to Sue," p. 724.

34. Theodore Lowi, *The End of Liberalism* (New York: W. W. Norton, 1969); Grant McConnell, *Private Power and American Democracy* (New York: Vintage Press, 1966).

35. *Public Interest Perspectives*, p. 64.

36. Quoted in Lazarus, *The Genteel Populists* (New York: Holt, Rinehart and Winston, 1974), p. 37.

37. See, for example, Michael Harrington, *The Twilight of Capitalism* (New York: Simon and Schuster, 1976); Michael Reagan, *The Managed Economy* (New York: Oxford University Press, 1963); John Kenneth Galbraith, *Economics and the Public Purpose* (Boston, Mass.: Houghton Mifflin, 1973).

38. A recent example is a lawsuit file by environmental groups to prevent the Carter administration from modifying strip-mining regulations promulgated by the Interior Department. See "Two Complaints," *New Republic*, 3 February 1979, pp. 5–6.

39. Lazarus, *The Genteel Populists*, p. 12.

40. See McConnell, *Private Power*; Samuel Haber, *Efficiency and Uplift* (Chicago, Ill.: University of Chicago Press, 1964); Samuel P. Hays, *Conservation and the Gospel of Efficiency* (New York: Atheneum, 1974).

41. Lowi, *The End of Liberalism*, and McConnell, *Private Power*.

42. Orren, "Standing to Sue," p. 724. A recent statement of this position can be found in Charles Lindblom, *Politics and Markets* (New York: Basic Books, 1977); also see Eckardt C. Beck, "Ending Pollution Blackmail," *New York Times*, 8 May 1978.

43. For an exhaustive study of the impact of citizen pressures on business decisions, see David Vogel, *Lobbying the Corporation: Citizen Challenge to Business Authority* (New York: Basic Books, 1978).

44. For example, following the defeat of CPA, Mark Green wrote that "until some version of public funding of public elections cuts the cord between business giving and members voting, citizen interests will forever compete at a disadvantage in the political marketplace" ("Why the Consumer Bill Went Down," *Nation*, 25 February 1978, p. 207).

45. See "Non-Profit Groups that Lobby Slated for Mail-Fee Break," *Wall Street Journal*, 1 June 1977.

46. One of the most notable instances of the withholding of tax-exempt status in order to handicap a public-interest group effectively destroyed the Project on Corporate Responsibility. See "The PCR and the IRS: A Case Study," *Economic Priorities Report* 5, no. 1 (1974): 36.

47. See James M. Perry, "Restrictive New Lobbying Rules?" *Wall Street Journal*, 3 April 1978. See also Gail Robinson, "Second Thoughts on Election Law," *Environmental Action*, 28 August 1978, pp. 9–11.

48. A public advocate noted in 1975, "We've stopped representing ourselves as representing 'THE' public interest. We represent significant public

interests which would otherwise not be adequately represented" (quoted in Lynn Cunningham et al., "Strengthening Citizen Access and Governmental Accountability" [Washington, D.C.: Exploratory Project for Economic Alternatives, 1977]).

49. Nader argues, "I think we can develop the broadest consensus behind a number of major or new procedural remedies or the deepening of old procedural resources. That consensus can make the public interest movement a force in society" (*Public Interest Perspectives*, p. 2).

50. Warren Weaver, Jr., "U.S. Information Act: Difficulties Despite Successes," *New York Times*, 8 August 1977.

51. C. Christian Hill, "Businesses Are Finding Environmental Law Can Be Useful to Them," *Wall Street Journal*, 9 June 1978.

52. Robert Lindsey, "Tax-Exempt Foundations Formed to Help Business Fight Regulation," *New York Times*, 12 February 1978.

53. The charge that public-interest activists are elitist is made with increasing frequency. See, for example, William Tucker, "Environmentalists and the Leisure Class," *Harper's*, December 1977, pp. 49–80.

54. See, for example, Marjorie Boyd, "The Protection Consumers Don't Want," *Washington Monthly*, September 1977, pp. 29–34; "Regulators and the Polls," *Regulation* (November–December 1978): 10, 11, 54.

Chapter Six

LOBBYING THE CORPORATION: CITIZEN CHALLENGES TO BUSINESS AUTHORITY

WHAT IMPACT has the corporate accountability movement had either on the political system or on the corporation? How do businessmen view this new source of political pressure and how has their perception changed over the last decade? To what extent have the expectations of those who initiated the citizen challenges in the late sixties and early seventies been realized? How are we to assess the reforms offered by the corporate accountability movement?

THE BUSINESS RESPONSE

For the most part, corporations take citizen demands, particularly when expressed through stockholder resolutions, with increasing seriousness. The demands are regarded as a permanent, though not necessarily legitimate, part of the political and social environment of the modern firm.

This represents a considerable change from James Roche's speech before the Detroit Economics Club in 1971, in which he accused the Project on Corporate Responsibility of seeking to destroy the free enterprise system.[1] Few executives would now publicly respond as did Henry Ford in 1970 when asked if he thought the Episcopal Church was justified in praying for General Motors to leave South Africa. Ford replied, "I don't think it's any of their goddamn business. It's none of our business how South Africans run themselves."[2]

By any objective criteria—the willingness of management to voluntarily include public interest resolutions in their proxy statements, the number of resolutions withdrawn after satisfactory negotiations with politically oriented investors, and the frequency of meetings between chief executive officers and activists—the acceptance of citizen pressures by business has increased considerably. A survey of *Harvard Business Review* readers taken in 1976 reported that 62.4 percent of the respondents believed that "the polling of shareholder opinions on sensitive social issues" can have either "some" or "very positive impact."[3]

For those corporations that have been repeatedly challenged on a particular issue by the same organization over a period of years, corporate activists have come to occupy a role not dissimilar to that shared by trade union representatives; both agreements and disputes take place within the context of a "working relationship." Generally the more experience a corporation has with citizen demands, the less anxiety such demands provoke. Thus, Tim Smith of the Interfaith Center noted in 1977:

> In the beginning we had most of our meetings with corporate public relations people. But now we find it easier to get through to the top man. . . . The rhetoric has changed dramatically. There is a growing tendency to give information when asked to review touchy questions.[4]

What accounts for this change? First, publicly held corporations tend to be very sensitive to any communication from their shareholders. One executive put it, "Anything from the stockholders, we have to take seriously."[5] AT&T's corporate secretary observed, "Even if a proposal does not carry in the voting, the size of the vote it gets can stimulate management to do something."[6] Viewed from the perspective of electoral politics, the votes gathered by shareholder activists appear rather inconsequential. However, when translated into the world of the corporation, 5 percent is a large number. A 5 percent decline in sales or the selling of 5 percent of a corporation's stock is economically very consequential. The process of historical expectations is also at work; having grown used to total shareholder acquiescence—save in the most extraordinary of circumstances—any lack of support is regarded as threatening.

In addition, shareholder activism makes the firm very vulnerable to bad public relations. What has induced a large number of firms to negotiate settlements with shareholder groups has simply been their concern about the publicity that shareholder public interest proposals receive.[7] During a period when management has been extremely sensitive to its public image, any possibility for avoiding adverse publicity cannot be dismissed. As a rule, executives try to avoid head-on confrontations with groups such as the church that can accomplish very little in the way of building public good will. Tim Smith reported that corporations hated to be seen as "doing battle with the church."[8] And Will Maslow of the American Jewish Congress observed:

> Billion dollar corporations are extremely sensitive to shareholder opinion. They do not wish to appear in an adversary position with the reputable and well-intentioned organizations offering such resolutions or to seem opposed to the good causes they are sponsoring. A stockholder's

resolution seems a questioning of management wisdom, a rift in the happy family of shareholders.[9]

The offer to withdraw resolutions thus provides activists with one of their few pieces of leverage: they can offer to spare management the publicity associated with a confrontation with a citizens' organization and at the same time keep the annual meeting from being dominated by criticisms of the company's social performance. These provide important incentives for an "out of proxy" settlement. The last thing most corporations want is a story about criticism of their social performance on the front page of the *New York Times* or in a report of their annual meeting. Richard Hays of the American Society of Corporate Secretaries observes that increased willingness of corporations to agree to shareholder demands is partially due to the fact that "a number of companies aren't happy with the negative image that they are always against anything shareholders propose."[10] George W. Coombe, assistant general counsel for General Motors— who, in his former position as corporate secretary, handled the company's negotiations with Campaign GM—noted in 1975:

> One thing that has helped considerably to quiet down the social issues is the pre-meeting dialogue. I have found most of the church people to be quite reasonable, once they understand what our problems are. Annual meetings, after all, are not the best forum for settling far-ranging disputes of this sort.[11]

The responses of General Motors, Exxon, and AT&T to shareholder proposals in 1977 dramatize some of the changes that have taken place in the six years since Campaign GM. A few years earlier a high official at GM had privately informed a church representative, "We cannot afford to support any resolution by a shareholder because it would show we are weak and willing to delegate management prerogatives." In 1977, however, two stockholder resolutions were voluntarily withdrawn by their church sponsors after GM agreed to meet their requests for additional information about the company's investments in Chile and South Africa. Exxon and AT&T went a step further. The world's largest energy corporation recommended that its shareholders support a resolution from the United Presbyterian Church asking for a report on its strip-mining activities. The last time the company supported a shareholder proposal was more than twenty years earlier—and that recommended that stockholders buy the company's products. AT&T, for the first time, also urged its shareholders to support a resolution requiring secret balloting at annual meetings—even though it had been defeated overwhelmingly on five previous occasions.[12]

Agreements reached privately with management provide perhaps the clearest index of the growing credibility of shareholder activists. Between 1974 and 1977, a total of ninety-eight shareholder resolutions were withdrawn by their proponents following negotiations with management. Equally significantly, the agreements reached in 1967–1977 were more likely to involve substantive changes in corporate policy—rather than simply additional disclosure.

Enlightened Self-Interest

There are other factors aside from public relations to explain why at least some relatively "enlightened" executives have become more tolerant of direct political pressures. Most importantly, citizen challenges serve to reduce somewhat the chronic isolation of executives, putting them more closely in touch with the pressures and concerns of the "outside world." John D. deButts, the chairman of AT&T, told a meeting of the American Society of Corporate Secretaries in 1976:

> It's been a long time since we've had what I would call an uneventful meeting. . . .
>
> Now you might expect me to deplore this development and the threat it poses to our ordered corporate ways. Actually, I do not. I do not because the annual meeting, contentious as it sometimes can be, provides an opportunity unique in the year's calendar, for management to respond, face to face, to the various constituencies to which it is in greater or lesser measure accountable. Striking a sound balance among the often competing interests of these constituencies—shareowners, customers, employees, the public at large—is the essence of the art of management. The Annual Meeting brings the entire process into dramatic focus.[13]

While their actual impact on corporate decisions is minimal, the increasing number of minority and women directors has also helped expose the corporation's top decision makers to a somewhat greater variety of perspectives.[14] Their very physical presence tends to encourage a greater awareness among the corporation's top officials and other board members of the impact of their policies on these groups. As Joan Ganz Cooney, president of the Children's Television Workshop and a member of the board of Xerox, First Pennsylvania Corporation, and Macy's Department Stores, put it: "My presence is a pressure."[15]

John Bunting, who appointed a black businessman, a black lawyer, a female television producer, and a college student to the board of the First Pennsylvania Banking and Trust Company, explains that his diverse new directors "influence me by their mere presence. The fact that I have a woman on my board reminds me of things that I should be paying attention to, even if she doesn't say a word. The same thing for Blacks." Bunting adds, "They have become management's 'window to the world.'"[16]

Patricia Harris, a black female lawyer who served on the boards of IBM, Chase Manhattan Bank, and Scott Paper Company prior to her appointment to Carter's cabinet similarly notes, "People who have always been in the power orbit . . . tend to get blinders."[17] The impact of the Reverend Leon Sullivan's public disagreement with his fellow board members on GM's investment in South Africa can also be seen in this context. Richard Gerstenberg, who succeeded James Roche as chairman of the board of GM, states, "We have some pretty good discussions at our board on the issues of our day. His [Sullivan's] presence has made us more conscious of some things than we might otherwise have been."[18]

Other corporate officials, particularly those responsible for negotiating with critics, have also noted that citizen challenges perform a useful service by forcing many important social and political problems to the attention of management. The Bank of America, as a response to its 1964 dispute with CORE, established two management committees with responsibility for researching and clarifying the bank's position with respect to citizen demands. These committees have not been dormant; the world's largest bank has been under virtually continuous citizen pressures since the mid-sixties on issues ranging from its lending policies in California to the presence of its branch in Saigon. James Langton, the bank's executive vice-president for social policy who has been responsible for negotiating with "third force" groups for over a decade, observes: "The protests have done a lot of good. They have forced issues to our attention that otherwise would be dormant and have taught us a lot about the complexity of many issues."[19] Langton's counterpart at Del Monte adds: "We are not perfect and these groups play a useful role by bringing our shortcomings to our attention."

The experiences of the American oil companies in Namibia are probably the most dramatic example of this informational exchange. The companies, acting on a straightforward economic calculus, were unaware of the tenuous legal foundations of their investment until the Interfaith Center brought it to the attention of the public. Critics of the role of U.S. corporations in South Africa discovered that most American executives were unaware of the working conditions of their employees; they had placed the management of their operations entirely in the hands of white natives. Similarly, the executives of the companies manufacturing infant formulas appear to be unaware of how their products were marketed in poor nations until this issue was raised through the efforts of various church groups and the Ford and Rockefeller foundations. In these last two cases, of course, it is likely that management would have preferred to remain ignorant of these aspects of their foreign operations. But activists raised issues with which the corporations will eventually have to deal, and it would be difficult to assert that continuing corporate ignorance served any useful purpose.

Even the act of preparing a rebuttal to citizen pressures can serve a useful management function; it often forces senior executives at least to think about the social and political dimensions of their profit-seeking efforts.[20] Indeed, one might argue that citizen groups have displayed a far greater sensitivity to changes in the relationship between economic and social issues than have most corporate executives. What is striking is how frequently social issues first raised by the corporation's critics have proven to be relevant to the long run economic welfare of the firm. For example, shareholder activists raised the issue of the composition and independence of the corporate board before it became an issue of widespread concern within the business community and urged the repudiation of the "Wall Street Rule" three years before the financial community began to recognize that rule's inadequacy. Moreover, because of the frequency with which citizen challenges anticipate the agenda of the governmental process, they offer businessmen a relatively inexpensive and highly reliable political forecasting tool. More often than not, the issues raised in proxy resolutions and consumer boycotts eventually become the subject of legislative proposals and administrative regulations—a dynamic of which some businessmen are very aware.

Continued Annoyance

Still, the willingness of management to take the concerns of citizen challenges seriously should not be exaggerated. Most businessmen continue to regard the entire phenomenon as tiresome and bewildering. As Richard Holton, former assistant secretary of commerce, noted in 1974:

> In reading over the management responses . . . one has the impression that all too frequently when a proposal arrives in corporate headquarters, the scenario goes something like this: The proposal is turned over to the general counsel . . . [who] . . . seeks out some minor clause in the

proposal that is unworkable or infeasible and recommends against the proposal because of this clause, rather than recognizing that the main thrust of the proposal may have merit. Or alternatively, the reaction may be that "this is already company policy and is therefore unnecessary."[21]

Businessmen particularly resent the tone in which demands raised by the church are made. An executive of a firm regarded by activists in the church as one of the more responsive privately labeled the activists "a pain in the ass." Another executive, who has negotiated extensively with clerical officials, said that he personally was very bothered by their "arrogance, singlemindedness and cavalier attitude toward the truth." A management consultant with a similar history of involvement in stockholder versus company confrontation told a reporter from *Dun's*:

> I think the question of morality is ill-served by the church groups. After all, they have themselves shown a certain deviousness by, for example, suddenly acquiring two shares of stock in some companies and immediately sending in a 14-page proxy proposal. Moreover, they seem unwilling even to consider the cost of the morality they preach.[22]

Businessmen also tend to regard the choice of targets by activists as arbitrary. An acceptable history of the politics of citizen challenges could be written focusing on the experiences of a dozen large—and visible—corporations. Most of the principal targets of citizen challenges are among the fifty largest firms, including Exxon, General Motors, Mobil, SoCal, IBM, Gulf, ITT, U. S. Steel, Occidental Petroleum, Eastman Kodak, Rockwell International, Dow Chemical, and Boeing. Many executives do not believe that these firms have behaved less "responsibly" than others (often competitors) in whom activists have been less interested.

Finally, the diversity and complexity of corporate accountability movements is frustrating to executives who often find themselves subject to demands by groups about whom they know nothing. Most citizen challenges do not represent a clear constituency; it is difficult for executives to judge how seriously to take them. To help remedy this, the Public Affairs Council in 1971 published a small booklet called *The Challengers*.[23] It briefly profiled sixty organizations "dedicated to changing the private sector in America." The directory was updated in 1975 to reflect the shift from mass protests to "less visible but highly organized day-to-day work."[24] In 1977, the council published more detailed profiles of twenty-five groups, including their size, budget, scope, purposes, method of operation, funding history, effectiveness, and political orientation. Citizen pressures and the corporate response to them are also the subject of a number of case studies that are available for use by business school faculty, through the Inter-Collegiate Case Clearinghouse. In addition, IRRC performs a clearinghouse function for the business community, as does the Human Resources Network.

The problem with such research efforts is that different groups emphasize different issues at different times in different ways to different corporations. Although the American Society of Corporate Secretaries has served as a sort of "command post" for public interest proxy proposals, the sharing of experiences by corporate officials still tends to be sporadic. Corporations still typically deal with citizen pressures in isolation from each other; with the exception of the Sullivan principles—which were endorsed by more than fifty firms—businesses have not attempted to define common positions vis-à-vis citizen activists as they have with issues before the governmental process.[25]

The Annual Meeting

What particularly upsets executives is the presence of protestors and critics at shareholder meetings. Even the relatively infrequent and innocuous appearance of "professional shareholders" or "shareholder democrats" in the fifties and early sixties—before the annual meeting became the setting for actual political conflict—disturbed business.* As *Fortune* editorialized in 1965:

> There is no reason that management must tolerate all these obstructions to the proper conduct of company business . . . "Corporate democracy" derives from the hoary notion that the corporation is constructed on a model of a democratic political state, with the shareholders as the electorate and the board of directors the legislature. In fact, however, a corporation is not a republic in miniature. It is a business organization in which the owners—the shareholders—have some clear rights. But those rights are not analogous in any important way to the rights of citizens in a democracy, and the board of directors does not really resemble a legislative body.[26]

*Ironically, it was management who pioneered the use of the annual meeting for purposes not related to the spirit of the securities law. During the thirty years following the Securities and Exchange Act, many corporations began to use the meetings as part of their marketing strategy. They reasoned that their stockholders, already predisposed to their corporation's welfare, would provide a receptive audience for the consumption of its products. Thus, the annual meeting of General Motors featured test drives in the firm's new sport cars, while the shareholders of National Dairy products were treated to pickles and cheese. The corporation's owners were treated like consumers long before public interest groups began trying to make shareholders into citizens.

Or as the vice-president of one major corporation, whose responsibilities included preparation for the formal gathering of the firm's
owners, put it: "I don't give a damn about the annual meeting. I'd
like to see the thing abolished. The object of our meeting is to end it
as fast as possible without making a fool of the chairman."[27] Given
this perspective, the views of most executives toward political activists at the annual meeting are predictable. A study of corporate responses to political protests at annual meetings concluded:

> None of the companies responding to the inquiry was particularly
> happy about the prospect of having its stockholders' meeting used as a
> forum for reform. To the larger corporations, annual meetings are
> merely one feature (and a relatively ineffectual one, some executives
> say) of their investor relations programs—one of many channels of
> communication through which stockholders may question management
> and be kept informed about various aspects of the business.[28]

The annual meeting may well be the only time when the corporation's chief officers interact with the public in a physical environment
that is not totally planned and controlled by them. True, the annual
stockholders meeting is still a far cry from the proverbial New England town meeting. (A better analogy, and one that is more consistent with the constitutional origins of the corporation, might be the
question period in the House of Commons.) On the other hand, it is
the one time when corporate executives are a captive audience of
their diverse publics; both the "corporation" and the "public" become, momentarily, real individuals, rather than abstractions. For
one day a year, the individuals who manage the most hierarchical
civilian institution in the United States are personally subject to the
irreverence that pervades so many other aspects of American life.

Consider, for example, the tone of this dialogue between S. J.
Ruskin, a shareholder from Los Angeles, and William Rockwell,
president of the board of Rockwell International, at the corporation's 1976 meeting in Beverly Hills.[29] Ruskin wanted to know why
the firm's business meeting and customer entertainment were done
"down there in the Caribbean." Rockwell replied, "I think it's very
convenient." Ruskin shot back: "Convenient to whom?" Rockwell's
president replied: "Convenient to us."

The 1977 meeting of J. P. Stevens was the setting for a somewhat
more serious dialogue. An employee asked the firm's president:

> Mr. Finley, my name is Mary Frances Bradley. I'm one of your
> employees from the Statesboro plant. I'd like to ask you a ques-
> tion on salary. The proxy statement says you were paid

$240,000 in 1975 and $380,000 in 1976. That's a 60 percent increase. The workers only got a 10 percent raise. Why?

FINLEY: Well, the best way I can explain it is that that was incentive compensation.

BRADLEY: Well, why don't we get it?[30]

What the political use of the annual meetings has done is to force corporate presidents and chairmen to respond to pointed—and at times angry—questions covering virtually every aspect of their social and political as well as economic policies during the preceding year. As a consequence, preparation for the annual meeting has become an increasingly burdensome, time-consuming, and nerve-racking task. As one investor relations specialist told *Forbes*: "Beneath their calm exteriors, most board chairmen are nervous as hell about going before their stockholders. You'd be surprised how much psychosomatic illness there is as meeting time approaches."[31]

Small wonder that many companies have sought to discourage the attendance of critics at shareholder meetings by scheduling their meetings on the same day (in 1976, for example, over 100 companies listed on the New York Stock Exchange held their meetings on April 27) and in relatively inaccessible locations. There is also some sentiment within the business community for actually abolishing the annual meeting—a measure that would be legal under the chartering law of Delaware, though not under the regulations of the New York Stock Exchange. To date, no major corporation has done so.[32]

THE CHALLENGE OF CORPORATE ACCOUNTABILITY

In the final analysis, however, the reaction of corporate executives is likely to have only marginal impact on the future development of this third arena. American businessmen as a group have never been particularly receptive to challenges to their autonomy, and it is unlikely that the proportion of responsive executives has grown significantly over the last decade. A more important question is: what does the ten-year history of the corporate accountability movement indicate about the future of public control of the corporation in the United States?

Most obviously, the corporate challenge effort has failed to accomplish one of its principal initial objectives; it has not succeeded in becoming a popular political movement capable of mobilizing the populace against the abuse of corporate power. For a brief period between 1969 and 1971, there was a general mood of euphoria among many observers of corporate accountability movement politics. Mary Davidov, the director of the New Left's most serious effort to organize against business, the Honeywell Project, confidently predicted in 1970 that within two years, 50 to 100 other defense contractors would be the focus of similar efforts that same year. Hazel Henderson, a prominent writer on environmental affairs, predicted in *Nation* that

> this new "movement for corporate responsibility" whose goal is to politicize . . . the corporation, could become the most significant political development in the 1970's . . . open[ing] an almost untapped channel for organizing new constituents.[33]

Henderson expressed the aspirations of many frustrated with attempts to change government policies when she reported that "many . . . believe that the corporation may prove more responsive to political pressures than has formal government."[34] Nader prophesized that, through Campaign GM, people would begin to realize that

> no street in any American city is safe from General Motors. . . . The role of the individual share owner questioning the corporation in terms of social responsibility will increase. . . . A whole new conception of citizenship—one including corporations—would come into being.[35]

There were two efforts to capitalize on the momentum generated by what many observers regarded as the concrete successes of Campaign GM and FIGHT. In order "to establish a constituency" and increase its "credibility clout"[36] in 1972, the Project on Corporate Responsibility decided to establish a Shareholder Joint Action Program. For an annual contribution averaging $25, the project would implement shareholder initiatives, particularly proxy challenges and litigation, on behalf of its membership. Interested individuals would supply the PCR with a list of the companies in which they held securities, and periodically communicate to it the kinds of social issues in which they were interested. On this basis the project would decide which companies to challenge and what demands to make to them.

The PCR's proposals were strikingly similar in principle to an organization that Saul Alinsky attempted to create as a result of his experiences with Eastman Kodak. Alinsky was confident that he had stumbled onto something important in 1968: "In all my wars with the establishment, I've never seen it so uptight. I knew there was dynamite in the proxy scare."[37] In order to build on his experiences with Kodak, Alinsky envisioned the creation of a national membership organization called "Proxies for People." Headquartered in either Chicago or New York, the organization would send out professional organizers to middle-class communities throughout the United States. The targets, issues, and policies would be selected by the national board, but the key to the strategy would be the active involvement of the membership of local chapters. They would meet to study corporate policies, make recommendations to the national organization, and select individuals who would personally attend shareholder meetings in their local areas.

Alinsky was critical of Campaign GM because "It's not doing anything to organize and involve people."[38] What intrigued him about the idea of "Proxies for People" was that it would be used as a device to organize the middle class. It appeared perfectly suited to precisely those people who, by virtue of their income and educational levels, composed the social base of the so-called conscience constituency. In contrast to much of the radical rhetoric of this period, it appealed not to people's guilt about their affluence, but rather to the potential access and influence that their economic standing gave them. Alinsky would use "People's Capitalism," the proverbial slogan of the New York Stock Exchange, to mobilize "the people." In the last chapter of *Rules for Radicals*, written shortly before his death, Alinsky predicted:

> Proxies can be the mechanism by which these people [the middle class] can organize, and once they are organized they will re-enter the life of politics. Once organized around proxies they will have a reason to examine . . . various corporation policies and practices, both domestic and foreign, because now they can do something about them.[39]

In short, proxies were for Alinsky what the wage relationship was for Marx: a social relationship in terms of which people could define their common interests and challenge those who did not share them.

Neither the PCR nor Alinsky ever expected that their campaigns would actually win a majority against management. They were well aware that in a capitalist society, the wealthy, by definition, owned a disproportionate share of corporate stock. Rather, by mobilizing some significant fraction of the approximately 30 million Americans who owned stock—most of whom owned relatively few shares—they hoped to balance the inequality of wealth by the legitimacy that a democratic society attributes to sheer numbers. Acting collectively, citizens could acquire influence in corporate affairs disproportionate to their total individual wealth. It was this premise that presumably underlay the following Alinsky scenario:

> I want to be able to move those stockholders meetings into Yankee Stadium—and this goes for all corporations. They will have their thousand

or so stockholders there, and we'll have 75,000 people from Proxies for
People. I want to see the chairman of the board—in front of the cam-
eras and the mass media, with 75,000 people voting "aye" on one of our
resolutions—announce that 98% of the stock is in his hands, votes
"nay," and they win. I want to see him look at 75,000 people and tell
them that they haven't got a damn thing to say about it.[40]

Moreover, just as the power of institutional investors over management was ultimately based on the possibility of their divesting their
shares in a particular corporation, so too would the influence of citizen investors derive in the final analysis from their ability to make
their demands through the government.

In retrospect, it appears that the expectations of both the PCR and
Alinsky were somewhat naive. Corporate accountability *per se* is too
abstract an issue to capture the public's imagination. Moreover, except for the small minority of stock owners whose financial status
would render them unlikely candidates to challenge corporate social
policies, the shareholder role is not a particularly salient one; it is
commonly seen as little more than a risky savings account. In addition, the number of individual shareholders has been steadily decreasing since 1971, and many of those who continue to own stock
do so indirectly through mutual and pension funds. Mutual funds
make the shareholder relationship even more nebulous; few holders
are likely to have any idea about which companies they "own." Not
only is the relationship of an employee or a retiree to a pension fund
equally distant, but the beneficiaries of most union pension funds
have little say as to how their stock is voted. Indeed, the trustee relationship even limits the voting rights of certain wealthy individuals.

Most importantly, even if large numbers of shareholders could be
persuaded to take an interest in the social policies of their firms, they
would probably be as likely to support management in order to protect their dividends as to vote in favor of public interest resolutions.
The regular presence at shareholder meetings of sizable numbers of
vocal supporters of management suggests that there is a promanage-
ment constituency that includes many small shareholders.*

Moreover, the very emphasis on vote totals that informs most public interest proxy contests discourages the mobilization of individual
shareholders. It is a far more efficient use of limited resources to
concentrate on securing the support of institutional investors. Thus,

---

*The apparent identity of interests between most shareholders and management
has tempted many corporations to seek to mobilize their shareholders to support public policies sympathetic to business. However, they have had no more success than
public interest activists.

although Campaign GM received its greatest support from small shareholders—an estimated 60,000 voted for at least one of its proposals—its emphasis on receiving at least 3 percent of the shares voted dictated its strategy of emphasizing institutional investors. To the extent that shareholder activists want to "win" in a numerical sense, they will be unlikely to emphasize popular participation.[41]

The Politicization of the Corporation

To the extent that citizen challenges have succeeded in mobilizing relatively sizable numbers of individuals—whether through the voting of proxies, attendance at annual meetings, support of consumer boycotts, or by involvement in demonstrations—for the most part they have done so in connection with a broader political effort. Popular participation in citizen pressures on business has occurred most often as a complement to the use of either one or both of the other principal mechanisms of public access to the firm—collective bargaining and state intervention. Thus, the greatest degree of popular involvement in citizen challenges occurred as a spin-off of the antiwar and civil rights movements, whose primary focus was the state. Similarly, shareholder meetings of several banks and utilities throughout the United States have been attended by relatively large numbers of people to protest their loan policies and rate structures. But these organizing efforts have taken place in connection with attempts to influence the government, particularly state legislatures and public utility commissions. With the exception of the early civil rights protests, virtually the only consumer boycotts that have apparently received widespread public support—and thus measurably affected company profits—have taken place as a supplement to union organizing drives. The successes of the United Farm Workers in organizing farm workers in Florida and California were largely made possible by one of the most extensive, well-organized, and lengthiest consumer boycotts in American history. A similar and equally successful nationwide consumer boycott was instrumental in forcing Farah Manufacturing Company to recognize the Amalgamated Clothing Workers Union.[42]

The Role of Unions

Since pension funds own approximately 33 percent of the equity capital of major American companies, the role of the trade union movement is critical to an assessment of the degree of future public participation in citizen challenge efforts.[43] In 1977, J. P. Stevens became the first corporation in America to be pressured simultaneously from four directions: by the state through the National Labor Relations Board and the courts; by its employees through a strike; by consumers through one of the most extensive boycotts ever organized by the AFL-CIO; and by investors through the most elaborate and well-organized proxy challenges to which any corporation has ever been subjected on a social issue.[44] Five church organizations affiliated with the Interfaith Center filed two proxy resolutions. One asked for a written report to shareholders on the company's labor policies and practices, and the other requested the board of directors to disclose their equal employment practices. The Interfaith Center campaigned aggressively for the proposals, sending a four-page report to 8,000 specially selected Stevens shareholders. The company's annual meeting in New York was attended by a record 500 shareholders, many of whom were activists from church and labor groups. Among those who attended was Coretta King, who quoted her late husband's statement during the Montgomery bus boycott: "Our struggle is not toward putting the bus company out of business but putting justice in business."[45] Outside 3,500 people representing a broad cross section of the left-liberal community—not dissimilar in political composition to those who had opposed bank loans to South Africa a decade earlier—demonstrated. When the votes were tallied, the two resolutions were supported by 5.8 percent and 5.59 percent of the shares voted, impressive totals considering the fact that Stevens stock is closely held.

In addition, the union initiated a novel form of citizen pressure: it began a campaign to isolate J. P. Stevens from the business community by eliminating the interlocks between its board and that of other companies. The union organizer of the "corporate campaign" stated that his goal was "to display our power to Wall Street so they would know that any institution tied to J P. Stevens would be held accountable. . . . No institution like J. P. Stevens can exist in a vacuum."[46] After considerable pressure, including a threatened withdrawal of union pension funds, James D. Finley, the chairman of J. P. Stevens, resigned from the board of Manufacturers Hanover Trust. Shortly afterward, David Mitchell, the chairman of Avon Products Inc., announced his resignation from the board of J. P. Stevens.

The union effort clearly represented a further stage in the politicization of the corporate board. Previously, activists had attempted to force corporations to add representatives of various constituencies to their boards; this was the first time they pressured particular board members to resign. The union's focus on financial intermediates as a means of challenging the policies of an industrial firm can also be seen as an extension of the strategy initially developed by

Campaign GM's Round II. What is less clear, however, is whether the corporate campaign against J. P. Stevens signaled an increase of union involvement in the politics of corporate governance. On paper, the potential power of unions is impressive. Approximately one-fifth of private sector pension monies—amounting to between 50 and 60 billion dollars—are more or less effectively controlled by unions or their representatives. Another $140 billion are administered by trustees established by state and local governments. These figures hardly suggested the emergence of "pension-fund socialism," since most pension fund monies remain firmly under the control of the federal government or corporate managements. They are, however, significant. But with the exception of TIAA-CREF and a handful of locals in New York and California, unions to date have shown remarkably little interest in using their funds to influence corporate policies either by proxy voting or selective investment. Significantly, various unions threatened to withdraw their funds from the control of Manufacturers Hanover Trust, but they did not seek to influence the bank's voting of its proxies. There has been some interest in the voting of proxies by the boards that administer the pension monies of local government employees, but that too remains limited: only five public employee pension funds subscribe to IRRC and only one state—Minnesota—systematically considers social issues in its proxy voting decisions. As long as this pattern persists, citizen challenges are likely to remain more an embarrassment to business than a major focus of popular opposition to it.

CONSTITUTIONALIZING THE CORPORATION

While the lack of widespread public participation has clearly limited the political impact of the corporate accountability effort, it has not proved a fatal handicap; indeed, many of the movement's most important effects on corporate policy and public opinion occurred after the atrophy of the social movements of the sixties. By any reasonable criteria the accomplishments of the relatively small number of individuals—numbering in the hundreds—who pioneered the creation of a third political arena for public pressures on the corporation, have been extremely impressive. In 1967, who would have thought that using annual shareholders meetings to raise criticism of the social and political impact of corporate policies would within a few years become the rule rather than the exception? Who, in 1969, would have predicted that the public interest proxy resolution proposed by an antiwar medical student would become a permanent part of the political and legal environment of the American corporation, used to address a broad array of issues by a wide variety of political factions? Who, looking at the level of shareholder support for Campaign GM in 1970 and 1971, would have imagined that within three years, a major proportion of public interest resolutions would either be voluntarily withdrawn by their participants or receive enough votes to make them automatically eligible for resubmission? And, as recently as 1970, who would have foreseen that this decade would witness the participation of institutional investors in the corporate electoral process?

By treating corporations as if they were governments, direct pressures on business have reflected and reinforced a relatively new and potentially important way of approaching the problem of corporate accountability. The logical extension of the politicization of the corporation is for the corporation's structure of authority to come to more closely resemble that of the government itself. The amount of government regulation of business is unlikely to diminish, but in the future it is likely to address itself not only to the substance of corporate policies, but to the processes by which those policies are made. Citizen challenges have already played a role in placing two related sets of issues on the agenda of the governmental process: the internal structure of authority of the investor-owned enterprise and the ability of citizens outside the corporation to scrutinize and question the deliberations of management. These concerns are reflected in the raising of issues such as the composition, authority, and selection of the board of directors, the responsibility of units within the firm for monitoring particular aspects of its social impact, the participation of shareholders in the formulation and discussion of corporate policies, and the degree of public access to information about business behavior.

Corporate activism also has been accompanied by a resurgence of interest among lawyers, economists, and political scientists in the relationship between the governance of the corporation and its social impact. Since 1970, a broad array of schemes have been proposed to make management more directly accountable to those whose stake in the corporation's performance is not primarily financial.[47] Among these suggestions are giving only one vote to each shareholder (a sort of application of the principle of *Baker v. Carr* to the private sector); granting standing to file a shareholder derivative suit to anyone adversely affected by management policies—not just shareholders; requiring cumulative voting; taking the control of the proxy machinery away from management; extending the ability of shareholders to initiate proposals; allowing shareholders' nominees for directors to be included in the corporate proxy statement; and adding society-oriented disclosure rules to the regulations of the SEC. Sev-

eral of these reforms are included in the versions of federal chartering proposals advanced by critics of corporate social performance
such as Ralph Nader and Donald Schwartz.[48]

There is also a growing interest among social critics of business in
institutionalizing changes in the board room that would both better
insure the financial integrity of the corporation and increase the
likelihood that business decisions would be more responsive to those
affected by them.[49] John Kenneth Galbraith, Christopher Stone, and
Robert Townsend have proposed that a certain number of directors
of major corporations be chosen by the government. Others propose
strengthening the independence and competency of the board without altering its selection procedures. For example, Schwartz wants all
directors to serve full-time, while Nader would like to prohibit inside
directors and make each director responsible for a particular aspect
of social conduct. An important underlying goal of all these proposals is to somehow convert the board into a sort of internal regulatory agency, capable of helping both the public and the government
more effectively monitor and intervene in corporate decisions.

What distinguishes these reforms from most of the scores of laws
regulating business that have been enacted by the federal government since 1960 is that they address themselves not to the substantive impact of corporate decisions, but rather to the procedures by
which these decisions are made. The strategy that informs them is a
simple one; it is to strengthen the ability of those directly affected by
corporate policies—acting either individually or collectively—to defend those interests that are inadequately protected by either the
regulatory process or the marketplace. They attempt to give individuals both inside and outside the firm increased financial and legal
resources in order to monitor and challenge corporate policies, without having to depend upon government officials. In a sense, they
seek to apply the principle of checks and balances to the operations
of the private sector. The proposed reforms represent a logical extension of the two central premises of citizen protests: the notion
that the corporation has become a public institution and that the
responsibility for making corporate decisions more accountable cannot be exclusively left to the government. They are an attempt to
wrestle with the central dilemma that confronts contemporary critics
of business: how do you increase public control of "big business" if
you are equally suspicious of "big government"? As Ralph Nader
told an interviewer in 1970,

> I have a theory about power. If it is going to be responsible or ex-
> tremely repressive, it has to be insecure, it has to have something to
> lose. That is why putting all economic power in the hands of the State

would be disastrous, because it would not be insecure. No matter where [power] is located, it's going to be abused if the pathways are not open for a broader spectrum of values that have power behind them demanding recognition.[50]

A survey of 200 social activists reveals a similar perspective:

> . . . attitudes in this study indicate the heavy premium social activists put on the establishment of new legislative machinery for giving "outside groups a more direct voice in helping to shape policy in the nation's boardrooms."

The survey concluded, "What . . . they appear to want . . . is legislation which would enable themselves or others to make corporations more socially accountable through more direct disclosure of their operations and/or broader representation on boards of directors of appropriate outside interests." (Strikingly, only 42 percent believe that "government regulation is the best way to make business more responsive to people's needs.")[51]

Donald Schwartz, Campaign GM's legal counsel, has clearly articulated the thinking behind this strategy. He told a conference at Berkeley on corporate responsibility that

> [Contemporary reformers] ultimately desire to relocate the power more within individual hands, *since they believe that shifting the power to government hands is no shift at all.* The objective . . . is to reduce the size of corporations and government regulations alike and *strengthen the position of individual private citizens who will act directly—not through institutions—* against corporate abuse.[52] [emphasis added]

Phil Moore, one of the campaign's directors, added:

> . . . most of all, we need a system of corporate governance . . . like our own [Constitution]—not one that solves problems, but that sets forth the process by which problems are solved. . . . In essence, the corporate constitution would open up the corporation to activism. It would create a system of access in which the anti-war activist, the Black activist, the environmental activist and the consumer activist could press their demands on the corporation.[53]

Thus, the principal way in which corporations and governments are becoming subject to similar standards is that both institutions are under pressure to allow the public a greater role in monitoring and participating in their deliberations. The suspicion of both private and public power has led contemporary reformers to seek to develop ways of increasing the vulnerability and scrutiny of decision makers in both sectors. This process is far more advanced in the public sector, particularly with respect to access to the regulatory agencies and the courts, but attention will increasingly focus on opening up the private sector. Those affected by the corporation in their roles as socially concerned investors and consumers are working for restraints on management prerogatives roughly similar to those that currently protect unionized workers.

THE LIMITATIONS OF CORPORATE ACCOUNTABILITY

All its brave rhetoric notwithstanding, the corporate accountability movement can hardly be regarded as a serious challenge to corporate authority in the United States. This is not primarily due to the lack of widespread participation in it by radicals and socialists—especially after 1970; that is a symptom rather than a cause.[54] Nor is it primarily a function of the extent to which the citizen challenge effort has become dominated by the use of the proxy mechanism. It is true that shareholder activism can be seen as a contemporary variant of nineteenth-century populism; for in both instances the preservation and expansion of private property rights are the basis of a challenge to the prerogatives of the corporation.

Yet this, too, is symptomatic. What is most striking about the corporate accountability movement is the modesty of its demands on business. This is most obviously true of the substantive issues that corporate activists have raised since 1970. Corporations could have yielded to virtually every demand without threatening either their profits or disturbing their power. The increased employment of women and minorities, the cessation of the production of particular weaponry, the disclosure of additional material about environmental impact, the willingness to lend money to inner city housing, the reform of the marketing of infant formulas in poor nations, the refusal to comply with the terms of the Arab boycott—these are hardly policies whose enactment would merit more than a footnote in the history of American business. Even the potentially most expensive demand—withdrawal of all investments from South Africa—would hardly cause more than a small ripple in most corporate balance sheets. Nader, who has closely followed the development of nongovernmental pressures on the corporation over the last decade, correctly observes:

> The managers of the investor owned corporation have so many things to give. Corporations could go on meeting the demands of activists challenging them directly at the current rate forever and still their wealth and autonomy would remain essentially unaffected.[55]

Neil Chamberlain's perceptive analysis of the significance of the most visible dimension of citizen pressures can be generalized to most of the demands of the movement. He writes in *The Limits of Corporate Responsibility*:

> The consequence of adding a public forum aspect to the annual meeting is to "open" the corporate system to the realities of a society that has altered markedly since the days when statutory and common law established the present legal form. In so doing it does not meet, but in fact turns back, demands for broader participatory roles; it requires no sharing of power. The government of the corporation remains firmly in place. All that has happened is that it has become more public in its operations, more attuned to those voices that it has tended to ignore in the past. Management retains its centralized control by making modest and incremental adjustments in its practices and procedures to palliate those who call for more sweeping change.[56]

The efforts of the corporate accountability movement can be understood in the tradition described by Berle in *The Twentieth Century Capitalist Revolution*. Developed in Normandy, this custom provided that anyone who felt he had suffered an injury at the hands of his neighbors, feudal officials, or even the Duke himself, could cry, "Ha! Rollo!" The Duke would then be required to listen to his grievance and judge its merit "according to the law of God and good conscience."[57] In reality, citizen pressures have challenged the judgment of management, not its power.

The potential impact of the procedural reforms proposed by corporate reformers must also be viewed critically. Would improving opportunities for shareholder participation actually affect the kinds of social and political decisions made by corporate managements? Given the current distribution of stock ownership, one is entitled to be extremely skeptical. Even if shareholder activism were made easier, there is little reason to assume that the corporation's social critics could look forward to having any more direct impact on corporate policies than they have had in the past. The overwhelming majority of individual shareholders and institutional investors remain exclusively oriented to the bottom line. The kind of concessions management might be prompted to make to dissident shareholders have been and will remain marginal.

The likely effect of the appointment by the government of "public" directors on the corporation's balance of power also appears rather minimal. Not only might their presence reduce the number of critical decisions made at board meetings—which are rather minimal in any event—but the danger of co-option is a real one. If officials in regulatory agencies responsible for the supervision of particular industries come to almost invariably share the perspectives of the industry they are responsible for regulating, what can we reasonably expect of officials responsible for monitoring the performance of just one firm? Leon Sullivan and Sister Scully notwithstanding, the performance to date of "public interest" directors is not a particularly encouraging one. None has developed an active political relationship with any of the corporation's constituencies. There is no question that the kinds of changes in the board room advocated by the corporation's social critics would complicate and, on occasion, actually modify the decisions of top management, but to expect any major change in corporate priorities is naive.

A similar analysis can be made of the effect of imposing increased disclosure requirements on corporations. The analogy between the impact of the mandatory disclosure of financial data and that of social data is a deceptive one. The first category of information goes to a small group of people who have a direct and unambiguous stake in its impact and who, most importantly, are readily able to translate it into a form that corporate executives take extremely seriously—the price of their stock. In contrast, reports of corporate social performance would presumably be for the benefit of the "public." It is true that public opinion can be an important political force, but there are limits to the public's attention span. How much more knowledge about the social conduct of the hundreds of corporations that dominate the American economy can the public be expected to absorb and act on politically? The public can react to occasional scandals, but can we really expect citizens to pay as close and continuous attention to reports of corporate social performance as the investment community does to that of corporate earnings?

This is not to say the increasing public access and scrutiny of the corporation will be without any impact; that conclusion is adequately refuted by the evidence presented in this book. Direct pressures on business can change corporate behavior, but they are capable of doing so primarily to the extent to which their demands on business expand or complement those required by law. The central premise of citizen activism—namely, that corporations have become, in effect, public institutions exercising a degree of power closely connected to or rivaling that of the state—is actually contradicted by the history of the corporate accountability movement itself. Paradoxically, its successes are due primarily not to the individual or collective efforts of citizens, but rather to the support of the state—the very institution whose alleged domination by business led to direct pressures in the first place.

Why has the corporate accountability movement been unable to offer an adequate vision of what "democratically accountable" corporations would look like? We come full circle: the limitations of citizen pressures on business are linked to their cause. The relative conservatism of the corporate accountability movement stems from its underlying ideology; the notion of the corporation as a governmental or public institution obscures more than it illuminates. The reason the efforts to apply to the corporation the same standards of public accountability that the modern democratic tradition applies to the state are doomed to frustration is because the two institutions are, in reality, fundamentally distinctive. The corporation is not simply another governmental or public institution; unlike the state, it confronts a set of constraints that are essentially economic in character. It is dependent for survival on its ability to accumulate capital in an extremely competitive domestic and international economic environment. As long as corporations remain dependent on private capital markets, there are real limits on their capability to consider nonpecuniary values in their decisions.

The notion of the corporation as a public institution or private government is both informative and misleading. It is informative in that it illuminates the extent to which the social impact of the corporation does resemble that of a government. But it is deceptive to the extent that it obscures the inability of the corporation to command compliance with its decisions. The reason that a corporation, unlike a democratically elected government, cannot be politically accountable to those affected by its decisions, is because the most important decisions made by any firm are out of the control of those who govern it; they are dictated by the imperatives of a market economy. As the range of responses to the demands raised by citizen pressures indicates, corporate managers are certainly not without discretion and many could act somewhat differently than they do. But the extent to which business executives could actually change the basic orientation of their companies is severely limited: corporate accountability is fundamentally limited by the inability of a privately owned firm to pursue objectives that are incompatible with long run profit maximization, however loosely that objective is defined: a politically accountable corporation in a capitalist system is a contradiction in terms.

There is a way in which corporations can be forced to make decisions not dominated by the logic of capital accumulation, but it cannot be achieved through "corporate accountability." It requires the direct intervention of the government. At best, corporate activists can supplement government regulation; what they cannot do is substitute for it. In the final analysis, who governs the corporation is less important than who controls the government. Moreover, in their intensive focus on the corporation—its structure, power, and conduct—corporate activists have paid insufficient attention to the dynamics, and difficulties, of the capitalist political-economic system within which it functions. The future of the corporation will be decisively influenced by the way in which the American political system deals with issues such as unemployment, inflation, resource scarcities, international competition, and uneven regional development. The corporate challenge movement has not and, indeed, cannot adequately address these fundamental issues because they can only be addressed through the governmental process.

Conclusion

What, then, is the significance of the corporate accountability effort? What difference has it made? Clearly, what is least important about citizen pressures has been their direct, substantive effect on corporate decisions. These have been, and are likely to remain, marginal. Their impact on public policy has been more substantial. They have played a relatively important role both in bringing a number of issues before the political process, and in increasing the effectiveness of government controls over business. Their emergence means that the dynamics of government regulation of business can no longer be understood with exclusive reference to the governmental process.

Far more importantly, citizen challenges have helped increase the visibility and public scrutiny of corporate decisions. The business corporation is far less an abstraction than it was a decade ago. A significant number of interested publics have become more aware of the relationship between their political and social concerns and the specific policies of particular corporations. Those who exercise authority within the corporation are thus under far more scrutiny—by the government, the press, the public, as well as by institutional investors—than they were in the mid-sixties. In the course of treating the corporation as if it were a government, citizen pressures helped politicize the environment of the firm. Moreover, the form that pressures on business have assumed is itself of political significance; they are a reflection of widespread public mistrust of both business and government.

Finally, citizen pressures have increased the opportunities for the expression of public opposition to corporate policies. What is most important about the challenges to Kodak, Dow Chemical, Honeywell, Gulf, and General Motors is not their impact, but the fact that they occurred at all. Corporations can no longer depend upon the government to shield them from public hostility. Rather, to the extent that they make decisions that are widely regarded as having important political, social, and moral implications, they must now be prepared to directly confront substantial and prolonged public opposition—in all its diverse and novel forms. The most fundamental contribution of citizen pressures has been to link the corporation more closely with the vitality and turbulence of the democratic process. Ultimately, citizen protests have less to do with increasing corporate accountability than with preserving and strengthening democratic participation.

NOTES

1. For a summary of the speech and public reaction to it, see "Corporate Performance and Private Criticism, Campaign GM: Rounds I and II," a case prepared by Mrs. A. J. Sproat under the direction of C. Roland Christensen (Boston: Harvard University, Inter-Collegiate Case Clearinghouse, no. 9-370-026), pp. 16–17.

2. Quoted in Timothy H. Ingram, "The Corporate Underground," *Nation*, September 13, 1971, p. 212.

3. Earl A. Molander, "Ethics and Responsibility in Business Organizations: Internal Reform vs. External Controls," paper presented at Business Ethics Workshop, Graduate Theological Union, Berkeley, California, February 18, 1977. According to the Opinion Research Corporation, "Most businessmen and financial editors . . . believe that stockholder activism will be beneficial to publically owned companies." Kenneth Schwartz, "How Social Activists See Business," *Business and Society Review*, no. 4 (Summer 1975), p. 73.

4. Carl Irving, "Business Is Getting Religion," *San Francisco Chronicle*, February 3, 1977, p. 11.

5. "Annual Meeting Time," *Forbes*, April 15, 1976, p. 40.

6. Ibid., p. 42. Mary Gardiner Jones, a former member of the FTC who serves on three corporate boards, notes:

I know from my own experience that corporate managements . . . pay close attention to the views expressed by their institutional nonprofit investors on the issues raised by their stockholders' proxy resolutions as well as to the number of votes which these resolutions receive. [Testimony before Subcommittee on Citizens' and Shareholders' Rights and Remedies, "The Role of the Shareholder in the Corporate World," Committee on the Judiciary, U.S. Senate, Ninety-fifth Congress, First Session, part I, June 27, 28, 1977.]

7. Roger G. Kennedy, "Portfolio Decisions," *Vital Speeches* 41 (January 15, 1975): 213.

8. Peter B. Roche, "Activist Shareholders Are Pushing Drive for More Disclosure About Firms' Ethics," *Wall Street Journal*, April 5, 1976, p. 26.

9. Will Maslow, "How You Can Fight the Boycott," reprinted from *Moment*

by the American Jewish Congress, New York, p. 2. Exxon reportedly was anxious to seek a compromise with the American Jewish Congress because, "it could not afford to offend Jewish customers and investors," "Annual Meeting Time," p. 40.

10. William D. Hartley, "More Concerns Willing to Enter Negotiations on Shareholder Resolutions," *Wall Street Journal*, March 23, 1977, p. 17.

11. John C. Perham, "Annual Meetings: Back to Basics," *Dun's Review*, (April 1975): 106.

12. Vartanig G. Vartan, "AT&T Finds Annual Meeting Needs Careful Staging," *New York Times*, August 18, 1977, p. 52. Its chairman had previously instructed his staff: "This year find something we can recommend a vote in favor of."

13. *Preparing for the Annual Meeting and Stockholder Proposals*, Proceedings of a Conference sponsored by the New York Law Journal, 1976, p. 16.

14. See David Vogel, "The Corporate Board: Membership and Public Pressure," *Executive* 3, no. 3 (Spring 1977): 8–11, for a more detailed discussion of the impact of social pressures on the composition of the corporate board; see also "The Corporate Machinery for Hearing and Heeding New Voices: A Panel Discussion," *Business Lawyer* 26 (1971): 195–222. A poll of corporate activists on the effectiveness of "public interest" directors found that 5 percent regard them as "very effective," and 32 percent see them as "only somewhat effective," while 28 percent view them as "very ineffective." Kenneth Schwartz, "How Social Activists See Business," p. 72.

15. "A Big Jump in the Ranks of Female Directors," *Business Week*, January 10, 1977, p. 50.

16. Peter Vanderwicken, "Change Invades the Boardroom," *Fortune*, May 1972, pp. 157, 200. For more on the role and presence of blacks on the corporate board, see Jonathan Kwitny, "Firms Find Integration in Their Boardroom Is Working Quite Well," *Wall Street Journal*, October 5, 1972, p. 1; and Milton Moskowitz, "The Black Directors: Tokenism or a Big Leap Forward," *Business and Society Review*, no. 3 (August 1972), pp. 73–80.

17. "A Big Jump in the Ranks of Female Directors," p. 50.

18. Kwitny, "Firms Find Integration," p. 1. For a discussion of Sullivan's impact on GM during the first five years of his tenure, see "The Black on GM's Board," *Time*, September 6, 1976, pp. 54–55.

19. Interview with James Langton.

20. See William L. Cary, "Greening of the Board Room," *New York Times*, August 4, 1971, section 3, p. 33; and "The Greening of the Board Room: Reflections on Corporate Responsibility—A Panel Discussion," *Columbia Journal of Law and Social Problems* 10, no. 1 (Fall 1973): 15–46.

21. Richard H. Holton, "Management Responses to Shareholders' Proposals," prepared for a Union Bank Seminar, May 29, 1974, pp. 12–13.

22. John C. Perham, "Annual Meetings—Dissidents on the Attack," *Dun's Review*, April 1976, p. 57.

23. Roger E. Celler, "The Challengers," Public Affairs Council, 1971.

24. Judith Cole, "The Challengers," Public Affairs Council, 1975, p. 3. For other efforts to inform the business community about the tactics of the pub-

lic interest movement, see "Managing Business' Social Concerns, I—Expectations and Pressures," Stanford Research Institute, 1972; and "Principal Activist Tactics," *Corporate Responsibility Planning Service*, Human Resources Network, September 9, 1977, no. 417. The latter report explicitly deals with shareholder activism.

25. An interview with John Holcomb of the Public Affairs Council helped clarify the difficulties corporations experienced in trying to respond to demands raised by citizen challenges.

26. Stephen Mahoney, "Will the Annual Meeting *Please* Come to Order," *Fortune*, May 1965, p. 141; see also "Shushing the Annual Heckler," *Business Week*, May 22, 1965, pp. 118–23.

27. Mahoney, "Will the Annual Meeting," p. 142.

28. Henry C. Egerton, "Shareholder Proposals as a Vehicle of Protest," *Conference Board Record*, April 1971, p. 51.

29. Bryon E. Calane, "Rockwell Listens to Roar of Holders Over Its B1 Bomber," *Wall Street Journal*, February 13, 1976, p. 6.

30. Mimi Conway, "Confrontation with Stevens' Board," *In These Times*, March 16–22, 1977, p. 8.

31. "Annual Meeting Time," p. 40.

32. For the argument that the annual meeting should be abolished, see J. B. Fugua, "End Annual Meetings," *New York Times*, November 3, 1973, section 3, p. 36.

33. Hazel Henderson, "Politics by Other Means," *Nation*, December 14, 1970, pp. 617–18.

34. Ibid., p. 618.

35. Quoted in "Campaign to Make General Motors Responsible," a case prepared by John W. Collins (Boston: Inter-Collegiate Case Clearinghouse, No. 9-371-660), p. 1; see also, Blumberg, "Politicization of the Corporation," p. 1561.

36. "Project on Corporate Responsibility," *News and Thought*, Summer 1972, p. 6.

37. Saul D. Alinsky, *Rules for Radicals*, p. 175.

38. "Proxies for People—A Vehicle for Involvement," *Yale Review of Law and Social Action* 1 (Spring 1971): 68.

39. Alinsky, *Rules for Radicals*, pp. 178–79.

40. "Proxies for People," p. 66.

41. Strikingly, a poll of 3,500 Presbyterians by the Church's Committee on Mission Responsibility through Investments taken in 1976 revealed that only 16 percent were aware that the church had filed public interest proxy resolutions.

42. See Sethi, "La Huelga Y La Causa (A) and (B)," *Up Against the Corporate Wall*, pp. 160–68, 340–55. For a discussion of the labor-management conflict at Farah, see "A Boycott Begins to Hurt at Farah," *Business Week*, June 2, 1973, p. 56; and "A Texas Pants Maker Loses to a Boycott," *Business Week*, March 2, 1974.

43. See Peter Drucker, *The Unseen Revolution: How Pension Fund Socialism Came to America* (New York: Harper & Row, 1976).

44. For the labor dispute involving J. P. Stevens, see Damon Stetson, "Church Groups Support Union Drive at J. P. Stevens," *New York Times*, February 15, 1977, p. 12; Mimi Conway, "Confrontation with Stevens' Board," *In These Times*, March 16–22, 1977, p. 8.

45. Quoted in Robert Friedman, "For J. P. Stevens Its Cheaper to Violate the Law than Recognize It," *Seven Days*, April 11, 1977, p. 11.

46. Quoted in Michael Jensen, "Union Strategist on Wall Street," *New York Times*, March 26, 1978, section 3, p. 5.

47. Donald Schwartz, "Federal Chartering of Corporations: An Introduction," *Georgetown Law Journal* 67 (1972): 71–121; Robert N. Shwartz, "A Proposal for the Designation of Shareholder Nominees for Director in the Corporate Proxy Statement," *Columbia Law Review* 74 (1974): 1139–74; Stephen Schulman, "Shareholder Cause Proposals: A Technique to Catch the Conscience of the Corporation," *George Washington Law Review* 40, no. 1 (1971): 1–75; Howard M. Friedman, "The Public Interest Derivative Suit: A Proposal for Enforcing Corporate Responsibility," *Case Western Reserve Law Review* 24 (1973): 294–329; Thomas J. Schoenbaum, "The Relationship Between Corporate Disclosure and Corporate Responsibility," *Fordham Law Review* 40, no. 3 (1972): 565–94; Melvin Aaron Eisenberg, "Access to the Corporate Proxy Machinery," *Harvard Law Review* 83 (1970): 1489–1526; William J. Feis, "Is Shareholder Democracy Attainable?" *Business Lawyer* 31 (1976): 621–43; David L. Ratner, "The Government of Business Corporations: Critical Reflections on the Rule of One Shareholder, One Vote," *Cornell Law Review* 56 (1970): 1–56.

48. See Ralph Nader, Mark Green, and Joel Seligman, *Taming the Giant Corporation* (New York: W. W. Norton, 1976); and Schwartz, "Federal Chartering."

49. Robert Townsend, "Let's Install Public Directors," *Business and Society Review*, no. 1 (Spring 1972), pp. 69–70; John Kenneth Galbraith, "What Comes after General Motors?" *New Republic*, November 2, 1974, pp. 13–17; Christopher D. Stone, *Where the Law Ends* (New York: Harper & Row, 1976), and "Public Directors Merit a Try," *Harvard Business Review*, March/April 1976, pp. 20–42; Nader, Green, and Seligman, *Taming the Giant Corporation*, pp. 115–39, especially 118–31; for an additional discussion of proposed reforms of the corporate board, see Phillip I. Blumberg, Eli Goldston, and George Gibson, "Corporate Social Responsibility Panel: The Constituencies of the Corporation and the Role of the Institutional Investor," *Business Lawyer*, March 1973, pp. 177–213; Melvin Aaron Eisenberg, "Legal Models of Management Structure on the Modern Corporation: Officers, Directors and Accountants," *California Law Review* 63 (1975): 373–439; Detlev Vagts, "The Governance of the Corporation: The Options Available and the Power to Prescribe," *Business Lawyer*, February 1976, pp. 929–38; Phillip I. Blumberg, "Reflection on Proposals for Corporate Reform through Change in the Composition of the Board of Directors: 'Special Interest' or 'Public Directors,'" in *The Unstable Ground: Corporate Social Policy in a Dynamic Society*, ed. S. Prakash Sethi (Los Angeles: Melville Publishing Co., 1974), pp. 112–34. No one has seriously proposed that directors be chosen by any group other

than shareholders, the government, or employees. The issue of worker participation in corporate governance is beyond the scope of this study.

50. Eileen Shanahan, "Reformers: Urging Business Change," *New York Times*, January 24, 1971, section 3, p. 1.

51. Schwartz, "How Social Activists," p. 73.

52. Donald Schwartz, "The Federal Chartering of Corporations: A Modest Proposal," in *The Unstable Ground*, ed. Sethi, p. 158.

53. Philip W. Moore, "Corporate Social Reform: An Activist's Viewpoint," in *The Unstable Ground*, ed. Sethi, p. 55.

54. With the exception of the issues of corporate military production and American corporate investments in South Africa, groups and individuals explicitly opposed to capitalism have tended not to participate in direct challenges to business. One of the few accounts of the movement for corporate accountability to appear in a radical publication was published by the North American Congress for Latin America in 1972 entitled, "Moving Against the Corporations," *NACLA's Latin American and Empire Report*, VI:9 (November 1972), pp. 20–25. For discussions of the relationship between radicals and counter-corporate politics, see "Why Your Radicals Zero in on Business," *Nation's Business*, July 1967, pp. 31–34; and David Vogel, "Corporations and the Left," *Socialist Review* 20 no. 2 (October 1974), pp. 45–66. For a highly exaggerated view of the role of the left in citizen pressures on business—which fails to distinguish between those who propose proxy resolutions and the Weathermen—see William Braznell, Jr., "The Radicals Are Coming—Are You Ready?" *Public Relations Journal*, December 1976, pp. 12–15.

55. Interview with Ralph Nader.

56. Neil Chamberlain, *The Limits of Corprate Responsibility* (New York: Basic Books, 1973), pp. 199–200.

57. Berle, *Twentieth-Century Capitalist Revolution*, p. 62.

Chapter Seven

THE ETHICAL ROOTS OF BUSINESS ETHICS

Introduction

While both public and scholarly interest in business ethics has increased significantly over the last decade, the subject of business ethics is not a new one; it is in fact as old as the western ethical tradition itself. Nor is public concern with the ethics of business novel. On the contrary, it has been a continual focus of public concern since the origins of the market economy in the west more than 750 years ago.

Unfortunately, much contemporary writing on business ethics lacks a historical focus. Aside from the obligatory references to Kant and Mill, it is relatively rare to find any serious discussion of concepts or ideas that date back more than a few decades. The writings of Aristotle as well as those of the medieval and Protestant theologians who thought long and hard about the ethics of business are rarely cited.[1] One also finds remarkably few references in the contemporary business ethics literature to the works of scholars such as Max Weber, Albert Hirschman and Michael Walzer—all of whom have written extensively about the ethical dimensions of capitalism.[2]

Significantly, there are hardly any histories of business ethics in America, although there is a rich secondary literature on this subject.[3] Nor do any of the widely used business ethics texts include an extended discussion of the history of the use of ethical concepts to evaluate business behavior in the United States, Europe or Japan during the last few centuries. The 1980s were certainly not the first period in American history when it was widely believed that the ethics of business left much to be desired: criticisms of the moral shortcomings and lapses of financiers, bankers and investors on Wall Street are a recurrent theme of American history.[4] Yet to date, no one has attempted to place the contemporary resurgence of criticism of the ethics of business within the context of the history of business-government-society relations in the United States.

The purpose of this chapter is to trace the historical roots of some of our current preoccupations with the ethics of business. My argument is that many of the contemporary criteria we use to assess the ethics of business date back several centuries. In many important respects, the ethical standards to which we hold business have remained remarkably constant over a relatively long period of time, though obviously many of the specific aspects of business conduct that trouble us are new. Moreover, many of our contemporary debates about the nature of business ethics can be traced back a number of centuries. By drawing upon this rich intellectual history, we will be in a better position to appreciate the nature and significance of many current concerns.

I will illustrate this thesis by focusing on three sets of tensions: the tension between ethics and profits, between private gain and the public good and between the results of capitalism and the intentions of businessmen.

ETHICS AND PROFITS

I want to begin by examining the relationship between ethics and profits or more specifically the relationship between virtue and economic success. The emergence of capitalism in 16th century Europe was closely associated with the Protestant reformation. In an important sense, Protestantism made business ethics possible. For to the extent that money-making was viewed as morally suspect—as it was in medieval Catholic theology—it was difficult to establish any moral standards for its pursuit. As St. Augustine put it, "the businessman . . . may conduct himself without sin, but cannot be pleasing to God."[5] "The Church's attitude toward trade was . . . nicely put in the saying: *Homo mercator vix aut numpuam Deo placere potest*—the merchant can scarcely or never be pleasing to God."[6] St. Thomas Aquinas regarded most forms of trade conducted for profit as inherently morally suspect. As he wrote, ". . . he who in trading sells a thing for more than he paid for it must have paid less than it was worth or be selling it for more."[7]

Catholic theologians did distinguish among types of economic activity. For example, they regarded producing a good for sale as less ethically suspect than either trading in goods or extending loans. But for the most part, business activity was regarded as beyond the moral pale: the only ethical advice Christ gave to the merchants and tradesmen he encountered was to abandon their work and follow him. A moral businessman was thus a contradiction in terms. In a way, it was no more possible to have been an ethical money-lender six centuries ago than it is now possible to be a socially responsible drug dealer.

For if an activity is regarded as inherently immoral, it is impossible to perform it in an ethical manner; the only responsible course of action is to disengage from it entirely. The contemporary moral case against such business activities as investing in South Africa, manufacturing and marketing cigarettes or producing strategic weapons thus represents an echo of the more sweeping medieval case against the pursuit of profit in general and finance in particular. Those who oppose these business activities on moral grounds believe that it is impossible for them to be performed in an ethical manner. Thus, during the intervening centuries the specific sources of profit that have been classified as inherently unethical has changed. But the moral standard by which we evaluate the ethics of many businesses and business activities has remained remarkably stable.

Not surprisingly, many medieval merchants did in fact act like contemporary drug dealers. After all, if one is engaging in an activity that is regarded as immoral to begin with, why should one care about performing it in an ethical manner? Pre-reformation capitalism was rooted in a "rampant individualism which knew few scruples. . . . The 'capitalist mentality of the medieval business classes rested on the dictum: 'A profit is a profit, however it is acquired.'"[8] For example, the merchants of the Italian city-states thought nothing of putting the diseased bodies of animals into the shops of their competitors in order to make them, their employees and their customers ill. And Queen Elizabeth knighted Francis Drake for plundering Spanish ships and killing their crews.

It was by morally sanctifying the pursuit of profit that Protestantism made business ethics possible. While traditional Christian theology viewed work at worst as a curse and at best as a distraction, Protestantism held that what a businessman did between "9 and 5" could be pleasing to God. Not only could one serve God by working, but also that the correct use of wealth was precisely to improve it for the glory of God. Consequently, the pursuit of profit and the pursuit of heaven become not only compatible, but mutually reinforcing. A diligent worker was less likely to be tempted by the devil. And being rewarded with financial success was now understood as a sign of God's favor. In short, the Reformation made it possible to be both an ethical individual and a successful businessman.

Calvin's radical doctrine of predestination was never widely shared, even among Protestants. But a more secular version of Protestant business ethics did become an important part of western popular culture. It is to the Protestant ethic that we owe our contemporary effort to understand the relationship between being a virtuous person—or an ethical corporation—and being financially successful—or profitable.

Irving Kristol has described 19th century America as "a society in which it was agreed that there was a strong correlation between certain personal virtues—frugality, industry, sobriety, reliability, piety—and the way in which power, privilege and property were distributed."[9] It was a society in which "success" was associated with "duty performed"—a point which was made repeatedly in the Horatio Alger novels that were read by literally tens of thousands of schoolchildren during the second half of the 19th century as well as in the widely quoted homilies of Benjamin Franklin. Kristol quotes from a description of a leading merchant by Theodore Parker, an influential theologian and Unitarian minister from Boston: "He had no uncommon culture of the understanding or imagination . . . but in respect of the greater faculties—in respect of conscience, affection, the religious element—he was well born, well bred."[10]

Kristol is correct to note that Americans during the 19th century were extremely interested in the relationship between good moral character and success in business. But he appears to have exaggerated the extent to which they invariably regarded the two as closely related. Certainly by the end of the century, many Americans did not share a very high opinion of the character of a number of successful 19th century industrialists. For example, in his *History of the Great American Fortunes*, published in 1909, Gustavus Myers described Jay Gould, an extremely successful financial operator, as a "freebooter," "a pitiless human carnivore, glutting on the blood of his numerous victims . . . a gambler destitute of the usual gambler's codes of fairness in abiding by the rules." This is scarcely the portrait of a man whose accumulation of wealth would have been pleasing to God.[11]

Contemporary discussions of business ethics focus less on questions of individual character than was true a century ago. Indeed, we appear to have almost completely lost sight of the fact that the word ethics is derived from the Greek term *ethikos*, which means, "character." (Hence Aristotle's admonition that techniques of moral reasoning should only be taught to those who were already of good moral character.) Because much economic activity now takes place through organizations, we have become interested less in the character of individual businessmen than in the decision-making processes of business firms. Consequently, we tend to use the terms corporate social responsibility and business ethics almost interchangeably.

In addition, contemporary discussions of business ethics, as well as ethics in general, are overwhelmingly cast in secular terms. The profound Judeo-Christian roots of the western tradition of business ethics are rarely examined. Even those theologians who write about business ethics rarely make any reference to the concepts of sin, evil or divine judgment. Nevertheless, we remain no less preoccupied with the relationship between morality and profits than with Weber's Calvinist merchants or Kristol's 19th century schoolchildren.

Indeed, one's assessment of the relationship between the two can be understood as a virtual litmus test of one's overall appraisal of the ethics of business in contemporary American society. Those who are highly critical of the ethical behavior of American business tend to assume that the relationship between ethics and profits is either random or negative. One indication of the public's poor opinion of the contemporary ethics of American business is that significant segments of the American public believe that companies are likely to behave irresponsibly in order to increase their levels of profitability. And there are certainly Americans who believe that financially successful firms are apt to be less ethical than those on whom the invisible hand has not bestowed material blessings. The latter's view of the ethics of business bears a striking similarity to that held by Augustine and Aquinas, though their reasoning may differ.

On the other hand, a secular variant of the Protestant ethic has now been revived by the mainstream business community. The reports on business ethics issued by such organizations as the Business Roundtable and Touche Ross argue that good ethics is good business.[12] They purport to demonstrate that not only is it possible to be both virtuous and successful, but that the former is a necessary condition of the latter. As the Roundtable statement puts it, ". . . there is no conflict between ethical practices and acceptable profits. Indeed the first is a necessary precondition for the second."[13] Former SEC commissioner John Shad echoes this perspective: "ethics Pays. It's smart to be ethical."[14]

Their position is *not* that socially responsible firms will invariably be profitable. But then neither did the Protestant clergy in either 16th century Europe or 19th century America preach that good people will invariably prosper, or for that matter, that good people were assured of salvation. Rather, what both they and the contemporary leadership of the American business community are asserting is that being "good" or "responsible" is a necessary, though not sufficient condition for succeeding in the marketplace. In other words, while not all virtuous firms and individuals will be successful, all who are successful are likely to have been virtuous.

There is also an implicit corollary which is equally important, namely that those who behave badly will be punished. For the Roundtable, Touche Ross and John Shad, this punishment takes the form of customer or employee dissatisfaction, criticism in the media, both presumably resulting in reduced profits, and, in extreme cases, civil or criminal prosecution. For the Protestant clergy punishment was deferred to the afterlife, though its form was both more consequential and enduring than that commonly meted out by secular authorities and the market. Numerous scholars have attempted to measure the relationship between the social responsibility of a company and its financial performance.[15] Yet while this research is important, in another sense it is also beside the point. After all, the appeal of Calvinism or Horatio Alger did not rest on the demonstrated validity of their causal models. It may make more sense to regard the Business Roundtable's statement as the contemporary, secular equivalent of a Protestant sermon. Like many, if not most of the statements on business ethics made by businessmen, its real purpose is to exhort the business community to improve its moral behavior. And just as the Protestant clergy held out the promise of salvation as a reward for virtue, so does the Roundtable, and virtually all executives, hold out the promise of improved profits as a reward for more ethical business conduct.

While it is true that, in principle, the validity of the latter can be demonstrated in a way that the former cannot, in the final analysis both rest on faith. Equally importantly, both predictions are meant to be self-fulfilling. Thus, if large numbers of executives are to be persuaded that "good ethics is good business," the two in fact are likely to turn out to be positively correlated. Alternatively, if many executives continue to believe that there is a trade-off between the two, then the ethics of business are less likely to improve measurably.

In sum, what is significant is not whether or not ethics and profits are in fact correlated but the fact that our interest in their relationship has a long and distinguished history. The debate over the nature of the relationship between ethics and profits remains central to our appraisal of the moral legitimacy of business. The real significance of the Protestant ethic was its role in legitimating capitalism. Likewise, the contemporary efforts of the business community to equate ethics and profits can in part be understood as a component of their attempt to firm up the moral legitimacy of our contemporary business system. Alternatively, those who argue that a good person cannot succeed in business or that a socially responsible company is handicapped in the marketplace are challenging the ethical foundations of our market economy; they in effect are arguing, as did many medieval Catholic theologians, that an ethical businessman is an oxymoron.

The significance of the emergence of ethical or socially responsible investment funds and programs can also be understood in this context. For like Calvin's sermons and Alger's novels, these funds appeal to the desire of the public to be *both* virtuous and prosperous. They are based on the assumption that not only is there no trade-off between the two, but that in many cases they are mutually reinforcing. For all the progressive political rhetoric that surrounds these funds, their core assumptions are actually quite similar to those of the Business Roundtable. And like the Roundtable, their depiction of the relationship between ethics and profits is also meant to be self-fulfilling: presumably if many investors act on the belief that a responsible firm is also likely to be more profitable, then the price of its shares will rise accordingly. The popularity of these funds suggests that moral issues that troubled Aquinas and Calvin remain: evidently many people are still searching for a way to accumulate capital without sin.

PRIVATE GAIN AND THE PUBLIC GOOD

The notion that successful businessmen were, or at least could also be good human beings constituted one important dimension of the original moral case for capitalism. A second dimension involved a new understanding of the relationship between economic success and the public good.

In pre-market economics, the acquisition of wealth was primarily a zero-sum game. One became wealthy primarily by taking resources from others, usually in the form of taxes or warfare. What made capitalism unique was its claim to have developed a mechanism through which it was possible for an individual to acquire wealth which not only did not make others worse off but actually made them better off! This mechanism was, of course, the market. In principle, in an economy organized according to market principles, the only way to acquire wealth is to satisfy the material needs of others; profits are the reward the businessman receives for successfully fulfilling the legitimate expectations of his employees, customers, and investors.

Wealth accumulated through the market does not subtract from the total volume of goods and services available through the market system: the consumer is no more worse off for having exchanged his money for a commodity than the merchant is poorer because he now has fewer goods and more money. Thanks to the miracle of the market, both are better off than they otherwise would have been, though not necessarily in the same proportion.

Prior to capitalism, virtually all profit tended to be regarded as profiteering; it appeared to be rooted in extortion rather than fair exchange. Accordingly, it was morally suspect. What capitalism did was make money-making ethical. The claim that capitalism was the world's first fair economic system was predicated on the understanding that the merchant, unlike the Roman warrior or the feudal lord, actually *deserved* the material wealth he had accumulated. In short, capitalism was the first social system for which it was possible to claim that the wealthy received their wealth as their just reward for performing a socially useful function.

Centuries after the origin of capitalism, we continue to judge the acquisition of wealth by this standard. Thus, for many free-market oriented economists, the moral case against government intervention in the economy is that it divorces the acquisition of wealth from service to the needs of society as expressed through the market. Protective tariffs, subsidies, tax breaks, legally sanctioned cartels and monopolies—all can be viewed as contemporary versions of mercantilism, the system of business-government relations whose abuses and inequities Smith exhaustively chronicled in *The Wealth of Nations*. Government intervention does, of course, create wealth; that is precisely why Washington is filled with so many thousands of lobbyists. But the moral claim of its critics is that much of the wealth it creates is extorted rather than earned; it reflects political influence rather than social contribution.

Many contemporary economists and political economists tend to regard the government as the primary, if not the exclusive source of illegitimate wealth in contemporary capitalist societies. Even though this perspective tends to overlook the numerous regulations and public expenditures that clearly do make society better off, this focus is not an unreasonable one. It is difficult to read the daily papers without coming across yet another example of a banker or developer who has used his political influence to acquire large sums of money—in each case clearly making significant numbers of his fellow citizens worse off. Adam Smith would surely have not been surprised by the recent scandals at HUD or in the Savings and Loan industry. He would likely have regarded them as an inevitable outgrowth of a system of political economy that rewards political privilege rather than economic performance.

However, for much of the American public, government is not the only source of illegitimate wealth. Many citizens do not share the belief of neo-classical economists in the inherent morality of wealth accumulated through the market. Rather, they are prepared to subject profits earned through the market to the same ethical standards that Smith employed in his critique of the profits derived from mercantilism.

Consider, for example, the response of the American public to the increased earnings of the major integrated oil companies following the oil price rise of 1973. Were these profits deserved? The answer given by the vast majority of gasoline consumers was a resounding "no." Responding to pressures from the electorate, the federal government immediately established price controls on energy prices in an effort to limit oil company profits. And when energy prices were subsequently deregulated, the government imposed a "windfall" or "excess" profits tax on the integrated oil firms in order to prevent them from financially benefitting from the removal of price controls.

Now, from the point of view of neo-classical economics, the notion of an "excess" or "windfall" profit is absolutely without meaning. (One is reminded of the *New Yorker* cartoon in which an elderly executive reading the paper at his club turns to his friend and exclaims: "In all my many years in business, I have yet to see an excess profit!") Rather, these terms only make sense as moral categories.

Why did much of the American public regard the oil companies' earnings as an example of "profiteering"? In other words, why did they consider them to be "undeserved"? There were a number of reasons, but two seem particularly significant. First, they did not appear to reflect any additional effort on the part of the industry. The oil companies, after all, did not report increased earnings in 1974 because they had discovered new oil reserves or improved their operating efficiency. Rather, their increased earnings essentially reflected inventory profits: substantial wealth was being transferred to them for no other reason than that a group of Arab oil ministers had suddenly discovered how to form a successful cartel. Their profits were due less to their economic contribution than to the fact that they happened to be in the right place at the right time; in short, their "fortunes" were due only to their having been fortunate.

Secondly, the good fortune of the oil producers had important distributive consequences: it was accompanied by substantial suffering on the part of American consumers. Indeed, the two appeared to be almost physically linked: it was as if the increased price of gasoline at the pump represented a direct transfer of wealth from consumers to shareholders and executives. The proposed deregulation of energy prices promised to raise gasoline prices still further: many regarded it as unfair for a small group of executives and stockholders to benefit as a result of the sacrifices of millions of ordinary Americans.

Not surprisingly, the maintenance of price controls on energy in the United States throughout the 1970s evokes the medieval concept of the "just price." This term of course also has no economic meaning. Rather, it derives from the notion, widely shared in medieval Europe, that those who controlled access to certain critical commodities, particularly when their control was due to an "act of God" rather than their own initiative, were not entitled to all the profits that the "normal" workings of the market allowed.

Questions about social contribution and fairness have also been raised in connection with the profits received by investment bankers as payment for their efforts to restructure the American economy. Robert Reich has described a segment of the American financial community as, "paper entrepreneurs."[16] Like "windfall profits," "paper entrepreneurship," is a term of moral opprobrium rather than economic analysis. Reich's criticism of the various financial intermediaries who have made large fortunes by buying and selling and putting together and breaking up existing companies is remarkably similar to the medieval church's strictures against usury.

The Church, although it frowned upon all forms of money-making, was particularly critical of banking or money-lending. It argued that it was wrong for someone to be paid back more money than they had lent since the commodity that they lent had not been improved in any way. Gold and silver were essentially "sterile": they represented a convenient way to measure wealth, but they themselves were incapable of adding to the resources available to sustain life. Accordingly, while the farmer or craftsman was entitled to charge for their labors, a banker was not.

This, of course, is precisely why Reich is so critical of the profits earned by Wall Street firms from restructuring the American economy. Reich regards corporations as the exclusive source of "real" wealth: their profits are legitimate because they derive from their efforts to deploy human and material resources to meet various private and public needs. Those, however, who make their living from buying and selling these companies are in a different moral category: paper entrepreneurs are predators, not creators of value. (The authors of *Manufacturing Matters; The Myth of the Post-Industrial Economy* also offer a moral hierarchy of the sources of business profits: only they view manufacturing firms as the ultimate source of "real" national wealth.[17]) Reich views wealth derived from shuffling paper in much the same way that the Church fathers regarded the interest generated by lending specie.

As in the case of the oil company profits in the 1970s, the extraordinary profits earned by lawyers and investment bankers as well as some managers and stockholders during the 1980s, also raises the issue of fairness. If restructuring is essentially a zero-sum game, as its critics allege, then the wealth accumulated by its beneficiaries must be counter-balanced by a reduction in wealth on the part of various other constituencies. The latter includes not only the holders of various financial assets, but, more importantly from the point of view of the public, large numbers of employees. Paper entrepreneurship appears unfair to significant segments of the American public because it has made some better off by making others worse off—which is precisely the pre-capitalist definition of profiteering.

More generally, the public's appraisal of the ethics of restructuring has to do with their perception of its contribution to economic efficiency and productivity. If, on balance, the dramatic changes in the governance of the American economy that took place during the 1980s resulted in making American business *less* productive and efficient, then the profits earned from this activity are clearly not deserved; after all, the moral case for profits rests on their status as a reward for activities that *increase* society's overall material abundance, not those that subtract from it. Alternatively, if paper entrepreneurship has, on balance, contributed to strengthening the long-term performance of the American economy, then its critics are as short-sighted as the medieval church when it prohibited the payment of interest on the grounds that "time belonged to God."

It is in this context that the legitimacy of the substantial fortune accumulated by Michael Milken should be viewed. Milken's defenders have pointed out that as a proportion of the amount of money he was able to raise for companies through the sale of junk bonds, his compensation, though larger in 1988 than the profits of all but a handful of corporations, was not excessive. On the other hand, the amount of Milken's personal wealth was specifically referred to in the opening pages of the U.S. Attorney's indictment of him for violating the securities laws. Both of these statements miss the point. At issue is not the size of Milken's fortune but who benefitted from his accumulation of it. (Obviously, because Milken violated the law, he deserves to be punished. But while how much he gained as a result of his illegal activities might affect his sentence, it certainly is irrelevant to his guilt or innocence; in a capitalist system, making a lot of money is not a crime.)

If one judges the development of junk bond financing to have made a positive contribution to the ability of large numbers of American corporations to accumulate the funds they need to grow and expand, then Milken's compensation cannot be considered unreasonable. On the other hand, if one regards junk bond financing as having amounted to little more than asset reshuffling at best, and asset stripping at worst, then Milken's compensation was not deserved—regardless of its amount. In this context, it is striking that in the movie "Wall Street" the unethical trader played by Michael Douglas explicitly justifies his financial machinations in zero-sum terms.

As he puts it, "It's a zero-sum gain. Somebody wins and somebody loses. Money isn't gained, it's transferred. I create nothing I own." It would be hard for anyone to come up with a clearer ethical indictment of the ethics of restructuring.

It is important to stress that in each of these cases, the morality of profits has nothing to do with their magnitude. It is true that if the sums made by the oil industry and investment bankers were not significant, hardly anyone would care whether or not they were deserved. But many athletes, entertainers and "real" entrepreneurs make substantial sums of money without their ethics being called into question by the public. And certainly during the 1980s many high-tech firms reported increases in profits comparable to that enjoyed by the oil industry during the previous decade. And yet no one has ever suggested subjecting them to a "wind-fall" profits tax.

In this context, it is also worth noting that many homeowners in New York, Washington, D.C., and California have experienced a dramatic increase in wealth due to their good fortune in having bought a home in the right place at the right time. Their profits are clearly no more—or less deserved—than those of the oil industry. And yet no one has ever proposed subjecting them to a "windfall home profits tax," although Henry George, who wrote before home ownership became widespread, advocated a tax on land for precisely this reason. And while housing is no less a critical commodity than energy, no one outside of Berkeley, California, has seriously proposed the establishment of price controls on the sale of private homes. Evidently, the public's view of business ethics is not immune to calculations of its own material interests.

The distinction between the wealth accumulated by Bill Cosby and Apple Computer on one hand, and Michael Milken and Exxon on the other has no basis whatsoever in economic theory. Rather, it rests on a moral distinction that dates back several centuries. Medieval economic thought, although all but forgotten except by a handful of scholars, continues to exercise an important hold on our collective moral imagination. For some products, sold under certain circumstances, significant segments of the public continue to believe in the concept of a "just price." And they also continue to hold that not all wealth or profits are created equal; some are more deserved than others.

INTENTIONS AND RESULTS

Adam Smith wrote in *The Wealth of Nations*:

> It is not from the benevolence of the butcher, the brewer, or the baker, that we expect our dinner, but from their regard to their own self-

interest. We address ourselves, not to their humanity but to their self-love, and never talk to them of our own necessities but of their advantages.[18]

These often quoted lines capture the moral contradiction that lies at the heart of capitalism: capitalism is a system in which morally dubious intentions combine to produce morally beneficial results. On one hand, we do get the food that we need to survive—certainly no mean accomplishment in a world in which hunger was once commonplace. But on the other hand, the way we achieve this happy outcome is by paradoxically assuming that the providers of food are indifferent as to whether or not we are actually fed.

If one judges the ethics of capitalism by its results, then the system deserves our unequivocal moral approbation. By any conceivable indicae, appealing to the self-interest of humanity "works": market economies have produced more wealth and greater economic security for more individuals than even their most ardent defenders in the 18th and 19th centuries ever thought possible. The performance of capitalism with respect to improving the quality of life is equally impressive. And no other economic system has proven even remotely as compatible with liberty and democracy.

Yet, to borrow from the title of Irving Kristol's collection of essays, while capitalism may deserve "two cheers," it evidently does not appear to merit "three." Why not? I think the explanation has to do with the appeal to self-interest that is at the core of the modus operandi of a market economy.[19] The issue of motives constitutes the moral Achilles heel of capitalism. Notwithstanding its impressive results, many remain uncomfortable with a system of political economy in which the relationship among economic actors is essentially based on selfishness.

There have been a number of efforts to address this moral issue, none of them very satisfactory. In *The Passions and the Interests*, Albert Hirschman presents the ideas of a number of 18th and 19th century thinkers who argued the moral case for capitalism on the basis of the ethical superiority of its motives.[20] They favorably contrasted a society in which people sought to maximize their interests with one in which people were ruled by their passions. As Montesquieu wrote, ". . . it is fortunate for men to be in a situation in which, though their passions may prompt them to be wicked, they have nevertheless an interest in not being so."[21]

Now it may well be the case, to cite Samuel Johnson's famous epigram, that, "there are few ways in which a man can be more innocently employed than in getting money."[22] Certainly, when one compares the profit motive to the wide range of homicidal and genocidal passions that have motivated the behavior of no small number of individuals in the course of human history, the case for the moral superiority of the former is clear. Keynes' judgment is surely correct: "it is better that a man should tyrannize over his bank balance than over his fellow citizens."[23] Would that Hitler or Stalin were profit-maximizers!

However, the last few centuries have also demonstrated that far from calming men's passions, the pursuit of money can just as easily inflame them. Connie Bruck's portrait of Michael Milken reveals a man driven not so much by the rational pursuit of self-interest as a possessed megalomaniac—hardly the kind of individual that one presumes Montesquieu had in mind.[24]

Moreover, while the pursuit of material self-interest may be preferable to some motives for human activity, it is hardly superior to many of them. Much of the ethical appeal of socialism in the West has derived precisely from the moral superiority of the motives that it has proposed to substitute for the pursuit of material self-interest. It remains far more uplifting to exhort people to "love one another" than to "maximize their utilities," even though the latter may in fact be more socially beneficial. And it is worth recalling that of the seven deadly sins, three, namely greed, envy and gluttony play a central role in the proper functioning of market economies. Economists have persuaded us of their utility; but our need to rely upon them so heavily still makes many uneasy.

Perhaps the most audacious effort to reconcile the motives of capitalists with the results of capitalism can be found in George Gilder's *Wealth and Poverty*.[25] Gilder argues that capitalism begins, not with material self-interest, but with "giving." Because the investor has no guarantee of return on his investment, his investment effectively constitutes a gift to the community. And like the gifts of the South Sea Islanders, it is given in the hope that it will be reciprocated. This argument has persuaded no one: as one of his numerous critics put it, Gilder's attempt to equate giving and investing is as likely to give philanthropy a bad name as capitalism a good one.

Yet at the same time, his analysis, perhaps unwittingly, also helps make sense of both the pervasiveness and widespread public appeal of corporate philanthropy. In fact, corporate philanthropy fits Gilder's model far better than does business investment. For philanthropy clearly takes the form of the giving of gifts, without any guarantee of return. Yet at the same time, the gifts given by corporations are commonly understood to be motivated not simply by altruism, but by the firm's long-term interests. They thus represent a kind of happy medium between a genuine gift, whose primary purpose is to improve the welfare of the recipient, and an investment, whose only purpose is to maximize the wealth of the investor.

Not surprisingly, corporate philanthropy has been criticized from both the left and the right. One set of critics have attacked it for failing to serve the objectives of the firm's stockholders: they argue that too much corporate philanthropy goes to organizations and institutions that are hostile to business. Another group of critics attack it for precisely the opposite reason: they question its legitimacy on the grounds that its *real* purpose is to improve the image of the company and thus it is misleading to describe it as philanthropic. The paradox of corporate philanthropy is that the more the public perceives it as altruistic, the more effectively it serves the self-interest of the company that provides it.

Michael Novak's *The Spirit of Democratic Capitalism* represents another contemporary effort to improve the moral status of capitalism by redefining the motives that underlie it. Novak notes that, "like prudence in Aristotelian thought, self-interest in democratic capitalist thought has an inferior reputation among moralists."[26] He argues however that it is misleading to equate "self-interest" with greed or acquisitiveness. Rather, self-interest also encompasses "religious and moral interests, artistic and scientific interests, and interests in peace and justice," as well as concern for the well-being of one's family, friends and country.[27]

But while it is certainly true that much behavior in capitalist societies is self-interested rather than selfish, this is decidedly not the case for those activities that fall within the sphere of economics. The predictive power of neo-classical economics rests precisely on the fact that consumers, investors and employers do define their self-interest primarily, if not exclusively, in pecuniary terms. It is possible to deplore the extent to which our economic system rests on economic self-interest; it is not however appropriate to deny it.

The doctrine of corporate social responsibility also can be understood as part of this ongoing effort to reconcile the "intentions" and "results" of capitalism. It does this in part by fudging the issue: no small part of the nearly universal appeal of the doctrine of corporate social responsibility rests on the fact that there is no agreement as to what is meant by it. Proponents of corporate social responsibility do not deny the legitimacy of the profit motive. Rather they seek to redefine it in a way that also encompasses other, more public spirited purposes. The notion of the "corporate conscience" represents an attempt to humanize the firm, to endow its managers with a range of motivations that are not restricted to the selfish pursuit of wealth. Likewise, the adjective "enlightened" in the commonly used phrase "enlightened self-interest" is clearly meant to soften the harshness of the noun that follows it, while the term "self-interest," taken directly from Adam Smith, is presumably intended to serve as a euphemism for selfishness.

But the use of this phrase begs a critical issue. For what happens when there is a conflict between the concerns of a manager for the welfare of society and the material interests of a company's shareholders? The response of the free-market oriented position is clear: since society is best served when executives intend to maximize the interests of their shareholders, the latter's preferences should be given priority. Indeed, one important conservative criticism of corporate social responsibility is precisely that it gives businessmen "credit" for serving society only when they are engaged in activities that are *not* primarily motivated by shareholder interests, thus undermining a central moral *raison d'etre* of a market economy.

The response of the advocates of corporate responsibility is to deny that there is a tension between the intentions and results: common to virtually every exposition of the doctrine of corporate social responsibility is the belief that, in the long-run, what is in the interests of "society" is also in the interests of business and *vice-versa*. Thus those firms who intend to do good will also wind up doing well. This is also the position of the socially responsible investment movement. Much of the popularity of "socially responsible" investment vehicles rests on their claim to have resolved the tension between "bad" intentions and "good" results that characterizes a market economy: they enable investors to hold on to their good intentions without sacrificing their rate of return. And much of the claim for the need to instruct businessmen in ethics rests on a similar social vision.

This position is evidently an appealing one, but unfortunately it is not terribly persuasive. For if corporate social responsibility amounts to nothing more than enlightened self-interest, then why would anyone need to devote any special effort to understand it or to urge others to pursue it? For that matter, what would be the point of teaching ethics to present or future managers? Why not simply teach them how to become more intelligent or sophisticated profit maximizers? Likewise, if socially responsible funds offer their investors market rate of returns, then what is the point of creating them?

The fact that so much effort is devoted to preaching to both executives and investors about their social and moral responsibilities suggests that more than two centuries after Adam Smith, we are still uncomfortable with an economic system that relies so heavily on the motive of selfishness to achieve its goals—however laudable. The moral paradox that Adam Smith so insightfully described more than two centuries ago remains with us; we are no closer than he was to resolving it.

Conclusion

This essay has attempted to retrace some of the historical roots of the ways in which we now think and talk about the ethics of business. It has done so by focusing on the terms of public discourse about a wide range of contemporary issues in business ethics. In this sense, it really represents a kind of introduction to the *politics* of business ethics. By comparing various contemporary and historical examples of business conduct in a wide range of areas, I have attempted to explore why, how and under what circumstances various aspects of business activity have come to be viewed by significant segments of the public as either ethical or unethical.

Admittedly, the specific ethical standards for which we hold managers and their companies responsible have changed considerably in recent years. Many of the contemporary moral controversies that surround the activities of business were unanticipated two decades ago, let alone during the 13th or 17th centuries. And doubtless others will subsequently emerge that we cannot now imagine. But too much contemporary writing on business ethics is dominated by a focus on current events. We are too ready to assume that the ethical dilemmas that business now faces are somehow unique or unprecedented.

However, many of the problems and issues that those who currently write about business ethics are attempting to address are not new. Rather, they are rooted in the nature of a market economy, if not in human nature itself. This does not make our contemporary concerns or standards any the less valid; on the contrary, by emphasizing their deep roots in the western ethical tradition, it underlies their importance. The contemporary literature on business ethics can thus be understood as part of an ongoing moral dialogue with deep secular and religious roots.

The relationship between ethics and profits, the connection between private gain and the public good and the tensions between the motives of economic actors and the results of market competition—these concerns have been with us for centuries. Our ability to understand many aspects of contemporary business ethics can be enriched by examining the ways in which previous generations of ethicists, religious as well as secular, have wrestled with many of the same dilemmas that now confront us.

NOTES

1. The most important exception to this generalization is Peter Drucker, "What is 'Business Ethics'?" *The Public Interest*, Spring, 1981, pp. 18–37. Unfortunately, virtually the only occasion when this article is cited is when someone wishes to criticize it.

2. This omission is particularly striking in Amitai Etzioni, *The Moral Dimension* (New York: Free Press, 1988).

3. One notable exception is Saul Englebourg, *Power and Morality; American Business Ethics, 1840–1914* (Westport: Greenwood Press, 1980).

4. See for example, Maury Klein, *The Life and Legend of Jay Gould* (Baltimore: Johns Hopkins, 1986). For a fascinating history of American business values, which includes material both sympathetic to and critical of business, see Peter Baida, *Poor Richard's Legacy: American Business Values from Benjamin Franklin to Donald Trump* (New York: William Morrow and Company, 1990).

5. Quoted in Gordon Marshall, *In Search of the Spirit of Capitalism* (New York: Columbia University Press, 1982), p. 34.

6. Robert Heilbroner, *The Making of Economic Society* (Englewood Cliffs: Prentice-Hall, 1962), p. 39.

7. Quoted in Paul Blumberg, *The Predatory Society* (New York: Oxford University Press, 1989), p. 5–6.

8. Ibid., p. 104.

9. Irving Kristol, *Two Cheers for Capitalism* (New York: Basic Books, 1978), p. 261.

10. Kristol, op. cit., p. 261.

11. Quoted in *Jay Gould*, p. 1.

12. See David Vogel, "Ethics and Profits Don't Always Go Hand in Hand," *Los Angeles Times*, December 28, 1988, Part II, p. 7.

13. Ibid.

14. Ibid.

15. See for example, Jean McGuire, Alison Sundgren, and Thomas Scheenweis, "Corporate Social Responsibility and Firm Financial Performance," *Academy of Management Journal*, vol. 31, no. 4, pp. 854–71.

16. See for example, Robert Reich, *The Resurgent Liberal* (New York: Times Books, 1989), chapter 2.

17. Stephen S. Cohen and John Zysman, *Manufacturing Matters; The Myth of the Post-Industrial Economy* (New York: Basic Books, 1987).

18. Adam Smith, *An Inquiry into the Nature and Causes of the Wealth of Nations* (New York: Modern Library, 1937), p. 14.

19. A similar point is made in Joseph Schumpeter, *Capitalism, Socialism and Democracy* (New York: Harper and Row, 1950).

20. Albert Hirschman, *The Passions and the Interests* (Princeton: Princeton University Press, 1977).

21. Ibid., p. 73.

22. Ibid., p. 58.

23. Ibid., p. 134.

24. Connie Bruck, *The Predators Ball* (New York: Simon and Schuster, 1988).

25. George Glider, *Wealth and Poverty* (New York: Basic Books, 1981).

26. Michael Novak, *The Spirit of Democratic Capitalism* (New York: Simon and Schuster, 1982), p. 93.

27. Ibid., p. 94.

Chapter Eight

WHEN CONSUMERS OPPOSE CONSUMER PROTECTION: THE POLITICS OF REGULATORY BACKLASH

THE POLITICS of health, safety and environmental regulation in the United States primarily revolve around conflicts between business and non-business constituencies over the creation, enforcement and renewal of the numerous regulatory statutes enacted since the early 1960s. Business interests have generally tended to oppose these forms of 'social' regulation on the grounds of their high costs. Consumer and environmental organizations have, in turn, generally supported increased restrictions on business in order to protect the health and safety of the public and increase the supply of various public goods. However, not all political conflicts over social regulation have followed this pattern.

Some scholars, in an effort to explain the political resiliency of health, safety and environmental regulation during the 1970s and 1980s, have noted that the business community has by no means been united in its opposition to social regulation. On the contrary, various firms and industries have on occasion supported the retention, or even the strengthening of protective regulations when they have seen them as a source of competitive advantage (see, for example, Leone 1989 and McCormick 1989). Other studies have documented that business has not been the only source of opposition to government regulation of corporate social conduct. For example, unions and state and local governments have at times cooperated with business interests to oppose federal controls that threaten the economic interests of their members or constituents, particularly in the area of environmental regulation. (See Vogel 1984.)

This chapter explores yet another dimension of the politics of protective regulation. It examines four controversies in which the primary opposition to health and safety regulation came from consumers. In each case, significant numbers of individuals whom the regulation was designed to protect campaigned successfully to have it withdrawn or changed. These cases depart from the typical pattern of consumer politics in two respects. First, the established consumer movement, which supported these health and safety rules, found itself opposed not by business but by consumers. Secondly, in three of the four cases, business played virtually no role in the effort to reduce the scope of government regulation, while in the fourth its role was marginal.

In 1974 Congress responded to the complaints of many motorists by forbidding the National Highway Traffic Safety Administration (NHTSA) requiring that all new automobiles be equipped with an engine-interlock system. (Foreman, Jr., 1988: 120–126, Mashaw and Harfst, 1990: 124–140, 202–223.) Two years later, Congress yielded to the protests of large numbers of motorcyclists by repealing a NHTSA rule that required states to forbid motorcyclists or their passengers from riding without a helmet. (Mashaw and Harfst, 1990: 229–230.) In 1977 Congress responded to a grass-roots effort organized by the American Diabetes Association and supported by the manufacturers and business consumers of low-calorie products by overturning the Food and Drug Administration's ban on the artificial sweetener, saccharin. (Cummings 1986: 130–136, Forman 1988: 138–141.) Finally, beginning in 1987, the Food and Drug Administration began to yield to pressures from the gay community and its supporters by agreeing to streamline its procedures for the testing and approval of new drugs designed to fight AIDS and other fatal diseases (Vogel 1989a).

Each of these cases has been examined by scholars and this article draws in part on their research. No one however has explored the links among these four cases nor attempted to assess their significance for our understanding of the politics of protective regulation. This article briefly summarizes the emergence and outcome of these four conflicts and then attempts to place them in a broader context, in order to address the question: why have there been so few cases of successful consumer opposition to health and safety regulation?

Seat Belts

In 1967 the National Highway Traffic Safety Administration, acting under the authority of the National Traffic Safety and Motor Vehicle Safety Act of 1966, required the installation of seat belts in all new vehicles. Two years later, frustrated by the continued low rate of seat belt usage, the agency began to explore the option of requiring the installation of passive-restraint systems that would automatically protect vehicle occupants. In 1971 the agency announced that it intended to require inflatable air bags to be installed on all vehicles beginning in 1973. After automobile manufacturers complained that they needed additional time to comply with this requirement,

NHTSA proposed that, as an interim measure, seat belt systems with ignition interlocks be placed on all new vehicles beginning in 1974.

Automobile manufacturers were divided about the merits of the interlock proposal; on balance they strongly preferred it to the mandatory installation of air bags. General Motors expressed concern that consumers might 'become so annoyed by the inconvenience of the starter interlock feature that they would have the entire system disconnected' (Foreman 1988). GM also worried about the reliability of the interlock device; its engineers predicted that many cars would not start even after the occupant's belts were buckled. Ralph Nader's Center for Automobile Safety opposed the interim rule, arguing that seat belts were significantly inferior to air bags as a means of protecting drivers and their passengers, especially small children. Nader's Center also shared GM's concerns about the reliability of the ignition interlock system. Nonetheless, most auto safety advocates supported the agency's compromise proposal since it offered an immediate way of increasing seat belt usage and thus reducing automotive injuries.

The Department of Transportation did modify its original proposal slightly. It permitted the interlock system to be bypassed in an emergency by installing an 'override' button under the hood. It also added a built-in delay feature that enabled the car to be restarted for up to three minutes after the ignition had been turned off. (The provision was designed to make life easier for parking lot attendants.) On the other hand, in order to prevent drivers and their front-seat passengers from bypassing the system by keeping their seat belts permanently buckled—as many had done to get around the existing buzzer-and-light warning system—NHTSA required that a device be installed that prevented the car from starting unless the car's occupants sat down immediately before fastening their seat belts.

In the summer of 1973, a few months before the 1974 model cars were due to go on sale, the Department of Transportation mounted a major public relations campaign to inform car buyers of the new policy. A spokesman for the NHTSA stated, 'We've got about two months to tell 200 million people about the interlock (Karr 1973: 12), adding that the Department was concerned that if people first became aware of the system after having purchased the 1974 model cars, they would become extremely angry.' Nonetheless the public began to complain about the new safety device as soon as the 1974 model automobiles left the showroom. *The New York Times* reported that 'a check of new car owners around the country shows that the government-mandated safety device is almost universally disliked' (Quotes from Irvin 1974: 20). Dealers reported that most new car owners found the system 'objectionable.' While no statistics were released by either the manufacturers or the Department of Transportation as to the actual failure rate—automobile engineers had predicted a rate of 3 per cent—there were widespread reports of defects.

New car owners began discontinuing the interlock systems almost immediately. Their actions were not illegal. It was only against the law for a manufacturer or a dealer to deliver a car with the interlock device deactivated. A survey of new car owners conducted by the Ford Motor Company in April 1974 reported that one-third had removed the interlock device. By August, apparently one million motorists—or about four out of every 10 new car owners—had disconnected the system. One car owner explained, 'It spoiled the whole feel of the car. I felt like I was strapped in a high chair all the time' ('Drivers . . .' 1974: 30). Nevertheless, the majority of new car owners did not disconnect the safety device and, as a result, seat belt usage was higher than ever before (Minor 1984: 8). During the first six months of 1974, automobile deaths were 6,000 lower than they had been during the previous year. NHTSA publicly attributed this reduction to the interlock system, though it is likely that the reduction in driving due to the 1973 energy crisis also played a role ('Drivers . . .' 1974).

During the summer and fall 1974, members of Congress began to receive an increasing volume of mail from constituents angry with the new regulation. Most appeared to regard it as a 'clear case of Washington bureaucrats gone berserk' (Foreman 1988: 124). *Motor Trend* reported that 76 per cent of drivers polled were opposed to the interlock while Hertz officials stated that drivers had ripped out the systems on a majority of their rental cars (Marshaw and Harfst 1990: 135).

While there was no organized lobbying against the interlock system, members of Congress were well aware of their constituents' hostility toward the new safety regulation. On 11 July 1974 the House Interstate and Foreign Commerce Committee issued an amendment to the National Highway Traffic Safety Act that gave manufacturers the option of substituting a sequential warning system for the interlock device; purchasers could then choose between the two. The sequential warning system activated a buzzer and warning light if the seat belt was not fastened, but the car still started. However, by the time the bill reached the floor of the House, even this modification no longer appeared to be sufficient.

Representative Louis Wyman (Rep-N.Y.) offered a 'citizens' rights' amendment that allowed the automobile manufacturers to offer either a sequential warning system or a passive restraint system but forbade the Department of Transportation from requiring either. His amendment only permitted DOT to require that manufacturers install a dashboard light that would flash if seat belts were not fastened. 'The Wyman amendment caught safety activists by surprise. . . . The rhetoric of prudent paternalism was no match for visions of technology and "big brotherism" gone mad' (Mashaw and Harfst 1990: 135). The House approved the Wyman amendment by a vote of 339 to 40.

A roughly similar measure was introduced by Senators Thomas Eagleton and James Buckley. It was strongly opposed by Senators Magnuson and Hartke and other members of the 'safety coalition' in the Senate, but was subsequently passed by a vote of 64–21. Even the majority of the Senate Commerce Committee, which had played a central role in the enactment of the automotive safety legislation during the mid 1960s, voted for the Eagleton-Buckley amendment. (Pertschuk 1982; 5–28, and Calvert, Moran and Weingast 1987.) Legislation forbidding the NHTSA from requiring technology that interfered with the ability of motorists to decide whether or not they wore their seat belts was subsequently signed into law by President Ford.

MOTORCYCLE HELMETS

In 1967 NHTSA issued an additional series of vehicle safety standards designed to implement the National Traffic and Motor Vehicle Safety Act of 1966. One of these standards required the states to enact legislation requiring the mandatory use of safety helmets and eye protectors by motorcycle operators and their passengers. States that failed to do so faced a reduction of federal highway funds. By 1975 all but three states had adopted the mandatory helmet requirement. This regulation was subsequently upheld by a U.S. Circuit Court, which ruled that government had a legitimate interest in protecting its citizens from injury. This court held that 'we do not find the right to ride helmetless to be a personal right that can be deemed fundamental or implicit in the concept of ordered liberty' ('Lid Put . . .' 1976: E3).

The mandatory helmet requirement proved very unpopular among many motorcyclists and they held noisy demonstrations at a number of state capitals. But fearful of losing federal highway funds, only two states repealed their mandatory helmet laws. Consequently, the motorcyclists decided to focus their attention at the federal level. They established an organization called ABATE (A Brotherhood Against Totalitarian Enactments) which, along with the American Motorcycle Association, sought to persuade Congress to overturn the NHTSA rule.

In September, 1975, Senator Jesse Helms of North Carolina introduced legislation forbidding the NHTSA to require the states to mandate helmet use. He argued, 'The government has no business telling the individual when he can or cannot wear a helmet when only the individual's personal safety is involved' (McCarthy 1976). His position was supported by Senator James Abzourek, who stated that, 'people rightfully resent laws which protect them only from themselves' (Mashaw and Harfst 1990: 229). The editor of *Road Rider* urged motorcyclists to demonstrate their support for the Helms proposal: 'Right now we've got to scream our mandatory helmeted heads off to stop the feds and their murderous "safety" drive' (McCarthy, 1976).

In November, a large band of angry motorcylists drove through the streets of Washington, D.C., and loudly circled the nation's capital. A group of motorcyclists subsequently attended a Senate hearing on the Helms legislation. One senator took a look at the hundreds of people crowded into the hearing room, put his hand over his microphone, turned to one of his colleagues and stated, 'If these are the kind of people whose (expletive deleted) lives we are trying to protect, let's rescind the regulation and let the (expletive deleted) motorcyclists get their (expletive deleted) skulls bashed in' (confidential interview with author).

There was no active lobbying in support of the requirement, though it was backed by a number of insurance companies and indeed surveys reported that most motorcyclists favored it. On 16 May 1976, President Ford signed the Federal Aid Highway Act, which among other provisions, ended the Federal Government's authority to withhold highway construction funds if states did not enact mandatory helmets.

Between 1977 and 1980, motorcyclists demonstrated at a number of state capitals to urge repeal of state mandatory helmet laws. Joan Claybrook, who became head of NHTSA in 1977, noted, 'many states . . . interpreted the repeal of our authority to impose sanctions as a signal to revoke their helmet laws' (Knight, 1980: F1). By 1980, only 21 states, plus the District of Columbia, still required the use of helmets. The result was a significant decline in their use. According to federal researchers, more than 95 per cent of motorcyclists continued to wear helmets in states that keep their use mandatory, but only 55 to 60 per cent still wore them in states that had made them voluntary.

The impact of this change in federal regulatory policy was dramatic. Motorcyclist deaths had declined 40 per cent after the state mandatory helmet laws went into effect in the late 1960S. But between 1976 and 1979, deaths due to motorcycle accidents increased by 46 per cent. In 1976, motorcycle accidents claimed 3,312 lives; in 1979, they resulted in 4,850 fatalities. There was a two to threefold increase in the frequency of head injuries in states that had replaced their laws and almost a fourfold increase in the severity of head injuries among motorcyclists in those states that had repealed their laws (Knight 1980). According to one study, the repeal led to a $16 to $18 million increase in unnecessary medical expenditures, a significant share of which was borne by taxpayers, since many motorcyclists had little or no health insurance (Brody 1980).

SACCHARIN

On 9 March 1977 the Food and Drug Administration announced that it proposed to ban the use of saccharin in all foods, beverages and cosmetics sold in the United States. The FDA's decision was mandated by the Delaney clause, an amendment to the Food, Drug and Cosmetic Act which stated that 'no additive shall be deemed to be safe if it is found to induce cancer when ingested by man or animal' (Cummings 1986: 133).

While saccharin had been used as an inexpensive substitute for sugar in the United States since the turn of the century, its use was initially restricted in various ways by all but three states. These restrictions were primarily the result of pressures by soft drink bottlers and food processors who feared competition for their higher-priced sugar products. However, during the 1960S as a distinctive market began to develop for diet drinks and food products, the restrictions were repealed. As a result, between 1961 and 1977 saccharin consumption increased at the rate of nearly 25 per cent per year.

The public's increased use of saccharin brought the food additive to the attention of regulatory officials. In 1968, the National Academy of Sciences issued a study reporting that while consumption of saccharin at the level of one gram or less per day appeared to be safe, additional research was warranted. In the early 1970S, a number of animal experiments were conducted with saccharin, two of which found that the artificial sweetener increased the incidence of bladder tumors in male rats, especially in the second generation (GAO 1976). The National Academy of Sciences was asked by the FDA to review these studies and in 1974 the Academy concluded that the scientific evidence was inconclusive.

However, in 1977, the Health Protection Branch, the Canadian equivalent of the FDA, released the results of an extensive and highly sophisticated two-generation study of rats. It confirmed earlier reports that a diet of 5 per cent saccharin had increased the incidence of bladder tumors in male rats. Subsequently, saccharin was banned in Canada, and shortly afterward, acting on the basis of the Canadian study, the FDA proposed that its use be prohibited in the United States as well. However the FDA indicated that it would consider applications for marketing saccharin as an over-the-counter drug.

Donald Kennedy, the FDA's new director, explained, 'our intention is to eliminate the risk of cancer from unnecessary uses of saccharin while continuing its availability for people who may need it for medical purposes' (CQA 1977: 496). The ban was expected to become effective following the mandatory 60-day period for public comments.

Eight years earlier, in 1969, the FDA had banned the use of the other commonly used sweetener, namely cyclamates, on similar grounds. Both consumers and the food industry had preferred saccharin to cyclamates, since the former had no aftertaste and was more versatile. The FDA's ban thus created little difficulty for either the manufacturers or consumers of diet products, since most firms were able to switch immediately to saccharin. Ironically, subsequent research revealed that cyclamates were indeed safe (Cummings 1986: 128). However, because the ban on cyclamates remained in effect, prohibiting saccharin meant that no artificial sweetener was now available. The Canadians did not face this problem since they had not earlier banned cyclamates; consequently, the saccharin ban created no controversy in Canada.

Congress was immediately deluged with an avalanche of complaints from many consumers who claimed they needed saccharin because of illness or obesity. 'Some members reported receiving more mail and phone calls on this than on any other issue in years' (CQA 1971: 495). The FDA was also swamped with protest mail. One official stated, 'We've been getting about 1500 letters a day, the largest amount of mail we've ever had on a single issue' ('Saccharin-Product . . .' 1977: 72). Citing her 'inalienable right to live a normal healthy life,' a diabetic in Louisiana sued the FDA to block the proposed ban. The *New Republic* (1977: 7) noted, 'Consumers have not been so angry at their protectors since Ralph Nader had the government put buzzers on seat belts.'

Both the American Diabetes Association and the Juvenile Diabetes Foundation announced their opposition to the proposed ban. The latter organization contended that without easy access to saccharin-sweetened drinks and foods, the nation's 300,000 children affected with diabetes would be further denied a normal childhood (Cummings 1986). Several doctors also expressed their disapproval of the ban. Dr. Oscar Crawford, a member of the National Diabetes Advisory Board, asked at a news conference held at the Department of Health, Education and Welfare: 'As we try to solve one problem, are we creating other problems that are worse from a public health standpoint?' (Weintraub 1977: 11). The American Medical Association subsequently voted to oppose the ban.

Opposition to this regulation also came from the business community. It was led by the Calorie Control Council, an organization primarily funded by bottlers of low-calorie soft drinks. The Council's president called the FDA action 'an example of colossal government overregulation in disregard of science and the needs and wants of consumers' ('How Sweet . . .' 1977). The soft drink industry had failed to mobilize against the banning of cyclamates in 1969 because a substitute artificial sweetener existed, namely saccharin. But the FDA's ban on saccharin threatened to destroy the market for low-calorie drinks, which represented about 11 per cent of all soft drink sales.

The Calorie Control Council hired the public relations firm Hill and Knowlton to organize a major media campaign against the FDA decision. They questioned the scientific basis of the FDA's decision, noting that the rats in the Canadian study had been fed the equivalent of 800 cans of diet soda or 4,000 packets of saccharin a day. Moreover, in the more than 80 years that people had been consuming saccharin, not a single case of an adverse effect on a human being had been reported (*New York Times* 1977: IV:8).

Within a week of the FDA's announcement, a dozen bills were introduced in the Congress to either amend the Delaney clause or make saccharin an exception to it. Pressures on Congress intensified throughout the summer (Lyons 1977: A18). Both the House and the Senate subsequently passed legislation suspending the FDA's ban on saccharin. The differences between the House and Senate versions primarily revolved around the exact language that would be required to be placed on saccharin products and posted in retail stores where saccharin products were sold. On both issues, the House gave in to somewhat stricter requirements of the Senate. A number of bills were subsequently introduced to repeal the Delaney clause, but none were ever acted upon. Congress, however, has continued to renew its prohibition of the FDA's banning of saccharin each time the previous restriction has expired, even though an additional artificial sweetener, Aspertame, was subsequently approved for use.

DRUG APPROVAL AND AIDS

The 1962 Kefauver amendments to the Food, Drug and Cosmetic Act, tightened the procedures for the approval of new prescription drugs in the United States. The average cost of developing a new drug increased from $1.3 million in 1960 to $50 million in 1979. In 1979, it took the average drug approximately 10 years to get through the FDA's testing process, four times longer than before 1962 (AEI 1979: 35–36).

Compared to other nations, such as Great Britain, West Germany and Switzerland, American regulatory procedures were now both more expensive and more time-consuming. Nearly four times as many new medicines were introduced in Great Britain as in the United States during the 1960s (AEI 1979). A subsequent study by the Government Accounting Office (GAO) tracking the introduction of 14 significant new drugs, found that 13 were available in Europe years before they were approved for use in the United States. A West German study reported that while the United States remained, by a wide margin, the leading producer of new drugs, it ranked ninth out of twelve countries studied in being the first nation to make drugs available to its citizens (AEI 1979).

In 1979 the House Committee on Science and Technology held 'the first hearings in the history of the FDA that were designed to show that the agency was overly cautious, rather than not cautious enough in regulating new drugs' (Foreman 1988: 45). The following year, Democratic Representative James Scheurer of New York, the chairman of a House Science and Technology Subcommittee, wrote (*New York Times* 22 May 1980): 'The Food and Drug Administration is contributing to needless suffering and death for thousands because it is denying them life-saving and life-enhancing drugs that are available abroad far sooner than they are here.' The FDA's requirements for approving new drugs remained unchanged. Congress showed no inclination to amend the 1962 amendments, and, equally important, FDA officials remained unwilling to interpret them more flexibly.

The explanation for the agency's commitment to the regulatory status quo is straightforward: the political costs to the FDA of approving a drug that turned out to be unsafe or ineffective were far higher than those incurred by delaying the approval of a drug that turned out to be safe. Those who suffered as a result of America's drug lag were not politically organized; indeed, with a handful of individual exceptions they did not even realize they were being deprived of potentially effective new drugs. On the other hand, should the FDA approve a drug that turned out to be unsafe or ineffective—as it still did on occasion—the agency would find itself subject to widespread congressional and public disapproval. These 'victims' were readily identifiable and had powerful allies in Congress, the public interest movement and the press. As a former FDA Commissioner observed: 'The message to the agency staff was very clear. Whenever a controversy over a drug is resolved by approval, the agency and the individuals involved will likely be investigated. Whenever a drug is disapproved, no inquiry will be made' (Kelly 1981: 100).

However, in the mid-1980s, the politics of the drug approval process in the United States changed dramatically. This change was precipitated by the emergence and spread of AIDS, a fatal disease that initially disproportionately affected male homosexuals. Three factors made the politics surrounding the medical treatment of AIDS unique. First, unlike virtually all of the diseases whose sufferers had previously been adversely affected by the drug lag, AIDS was fatal. Second, because the disease was new, no existing drugs were available to treat it. Third, and most importantly, those who suffered from the delay in the FDA's approval of drugs to treat AIDS were politically articulate. Not only did they know who they were, but they were part of a broader, politically organized network, namely the gay community and its supporters.

In a response to public pressure, the FDA agreed to modify its usual drug approval procedures, in order to make at least one drug available for the treatment of AIDS. In 1987, AZT was approved in only 18 months—faster than any other drug in FDA history. Yet this action failed to mollify the agency's critics. Larry Kramer, a founder of the Gay Men's Health Crisis, the largest self-help AIDS organization in the United States, charged that 'there is no question on the part of anyone fighting AIDS that the FDA consists of the single most incomprehensible bottleneck in American bureaucratic history—one that is actually prolonging the roll call of death' (Kiely 1987: 13). Ben Schatz, director of the AIDS Civil Rights Project of National Gay Rights Advocates, stated: 'We feel the FDA is conducting business as usual when they should be waging war. There is a lot of ego on the line in the scientific establishment and in the AIDS industry. The decisions are not being made strictly based on human compassion' (Spector 1987: 29). AIDS demonstrators picketed government offices carrying signs reading 'The FDA is killing us' ('First ...,' 1987: 22).

In June, 1987, the FDA put into effect new rules designed to expedite the availability of experimental drugs for very sick patients.

'These new procedures represent the sharpest change in 25 years in the way new drugs are approved' (Chase 1987: 1). Under the previous drug approval system, while companies could make experimental drugs available to gravely ill patients, they were not allowed to charge for them until they had been officially approved for use. But under the new rule companies needed only to show that there was a 'reasonable basis for concluding the drug may be effective and that it wouldn't expose patients to significant additional risks' (Chase 1987). Then, subject to the FDA's approval, they could sell the drug, though only at a price necessary to cover their costs.

Young described the new procedures as a way 'to get breakthrough drugs to the American people', before their safety and effectiveness was proved. He stated, 'Where a person is going to die in months, and where patient and doctor are informed, we can take a bit more of a risk.' The following month, the FDA made another policy change as a response to criticism from AIDS patients. and their supporters. Dr. Young appeared before a hostile audience of AIDS patients in Boston to announce that the Commission would allow people with AIDS to import drugs from foreign countries that were not yet approved for sale in the United States. However, in order to prevent these drugs from being disseminated commercially, AIDS patients could only bring in enough drugs to provide about three months of treatment. While Young stated that the FDA had made considerable progress in speeding up the clinical trial of drugs in making them far more easily available to patients with life-threatening diseases, he added, 'In the meantime, I'm not going to steal the hope of AIDS victims by denying them drugs from abroad' (Boffey 1987: 1).

On 25 July 1988, the Presidential Task Force on Regulatory Relief met with Frank Young. It was concerned that the FDA's previous efforts to make experimental drugs available to desperately ill patients was having little impact. Vice President Bush, who headed the Task Force, urged Young 'as quickly as possible' to develop 'new administrative and legislative proposals' to speed up the availability of new drugs for life-threatening conditions. A counselor to the vice-president stated: 'We want to vary the regulatory hurdles depending on the seriousness of the disease. Maybe you should lower your standards. You're dealing with a disease that's certain to result in death' (Boffey 1987). In response, the FDA began to explore an administration proposal described as 'one of the most significant revisions in drug regulation in several years' (Boffey 1987). In essence, this proposal suspended the third stage of testing of new drugs for desperately ill patients. This stage involved giving the drug to a large number of patients and giving an equal number of placebos, in order to obtain a statistically meaningful measure of the drug's effectiveness. The previous two stages involved the dispensing of the drug to both healthy individuals and a limited number of patients for which it was prescribed in order to monitor it for toxicity and significant side effects. Placebos were also used in Phase II. The third stage typically added two to three years to the drug's approval time. However, according to the FDA's own data, only ten per cent of the drugs that successfully completed Phase II failed to complete Phase III as well.

In its draft proposal, the FDA for the first time officially sanctioned the concept of risk-benefit analysis. It stated: 'The agency recognizes that safety is not absolute (i.e., no drug is free of risk), but must be assessed in light of what condition the drug treats. This is particularly true in the case of drugs to treat life-threatening diseases, where drugs that are quite toxic may nevertheless be considered safe under the circumstances' ('Relief . . . 1988: 26). On 20 October 1988, the FDA announced a new drug approval process that it estimated would reduce the time necessary for the approval of promising drugs by one-third to one-half. The agency's new rules, modeled after the process used to approve AZT, eliminated the lengthy third stage of the traditional three-part clinical trials for promising drugs designed to treat life-threatening illness for which there existed no satisfactory treatment. While prompted in large measure by the Commission's slow rate of approval for drugs designed to treat AIDS, the new policy also was designed to speed the commercial availability of drugs for a number of other illnesses, including certain cancers, heart diseases, and brain seizures. The vice president of clinical research and development for a drug company declared that in his opinion Administrator Young had 'used the AIDS epidemic as a weapon to facilitate what he has wanted to do all along' (Russell 1988: C1).

IMPLICATIONS

These four cases do not exhaust all instances of successful opposition to government social regulation in the United States on the part of consumers. Yet on balance it is clear that in spite of the significant growth in the scope of social regulation of business over the last quarter century, there have been relatively few cases of citizens mobilizing to oppose government health and safety regulations. To the extent that organizations representing consumers have participated in the regulatory process, it has normally been to expand, not reduce or restrict, the scope of protective regulation (Nadel 1971).

Why? What specifically did the four regulations we have examined have in common? And what distinguished them from most other health and safety regulations? One important distinguishing feature of these regulations was their unusually high visibility to individual consumers. Obviously, many government regulations do directly intrude on the daily lives of citizens. Regulations restrict the range of products consumers can purchase, require them to read various disclosure statements and make it more difficult to open containers containing hazardous products. But for the most part the burdens these regulations impose on individual consumers are trivial. The saliency of a regulation must be unusually high for consumers to be motivated to oppose it.

Few rules promulgated by the American government over the last quarter century have been as intrusive as either the seat belt interlock system or the mandatory helmet requirement. Both required consumers to alter their behavior each and every time they began using a product that was extremely important to them and which they used on a regular basis. Likewise, for dieters and diabetics, saccharin was a product they consumed several times a day and on which they had come to rely to protect their health. For individuals afflicted with AIDS, the FDA's interpretation of the 1962 Amendments was literally a matter of life and death.

Secondly, consumers opposed these regulations not because of the low financial costs of complying with them, but because they interfered with their freedom of choice. They could not comply with these regulations simply by paying more. Drivers could not choose not to wear their seat belts, motorcyclists were deprived of the option of riding without a helmet, diabetics could no longer consume products that tasted sweet without impairing their health and individuals with AIDS were not able to purchase drugs that might prolong their lives. In short, they had no opportunity to exit; their only alternative was to use their voice.

Not only did these regulations significantly restrict the choices available to consumers, but they did so in ways that many consumers believed made them worse off. Consumers felt that they were in a better position than the government to know what was in their self-interest. Significant numbers of motorists felt that the inconvenience of having to fasten their seat belts before starting their automobile engine outweighed the possibility of a reduction in their likelihood of being injured after an automobile accident. Likewise, many motorcyclists felt that the restriction made them worse off by reducing their visibility and hearing or interfering with the pleasure they experienced from riding a motorcycle. (Ironically, as health and safety regulations go, the interlock system and the mandatory helmet requirement were both extremely effective.) In the case of saccharin, it was not merely the fact that large numbers of individuals had been consuming this particular food additive for many years without any discernible negative impact on their health that led to protest over the FDA ban. Rather, what distinguished the proposed saccharin ban was that many of its intended beneficiaries believed that it actually impaired their health. The ban protected them from a danger that they regarded as remote, while increasing their exposure to a set of hazards that they viewed as both serious and immediate. The cost/benefit calculation for individuals afflicted with AIDS was even more striking. It was difficult for AIDS patients to understand how the FDA's drug approval procedures protected their health; the agency's strict drug approval policies appeared to effectively undermine the only possibility they had of continued life.

A third reason why consumer opposition to consumer protection regulation has not occurred more frequently has to do with the nature of the political process. While policy-makers are often prepared to enact regulations that antagonize business, particularly during periods of relative prosperity, they generally seek to avoid promulgating protective regulations that will upset large numbers of voters— as each of these four regulations clearly did (Vogel 1989; Weaver 1986). Accordingly, they have attempted to design health and safety regulations in such a way as to minimize their interference with the daily lives and freedom of choice of individual consumers. Their strategy has centered on placing the largest possible share of the 'burdens' of compliance on companies, inconveniencing and restricting the freedom of producers rather than consumers.

Thus, it is companies who have to install additional safety equipment on their products, file environmental impact assessments, install expensive pollution abatement equipment and quarrel with government scientists' assessments of the risks of various food additives. These requirements are burdensome, but the public is by and large indifferent for the simple reason that they themselves are not inconvenienced. All they have to do is pay for them.

This principle extends to other areas of regulation as well. There is no federal HSHA (Household Safety and House Administration) to inspect houses and apartments for the violations of safety rules, even though more accidents occur in homes than in factories and offices. OSHA has sought to require companies to 'engineer out' the risks posed by hazardous workplace equipment instead of inconveniencing workers by requiring them to wear hardhats, ear muffs or respirators. Likewise, while many individuals engage in leisure activities such as rock climbing or hang gliding that are at least as hazardous as the use of any particular consumer product, the Consumer Product Safety Commission (CPSC) has made no effort to ban or restrict any individual hobbies. Indeed, the 1972 legislation that established the CPSC specifically forbade the agency from regulating the use of what is clearly the most dangerous consumer product, namely firearms, lest it interfere with the 'right' of America to bear arms. While cigarette smoking is a far more important cause of cancer than industrial emissions, it is the latter that has borne the brunt of the American government's regulatory efforts to reduce cancer rates (Efron 1984).

Significantly, even though the effectiveness of the catalytic convertor declines with usage, it was not until more than a decade after emission requirements were first imposed on automobile manufacturers that all motorists were required to have their cars' emission systems regularly inspected. Ironically, although California was the first state to impose automobile emission standards and the only state specifically allowed by Congress to require automobile emission standards stricter than those established for vehicles sold in the remainder of the United States, it was among the last states to comply with this requirement. Likewise, the air quality in a number of American cities could be measurably improved if the use of motor vehicles by their residents was curtailed. Yet the EPA has thus far stopped short of requiring cities to regulate automotive usage by restricting the location of shopping centers, stadiums and highways or by imposing additional tolls on motorists or additional taxes on gasoline (Vogel 1984). Instead, the burden of reducing automotive emissions has been placed exclusively on automakers and energy companies.

It is certainly true that many or most of the costs of compliance with protective regulations are passed on to consumers in the form of higher prices. But the public appears to be largely indifferent to the substantial sums of money that the government requires companies to spend on protecting their health and safety. The public's response to regulation is shaped less by the distribution or magnitude of the costs of compliance than by the *saliency* of the costs. Not only are the increased costs of any individual product generally too modest to be noticeable to consumers, but even more importantly, the costs of compliance by business are hidden. Social regulation is an indirect tax. And like other indirect taxes it rarely provokes political resistance from those who have to pay it. Consequently, since the significant expansion of social regulation in the late 1960s and early 1970s, not once has the public mobilized to oppose a specific health and safety regulation on the grounds that it is too expensive. On the other hand, the American electorate has consistently expressed its lack of support for direct taxes on various products in order to accomplish various environmental objectives. Taxes on products are highly visible to consumers; expenditures by companies are not.

In short, policymakers are confronted with an electorate that generally supports health and safety regulation—provided that they themselves are not inconvenienced. Accordingly, they have attempted to design regulations so as to place the major direct costs of compliance on companies and to make the costs and restrictions imposed on consumers as subtle and invisible as possible. This enables them to claim credit for protecting the public's welfare, but to avoid being blamed for interfering with their daily lives (Weaver 1986). From this perspective, these four controversies owe their origin to a series of miscalculations on the part of government officials. What then went wrong?

In the two NHTSA cases, public officials made the mistake of taking too literally the public's clearly expressed interest in reducing injuries from the use of motorized vehicles, which had led Congress to establish the agency in the first place. As long as the NHTSA placed the entire burden of improving driver safety on the automotive manufacturers, the public was willing to do its share by paying higher car prices. But once the federal government began demanding that the public also change its behavior, willingness to support the agency's efforts to fulfill its legislative mandate diminished rapidly. The two NHTSA rules directly interfered with the 'freedom' of drivers and motorcyclists, which many evidently judged to be more important than their safety.

In the case of the saccharin ban, the FDA was simply complying with the provisions of the Delaney amendment, which required it to give absolute priority to reducing the incidence of cancer from the use of food additives. Additives had been previously banned under the terms of this amendment without provoking public opposition. Saccharin was unique because it was the only artificial sweetener available to the public at the time it was banned. The statutory authority under which the FDA functioned explicitly forbade it from weighing the costs and benefits of food additives. The agency's inability to anticipate the public's reaction to its ban was thus imposed by Congress.

In the case of drug approval policies, the FDA found itself confronted by consumers whose policy preferences differed markedly from organizations representing consumers who had pressured it in the past. All previous criticism of the FDA's drug approval policies from consumer groups and Congress had focused on the laxity of the agency's drug approval standards. Never before had those who suffered from the non-approval of particular drugs been politically mobilized. The FDA was thus caught off guard by its failure to recognize the emergence of a new consumer constituency, with a radically different set of demands.

However it is one thing for many citizens to be upset about a particular government regulation; it is quite another for them to be able to persuade Congress or a regulatory agency to repeal it. Why were consumers able to get these decisions reversed, in most cases rather quickly? For that to have happened, two additional conditions were necessary.

First, the consumers who opposed these regulations had to become politically mobilized. In spite of the barriers to collective action that are inherent in the consumer role, consumers had become politically organized during the late 1960s and the early 1970s. By the mid 1970s, America had a politically influential consumer movement; indeed this movement had played a critical role in pressuring policymakers to promulgate the very regulations whose repeal this article has described (Nadel 1971; Pertschuk 1982). Obviously this vehicle of consumer representation was not available to consumers who wanted to reduce or weaken health and safety regulations. On the contrary, in each of the four cases we examined, the established consumer movement was on the side of the regulatory agency. Thus protesters had to develop or make use of alternative political vehicles.

In the case of the interlock system, there was no organized interest-group opposition. Congress primarily responded to a spontaneous outpouring of constituent opinion, expressed primarily through letters and editorials. In a sense, the repeal of the interlock provision can be understood as an example of constituent service, multiplied several hundred-thousand-fold. This is a role in which congressmen excel (Fiorina 1977). In the other three cases, consumers had important organizational advantages to help them convert their personal resentments into political action. Unlike the consumers of most products, both motorcyclists and AIDS sufferers already had a highly developed sense of collective identity. They had a number of existing vehicles for communicating with one another that they could use to pressure policymakers. Motorcyclists had their own clubs and magazines and many individuals with AIDS were active in the gay community, which was already highly politicized prior to the spread of this disease. Diabetics were not only represented by two organizations, each of which had both chapters and a magazine, but they also had an additional means for overcoming the free rider problem, namely the entrepreneurial skills and financial resources of the corporate consumers of saccharin.

There is an additional set of factors that helps account for the success of the consumers opposed to these particular regulations. In each of the four cases, both the costs and benefits of compliance were divisible. Following the decision of Congress to overturn the two NHTSA rulings, the drivers of new automobiles were still able to fasten their seat belts and risk-averse motorcyclists were still free to put on helmets. Likewise, after the ban on saccharin was removed, consumers were still free not to consume this particular food additive. And following the streamlining of the FDA's rules for approving new drugs, nothing prevented the victims of AIDS and other fatal diseases from restricting their medication to those pharmaceutical products that had been approved according to a strict interpretation of the Kefauver Amendments.

It was precisely the fact that compliance with each of these regulations *could* be made voluntary that enabled their opponents to claim that the government was interfering with their 'freedom' or 'rights.' In three of these four cases, the regulations were challenged on constitutional grounds, even though the courts proved unsympathetic to the plaintiffs. In fact, virtually all health and safety regulations restrict the rights and freedom of some individuals. However, for the most part, these regulations are unavoidable: it is impossible for some to be 'free to choose' without at the same time making others less 'free'. What is 'freedom' in the eyes of a regulation's supporters constitutes coercion to those who believe that a particular regulation is unnecessary to protect their health or safety.

An additional important reason why Congress, as the ultimate regulatory court of appeals, was able to respond to the complaints of large numbers of consumers with such alacrity was because doing so did not endanger the health and safety of any other readily identifiable groups of constituents. In each case, the demands of the opponents of the regulation were extremely narrow and limited. They only wanted to repeal or modify the regulations that directly affected them. The fact that there were limited negative externalities also served to limit the political effectiveness of the organized consumer movement; the latter could not demonstrate how innocent third parties would be hurt by the repeal of these particular regulations.

What makes these four cases unusual is precisely that their politics cannot be understood in terms of Wilson's (1980) cost/benefit framework. Unlike most regulatory policies, both the benefits and the costs of these regulations and their repeal were borne by the same individuals. Nor would these policies be classified as 'regulatory' in Lowi's (1964) three-part typology of the policy process; they are more accurately defined as 'distributive'. They thus presented legislators with an opportunity rarely offered in regulatory politics: they could make many of their constituents better off without making any others worse off. As Moe (1989: 278) writes, legislators value 'particularized' control: 'they want to be able to intervene quickly, inexpensively, and in ad hoc ways to protect or advance the interests of particular clients in particular matters'. These cases clearly provided opportunity to do precisely that.

In this context, it is worth noting that each of these four cases of regulatory 'backlash' involved consumer protection rather than environmental protection or occupational health and safety. It is extremely difficult for the latter two kinds of regulation to be implemented on a voluntary basis. Individuals cannot be selectively exposed to pollution or hazardous wastes. Likewise, in most cases, it is impossible for some workers to be exposed to increased workplace hazards without also increasing the dangers experienced by others who may be more risk-averse. Significantly, the recent wave of restrictions on the freedom of individuals to smoke when and where they want rests precisely on the argument that secondary smoke exposes non-smokers to harm.

Each case has been drawn from the United States. However, America is not unique in the scope of its regulatory controls over business. Why then have no similar kinds of conflicts emerged in other nations? The answer to this question illuminates some of the distinctions beween the politics of protective regulation in Europe and the United States. First, regulatory authorities in other nations enjoy substantially more discretion and autonomy than their counterparts in the United States (Vogel 1986). Their decisions are not as constrained by regulatory statutes. No other nation has a stature similar to the Delaney clause, which explicitly requires regulatory officials to ban all carcinogenic food additives. Nor has any other legislature enacted a law similar to the Kefauver amendments, which made the American drug-approval process so time-consuming in the first place. Accordingly, one reason why consumers elsewhere have not complained as much as their counterparts in the United States may be that they have had less to complain about; their regulatory officials have been better able to make policy on a case by case basis.

A second distinction has to do with political culture. Appeals to individual freedom and individual rights resonate especially strongly in American political culture (Huntington 1981). Thus even when the governments of other nations do intrude on individual rights, such as by requiring the wearing of motorcycle helmets, their citizens are less likely to regard these rules and regulations as unreasonable, let alone unconstitutional. The exercise of paternalism by government is more likely to be regarded as illegitimate in the United States.

A final distinction has to do with political institutions. Even if substantial numbers of consumers in Europe or Japan resented a particular regulation, their opportunities to use either the legislative or administrative process to redress their grievances would be limited by their lack of access to the policy process. The latter would be likely to be restricted to officially recognized consumer groups, meaning that the narrower groups of 'unofficial' consumers who were so successful in the United States would be less able to successfully challenge regulations that were supported by broad, mainstream consumer organizations. Consumer backlash is less likely to occur in a corporatist political system.

REFERENCES

American Enterprise Institute (AEI) (1979) *Proposals to Reform Drug Regulation Laws*. Washington, DC, AEI.
Boffey, Philip (1987) FDA will allow AIDS patients to import unapproved medicines, *New York Times*, p. 1.
Brody, Jane (1980) Personal health, *New York Times*, 9 July.
Calvert, Randall L., Mark J. Moran & Barry R. Weingast, 'Congressional Influence over Policy Making: The Case of the FTC', in Mathew D. McCubbins & Terry Sullivan, *Congress: Structure and Policy*. Cambridge: Cambridge University Press, 1987, pp. 493–522.
Cancer and your sweet tooth, *New Republic, March 26, 1977*, p. 7.
Chase, Marilyn (1987) FDA rules changes may rush new drugs to very sick patients, *Wall Street Journal*, October 5, p. 1.
Congressional Quarterly Almanac (CQA), 1977. Washington, DC: CQ.
Cummings, Linda (1986) The Political Reality of Artificial Sweetness, in Harvey Sapolsky (ed.), *Consuming Fears*. New York: Basic Books.
Drivers disconnecting seat belt locks, *New York Times*, August 18, 1974.
Efron, Edith (1984) *The Apocalyptics*. New York: Simon and Schuster.
Fiorina, Morris (1977) *Congress: Keystone of the Washington Establishment*. New Haven: Yale University Press.
First do no harm, *Wall Street Journal*, December 21, 1987.
Foreman, Christopher H. Jr. (1988) *Signals from the Hill: Congressional Oversight and the Challenge of Social Regulation*. New Haven: Yale University Press.
Frieden, Bernard (1979) *The Environmental Protection Hustle*. Cambridge: MIT Press.

How sweet it was, *Wall Street Journal*, March 14, 1977.

Huntington, Samuel (1981) *American Politics and the Promise of Disharmony.* Cambridge: Harvard University Press.

Irvin, Robert (1974) The interlock system: A 'devillish contraption', *New York Times*, April 7, p. 20.

Karr, Albert (1973) Seat-belt interlock for 1974-model autos poses a PR problem, *Wall Street Journal*, July 3, p. 12.

Kelley, John (1981) Bridging America's drug gap, *New York Times Magazine*, September 13, p. 100.

Kiely, Thomas (1987) Rushing drugs to market, *Technology Review*, August/ September.

Knight, Jerry (1980) Motorcycle deaths jump after helmet law repeal, *Washington Post*, April 12, p. F1.

Leone, Robert (1986) *Who Profits: Winners, Losers and Government Regulation.* New York: Basic Books.

Lid put on cyclists riding bareheaded, *Washington Post*, January 10, 1976, p. E3.

Lowi, Theodore (1964) 'American Business and Public Policy: The Politics of Foreign Trade', *World Politics*, Vol. 16 (July).

Lyons, Richard (1977) Depth and finesse of lobbying against saccharin bill expected to result in a 19-month postponement, *New York Times*, October 5, p. A18.

Mashaw, Jerry and Harfst, David (1990) *The Struggle for Auto Safety.* Cambridge: Harvard University Press.

McCarthy, Colman (1976) Should the helmet be outlawed? *Washington Post*, January 16.

McCormick, Robert (1989) A Review of the Economics of Regulation: The Political Process, in Roger Meiners and Bruce Yandle (eds.), *Regulation and the Regan Era.* New York: Holmes & Meier, pp. 16–37.

Minor, Michael (1984) Accident Risk and Automotive Safety: Safety Belt Use in the U.S., *Proceedings of the First U.S.–Japan Workshop on Risk Management*, Tsukuba, Japan, October 28–31.

Moe, Terry M. (1989) 'The Politics of Bureaucratic Structure', in John E. Chubb & Paul E. Peterson (eds.), *Can the Government Govern?* Washington, DC: The Brookings Institution, pp. 267–329.

Murray, Chris (1977) Environmentalists fight for Delaney clause, *Chemical and Engineering News*, May 23, p. 16.

Nadel, Mark (1971) *The Politics of Consumer Protection.* Indianapolis: Bobbs-Merill.

New York Times, advertisement, May 1, 1977, Section IV, p. 18.

Pertschuk, Michael (1982) *Revolt Against Regulation.* Berkeley: University of California Press.

Relief from suffering, *Wall Street Journal*, September 19, 1988, p. 26.

Russell, Sabin (1988) Speedier approval of drugs hailed, *San Francisco Chronicle*, October 21, p. C1.

Saccharin-produce plant going full tilt under load of orders (1977), *New York Times*, March 30, p. 72.

Scheurer, James (1980) The FDA: Too slow, *New York Times*, May 22, p. 35.

Spector, Michael (1987) When time and testing clash, *Washington Post National Weekly Report*, November 7, p. 29.

U.S. Government Accounting Office (1976) *The Need to Resolve Safety Questions on Saccharin*. Washington, DC: U.S. Government Printing Office.

Vogel, David (1984) A Case Study of Clean Air Legislation, 1967–1981, in Betty Bock et al. (eds.), *The Impact of the Modern Corporation*. New York: Columbia University Press, pp. 309–86.

—— (1986) *National Styles of Regulation*. Ithaca: Cornell University Press.

—— (1989) *Fluctuating Fortunes: The Political Power of Business in America*. New York: Basic Books.

—— (1989a) 'AIDS and the Politics of Drug Lag', *Public Interest*, Summer, pp. 73–85.

Weaver, R. Kent (1986) 'The Politics of Blame Avoidance', *Journal of Public Policy*, 6, 4.

Weintraub, Barnard (1977) Saccharin ban stirs demand to curb FDA, *New York Times*, March 12, p. 11.

Wilson, James Q. (1980) *The Politics of Regulation*. New York: Basic Books.

PART THREE

The Dynamics of Business Power

Chapter Nine

POLITICAL SCIENCE AND THE STUDY OF CORPORATE POWER: A DISSENT FROM THE NEW CONVENTIONAL WISDOM

THE WAY political scientists write about business has changed substantially over the last two decades. Prior to 1970, hardly any members of our discipline viewed the business corporation as posing a unique problem for either democratic theory or practice. Only a handful of political scientists dissented from the then prevailing pluralist orthodoxy, and their writings had relatively little impact on the remainder of the discipline.[1] Even scholars such as Kariel, McConnell or Lowi, who explicitly questioned the pluralist description of American politics, did not regard business any differently from the way they viewed a variety of other interest groups, including organized labour and farmers.[2]

However, over the last fifteen years, the intellectual—and political—centre of gravity of the discipline has noticeably shifted. While all the American government textbooks published during the 1950s and 1960s reflected the ideas of pluralists such as David Truman and V. O. Key, Jr., since 1974 a steady stream of American politics texts have been published that are highly critical of corporate capitalism and of the impact of business on the American system.[3] Of greater intellectual significance has been the highly visible 'conversion' of two of the discipline's most prominent pluralists, Robert Dahl and Charles Lindblom. In their new preface to *Politics, Economics, and Welfare*, published in 1976, Dahl and Lindblom confessed that

> In our discussion of pluralism we made another error—and it is a continuing error in social science—in regarding businessmen and business groups as playing the same interest-group role as other groups in polyarchal systems, though more powerfully. Businessmen play a distinctive role in polyarchal politics that is qualitatively different from that of any interest group. It is also much more powerful than an interest-group role.

They added,

> . . . common interpretations that depict the American or any other market-oriented system as a competition among interest groups are seri-

ously in error for their failure to take account of the distinctive privileged position of businessmen in politics.[4]

Dahl first described the business corporation as an essentially public—or political—institution in *After the Revolution*, published in 1970.[5] Since then he has published two monographs, *Dilemmas of Pluralist Democracy* and *A Preface to Economic Democracy* (the latter title presumably a derivative of his *Preface to Democratic Theory* published two decades earlier), which argue that corporate power is not subject to democratic standards of accountability.[6] While Lindblom's *Politics and Markets* presents, as its subtitle indicates, a wide ranging analysis of 'the world's political-economic systems', it is best known for its last two sentences: 'The large private corporation fits oddly into democratic theory. Indeed, it does not fit.'[7] The book itself is arguably the most widely known and influential study of American business–government relations by an individual identified with our discipline to appear in the last quarter-century.

Two decades ago one could not write about interest-group politics in America without referring to Dahl's *Who Governs?* Today it is impossible to discuss the power of business in America without footnoting *Politics and Markets*. Since the publication of *Politics and Markets* a decade ago, a total of sixteen articles have been published in American and British political science journals that explicitly discuss the political power of business.[8] Four of these are review essays. Of the remainder, fewer than half either implicitly or explicitly take issue with Lindblom's description of the political influence of business in either the United States or Great Britain. The majority, although written from a variety of perspectives, essentially echo what has become a new conventional wisdom. This was summarized by David Menninger in a recent essay in *PS* on 'Political Science and the Corporation'. He wrote:

> While they may not reject outright the American formula of popular government and private enterprise that has prevailed thus far, political scientists are likely to judge the large corporation's concentration of resources and wealth to be an anomaly that upsets the balance between democracy and capitalism.[9]

Twenty years ago, the number of political scientists who shared this judgement could be counted on the fingers of one hand; this is clearly no longer the case. The purpose of this essay is critically to evaluate this new understanding of the political significance of the large corporation.

The contemporary writings of political scientists on corporate power fall into three broad categories. One argues that the largely privately owned business corporation undermines democracy because its internal structure of authority is undemocratic. Since those who control it are elected by stockholders rather than employees, the individuals most affected by the firm are denied any meaningful say in its governance. A second set of arguments focuses on the relationship between business and government. Its central contention is that pluralist democracy is flawed because business occupies a 'privileged position'. Not only do business firms enjoy disproportionate access to political resources, but the dependence of the citizenry on the economic decisions made by corporate executives means that government officials must constantly defer to the former's preferences. As a result, needs and preferences of business define the parameters within which public policy is debated and implemented. The first perspective is primarily associated with the work of Robert Dahl, the second with the writings of Charles Lindblom. There is also a third approach, which can be characterized as Marxist or neo-Marxist. It is reflected in two articles that have appeared recently in the *American Political Science Review*.[10] This perspective incorporates the insights of the first two, but goes a step further in conceiving of the capitalist mode of production as itself a system of power. Its central contention is that a political economy based on private ownership of the means of production and marketplace exchange restricts the liberty and freedom of those who are not members of the capitalist class.

This chapter does not deal with the neo-Marxist approach. It focuses mainly on the work of Charles Lindblom, since his work has been the most influential. It begins, however, by examining briefly Dahl's writings on the nature of the corporation as a private government.

THE CORPORATION AS A PRIVATE GOVERNMENT

Dahl argues that corporations should be seen as political systems, whose leaders exercise great power, influence and control over employees, consumers, suppliers and (at least) local economies. As social enterprises, corporations should be subject to social control. As political systems operating within a democratic polyarchy, they should be governed by democratic processes. According to Dahl, there are no overriding philosophical or practical justifications for capitalist control, or even ownership, of corporations. The arguments that Locke and Mill offered for the rightful ownership and control of the fruits of one's labour are more logically applied to corporate employees than to absentee shareholders. The ability of corporations to attract equity capital stripped of voting rights is amply demonstrated by the abundance of preferred stock. Most of America's largest corporations, and all of its commercial banks, obtain a majority of their capital from bondholders and lenders who have, and expect, no governance role or ownership rights. This attenuation of the traditional link between ownership and control further undermines the argument that ownership (or the provision of capital) conveys an inalienable right of control.

Dahl therefore finds it disturbing that a substantial proportion of the citizenry 'live out their working lives, and most of their daily existence, not within a democratic system but instead within a hierarchical structure of subordination'.[11] The argument that corporate employees have the freedom to exit the hierarchy and seek employment elsewhere ignores the often substantial costs of dissent. An individual who leaves a corporate hierarchy may sustain significant search and relocation costs and may sacrifice seniority, status or uninvested pension benefits. And the only realistic alternative for most individuals is employment in yet another undemocratic hierarchy. Worse still, the individual who chooses to exit has no 'right' to membership in another firm or to employment of any kind.

The obvious solution is to extend the criteria of procedural democracy to the government of firms. Meaningful reform will require the imposition of both internal and external social control mechanisms. To ensure that corporate decisions are influenced by those most heavily affected by them, Dahl advocates worker management (and social or worker ownership). He argues that the fact that such arrangements have not arisen widely in the past should not be taken as evidence that they are unworkable. It merely reflects the superior bargaining power that owners of capital have historically enjoyed over workers and other societal interests.

Dahl's contention that the decisions made by privately owned corporations are profoundly public or social in character is neither novel nor especially controversial. The doctrine of corporate social responsibility, first articulated in the United States at the turn of the century, and echoed repeatedly by each generation of executives since, explicitly recognizes that corporations have ceased to be private institutions. More importantly, the argument that the corporation, because of its status as 'private property', should therefore have its decisions and internal authority structure immune from public scrutiny or control is no longer made or believed by anyone—save libertarians. The undermining of the concept of limited government in American mainstream political discourse has meant that everything the corporation does is now, in principle, the public's business: contemporary conservative criticisms of government control over business rest today primarily on pragmatic grounds, not ideological ones.

The contention that 'neither in theory nor in practice are corporate governments democratic' is also unexceptionable.[12] Yet this does not make the corporation unique: every single non-government institution can be described in similar terms. Universities, foundations, labour unions, many professional and trade associations, religious and charitable institutions and organizations—even public interest groups—all exercise political power, and none is governed according to democratic principles or precepts. In its internal structure of authority, the corporation is actually quite typical of the institutions and organizations that characterize democratic societies.

In fact, given Dahl's criterion for democracy, namely that an institution is non-democratic unless those who work for it are able to hold those who govern it accountable, the government itself is not run according to democratic principles. After all, government employees do not choose their superiors, nor are they formally consulted about the most important decisions taken by the departments or bureaucracies in which they work. But no one considers that the structure of the military is a threat to democracy because soldiers are not allowed to set military policy or that the Army Corps of Engineers is a threat to democratic rule because its employees can no longer set the nation's conservation policy. Quite the contrary, these organizations are compatible with a democratic form of government precisely to the extent that those who govern them are *not* accountable to those employed by them.

Dahl does acknowledge that the corporation is one among a large number of institutions that exercise authority in our society. But he wishes to reform the internal structure of authority of only one of them, namely, the 'privately owned and controlled economic enterprise'.[13] However, he never explains the basis for this distinction. Why, if our society is to be made democratic, is it essential that General Motors be governed democratically by its employees, but not the Catholic Church, Yale University, the Ford Foundation or, for that matter, the American Political Science Association? Certainly it cannot be on the basis of their size or social impact—though clearly these criteria would exclude the APSA. Both Yale University and the Ford Foundation are at least as large and powerful as any one of hundreds of *Fortune* 500 companies. Nor can it be because the corporation is particularly undemocratic: it is certainly no less democratic than the Catholic Church and probably only marginally less democratic than a university. (Of all non-governmental institutions, the university probably comes the closest to being democratically governed by its workers, with the important caveat that self-government is restricted to tenured faculty.)

Why, then, does Dahl not insist that universities, religious institutions, foundations and professional associations be governed by their employees? Presumably because he recognizes that there is a tension between the purposes for which these organizations were established and the interests of their employees. This is most obvious in the case of the Catholic Church, whose entire *raison d'être* is based on the deference of the clergy and the laity to the Church hierarchy and, by extension, to God. But it is only marginally less true in the case of Yale University and the Ford Foundation. The purpose of the former is, in principle, to create and disseminate knowledge, the latter to disperse the funds given to it by Henry Ford in order to further various social objectives. There is no reason to assume that the ability to make the decisions necessary to achieve these purposes is randomly or equally distributed among all of their employees. Hence, the trustees of each institution have established an internal division of authority in which some individuals have more power with respect to particular decisions than others. The internal structures of both the Sierra Club and Common Cause follow from a similar logic.

But why, then, is Dahl unwilling to grant the same deference to the managers or the board of directors of the business corporation? Is it not significant that not one single institution—whether public or private, profit-seeking or eleemosynary in modern capitalist societies—is governed by those who work for it? Instead, each is controlled by some other group of individuals—stockholders and consumers in the case of business, citizens in the case of government, their membership in the case of voluntary organizations and trade unions, faculty in the case of universities, trustees in the case of foundations—precisely because the accountability of each to its constituency or constituencies is central to the fundamental purposes for which it was established. Far from making our society more democratic, the control of any of these institutions by their employees would undermine democratic accountability. Thus we judge the Teamsters to be an undemocratic union precisely *because* it is controlled by its employees rather than its members. And, by like token, governmental agencies are considered unaccountable to the public to the extent that their policies are dictated by their employees rather than politicians or political appointees.

This criticism of the case for worker ownership does not mean that we should abandon attempts to make the workplace less authoritarian. Although the legal structure of corporate ownership has remained relatively stable throughout the history of capitalism, the rights of workers *vis-à-vis* managers have steadily increased. The most important change has been the legal recognition of the right of workers to join unions, although a decreasing proportion of workers in both the United States and Great Britain have chosen to do so. In addition, over the last two decades, the federal government has limited the ability of managers to discriminate among employees on the basis of sex, race, religion and age, and established regulations designed to protect their health and safety. More recently, the courts in some states have shown an increased willingness to protect non-unionized employees from arbitrary dismissals and demotion and in some cases to protect their rights of free speech. While the rights of workers tend to be greater for those who work in the public sector, there is no reason why similar rights cannot be extended to workers in the private sector, thus making the internal authority structure of business resemble more closely that of the government.

THE PRIVILEGED POSITION OF BUSINESS

So much for Dahl. Lindblom in *Politics and Markets* argues that the pro-business slant of public policy is not merely the result of business's superior economic and political resources or of its ability to bring those resources to bear on particular political decisions, though these factors obviously do matter; rather, business enjoys a privileged position within the political economy because of its unique relationship to the public welfare. This relationship sets it on a plane apart from other interests and institutions that compete for political influence. Corporate leaders hold a privileged position in polyarchies because society has placed in their hands the responsibility for mobilizing and organizing society's resources. In this capacity, corporate executives 'decide a nation's industrial technology, the pattern of work organization, location of industry, market structure, resource allocation, and, of course, executive compensation and status'.[14] This broad category of major decisions is removed from the agenda of government and thus from polyarchal control. Our constitutional protection of private property rights compounds this problem, since it prevents public control over corporate decision making from being exercised directly.

Corporate owners and their executives must therefore be induced to perform their primary social functions rather than be commanded to do so. These inducements may take the form of delegated monopoly rights, limited liability, rights of way, subsidies, tax incentives, infrastructural services such as public works and education, insurance, military protection of investments, rights to transfer costs of pollution or other externalities to third parties, etc. All of these inducements impose costs—in the form of taxes, eminent domain, uncompensated damages, extracted consumer surplus and the like—on non-corporate interests in society.

These costs have historically been the *quid pro quo* for economic development and expansion, employment and affluence. They amount to a social contract, whose terms and enforcement are issues of constant, though constrained, public debate and struggle. This contract constitutes the framework for what Lindblom characterizes as the prison of the marketplace. In this metaphor, public demands are held hostage to business requirements for inducements. This view of the market as prison requires 'no conspiracy theory of politics, no theory of common social origins uniting government and business officials, no crude allegation of a power elite established by clandestine forces'.[15] For businessmen, 'Simply minding one's own business is the formula for an extraordinary system for repressing change'.[16]

The consequences of prolonged life in this prison include a remarkably rigid maldistribution of income and wealth, environmental degradation, unabated poverty and the persistence of considerable autonomy for corporate leaders, even as the social impact of corporate decision making becomes increasingly pervasive. The slightest reforms that run counter to business interests are enacted only after a ransom is paid in the form of new inducements. Escape from the market prison would require an awareness among the prisoners themselves that (1) they are imprisoned and (2) they hold the cellblock keys. Such an awareness, however, is constantly being underminded by corporate attempts to mould citizen volitions:

> Consider the possibility that businessmen achieve an indoctrination of citizens so that citizens' volitions serve not their own interests but the interests of businessmen. Citizens then become allies of businessmen. The privileged position of business comes to be widely accepted.[17]

Since the mechanisms of mass acculturation rest in corporate hands (either through direct ownership or through media dependence on advertising revenues), an indoctrinated public opinion can be traced to the structural relations of capitalism. This subtle manipulation of civic consciousness is achieved by systematically intertwining private enterprise with the concepts of nation, democracy and liberty. This serves to legitimize the privileged position of business and to remove it, along with other grand issues such as private property, corporate autonomy and distributive equity, from the public agenda. Thus, what is often seen as the quasi-democratic give and take of interest group politics should be understood to apply only to secondary issues. These are issues on which a broad consensus does not exist within the business community. As these issues reach the political agenda, the public is subjected to competing messages from various business interests. A divided business community is forced to join coalitions and compromise with other societal interests. This can then be conveniently cited as evidence of the limits of corporate power, and further reinforces the myth that democratic pluralism is alive and well.

This bias prevents active consideration of the possibility that a more democratic policy-making process might require modification or even elimination of the market as an organized mechanism. It is a natural consequence of a system of incentives manipulated by corporations that is able to offer research funds and endowed faculty chairs to co-operative intellectuals willing to legitimize the status quo. Lindblom concludes that American political theorists who do come to grips with the fact that the market imprisons the policy-making process should at least entertain the notion that fuller democracy might require the elimination of the market as the primary means for allocating society's resources.

The essence of Lindblom's argument is that businessmen are uniquely powerful because the government relies upon them to organize society's economic activities. But, while this makes the government dependent on the decisions of businessmen, it also makes businessmen at least as dependent on the decisions of government. They must depend upon government to protect and safeguard their property rights, to create and maintain a sound currency, to assert and protect their interests in the world economy, to enforce 'reasonable' regulations, not to tax them excessively, etc. In the real world, neither business nor government get all they want from each other: government officials are usually dissatisfied with the economy's rate of growth while businessmen invariably argue that their profits would be higher if the government was more responsive to their needs.

It is not obvious whose leverage is greater. A lack of business confidence can lead to unemployment, which frequently, though not always, hurts elected officials. But, by like token, various government policies—such as inflating the currency, refusing requests for protectionism, increasing taxes or imposing costly environmental controls—can also reduce the wealth of businessmen. These latter examples are not hypothetical: throughout the history of democratic capitalism, the profits of particular companies and industries, as well as corporate profitability in general, have been adversely affected by various public policies.

Nor is the threat on the part of businessmen to withhold additional investment unless their demands are met as powerful as it is frequently portrayed. For one, its power is fundamentally limited by the fact that it cannot be employed without also hurting capitalists themselves. An economic showdown not only hurts workers; it also interferes with the ability of investors to protect their wealth. In this sense, a 'capital strike' is precisely similar to a strike by workers: both hurt their adversaries, but not without also hurting those who employ them. It is true that some capitalists, unlike workers, can readily transfer their resources to a more favourable jurisdiction. But this is not true of all capitalists: many industries, such as those involved in the extraction of natural resources or which provide services directly to consumers, have relatively few geographical options. Moreover, the power of capital to 'flee' is counterbalanced by the ability of consumers to purchase the goods and services produced by the capitalists of another country.

Equally importantly, the dependence of the economy on 'investor confidence' is limited by the fact that the GNP is made up of three components—investment, consumption and government spending—each of which is important. Companies, after all, can be given every incentive to invest, but unless businessmen have reason to believe that consumers are willing to purchase what they produce they are unlikely to expand production. In fact, not only is the economy no less dependent on consumer confidence than on investor confidence, but the economic effects of the former show up more quickly. At the same time, given sufficient consumer demand, companies are likely to increase their investments—regardless of whatever obstacles politicians may place in their way. (The investments made by businessmen working in the underground economy fall into this category: they take place not as a result of inducements by government but in the face of every effort by government to discourage them.) And government is by no means completely dependent on either consumer or investor confidence to stimulate the economy; not only can the Federal government in the United States contribute to consumption through increasing its own spending, but state and local governments control several tens of billion dollars' worth of pension-fund assets which can be used either to begin new companies or expand existing ones.

The ability of companies to threaten to withhold making new investments in order to force the government to make public policies that preserve or restore 'business confidence' is also constrained by the business cycle itself. When the economy collapses for a prolonged period of time—as occurred in the early 1930s—it becomes rather difficult for companies to insist on the importance of 'investor confidence'. The fact that business was generally blamed for the Great Depression significantly weakened its ability to 'veto' new government initiatives after 1934: it was rather awkward for companies to threaten to increase unemployment when 25 per cent of the work-force was already unemployed. On a lesser scale, a similar development took place during the mid-1970s: having been blamed for causing the 'energy crisis', the oil industry was scarcely in a position to insist upon additional concessions—lest the nation's supply of oil be disrupted! On the other hand, when the economy is performing relatively well, politicians are less likely to take seriously corporate complaints about the excessive burdens of government intervention. This was the case during both the Progressive Era and the period between the mid-1960s and the mid-1970s. As a result, controls on business tend to be increased both when the economy is doing very poorly—and when it is doing very well. It is when its performance lies somewhere in between—as occurred during the latter part of the 1970s and the first half of the 1980s—that politicians become more willing to defer to business preferences.

Nor is it true that governments in capitalist democracies are afraid to support policies that increase unemployment. The Thatcher Government, for example, has done precisely that—and was re-elected. President Reagan, in his first two years in office, tolerated the highest levels of unemployment in the United States since the Great Depression and was overwhelmingly re-elected even though unemployment in 1984 was, by historic standards, extremely high. The Reagan Administration has also presided over what is estimated to be a permanent loss of two million industrial jobs due to imports—and yet it has for the most part resisted pleas from both businessmen and workers to increase American tariffs. And it supported a tax reform bill with significant 'adverse effects'—in terms of both profits and unemployment—on one of the nation's most important industries, namely construction.

The structuralist analysis of corporate power is unpersuasive for another reason: it tends to reify business. Even though the government may have to provide inducements to business to enable the economy to grow, it does not follow that it has to provide inducements to any particular business or industry. After all, segments of the economy can perform poorly even when the economy as a whole is doing relatively well (and the reverse is also true). The government can—and in fact does—discriminate among businesses. Government spending, tax, trade and industrial and regulatory policies invariably favour particular sectors, industries, regions, products and even plants over others. (Indeed, competing to increase their share of benefits from government is among the most important purposes of corporate political activity.) Just as firms can play off different governmental units against each other, so government officials can play off different segments of business against each other. This latter process also tends to increase the power of non-business constituencies, since their support may be critical in enabling certain segments of business to gain a competitive advantage over others.[18]

One can carry this analysis a step further. Not only is the government not vulnerable to the threats of any particular businessmen; it does not even have to satisfy most of them. Instead it can choose to concentrate its inducements on those of its citizens who are not currently businessmen but would like to assume this role. It can, in effect, write off virtually every existing company, providing there are others interested in taking their place. This is obviously an exaggeration: economies do not transform themselves overnight. But it is worth noting that, in the aggregate, *Fortune* 500 companies have not created one single net job in the United States in the last quarter of a century. Virtually all new employment—other than in the public section—has been created by relatively new companies. To the extent that the government, as Lindblom asserts, is dependent on business to provide employment, it would be well advised to ignore every single demand made on it by a manufacturing company and instead defer always to the interests of firms in the service sector, since it is from them that virtually all new jobs have derived. The typical service firm is a relatively small, independently owned business employing less than twenty employees. Are these the companies Lindblom has in mind when he speaks about the dependence of government on business to create jobs?[19]

More fundamentally, if governments were actually responsive to even a significant proportion of political demands made by existing companies, the economy would stagnate. There would be no bankruptcies, no imports to compete with domestic producers, no industries or regions in decline, no reductions in existing tax breaks or subsidies, no changes in government procurement or spending policies. This state of affairs more accurately characterizes state socialist societies than capitalist ones. It certainly does not accurately describe the contemporary American political economy. One can, of course, cite a large number of public policies whose purpose is to preserve the economic status quo; but these must be placed alongside the economic deregulation of airlines, railroads, trucking and telecommunications, the Reagan Administration's resistance to demands for increased protectionism and the 1986 tax reform bill. Each of these policies—deregulation, free trade and tax reform—has or will undermine the profitability of countless firms and industries, although presumably strengthening the overall performance of the economy as a whole. If politicians wish to encourage economic growth, they would be well advised to ignore rather than defer to what most business lobbyists want from them.

The fact that there are so many different businesses significantly increases the flexibility of public policy. For there are scarcely any tasks that the government might wish to undertake that it cannot find some businessman willing to perform in the expectation of making money. Do we wish to reduce pollution? Such a policy will certainly reduce the profits of those firms that pollute. But the money they are forced to spend on pollution-control equipment in turn represents a source of profit for the manufacturers of pollution-control equipment. Do we wish drug and cosmetic companies to do more testing on their products before they market them? The costs imposed on these firms, in turn, represent a business opportunity for companies that specialize in running laboratory tests. Do we wish to divert resources from the production of weaponry to health care? The result will be that the profits of defence contractors will decline and those of health-care suppliers increase.

This dynamic also operates at the local level. California, for example, has enforced extremely strict land-use controls, which have had the effect of discouraging a number of industrial firms from locating or expanding their facilities in that state. Has this hurt the California economy? Not at all: it has simply resulted in a relative decrease in the number of traditional manufacturing jobs and an increase in high-tech and service sector employment. The cities of Santa Monica and Berkeley have enacted what are arguably the most 'anti-business' regulations of any community in the United States. Have their economies suffered? Not in the slightest. Because of their location and other attractions, there are no shortages of businesses that are eager to locate within their boundaries. Companies do have the right to decide where they will invest, but governments also can determine what kinds of investments they wish to permit or induce.

Lindblom writes:

One line of reform after another is blocked by prospective punishments. An enormous variety of reforms do in fact undercut business expectations of profitability and do therefore reduce employment. Higher business taxes reduce profitability. Bearing the costs of pollution control reduces profitability. Building safer automobiles reduces profitability. Countless reforms therefore are followed immediately— swiftly—by the punishment of unemployment.

... the conflict between reform and its adverse effects on business that punish us through unemployment is a long-standing and real repressant of change. As for the ubiquity of punishment, its swiftness and severity, there is nothing like it elsewhere in the social system. Nowhere else is there so effective a set of automatic punishment established as a barrier to social change.[20]

Change a few words from these paragraphs and you have the kind of rhetoric that has been a staple of business political discourse in the United States for the last century. Fortunately, most of the time politicians in the United States and other capitalist countries have not found it persuasive. The income tax, social security, the legalization of labour unions, the establishment of TVA, unemployment insurance, Medicare, environmental and consumer protection, federal regulation of the securities markets—each of these reforms was bitterly opposed by businessmen precisely on the grounds Lindblom cites. Yet each has been enacted and 'grass has not grown in the streets'. A capitalist economy is far more flexible and malleable than either Lindblom or most businessmen assume: companies somehow find a way to prosper and grow—despite the political rhetoric of those who own and control them. In fact, far from 'countless reforms [being] followed immediately—and swiftly—by the punishment of unemployment', the opposite has in fact been the case: either, as during both the Progressive Era and the period between 1965 and 1977, reforms have taken place during a period of relative prosperity or, as during the 1930s, they have contributed to economic recovery. To suggest that 'businessmen sometimes learn to live with reforms' must rank as one of the classic understatements of contemporary political analysis.

If one surveys the public policies of the democratic capitalist nations in the postwar period, one is struck not by how narrowly constrained have been the imperatives of a privately owned economy but by how varied they have been. Capitalist economies have prospered with virtually no government ownership of the means of production and with an extremely large public sector, with market-based capital markets and with politically directed ones, with very weak labour unions and with very strong ones, with virtually no environmental protection laws and with extremely strict ones, with extremely generous welfare states and with very limited ones, with regressive tax policies and with progressive ones. And, by like token, capitalist economies have done poorly under all these varied public policies as well. In short, the relationship between any particular set of reforms and economic growth or corporate profitability is by no means as clear-cut as Lindblom implies.

If there is anything the postwar experience has taught us, it is how difficult it is to predict the impact of particular public policies on corporate profitability. Economics is a notoriously inexact science: most of the time we do not know what will be the impact of various policies on business activity. Who, for example, a decade ago would have predicted that the United States could run the largest government deficit in its history and that prices would be declining? Or that it could run the largest trade deficit in the history of capitalism without increasing unemployment? Can anyone really say with certainty what will be the long-term economic impact of the Tax Reform Act of 1986? Likewise, the environmental laws of the early 1970s were enacted without anyone having any idea as to the cost of their implementation.

In addition, even if politicians are persuaded by businessmen that a particular set of policies is necessary to increase economic growth, they can still refuse to enact them. Democratic governments can and do choose to accept lower growth rates in order to achieve other public policy objectives. These range from protecting the livelihood of small, inefficient farmers, as in Japan and France, maintaining the income levels of the elderly, as in Western Europe and the United States, or spending a significant share of GNP on the military as in the United States, Great Britain, and Sweden. With the exception of Japan, no democratic capitalist nation in the postwar period has made increasing its share of world GNP its most important priority. There are literally hundreds of policy changes that any capitalist government could make that would be likely to increase the rate of corporate investment—and thus presumably enhance corporate profits, improve economic growth rates and reduce unemployment. They do not choose to enact them for a simple reason: the electorate is not interested in making the sacrifices they would entail. The power of business is fundamentally limited by the fact that many individuals, both in their personal lives and in their roles as citizens, do not share businessmen's single-minded commitment to the maximization of wealth.

Moreover, even if it were true that, whatever the extent of its commitment to economic growth, the government was uniquely dependent on the decisions of business managers to perform this task, this by itself would not make business uniquely privileged. For creating wealth is not only one among many responsibilities of government, but it is not even the most important task for which we hold politicians responsible. Clearly the most important responsibility of government officials is to protect the physical safety of their citizens—both from other citizens and from invasion. The former task is generally entrusted to the police, the latter to the military. Does this mean that police officers and generals enjoy a privileged position, even in formally democratic polities? Of course it does: just as the economy may perform poorly if companies are not given sufficient incentives to invest, so there may be widespread civic unrest—or even worse, the loss of a nation's very sovereignty—if the claims of the police and the military are ignored. Since these latter two outcomes are at least as consequential as anything with which business executives can threaten politicians, the position of the police and the military must be considered at least as privileged as that of business.

Because we live in a highly specialized society, different social tasks are entrusted to different groups of individuals. Government, for example, is held responsible for safeguarding the public's health. This, in turn, makes government officials dependent on the skills and commitment of a certain category of medical personnel; if the latter cannot be induced to perform their tasks—such as, for example, finding a cure for AIDS—tens of thousands of citizens will find their lives endangered. Similarly, if the government wishes to develop more advanced nuclear weapons, put a man on the moon or design a Star Wars defense system, it makes itself dependent on the relatively small handful of individuals who possess the appropriate scientific and technical skills. Indeed, since the number of these individuals is far smaller than the number of businessmen, each of them is proportionately even more powerful than is each businessman. And, unlike those who currently occupy the role of businessman, they cannot be as readily replaced.

It is not simply businessmen who claim that unless they are given sufficient resources dire consequences will follow. The head of every single governmental agency and non-profit institution makes the identical argument. Thus educators inform us that unless we spend more resources on schools the next generation will be illiterate, and military officials regularly tell us that unless they are given more advanced and expensive weaponry the sovereignty of the nation will be endangered. Their threats are no more—or less—credible than those of business executives. Nor are the potential consequences of ignoring their demands necessarily any less severe. Indeed, on balance, the adverse social consequences of some government em-

ployees not being given sufficient incentives or resources to discharge their various responsibilities would in many cases be much
more immediate—and potentially catastrophic—than those of businessmen not being provided with sufficient incentives to make additional investments.

Dahl and Lindblom argue that an important source of the unique
power of businessmen is that they must be induced, rather than
commanded, to perform the 'many organizational and leadership
tasks that are delegated to them'.[21] But, again, how does that make
businessmen unique? Our society relies upon a system of inducements to perform an infinite variety of tasks. The electoral system
itself functions by inducing politicians, largely in the form of offering them the prospect of being elected or re-elected, to be accountable to the citizenry. Contrary to Lindblom's assertion that 'government officials . . . are directed and controlled through a system of
commands',[22] these politicians, in turn, must provide inducements to
various public agencies, largely in the form of allocating resources to
them. Otherwise, the latter may not assist them in carrying out their
electoral promises. Similarly, government agencies cannot command
citizens to work for them: they must offer them inducements in the
form of wages and various other benefits or privileges. Indeed, since
the abolition of the draft in the United States, even the military must
now induce rather than command a certain proportion of the population to serve in the nation's armed forces.

Inducements pervade the relationship between the government
and a wide variety of institutions, not simply business. If the nation
wishes to produce more engineers, it cannot issue commands to
schools of engineering; it must somehow induce their deans to expand their enrollments. The United States currently faces a national
shortage of teachers. Will this shortage be ameliorated by the government 'commanding' more individuals to pursue careers in education or by providing them with 'inducements' to do so? Similarly, if a
society wishes to increase or decrease its rate of population growth, it
can scarcely command families to have more or fewer children;
rather, it must provide them with various inducements to do so. And
if the government wishes individuals to save more and spend less (or
vice versa) it also is hardly in a position to command them to do so;
rather, through either exhortation or changes in the tax code, it
must provide them with appropriate inducements.

Moreover, businessmen themselves must rely upon inducements if
they are to increase their own wealth. They must induce investors or
lenders to supply them with capital and other businessmen to sell
them supplies. They also must induce individuals to work for them,

and they must provide these individuals, once employed, with incentives to be diligent, creative and productive. Just as they cannot command capital or labour, neither can they command consumers to purchase their products or services. They must induce them to do so. That is why 'command' economies do not make much use of advertising.

Inducements are equally critical for the non-profit sector. Trade associations, public interest groups, political parties, private social welfare organizations, cultural institutions, universities—none of these organizations can 'command' the resources they need to carry on their objectives. Rather, they must induce the public to volunteer their time and money if they are to survive and grow. In short, inducements pervade our entire society: they characterize relationships within the political system, between government and a variety of non-government actors and within both the market economy and the non-profit sector. They define not a market economy, but a non-totalitarian one.

This last point is extremely important. Democratic governments generally do not command businessmen to produce goods and services. But, by like token, they do not issue commands to workers, telling them where to live or what occupation to follow. Nor do they issue commands to consumers, telling them what and how much to purchase. They also do not issue commands to university professors instructing them what to teach or to journalists informing them what to publish. Nor do they command their citizens not to travel abroad or emigrate. In short, there is nothing atypical about the relationship between business and government: democratic governments treat businessmen no differently from the way they treat anyone else. And command economies treat everyone else the way they treat 'businessmen'.

Of course, democratic governments do not rely exclusively upon inducements, any more than state-socialist societies rely exclusively upon commands. They also enact innumerable laws and regulations that impose constraints on the behaviour of both individuals and institutions. These laws and regulations are backed up by the coercive power of the state, though their enforcement obviously varies. A major portion of these rules and regulations affects the conduct of businessmen. The government commands companies to pay a share of their profits in taxes, treat women and minorities fairly, not to export particular products to various countries, to disclose their financial status to prospective investors, not to pay their workers less than a specified wage and to install various safety equipment on their machinery. Through its controls over land-use, it forbids companies from locating in specified areas, and through the power of eminent domain it can expropriate private property for public purposes. For specific sectors of the economy, the government tells businessmen how much to produce, and for other sectors what services it must provide to customers, and at what cost.

Moreover, the line between a 'command' and an 'inducement' is not as sharp as Lindblom's analysis implies. Commands can be regarded as inducements in the sense that one is 'induced' to comply with them in order to avoid paying a fine or going to prison. Similarly, if the inducements offered by the government are sufficient to change behaviour, then they, in effect, have the authority of a command. In any event the distinction between them does not appear to be particularly critical. What is more important is that both, whether employed separately or in combination, provide democratic governments with a substantial capacity to affect the way the private economic sector allocates its resources.

In this context, it is worth noting that the number of commands the American government has issued to business has recently increased: over the last two decades, Congress has imposed more restrictions on corporate than in the entire previous history of the United States.[23] These increases in government regulation of corporate social conduct are significant for a number of reasons. First, they have significantly narrowed the boundaries of managerial discretion: each new rule and regulation has imposed an additional restriction on the prerogatives—and thus the power—of management. Secondly, unlike in the past, when many government regulations were initiated by various industries, these regulations were adopted over the strong opposition of most of the industries immediately affected by them. None was initiated by business: their adoption reflected a relative erosion in the ability of business both to define the public policy agenda and to determine the outcome of specific legislative, administrative and judicial decisions. Thirdly, in no other capitalist democracy has the making and enforcement of government regulation of corporate social conduct provoked as much contention between business and government as in the United States. Compared to those of other capitalist governments, the laws enacted by the American federal government between the mid-1960s and the late 1970s tended to be unusually strict, detailed and ambitious.[24]

Have these laws actually been enforced? Enforcement has been uneven, but it has been far from non-existent. Overall, American industry has, over the last decade, devoted 5 percent of its investments to complying with occupational health, safety, and pollution-control standards. These expenditures have reduced both industrial productivity and corporate profitability from what they would otherwise have been. But as a result the United States has dramatically reduced air pollution, improved the health of workers in a number of industries, significantly curtained discrimination against women and minorities, reduced the numbers of consumers killed or injured by a variety of products and increased the amount of land protected from industrial development. And it has done so not by providing companies with additional inducements but by threatening companies with, and frequently imposing on them, penalties for noncompliance. Moreover, America's commitment to these objectives persisted throughout the 1970s, a decade in which the overall performance of the economy was relatively weak.

One might of course reply that these regulations are of secondary significance: they do not fundamentally threaten the structure of power and privilege of the private sector. Yet reforms under capitalism have a recurrent tendency to look more benign in retrospect than at the time when they were initially proposed. Following the 1895 Supreme Court decision declaring the federal income tax unconstitutional, the *New York Times* declared that, 'The fury of ignorant class hatred, which has sufficed to overthrow absolute power in other lands . . . has dashed itself in vain against the Constitution of the United States, fortified by the institutions which a free people have established for the defense of their rights'. The *New York Sun* editorialized: 'The wave of socialist revolution has gone far, but it breaks at the point of the ultimate bulwark set up for the protection of our liberties'.[25] Sixty years ago, allowing workers to join unions or establishing a government-sponsored pension plan was regarded as a fundamental challenge to the prerogatives to management and a major threat to private property rights. Two decades ago, restricting management prerogatives over such critical decisions as whom to hire, fire and promote, where to locate production facilities, what to produce, what kinds of safety equipment to install, how much to pollute, etc., was viewed in similar terms. That executives have continued to make investments in spite of these reforms does not mean that managers have not lost power; it simply means that they have been able to adjust to having less of it.

If these 'reforms' do not 'count', what would constitute a 'significant' challenge to the power and privilege of business? Lindblom specifically mentions five 'grand issues of politico-economic organization' that businessmen have, through 'their disproportionate influence', been able to keep off the political agenda. They are:

> private enterprise, a high degree of corporate autonomy, protection of
> the status quo on distribution of income and wealth, close consultation

between business and government, and restriction of union demands to those consistent with business profitability . . .[26]

Let us consider each of them. The first, as Lindblom himself acknowledges, has been extensively discussed in Europe, so its absence from the political agenda in the United States can hardly be attributed to the power of 'businessmen' *per se*, only, at most, to the power of business in a particular capitalist country. In any event, given the history of government ownership in Western Europe, it is by no means obvious that the ownership status of the large business enterprise is of much political significance. Indeed, as Lindblom notes elsewhere, the constraints under which public-sector managers operate do not seem appreciably different from those of private-sector ones.

A 'high degree of corporate autonomy' is a rather vague phrase. While it is true that Americans do not publicly discuss the issue of corporate autonomy *per se*, they debate it rather extensively with respect to specific areas of corporate decision-making; that is precisely what the controversy over government regulation of corporate social conduct in the United States is all about. In Japan, many corporate investment decisions have been constrained by the government, while corporate labour policies are restricted by the governments of a number of European social democracies. Whether corporate autonomy, on balance, remains 'high' depends upon one's frame of reference; clearly, though, it has diminished considerably in every capitalist democracy. In any event, it has certainly been the subject of intense political debates and public scrutiny.

Lindbolm's fourth grand issue, the 'close' consultation between business and government, has also been extensively debated; indeed, it has been one of the most salient political issues in the United States over the last two decades. It is impossible to read a daily newspaper without coming across a new exposé of the close ties between business and government. More recently, many students of the American political economy have argued that linkages between the federal government and the private sector are inadequate and need to be strengthened; they want America to adopt a set of policies toward industry similar to those of Japan.[27] It is difficult to know what to make of Lindblom's last grand issue: 'the restriction of union demands to those consistent with business profitability', since this does not appear to have anything to do with government. However, union contracts have frequently reduced corporate profitability: the share of the corporate 'surplus' that was allocated to wages significantly increased in the United States during the 1970s. Indeed, in an essay on American economic policy in the postwar period, Karen

Orren has suggested that it is organized labour, not business, whose political position has been 'privileged'.[28]

We are left then with the distribution of income and wealth—an issue that, admittedly, has not been the subject of much public discussion in the United States. But what is actually meant by the 'status quo on distribution of income and wealth'? If it means that the same individuals—or their families—are able to maintain their existing share of the nation's wealth and income, then it is hard to understand why preserving the economic status quo would be in the interest of businessmen. After all, the entire purpose of engaging in business activity is to alter the status quo, i.e., to increase one's own share of income and wealth and reduce that held by others. (This of course is true internationally as well as domestically.) On the other hand, if by preserving the status quo Lindblom means to imply a static overall distribution of income and wealth, again it is not obvious why businessmen should favour such a policy. After all, the distribution of wealth and income among businessmen varies enormously: many small businessmen are in fact poorer than many workers. Why would not small businessmen want less inequality? Moreover, companies that depend on large numbers of consumers to purchase their products and services might well be better off if there were less income inequality since that would increase their sales.

More generally, even though business may, in some objective sense, benefit by having various issues kept off the political agenda, it does not follow that their status as non-issues can be attributed to the political power of business. Consider another 'non-issue': should Catholics be prohibited from occupying positions of responsibility in business and government in the United States? This question is not seriously debated in the United States. Politicians never mention it, and it is ignored by the mainstream media to a far greater extent than any of the 'non-issues' on Lindblom's list. Who benefits disproportionately from keeping this issue off the political agenda? Obviously Catholics do. Can we therefore assume that the lack of extensive public discussion of this issue reflects the political power and influence of American Catholics? Only in the most limited sense; it is much more attributable to a broad and deeply rooted consensus among Americans that the case for discrimination in employment based on religion is not an appropriate subject for public discussion. The fact that Catholics clearly benefit from this consensus does not mean that they created it or that they possess the power to prevent it from being underminded.

There are in fact an infinite number of policy alternatives Americans do not publicly discuss, ranging from restoring slavery to nationalizing private universities. None of them is neutral: in each case a particular subset of the population disproportionately benefits from public silence about them. If businessmen are 'privileged' because Americans do not publicly discuss alternatives to capitalism, then by like token, blacks are privileged because we do not debate restoring slavery, private universities are privileged because we have not seriously considered nationalizing them and Catholics are privileged because we do not debate the merits of banning them from public and corporate employment. In short, businessmen are not unique. We all benefit by keeping various issues off the political agenda.

Lindblom does, of course, acknowledge that the agenda of all capitalist societies has not been uniform. For example, he notes that the issue of government ownership has been much more salient in Europe than in the United States. But he fails to appreciate the extent to which this undermines his entire argument about 'circularity'. For, if issues that threaten the prerogatives of businessmen have been seriously debated in some capitalist societies, then the ability of business to control the political agenda is *not* an inherent characteristic of a capitalist polyarchy. Rather, it must be due to the fact that the power of business is not uniform but rather varies, both among different capitalist societies and over time. But that is precisely the pluralist argument.

AGENDA FOR FUTURE RESEARCH

Clearly businessmen exercise considerable power over their employees, the political system and the economy as a whole. However, this article has suggested that the way political scientists have gone about analysing the power of business suffers from serious shortcomings. How then should we go about studying corporate power?

First, we need to take seriously Dahl's notion that the corporation is in fact a private government. But we need to do more than simply accept this: we need to describe how power is actually distributed in the corporation. Are corporations actually institutions in which the many are regularly 'chained in submission to the few'?[29] How much mobility is there within them? How are wealth and income distributed among their employees and according to what criteria? How much freedom are individuals actually able to exercise at different levels of the corporate hierarchy? Moreover, if we are to search for ways of making corporations more democratic, we need to determine which decision-making units are the most appropriate. Should we focus on altering the authority structure of the work unit, plant, division or all of a company's production units within a particular geographic region?

Clearly businessmen exercise political power. But that is hardly the issue: in a democratic society, *all* citizens are, in principle, in a position to exercise power. Presumably, Lindblom does not believe that businessmen should have *less* power than anyone else. The issue is: do they wield power out of proportion to their numerical representation in our society? Before we can answer this question, we must first specify how many of them there are. Who actually qualifies as a 'businessman'? If they are defined as those individuals who are responsible for organizing a nation's production of goods and services, then we would have to include not only senior corporate executives but also middle managers and small businessmen, including those who are self-employed. On the other hand, if businessmen are defined as those who own a share of the means of production, then we would have to include all those who own their own companies, participate in limited partnerships or hold shares in enterprises managed by either themselves or other people. If one includes all those who own corporate stock, whether individually or through pension funds, then a majority of all households in the United States might contain a 'businessman'. In any event, either definition encompasses tens of millions of people.

Determining what proportion of citizens are 'businessmen' is critical to any assessment of the relationship between business power and democratic rule. For the privileged position of businessmen is more threatening to a democratic polity if only 1 per cent of households contain a businessman than if 20 or 50 per cent qualify. Certainly not all these businessmen are equally powerful. But then we need to specify which subsets wield disproportionate political power.

We next need to describe the scope of their power. Obviously businessmen are not in a position to exercise disproportionate power with respect to all decisions. Their opinion, for example, as to whether or not the United States should permit abortions or provide aid to the rebels in Afghanistan presumably carries no more weight than that of any other group of citizens concerned about these issues. On the other hand, they might well be able disproportionately to affect tax or regulatory policies. But what is the relative importance of the issues whose resolution they are in a unique position to affect as compared to those that they are not?

This is an extremely important question, since defining the relative importance of the scope of corporate power provides us with a basis for comparing the power of business with those of other institutions. Clearly there are scores of issues that a significant number of Americans regard as the most important facing their society on which the views of businessmen are irrelevant. For these individuals, the political power wielded by business is less important than that exercised by, for example, the Catholic Church or the National Association of Women. Presumably, the more critical we regard the issues in whose resolution businessmen are interested, the more power we are likely to attribute to business.

Once we have both specified the range of issues in whose resolution businessmen are particularly interested and defined their relative importance, we are in a position to examine directly the political power of business. Political power has two dimensions: the ability to control the political agenda, and the ability to affect the resolution of those issues that are subject to public debate. All power, however, is relative: we are not interested in whether or not businessmen are 'powerful' but in how their power compares to that of other interest groups, institutions and organizations. Political power is also relative in another sense: it can vary over time. In fact, the political power of business in the United States has changed substantially over the last quarter-century: it decreased between the mid-1960s and the mid-1970s and has significantly increased over the last decade.[30] While it is true that, at least in the United States, the times when business is relatively powerful exceed those when it is not, this does not make business unique: in politically stable societies, the power of most institutions and organizations is relatively unchallenged most of the time. Finally, the degree of political power wielded by business is not necessarily identical in different capitalist nations or within different political units of the same nation. If Lindblom chooses to characterize the political position of business in the United States as 'privileged', one wonders what adjective he would use to describe the political power of large companies in postwar Japan or in France of the 1950s and 1960s.

To understand the extent of corporate political power we need to study both history and comparative politics. The agenda of democratic politics has varied enormously—both over time and among different capitalist democracies. At some point in some capitalist nation, virtually every conceivable issue whose resolution would either significantly enhance, or reduce, corporate power has in fact been debated. Does the scope of the political agenda follow some pattern that we can identify? Do businessmen appear to have more control over certain political outcomes in some capitalist societies than in others? And within any particular capitalist society how do both the political agenda and political outcomes vary over time? How can we account for these variations? In short, how, and why, do some 'non-issues' become 'issues', and vice versa?

We can employ a similar approach to measure the ability of busi-

ness, as compared to that of other political actors, to affect the resolution of issues that do in fact come before the political process. This
approach, however, comes up against an important objection,
namely, that the 'defeats' experienced by business may be of only
marginal importance: they may not fundamentally threaten corporate prerogatives. In Lindblom's words, 'Pluralism at most operates
only in an unimprisoned zone of policy making'.[31] But those who
advance this argument need to define more precisely what a fundamental challenge to corporate power would look like. What, in short,
are the constraints that no capitalist state could successfully impose
upon business? And how do these constraints compare to those that
a democracy also cannot impose upon other interest groups, organizations and institutions?

It is also important that we clarify the appropriate unit of analysis
for measuring corporate power. Is the power of business best understood by examining the political influence of particular companies,
industries and firms above a certain size or all business? Those who
argue that business dominates the political process tend to emphasize the latter two categories, but the basis for their judgement is not
self-evident. For it is not the case that those issues that affect only a
particular firm or industry are necessarily less important than those
that affect all or most companies. Some issues on which the interests
of business are divided, such as tax or trade policies, may actually be
far more consequential than issues in whose resolution all firms have
a common stake, such as affirmative action. Moreover, if we exclude
from our purview all issues that fall into the former two categories,
we risk depriving ourselves of the great bulk of available data on
business–government relations. It is difficult to believe that the resolution of virtually every issue affecting business that actually comes
before the political process is irrelevant to our understanding of the
extent and scope of corporate power.

In sum, in order to describe the political power of business we
need to specify the businesses to which we are referring, the scope
and significance of the issues whose outcome they have influenced,
and when and where this power has been exercised. Doing this systematically will take us a significant step beyond the straightforward
pluralist models of the 1950s and 1960s. It will enable us to discern
the patterns that underlie the exercise of corporate political power
over particular issues in different capitalist polities during different
historical periods.

Politics and Markets has made a major contribution to our discipline
by making political scientists more aware of the political significance
of the business corporation. The controversies the book has pro-

voked have been both stimulating and productive; all those who study business–government relations owe Lindblom an enormous debt. Doubtless, business does have formidable resources to bring to bear on the political process and we need to understand better how it uses those resources to affect both public opinion and public policy. My contention is not that individual companies, trade associations and interindustry coalitions do not wield significant political power; of course they do. It is rather that we do not require a distinctive methodology for measuring the political power of business in capitalist democracies. Business is not unique. There is nothing about the nature, scope or magnitude of the power wielded by business that cannot be accounted for within the framework of a sophisticated model of interest-group politics.

NOTES

1. See, for example, Peter Bachrach, *The Theory of Democratic Elitism* (Boston: Little, Brown, 1967); Robert Engler, *The Brotherhood of Oil* (Chicago: University of Chicago Press, 1977); Michael Reagan, *The Managed Economy* (London: Oxford University Press, 1963).

2. See Henry Kariel, *The Decline of American Pluralism* (Stanford, Calif.: Stanford University Press, 1961); Grant McConnell, *Private Power and American Democracy* (New York: Alfred A. Knopf, 1967); Theodore Lowi, *The End of Liberalism* (New York: W. W. Norton, 1969).

3. See, for example, Edward Greenberg, *Serving the Few* (New York: Wiley, 1974); Ira Katznelson and Mark Kesselman, *The Politics of Power* (New York: Harcourt Brace Jovanovich, 1975); Mark Nadel, *Corporations and Political Accountability* (Lexington, Mass.: D. C. Heath, 1976); G. David Garson, *Power and Politics in the United States* (Lexington, Mass.: D. C. Heath, 1977); Michael Parenti, *Power and the Powerless* (New York: St. Martin's Press, 1978); Kenneth Dolbeare, *Democracy At Risk: The Politics of Economic Renewal* (Chatham, NJ: Chatham House, 1984); Edward Greenberg, *Capitalism and the American Political Ideal* (New York: M. E. Sharpe, 1985).

4. Robert Dahl and Charles Lindblom, *Politics, Economics, and Welfare* (Chicago: University of Chicago Press, 1976), p. xxxvi.

5. Robert Dahl, *After the Revolution: Authority in a Good Society* (New Haven, Conn.: Yale University Press, 1970).

6. Robert Dahl, *Dilemmas of Pluralist Democracy* (New Haven, Conn.: Yale University Press, 1982); *A Preface to Economic Democracy* (Berkeley: University of California Press, 1985).

7. Charles E. Lindblom, *Politics and Markets* (New York: Basic Books, 1977), pp. xxxvi, xxxvii.

8. Charles F. Andrain, 'Capitalism and Democracy Reappraised', *Western Political Quarterly*, xxxvii (1984), 652–54; Andrew Blowers, 'Master of Fate or Victim of Circumstance—The Exercise of Corporate Power in Environ-

ment Policy-Making', *Policy and Politics*, XI (1983), 393–415; Robert Dahl, 'On Removing Certain Impediments to Democracy in the United States', *Political Science Quarterly*, XCII (1977), 1–20; Thomas Dye, 'Oligarchic Tendencies in National Policy-Making: The Role of the Private Policy-Planning Organizations', *Journal of Politics*, XL (1978), 309–31; Lawrence B. Joseph, 'Democratic Revisionism Revisited', *American Journal of Political Science*, XXV (1981), 160–87; Lawrence B. Joseph, 'Corporate Political Power and Liberal Democratic Theory', *Polity*, XV (1982), 246–67; Charles E. Lindblom, 'The Market as Prison', *Journal of Politics*, XLIV (1982), 324–36; Edgar Litt, 'Why Democratic Pluralism Reduces Inequality in the United States', *Polity*, XVII (1984), 396–403; John Manley, 'Neopluralism: A Class Analysis of Pluralism I and Pluralism II', *American Political Science Review*, LXXVII (1983), 368–83; David Marsh, 'Interest Group Activity and Structural Power: Lindblom's *Politics and Markets*', *West European Politics*, VI (1983), 3–13; Michael Moran, 'Politics, Banks, and Markets: An Anglo-American Comparison', *Political Studies*, XXXII (1984), 173–89; Mark Nadel, 'The Hidden Dimension of Public Policy: Private Governments and the Policy-Making Process', *Journal of Politics*, XXXVII (1975), 2–34; Sidney Plotkin, 'Corporate Power and Political Resistance: The Case of the Energy Mobilization Board', *Polity*, XVIII (1985), 115–37; Larry Preston, 'Freedom, Markets, and Voluntary Exchange', *American Political Science Review*, LXXVIII (1984), 959–69; Kay Scholzman, 'What Accent the Heavenly Chorus? Political Equality and the American Pressure System', *Journal of Politics*, XLVI (1984), 1006–32; David Vogel, 'The Power of Business in America: A Reappraisal', *British Journal of Political Science*, XIII (1983), 19–43.

9. David Menninger, 'Business and Politics', *PS*, XVIII (1985), 210.

10. Manley, 'Neopluralism'; Preston, 'Freedom'.

11. Dahl, 'On Removing', p. 8.

12. Dahl, *Dilemmas*, p. 198.

13. Ibid.

14. Lindblom, *Politics and Markets*, p. 171.

15. Ibid., p. 175.

16. Lindblom, 'The Market as Prison', p. 326.

17. Ibid., p. 330.

18. For a detailed description and analysis of this phenomenon, see chap. 12 in this volume.

19. According to *The Economist*, 'two-thirds of all new jobs created in the United States between 1968 and 1976 were created by companies with 20 or fewer employees. This trend has continued. . . . About 1.4 million new businesses are now being created in America each year'; 'In Praise of Pizza Parlours', *The Economist*, 17 May 1986, p. 75.

20. Lindblom, 'The Market', p. 326.

21. Dahl and Lindblom, *Politics and Markets*, p. xxxvii.

22. Lindblom, 'The Market', p. 327.

23. See David Vogel, 'The "New" Social Regulation in Historical and Comparative Perspective', in Thomas K. McCraw, ed., *Regulation in Perspective* (Boston, Mass.: Harvard Business School, 1981), pp. 155–86.

24. See David Vogel, *National Styles of Regulation: Environmental Policy in Great Britain and the United States* (Ithaca, NY: Cornell University Press, 1986).

25. Arthur M. Schlesinger, *The American as Reformer* (Cambridge, Mass.: Harvard University Press, 1968), p. 80.

26. Lindblom, *Politics and Markets*, p. 205.

27. See, for example, Lester Thurow, *The Zero-Sum Solution* (New York: Simon and Schuster), 1985.

28. Karen Orren, 'Union Politics and Postwar Liberalism in the United States, 1946–1979', in Karen Orren and Stephen Skowronek, eds., *Studies in American Political Development*, vol. 1 (New Haven, Conn.: Yale University Press, 1986), pp. 215–56.

29. Manley, 'Neopluralism', p. 378.

30. See Vogel, 'The Power of Business in America'.

31. Lindblom, 'The Market as Prison', p. 331.

Chapter Ten

THE POWER OF BUSINESS IN AMERICA: A REAPPRAISAL

OVER THE PAST fifteen years, there has been a steady stream of books and articles on business—government relations describing the 'privileged position' occupied by the business corporation in the American political system.[1] Taking issue with the pluralist paradigm that dominated writing and research on American national politics in the two decades after the Second World War, these writers have argued that business is not simply another interest group.[2] Instead, they have suggested that its role in American society is more akin to that of a dominant class, power elite or private government: it thus possesses a degree of influence that invariably exceeds that of any other class or interest group. This appraisal of the political dominance of business in contemporary American society primarily rests on four sets of interrelated observations. These include the ability of business to define the political agenda; the extent to which business gains disproportionate benefits from the political process; the need for elected officials to maintain a high degree of 'business confidence'; and the superior capacity of business interests to mobilize political resources, work closely with each other and shape the climate of public and elite opinion.

The purpose of this chapter is to question the validity of this analysis by examining a particular period in recent American politics: the decade from the mid-1960s to the mid-1970s. When contrasted to either the previous quarter-century or the subsequent half-decade, this period witnessed a significant decline in the political influence of business. A loose coalition of middle-class based consumer and environmental, feminist and civil rights organizations, assisted on occasion by organized labour, aided by a sympathetic media and supported by much of the intelligentsia, were able to influence both the terms of public debate and the outcomes of government policy in a direction antithetical to the interests of business. While the evidence presented in this essay is too limited to resolve the numerous points of contention between pluralists and their critics, it does demonstrate the need to develop a more sophisticated understanding of the dynamics of corporate political influence than is revealed in much of the recent literature on the subject.

This chapter explicitly challenges the views of those who have tended to regard both corporate power and corporate ties with government as essentially static and stable—at least since a particular stage in the development of American capitalism, usually dated at either the turn of the century or following the Second World War.[3] Rather, its central contention is that both the political effectiveness and the political activity of business vary considerably over time and that a detailed analysis of these variations is critical to an understanding of the dynamics of the distribution of power in America. Part I offers a brief outline of the erosion of business influence between the mid-1960s and the mid-1970s. Part II documents the significant shifts in the extent and nature of corporate political activity that occurred as a response to this development. The third part briefly chronicles the resurgence of corporate influence that took place during the second half of the 1970s and analyses some of the factors responsible for this most recent shift in the relative political position of business.

THE DECLINE OF BUSINESS INFLUENCE

Control of the Political Agenda

In *The Semi-Sovereign People*, E. E. Schattschneider writes that 'the definition of the alternatives is the supreme instrument of power.'[4] More recently, the identification of political power with the ability to determine which sets of potential conflicts among the citizenry actually become objects of public controversy is associated with those critical of the pluralist paradigm. For example, Bachrach and Baratz criticize Dahl for assuming that the political controversies he witnessed in New Haven actually involved 'important decisions'.[5] Instead, they contend that implicit in each political system is a 'mobilization of bias', that severely limits the ability of those subversive of the status quo to enter the political arena.[6] As a result, critical challenges by powerful minorities are thwarted by a process of 'non-decision making and thus are unable to enter the relevant decision-making arena'.[7] In short, they argue, like many other Marxist and non-Marxist scholars, that a critical dimension of political power is the ability to prevent the emergence of issues which challenge the existing allocation of values, or, alternatively, to promote political controversies whose resolution is unlikely to harm or likely to support elite privilege.[8]

What happened to business's control of the political agenda during the period in which we are interested? By any possible index, it declined remarkably. Business found itself on the ideological defensive to a greater extent than at any time since the New Deal. Certainly, the liberal tradition was not seriously threatened; neither socialism nor fascism entered the mainstream of political discourse. However, a number of proposals were widely debated that did seriously threaten important corporate prerogatives. The most important of these included the establishment of a government mechanism to facilitate national economic planning—proposed by a prominent group of distinguished citizens in 1975 and subsequently the subject of considerable debate—and a proposal that all firms above a certain size be chartered by the federal government, first offered in 1971 by Ralph Nader and similarly the focus of intense discussion throughout much of the decade.[9]

Although neither came close to being enacted in the form in which they were originally prepared, both proposals—and a variety of less dramatic reforms associated with them—did publicly question a critical array of hitherto sacrosanct management prerogatives; the former, focusing on the economy as a whole, reflected widespread public concern about the ability of the marketplace and thus corporate managers to make appropriate allocations of capital. The latter raised the issue of corporate accountability by explicitly questioning the capacity of corporate executives to manage their companies under existing law and custom without causing undue harm to consumers, employees, stockholders and the general public. Even the issue of public ownership, which, like the former two issues, had lain dormant since the 1930s, re-emerged during this period: in 1974, a bill to establish a federal energy corporation that would have directly competed with the investor-owned oil industry failed by only a handful of votes in the Senate.[10]

If there is any one set of values with which business in America has identified, it is that of the virtue of unlimited industrial growth and economic expansion. Yet throughout this ten-year period, the economic and social benefits of a steadily increasing output of goods and services were subject to more extensive questioning than at any previous point in American history.[11] Beginning with the publication in 1962 of Rachel Carson's best-seller *Silent Spring*, the American public was exposed to a continual stream of revelations in the mass media about the alleged deleterious effects of various products and production processes on the health and safety of consumers, employees and the public—if not the well-being of the planet.[12] Each new scandal served to weaken further public confidence in the integrity and competence of those who managed large corporations. Thus the number of people expressing a great deal of confidence in the heads of large corporations stood at 55 per cent in 1966, declining to 29 per cent by 1973, 21 per cent by 1974 and 15 per cent by 1975.[13] The terms of public discussion of the issue of environmental protection, as it emerged as the focus of popular concern in the late 1960s, tended to be highly critical of business values in general and the performance of several important industries in particular.[14]

In general, from the mid-1960s to the mid-1970s, the dominant tone of political discourse and even much of popular culture assumed an adversarial relationship with all the major institutions in American society, including the large corporation.[15] Each of the social movements of the 1960s and early 1970s—the civil rights movement, the consumer movement, the anti-war movement, the women's movement, the environmental movement—drew their political support from roughly the same constituency: relatively young, well-educated, middle-class individuals, a disproportionate number of whom worked in non-profit institutions, including, but not confined to, government[16]—the most rapidly growing sector of the post-war economy.

More specifically, throughout this period most of the issues on the political agenda in which business had an interest were initiated not by business, but by those who represented constituencies whose objectives differed with those of the corporate sector. Environmental protection, occupational health and safety, consumer protection, price controls on energy, affirmative action, product liability, expansion of the welfare state, tax reform, prohibitions on corporate overseas payments, the regulation of multinational corporations, corporate government and accountability, the reform of campaign financing, 'corporate lawlessness', restrictions on corporate trade and investment practices overseas—not a single one of those issues was initiated by business interests—although individual companies and industries clearly differed in their appraisal of the threats posed by particular issue-areas. While a variety of subsidy programmes continued to be proposed by particular industries, this period exhibited a striking lack of political initiatives from the business community as a whole. Instead, the business community found itself fighting its political battles primarily on terrain defined by those who wanted to reduce its prerogatives.

The Resolution of Political Conflict

During this decade there was a significant increase in the amount of legislation—primarily in the regulatory area—that was adopted in spite of corporate opposition. Between 1965 and 1975 more than twenty-five major pieces of federal regulatory legislation in the areas of consumer and environmental protection, occupational health and safety and personnel policy were enacted by the Federal Government. The amount of federal personnel responsible for administrating these laws increased from 9,707 in 1970 to 52,098 in 1975, while direct federal expenditures on regulatory activity increased more than five-fold.[17] Most of this regulatory legislation focused on the abuses of particular industries such as meat processing, automobiles, drugs and advertising. However, an important segment was much more sweeping in its impact. Thus, between 1969 and 1974, the federal government adopted the National Environmental Policy Act, the Clean Air Act Amendments, the Occupational Safety and Health Act, the Consumer Product Safety Act, the Federal Water Pollution Control Act, the Noise Pollution and Control Act, the Equal Employment Opportunity Act, the Campaign Finance Amendments and the Employment Retirement Income Security Act—each of which directly affected the overwhelming majority of large corporate enterprises operating within the United States.

Students of regulation have frequently noted that the passage of regulatory statutes themselves are hardly indicative of a shift in public priorities away from those of business.[18] In fact, the history of corporate capitalism in America provides ample evidence that most government regulatory agencies, if they did not shortly become coopted by the industries they were charged with supervising, at least enforced policies that proved entirely compatible with the long-term prosperity and legitimacy of the corporations under their purview. While it is certainly true that the 'capture' theorists of regulation, such as Bernstein, never suggested that new regulatory agencies would be subverted by business immediately, the ability of so many diverse constituencies to challenge corporate control of so many regulatory agencies simultaneously is unprecedented in the history of American business-government relations. Indeed, in a number of critical areas, including personnel policy, occupational health and safety and consumer and environmental protection, controls over business in the United States were more stringent, and certainly as strictly enforced, than in any other industrial country. The mutual mistrust and antagonism that developed between the regulators and the regulated during this period has no parallel outside the United States, traditionally considered the most conservative or pro-business capitalist democracy.[19]

In marked contrast to most of the regulatory agencies established during the Progressive Era and the New Deal, many of the more recently established agencies have proved relatively insensitive to corporate priorities. Recent regulatory statutes are far more likely to contain provisions specifying detailed standards of corporate conduct, thus significantly narrowing the traditional gap between legislative intent and administrative enforcement.[20] In addition, the agencies themselves came under intense scrutiny by highly knowledgeable and effective public-interest lawyers and lobbyists fully aware that the passage of legislation is itself insufficient to change corporate behaviour.[21] Armed with a wide variety of legal and administrative remedies to enable them to participate actively in the formulation and implementation of regulatory decisions, they proved a highly effective counterpart to corporate lawyers and lobbyists.

James Q. Wilson wrote in 1980, 'the cost of obtaining effective access to the political process has been lowered dramatically in the last decade or two'.[22] Assisted by foundation grants, computerized direct-mail fund drives, liberalized standing requirements in the federal courts and various public subsidies, as well as by sympathetic press coverage, public-interest groups became important participants in the political process. Finally, the traditional revolving door between executives and public officials was supplemented—and in some cases supplanted—by the emergence of an equally symbiotic relationship between public-interest activists and regulatory agency personnel.[23]

One rough measure of the effectiveness of these new regulatory agencies in changing corporate priorities is the amount of corporate expenditures they have succeeded in dictating. Although there is substantial disagreement over both the direct and indirect costs of social regulation to business, the former, at least, appears to have been substantial. For example, in 1976, corporate expenditure on environmental protection was estimated at $7.8 billion while compliance with OSHA regulations was estimated at $3.2 billion.[24] It is true that many of these expenditures have involved net benefits to society as a whole, while some regulations have actually benefited particular firms, industries and regions.[25] Moreover, many of the costs of compliance with social regulations are either passed along to the consumer or are offset by forgone wage increases. Nevertheless, they have clearly involved real financial and administrative burdens for a substantial segment of American industry. Corporate spending to meet regulatory requirements is at least partially responsible for some of the decline in the rate of productivity increase that began in the late 1960s. According to one study, environmental and worker health and safety programmes cut conventionally measured productivity by 1.4 per cent between 1967 and 1975.[26] Government regulation is also related at least in part to a significant decline in corporate profit rates: while the average return to industry between 1947 and 1965 was 8.6 per cent, between 1970 and 1978 it averaged (when adjusted for inflation) approximately 5 per cent.[27]

When viewed in the context of the history of American business, the changes in the nature and scope of government regulation that occurred from the mid-1960s to the mid-1970s represented a significant transfer of decision-making authority from the private to the public sector; in this sense they were clearly 'important decisions'. While the costs of corporate compliance with social regulations remained marginal from the perspective of the economy as a whole, the increased politicization of private-sector decision making itself represented a major reduction in the autonomy of corporate managers throughout the American economic system. In effect, the traditional distinction between 'regulated' and unregulated industries became obsolete—particularly as the former gradually became freed from price and entry/exit controls. For the first time in American history, government regulators began routinely to shape and influence virtually every important decision made by nearly every large firm. Nearly every corporate department developed a counterpart in the regulatory bureaucracy: decisions as to what to produce, where to produce it, whom to hire and promote, how to allocate research and development funds and—even for a brief period—how much to charge customers and pay employees—became subject to a highly complex process of negotiations and bargaining between corporate officials and regulators, congressmen and judges.[28] Executives throughout the firm were constantly required to anticipate the decisions of regulatory agencies, Congress, and the courts—even if only to challenge them. As an article in *Fortune* concluded in 1975,

> through streams of legislation, spreading and minutely detailed regulation, frequent application of moral suasion, and various other means, the government is now present—either in person, or somewhat like Banquo's ghost, in disturbing spirit—at every major business meeting.[29]

Consider the changes in the fate of two of the nation's most important industries: automobiles and oil. Before the passage of the National Traffic and Motor Vehicle Safety Act in 1966, the automobile was completely unregulated by the federal government. With the major form of federal involvement in the automobile industry consisting of the subsidization of highway construction (apart from labour relations where the government's role was relatively passive), Ford Motor Company did not even have a full-time lobbyist. By the mid-1970s, nearly every aspect of the automobile was regulated, including its exhaust levels, fuel efficiency and safety; a major share of the car industry's research and development became devoted to compliance with government directives, while the cumulative impact of eighteen government-mandated specifications adopted between 1968 and 1974 was estimated to have increased the retail price of the average car by $300.[30] Edward N. Cole, retiring from the presidency of General Motors Corporation, complained in 1974 that 'The fun is gone . . . I wouldn't go into the automobile business again.'[31] While the oil industry was extensively regulated by the federal government from the 1930s, this regulation was largely initiated and supported by the industry itself; indeed the oil industry was generally regarded as the nation's most powerful. But this pattern began to change in 1973 with the passage of the Emergency Petroleum Allocation Act. As a result, the industry's control over both fuel allocation and fuel prices was usurped by the federal government—much to the industry's chagrin. It was also forced to accept a reduction in its depletion allowance, a goal for which the industry's critics had unsuccessfully struggled for at least two decades. While the oil industry was able to resist successfully efforts to force it to divest, overall industry–government relations were more strained during most of the 1970s than at any time since the Progressive Era.[32]

The focus of federal expenditures also shifted during this period. Relatively more of the funds dispersed by the government tended to go directly to individuals—often of moderate or low income—and less to corporations in the form of government contracts. Thus, while in 1950 federal social-welfare expenditure constituted less than a quarter of the national government's budget, by 1975 it represented nearly half—an absolute increase from $10.5 billion to $170 billion. At the same time, expenditure on military and space hardware—the most important sources of government subsidy to the private sector during the postwar period—steadily declined as a percentage of the federal budget.[33] And in 1969, a tax reform law was enacted that went directly counter to the interests of high-income tax payers by increasing the tax rate on capital gains.

Business Confidence

The most powerful political weapon of business is usually thought to be its ability to withhold additional capital investment if its political demands are not met. Since the prosperity of the United States as a whole as well as the growth rates of particular regions and communities are largely dependent on the rate and location of private investment, politicians would appear to have an important incentive to defer to corporate priorities: if they impose restrictions on business too severely, they find themselves in difficulty when they again face the electorate.[34] But during the period we are considering, this weapon appeared to have lost much of its effectiveness. It is hard to think of a single occasion when business was able to use efficiently this 'veto' to prevent an issue from coming before the political process, and there were only two occasions when it was able to use it to overturn a particular public policy decision.[35] To be sure, business continued to 'cry wolf' at every new invasion of its prerogatives. But the complaints of corporations appeared to have lost much of their credibility.[36] Indeed, given the heightened environmental consciousness of several states and communities, the prospect of additional corporate investment was often viewed more as a liability than an incentive.

More importantly, the 1974–75 recession, at the time the most severe since the 1930s, far from revealing the vulnerability of the citizenry to 'investor confidence', became the occasion for a major increase in left–liberal policy initiatives. Not only did the issue of national economic planning reappear on the political agenda, but Congress, defying the fears expressed by both President Ford and the business community about a new outburst of inflation, significantly increased federal spending in order to reduce unemployment.[37] Even more dramatically, the energy shortage of 1973 did not increase the power of the oil industry over public policy. On the contrary, the industry itself was held responsible by much of the public for both the increase in energy prices and the lack of adequate energy supplies; it was subject to more popular abuse and political criticism than at any time since the dissolution of the Standard Oil trust in 1911.[38] While approval for the Alaska pipeline was accelerated, there was no lessening of environmental constraints on energy exploration and production in any other region of the country. Moreover, taxes on the industry were actually increased in 1974.

THE MOBILIZATION OF CORPORATE POLITICAL RESOURCES

A critical component of the argument of those who contend that business dominates the governmental processes is that business invariably commands the political resources necessary to achieve its policy objectives. Through such devices as funding electoral campaigns, hiring influential lobbyists, securing access to the media, and promoting the interchange of personnel between the private and public sectors, corporate interests are said to be readily able to translate their potential for political influence into actual control over public policy. This perspective is not without some validity: since the rise of the national corporation a century ago, large firms have on the whole enjoyed relatively good access to policy makers. And these mechanisms of influence have played an important role. But it certainly needs to be qualified sharply for the period with which we are concerned. It is incapable of accounting for one of the most striking developments in the political history of business in this century: the unprecedented increase in the amount of corporate resources devoted to influencing the federal government either directly or indirectly. As G. N. Wilson observed, 'Businesses (in the early seventies) felt under attack from public interest groups, unpopular with the electorate as a whole, and short of friends in the Congress. A new political strategy was needed.'[39]

It was as a direct response to a significant shift in the balance of power between business and interests unsympathetic to business—both within and outside of government—that business began to reorganize its approach to the influencing of government policy. The changes in corporate political behaviour that began in the early 1970s were, at least until 1977, primarily defensive. They were a response to widespread feelings of political impotence within the business community as well as businesses' recognition of the extent to which recent increases in government regulation had made corporations more vulnerable to the public policy process. Without question, the increase in the scope and severity of government regulation is the single most important factor prompting these changes in corporate political activity.[40]

The degree to which, throughout most of the 1970s, business saw itself as functioning within the political shadow of its adversaries is reflected in the particular political strategies that business adopted. Almost without exception, they represent a mirror image of those pioneered earlier by the public-interest movement. Increasing the physical presence of corporate officials in Washington, using lawsuits as a device to influence the implementation of government regulatory policy, grooming chief executives to be comfortable when dealing with the public, organizing citizens at the grass roots, making more extensive use of coalitions and *ad hoc* alliances, enhancing the awareness of common interests among diverse organizations and constituencies, using the press as a forum for influencing public opinion, seeking allies in the universities, and even becoming somewhat less partisan—each of these strategies was in large measure consciously modelled on those successfully employed against business by the public interest movement. The most prominent exception was the creation of political action committees, since public-interest organizations did not make extensive use of campaign contributions. This strategy was in turn based on that of organized labour—of whose lobbying skills business has traditionally been most in awe.

Corporate Political Participation

The substantial increases in corporate political participation that occurred in the 1970s can be divided roughly into three categories: lobbying, corporate public affairs efforts, and grass-roots organizing. Between 1968 and 1978 the number of corporations with public affairs offices in Washington increased from one hundred to more than five hundred.[41] Their size also became larger: the typical Washington corporate office now contains six or seven individuals, as contrasted with one or two individuals in 1974. For example, the Washington office of General Motors consisted of three people in 1968; ten years later it had increased to twenty-eight. Trade associations also increased their Washington presence. In 1970 21 percent of all national associations were based in Washington; by 1978, 27 percent had Washington as their headquarters. In 1977 an average of one association a week relocated its main office to the nation's capital, bringing the total number of trade associations headquartered in Washington to 2,000. And in 1973, the National Association of Manufacturers moved its headquarters to Washington, D.C., as part of its effort to upgrade its lobbying activities.

The growing corporate physical presence in Washington has been accompanied by equally sizeable increases in the numbers of lawyers and accountants. The Washington, D.C., Bar increased from 16,000 in 1972 to 26,000 in 1978—in large measure due to the increased corporate demands for legal representation. Not only have Washington law firms increased in both size and number, but a significant number of major law firms from throughout the United States now have Washington offices. Similarly, large numbers of new accounting firms have opened up offices in Washington while those already in the city have doubled and tripled the size of their professional staffs. All told, there are currently 450 law firms and 234 accounting firms in Washington—largely serving corporate clients. Moreover, an increasing share of corporate public relations campaigns now take place in Washington.

The increasing attention of business to government relations is also reflected within the firm itself. A 1979 Conference Board study reported that

Ninety-two per cent of the government relations executives polled said that over the past three years, their companies' concern with and involvement in federal government relations had gone up. Of these respondents, 61 per cent said that this increase has been extremely strong.[42]

Moreover, government relations gained greater status within the corporate organization as its practitioners became more directly involved in corporate decision-making and increased their own rank within the managing hierarchy; in many corporations, the senior public affairs officer became a member of the corporate board. Corporations also began to devote considerably more resources to the monitoring and managing of 'emerging issues'—a clear reflection of their loss of control over the political agenda.[43] Alerting firms to the changes in the public expectations of business that generally precede new regulatory initiatives also became a prominent feature of management consulting.

Another index of the shift in corporate priorities was the steady increase during the 1970s in the personal involvement of chief executive officers (CEOs) in public affairs or external relations. The Conference Board study notes that, 'One of the most striking developments in recent years has been the increasing participation of the chief executive officers in the government relations effort.'[44] A 1976 study reported that 92 per cent of the CEOs polled indicated that they were spending more time on external relations than they were in 1972 or 1970, while a 1978 survey revealed that the chief executive officers of the Fortune 1000 devoted approximately 40 per cent of their time to 'public issues'—in contrast to 20 per cent only two years earlier.[45] More recent estimates placed this number as high as 50 per cent for 'the top people in most large companies'.[46] As John deButts, the former chairman of AT&T remarked in 1978: 'So vital . . . is the relationship of government and business that to my mind the chief executive officer who is content to delegate responsibility for that relationship to his public affairs experts may be neglecting one of the most crucial aspects of his own responsibility.'[47] The formation of the Business Roundtable in 1972 was a striking symbol of this heightened commitment: the RT is the first business lobbying organization to be based on the principle of the personal participation of the corporate CEO.

This critical change in the willingness of the chief executive officer to become personally involved in the governmental process was accompanied by a shift in the background and training of CEOs. The individual who epitomized the 'modern business leader', 'with one foot in the boardroom and the other in Washington', was Irving Shapiro, who was Chairman and Chief Executive Officer of DuPont between 1974 and 1981.[48] What distinguished Shapiro was that he was chosen largely because of his skills at governmental relations. Shapiro was the first individual with no background in science, engineering or finance to become head of DuPont in the firm's nearly 200-year-old history; he rose through the company's legal department. Not surprisingly, Shapiro emerged as one of the most visible and influential public spokesmen for the business community, enjoying particularly close ties with President Carter.[49]

Corporate CEOs chosen during the 1970s were likely to be more adept at communicating with the public than was true in the past. For example, three people headed General Motors during this decade: James Roche, Richard Gerstenberg and Thomas Murphy. Each of them can be readily distinguished from his predecessors by being progressively more politically sophisticated and articulate—a fact which strongly influenced each succession. Moreover, beginning in about 1974, an increasing number of CEOs began to receive formal training in dealing with the public and the press.[50]

Finally, beginning in the mid-1970s, a number of firms made extensive efforts to mobilize their 'natural constituencies', namely, their stockholders and present and former employees. These individuals were encouraged to make political contributions through corporate political action committees as well as to correspond with their congressmen on issues affecting the company. A quarter of the firms polled by the Conference Board had recently developed a stockholder programme; it is estimated that by the late 1970s corporations were spending between $850 and $900 million per year on these efforts.[51] The company in the vanguard of this effort is Atlantic Richfield which in 1975 began organizing 53,000 of its individual shareholders, 6,000 employees, and 2,000 of its retired staff into forty-five regional committees. These committees are encouraged to take stands on public policy issues paralleling those of ARCO's management and to become politically active in their communities; the company spends $750,000 per year on these efforts.[52]

Finally, the 1970s witnessed a dramatic increase in a relatively new form of corporate participation in the electoral process: the political action committee (PAC). The number of business-related PACs increased from 248 in 1974 to 1,100 in 1978. While business-related PACs still represent a minority of the sources of campaign finance— they were responsible for 17.3 per cent of all funds raised by congressional candidates in 1978—their relative importance has increased substantially. Thus, while the contributions of business-related PACs were slightly less than those of organized labour in the 1976 congressional elections, two years later they distributed nearly double labour's sum. Although the political significance of business-sponsored political action committees remains a subject of considerable controversy, the increases in both their numbers and size that took place between 1974 and 1978 provides another indication of the heightened interest of business in the political process.[53]

Corporate Class Consciousness

A second major change took place in business-government relations during the 1970s. In response to the success of left–liberal forces, the business community became more class conscious. Many thoughtful executives and observers of business have long deplored the short-sightedness of most business attempts to influence government. Oblivious to the long-term interests of business as a whole, corporations have usually tended to evaluate public policy issues exclusively in terms of their immediate impact on their own earnings. As one executive put it in 1975, 'We don't have a business community. Just a fragmented bunch of self-interested people. When a particular industry is in trouble . . . it fights alone and everyone else turns their back'.[54] This pattern continued: companies remained more likely to become concerned with those issues that promised to affect directly their own operations and rarely devoted scarce political resources to influencing political decisions that primarily affect other industries. But throughout the 1970s businessmen also steadily became both more aware of their common concerns and more willing to act on them.

The Business Roundtable represents the clearest symbol of the heightening of class consciousness among the American *haute bourgeoisie*. Established in 1972, the Roundtable is the first new inter-industry business organization to be established in a quarter-century. However, it is not simply a mechanism for increasing the effectiveness of corporate lobbying—although that has been among its most important achievements. Among its most critical functions is that of 'raising the consciousness of top management', by educating them about issues of significance to business as a whole and promoting 'the notion that the "CEO of the future" must inevitably be a public figure, not a "private executive"'. The Roundtable does not attempt to function as 'one great big trade association', faithfully reflecting the sum of the particular interests of its 190 corporate members; rather, it develops positions on a relatively small number of issues and then encourages its membership to participate actively in their resolution. To borrow Lenin's distinction, its role is more akin to that of a vanguard party than a trade union: the Roundtable deliberately seeks to avoid advancing the narrow economic concerns of particular companies and industries in order to address issues of a more general character.

The Roundtable was remarkably successful in imposing a modicum of discipline or 'class solidarity' on what has traditionally been a rather anarchic business establishment. The Policy Committee has at times proved able to encourage the organization's members to go along with the policy decisions of the Committee—even when they were not in the particular interests of their own company. Thus, when the Policy Committee voted 19 to 11 to oppose actively the labour law reform bill, even those firms that had strongly advocated a position of neutrality and would derive no benefit from its defeat instructed their lobbyists to work actively against the bill's passage.[56] Similarly, the Roundtable opposed legislation requiring a percentage of imported oil to be carried in American ships—a policy that was clearly in the interests of the domestic merchant marine industry but inflationary for the business community as a whole.

However, the Roundtable was only the most prominent indication of the greater willingness of executives to concern themselves with the interests of business as a whole. Another was the sizeable increase in the number of *ad hoc* coalitions formed to lobby on specific issues.[57] The left–liberal community has traditionally made widespread use of these coalitions, but until fairly recently the primary unit of corporate political activity was the trade association—concerning itself exclusively with issues that immediately affected its membership. Business coalitions have focused primarily on issues of general concern to the business community, such as labour law reform, tax policy, and the consumer protection agency bill. But what is even more striking was the establishment of highly effective coalitions concerned with issues that disproportionately affected particular industries, such as energy policy and picketing practices in the construction industry. As one building contractor noted, 'It took us three or four months just to get business to understand that common-situs was their fight. We worked harder on the business community during that time than we did on Congress.'[58]

If the increases in government regulation account for much of the initial upsurge in corporate political activity, then the shift in the nature of that regulation is responsible for the increased communal consciousness of American businessmen. In his seminal 1964 *World Politics* review essay, Lowi distinguishes among three kinds of public policy: distributive, regulatory and redistributive.[59] His typology is based on the differential impact of government policies: distributive policies affect particular firms, regulatory policies influence particular industries, and redistributive policies affect business as a whole. It would seem reasonable to assume that the political consciousness of the business community would vary along parallel lines. Thus, the more the political agenda is dominated by redistributive issues, the more likely are businessmen to think in terms of their class interests. Similarly, the more distributive issues predominate, the more likely businessmen are to evaluate political decisions exclusively in terms of the welfare of their own company.

At first glance, this hypothesis appears invalid. There does not appear to have been much change in the importance of the kinds of issues that would fall into Lowi's third category between the mid-1960s and mid-1970s. It is true that tax policy, collective bargaining rights and the scope of the welfare state—the three issues Lowi specifically mentions as redistributive—were on the political agenda during this period. But their saliency were hardly sufficient to account for the developments that we have described. The vast majority of public policies affecting business involved regulatory issues; this should produce a heightening of trade association consciousness, not class consciousness. But Lowi's categories need not be taken literally. For what happened *during the first half of the seventies was precisely that government regulation of business ceased to be primarily 'regulatory'; instead it became 'redistributive'.*

The critical political change that occurred in the 1970s was that government regulation ceased to be primarily industry-specific: it began to affect business as a whole. Nor was the change simply a matter of scope. The extensiveness of the wave of social regulation that began in the late 1960s meant that regulation began to affect not only the performance but the entire balance of power within the economic system. In essence, during the 1970s the fight over government regulation became the focus of class conflict for the first time in American history: it pitted the interests of business as a whole against the public interest movement as well as much of organized labour. The nature of the conflict over regulation became analogous to the struggle over the adoption of the welfare-state and the recognition of unions that defined class conflict during the 1930s.

The Control of Ideas

A third dimension of the corporate response to the gains made by left–liberal forces during the 1960s and 1970s took place on an ideological plane. In addition to increasing their lobbying efforts and co-operating more closely with one another, business also engaged in a major and unprecedented effort to influence the climate of intellectual and public opinion. The attempts of corporations to make the prevailing 'mobilization of bias' more congenial to their economic and political interests was directed at the media, the universities and research institutes.

The magnitude of the first of these efforts is unprecedented in the history of American business. It reflected a widespread perception among corporate executives that business, economic and political reporting had become biased against business and was indirectly to blame for many of the political setbacks experienced by corporate interests in Washington.[60] Among the most visible efforts on the part of business to counter distorted media coverage was an increase in advocacy advertising—i.e., the sponsorship of advertisements designed not to sell products or influence the public image of a company, but to persuade the public of the merits of a particular political perspective. Beginning in the early 1970s,[61] corporate expenditures on institutional advertising increased steadily. Companies spent approximately $100 million on advocacy advertising in 1975 and $140 million in 1976; all estimates point to a steady expansion of expenditure in subsequent years. The most active corporation, Mobil, spent $5 million in 1975 (the last year for which figures are available), more than three times its 1973 total. While more than thirty-five major corporations and trade associations launched public advocacy campaigns, energy and utility companies were the most active. The latter, along with their respective trade associations, began devoting approximately half of their advertising budget to political persuasion. By the end of the decade, major corporate advertisers were spending about one-third of all their advertising dollars on campaigns aimed at the public in their roles as citizens rather than consumers.

Corporations, concerned about the political and intellectual influence of academics critical of business power and performance, also increased their efforts to influence the content of university education and research. A growing number of business spokesmen, including David Packard and William Simon, began urging corporations to politicize their contributions to higher education. Rather than making unrestricted grants to private universities on the basis of their academic reputations, they suggested that corporations be more discriminating: they should channel funds to schools, departments, institutes or faculty that are likely to support corporate objectives and values. While there are relatively few instances of funds being withheld from educational or research institutions because of their 'anti-business' reputations, there has been a substantial increase in the amount of private and business funding earmarked for particular projects and programmes.[62]

Finally, as a direct response to the funding that public interest groups and various left-of-centre scholars have received from liberal foundations and institutes—most notably Ford and Brookings—business began to fund extensively their conservative counterparts. Previously established conservative institutes, such as the Hoover Institution and the American Institute for Public Policy Research grew dramatically in the mid-1970s.[63] Corporate grants also fostered new institutes, including the Institute for Contemporary Studies, established in San Francisco in 1974, and the International Institute for Economic Research in Los Angeles, created in 1975.[64] The volume and scope of their publications, which include newsletters, reports, magazines, books and pamphlets, have become highly visible to scholars and journalists interested in public policy issues affecting business. They played an extremely important role in publicizing the costs associated with the expansion of government regulation as well as in promoting public policies aimed at strengthening the supply side of the American economy.

THE RESURGENCE OF CORPORATE POLITICAL POWER

The political successes of business in the late 1970s fully paralleled those enjoyed by the public interest movement a decade earlier. The political turning point for business was 1977. In that year large corporations and their allies defeated the most important legislative goals of both the consumer and labour movements, namely, the establishment of an Agency for Consumer Advocacy and labour law reform. Both were the focus of more intense business lobbying than any other piece of legislation before Congress in a decade—possibly a generation. In addition, the building trade unions were frustrated in their effort to enact a bill to allow common-situs picketing, while the linchpin of the left–liberal political agenda, the Humphrey-Hawkins full employment bill, was gutted.[65]

What really signalled the end of a decade of reform was not so much business's improved ability to prevail on issues defined by labour and the public interest movement, but its success in restoring its influence over the direction and substance of the political agenda itself. The bill reducing capital gains taxation enacted in 1978 represents a classic piece of class legislation: it provided direct financial benefits for business as a whole and virtually no benefits to middle and lower income taxpayers. The passage of this legislation was an

extraordinary political achievement for business: it represented the
most important redistributive policy initiated by business in more
than a decade.[66] Moreover, it symbolized a shift in the entire debate
over tax policy, as the issue of 'tax reform' became supplanted by a
concern over the lack of adequate investment incentives in particular
and 're-industrialization' in general.[67]

Business also succeeded in reducing the impact of previously enacted regulatory policies. The stringency of the 1970 Clean Air Act
was modified for particular industries, although strengthened for
others, while small businesses were exempted from the jurisdiction
of the Occupational Safety and Health Administration. Shortly after-
wards, Congress succumbed to intense pressure from the funeral
directors' industry and from advertisers on television programmes
directed at children and moved to restrict the power of one of the
most aggressive regulatory agencies, the Federal Trade Commission.
These shifts in policy, while relatively minor, revealed the extent to
which business had succeeded in shifting the tone of the regulatory
agenda from one dominated by 'corporate abuses' to one preoccupied with 'regulatory reform.' More importantly, in 1979 the Federal government finally began to eliminate controls of domestic oil, a
goal for which the oil industry had fought since 1974, and to phase
out controls on natural gas pricing—a prime political objective of
the energy industry since the mid-1950s. Although the policies of
the Reagan administration are beyond the scope of this article, to
date they represent a continuation of each of these trends. Among
the most important of the policies enacted by the Administration in
its first year was to decrease and weaken an array of social regulations affecting business and to help enact tax laws which significantly
reduced the rates paid by companies, investors, and the rich.

What role did the changes in the scope and extent of corporate
political activity play in this resurgence of corporate influence over
both the tone of public debate and the substance of public policy? At
least initially, its role in reversing the declining political fortunes of
business appears to have been decisive. At least part of the political
successes of the public interest movement and its allies during the
1960s and early 1970s was due to the lack of effective political organization on the part of business. Faced with a largely sympathetic
political environment since the late 1940s, the business community
had become complacent. When public criticism of the social dimensions of corporate conduct emerged in the 1960s, executives at first
had difficulty appreciating its significance. After all, were they not
providing the public with what it most wanted, namely, a steady increase in real living standards? Moreover, for nearly half a century

business's primary political adversary had been organized labour. It was thus unprepared for the emergence of political opposition based on the middle classes, rather than in the trade-union movement. In addition, many corporate lobbyists assumed that they could continue to rely indefinitely upon the assistance of a handful of extremely powerful congressional leaders either to defeat or to delay indefinitely legislation to which they were strongly opposed—as they had successfully done since the late 1930s. Finally, beginning in 1969, the White House was occupied by an administration widely regarded as sympathetic to the concerns of business.

However, after President Nixon's resignation and the rise in Democratic representation in the congressional elections in 1974, the efforts of business to mobilize its political resources increased rapidly. By 1977, these had begun to produce results. Each of the business victories in that year was a product of considerable corporate lobbying. Thus, a coalition of more than 450 separate organizations was organized to defeat the establishment of the Consumer Protection Agency, while national firms chartered planeloads of small businessmen to come to Washington to lobby their congressmen to oppose the labour law reform bill; the Roundtable played a critical role in both these efforts. Similarly, the tax bill enacted in 1978 was the product of intensive business political activity directed at both Congress and the White House. In each case the superior political resources employed by business simply overwhelmed those of liberal or pro-regulatory constituencies.

Yet, at the same time, the significance of this increased corporate political activity must be put into perspective. Both the failures and successes of business over the last fifteen years cannot be understood apart from the broad shifts in the accompanying climate of public and elite opinion. Beginning in the mid-1960s not simply business, but nearly every institution in American society, including government, was subject to widespread criticism.[68] The political movements that so successfully challenged corporate prerogatives in the late 1960s and early 1970s both derived from and reinforced the 'adversarial' intellectual and cultural climate of this period. Together they were able to widen the political agenda, making possible the adoption of a wide variety of restrictions on corporations, the enactment of which would have been inconceivable at the beginning of the 1960s.

Similarly, the resurgence of business influence in the late 1970s did not take place in a social and intellectual vacuum. It was both preceded and paralleled by a general shift in the climate of public discussion about the appropriate role for government in the economy. By the early 1970s business spokesmen, conservative economists, and neo-conservative intellectuals had begun increasingly to voice public criticisms of the consequences of various government policies affecting business. They urged that reducing inflation be made a major priority, questioned the costs and benefits of government regulation, documented the growing lack of competitiveness of the American economy, and argued that more attention should be paid to increasing the rate of savings and investment. By the end of the decade, many of their concerns had begun to be shared, in varying degrees, even by opinion-leaders in the liberal community—as well as by a substantial segment of the American middle class.[69]

Critical to both these shifts in the relative political power of business was a change in the public perception of the strength of the American economy. The political successes of the public interest movement in the 1960s and early 1970s took place in an environment of relatively high growth rates. Indeed, after more than two decades of unparalleled economic expansion, the ability of the American business system to satisfy the material needs of the citizenry had almost come to be taken for granted. The public was willing to support policies for ameliorating the undesirable by-products of industrial growth, confident that whatever burdens these might place on the private sector were well within its capacity to absorb.

However, as a result of the widely publicized economic difficulties experienced in the late 1970s by two of the nation's largest industries, steel and automobiles, public confidence in the underlying strength of the United States economy was dramatically undermined. While large sectors of the public continued to support particular regulatory programmes, the public-interest movement found itself on the defensive for the first time since its emergence in the mid-1960s. On the other hand, executives and conservative economists, who had been urging public officials to support policies aimed at improving the balance sheets of American corporations for nearly a decade, now found the public considerably more responsive to their arguments. The change in the climate of public opinion from the mid to late 1970s is striking. Thus, while the first Arab oil embargo resulted in an increase in government controls over the oil industry, the second—following the revolution in Iran in 1979—led to the lifting of price controls. Similarly, while the 1974–77 recession resulted in an increase in government spending to sustain consumer demand, the difficulties experienced by the economy in the late 1970s created an environment conducive to a series of tax cuts for companies and investors.

Seen from this perspective, Lindblom is partially correct: business is in a uniquely privileged position to persuade the public that the satisfaction of its demands is essential if high growth rates are to be restored. But there is nothing automatic about the political impact of this 'business confidence' weapon; indeed like the effects of investment itself, it may work only after a considerable time lag. It is also apt to have limited political significance in a relatively prosperous period.

CONCLUSION

Perhaps there is no need to choose between the pluralist and Marxist–power elitist appraisals of the relative power of business in the American political system. The validity of their respective analyses may simply depend on the time-frame one is examining. Thus, a pluralist perspective does offer a relatively accurate description of American politics from the late 1960s to the mid-1970s. Similarly, the relative influence of business in the twenty years following the Second World War is quite accurately described by scholars writing within a Marxist or elitist paradigm. The more critical question is: What factors contribute to relative increases and decreases in the control of business over government?

In principle, this question is at the heart of the intellectual agenda of Marxism. One of the earliest and most sophisticated Marxist critiques of pluralism explicitly criticized pluralist scholars for trying to measure power empirically instead of seeking to explain '*changes* in the association of values in society'.[70] Yet scholars working within a Marxist framework have tended to ignore this issue. The Marxist concept of 'monopoly capitalism', like its Galbraithian counterpart, 'the new industrial state', assumes the integration of big business and the national government to be the defining feature of the contemporary American political economy. But this framework renders completely inexplicable the dramatic increase in corporate political activity described in this chapter. If business and government were already so closely linked, then why would corporations have increased their political involvement so substantially? And if business already enjoyed ideological hegemony why did corporations so dramatically accelerate their efforts to re-shape public and intellectual opinion? Moreover, the Marxist concept of 'class consciousness', although in principle equally applicable to either the dominant or subordinate class, has been employed by Marxist scholars almost exclusively to understand the changes in consciousness of the latter. Yet the evidence presented in this chapter suggests that the class consciousness of the bourgeoisie also varies over time. This is an issue in which present-day Marxists, although not Marx himself, have unfortunately demonstrated relatively little interest.

Although most pluralists have been uninterested in the broader dynamics of social change, a pluralist analysis is relatively consistent with the political developments described in this chapter. Ironically, while those who challenged corporate prerogatives during the late 1960s and early 1970s were highly critical of the pluralist paradigm, their successes in increasing public controls over business does, in fact, confirm the pluralist vision. The political system did, in fact, prove highly responsive to anti-business political forces. On the other hand, although pluralism is, in theory, sensitive to the shifting currents of political influence, pluralist analyses do not illuminate the parameters within which political conflict itself takes place. By focusing on the influence of business in particular policy disputes, pluralists have tended to pay insufficient attention both to the boundaries of corporate political influence and to the processes by which political agendas themselves are formed. How powerful is business when it is politically dominant and how weak is it when it is on the defensive? How precisely does the 'conventional wisdom' change over time? These questions remain critical for any overall assessment of the political influence of business in America—or indeed that in any capitalist democracy.

NOTES

1. These books include Peter Bachrach, *The Theory of Democratic Elitism* (Boston: Little, Brown, 1967); G. William Domhoff, *Who Rules America?* (Englewood Cliffs, N.J.: Prentice-Hall, 1967); Ralph Miliband, *The State in Capitalist Society* (New York: Basic Books, 1969); Peter Bachrach and Morton S. Baratz, *Power and Poverty: Theory and Practice* (New York: Oxford University Press, 1970): Marvin Surkin and Alan Wolfe, eds., *An End to Political Science* (New York: Basic Books, 1970); Matthew A. Crenson, *The Un-Politics of Air Pollution* (Baltimore: Johns Hopkins Press, 1971); Edward Greenberg and Richard Young, *American Politics Reconsidered* (North Scituate, Mass.: Duxbury Press, 1973); Edward Greenberg, *Serving the Few* (New York: John Wiley, 1974); Ira Katznelson and Mark Kesselman, *The Politics of Power* (New York: Harcourt Brace Jovanovich, 1975); Mark Nadel, *Corporations and Political Accountability* (Lexington, Mass.: D. C. Heath, 1976); Arthur S. Miller, *The Modern Corporate State* (Westport, Conn.: Greenwood Press, 1976); Robert Engler, *The Brotherhood of Oil* (Chicago: University of Chicago Press, 1977); G. David Garson, *Power and Politics in the United States* (Lexington, Mass.: D. C. Heath, 1977); Charles Lindblom, *Politics and Markets* (New York: Basic Books, 1977); Michael Parenti, *Power and the Powerless* (New York: St. Martin's Press, 1978). The quote itself is taken from Lindblom,

Politics and Markets. See especially Chap. 13, 'The Privileged Position of Business', pp. 170–88.

2. Among the most influential statements of the pluralist perspective are David Truman, *The Governmental Process* (New York: Alfred A. Knopf, 1951); Robert Dahl, *Who Governs?* (New Haven, Conn.: Yale University Press, 1961); Nelson Polsby, *Community Power and Political Theory* (New Haven, Conn.: New Haven University Press, 1963); Arnold M. Rose, *The Power Structure* (New York: Oxford University Press, 1967); and Edwin Epstein, *The Corporation in American Politics* (Englewood Cliffs, N.J.: Prentice-Hall, 1969).

3. The former is generally referred to as 'monopoly capitalism'. See, for example, Paul Baran and Paul Sweezy, *Monopoly Capital* (New York: Monthly Review Press, 1966). The later time-frame is associated with a Galbraithian notion of a 'new industrial state'. See John Kenneth Galbraith, *The New Industrial State* (Boston, Mass.: Houghton Mifflin, 1967).

4. E. E. Schattschneider, *The Semi-Sovereign People* (New York: Holt, Rinehart and Winston, 1970), p. 68.

5. Bachrach and Baratz, *Power and Poverty*, p. 15.

6. Ibid., p. 43.

7. Ibid., pp. 33, 34.

8. See, for example, the various essays in Philip Green and Sanford Levinson, eds., *Power and Community* (New York: Vintage, 1969), and William Connolly, ed., *The Bias of Pluralism* (New York: Atherton Press, 1969). Lindblom, *Politics and Markets*, also makes much of this contention. See especially Chap. 15.

9. For the former issue, see, for example, *The Politics of Planning* (San Francisco: Institute for Contemporary Studies, 1976); Wassily Leontief and Herbert Stein, *The Economic System in an Age of Discontinuity* (New York: New York University Press, 1976); Initiative Committee for National Economic Planning, 'For A National Planning System', *Social Policy* (March/April 1975), pp. 17–19. For the later controversy, see Ralph Nader and Mark Green, eds., *Corporate Power in America* (New York: Grossman, 1973); Ralph Nader, Mark Green and Joel Seligman, *Taming the Giant Corporation* (New York: W. W. Norton, 1976); Donald Schwartz, 'The Case for Federal Chartering of Corporations', *Business and Society Review* (Winter 1973–74), 52–58; Peter Aranson, 'Federal Chartering of Corporations: An Idea Worth Forgetting', *Business and Society Review* (Winter 1973–74), 59–64; and Robert Hessen, *In Defense of the Corporation* (Stanford, Calif.: Hoover Institute Press, 1979). For more on the general debate over corporate government and accountability, see Neil H. Jacoby, *Corporate Power and Social Responsibility* (New York: Macmillan, 1973); Christopher Stone, *Where the Law Ends* (New York: Harper and Row, 1976); William Dill, ed., *Running the American Corporation* (Englewood Cliffs, N.J.: Prentice-Hall, 1978), and David Vogel, *Lobbying the Corporation: Citizen Challenges to Business Authority* (New York: Basic Books, 1978).

10. 'Reserved', *New Republic*, 9 November 1974, pp. 5–6.

11. For a good perspective on this development, see Chester L. Cooper,

ed., *Growth in America* (Westport, Conn.: Greenwood Press, 1976), especially Samuel Hays, 'The Limits to Growth Issue: An Historical Perspective', pp. 115–42.

12. Rachel Carson, *Silent Spring* (New York: Houghton Mifflin, 1962).

13. Quoted in Leonard Silk and David Vogel, *Ethics and Profits* (New York: Simon and Schuster, 1976), p. 21.

14. See Walter Rosenbaum, *The Politics of Environmental Concern* (New York: Praeger, 1973).

15. The phrase 'adversarial culture' is originally Lionel Trilling's. For a comprehensive description and analysis of its manifestation in American life in the 1960s and early 1970s, see Daniel Bell, *The Cultural Contradictions of Capitalism* (New York: Basic Books, 1976). For particular examples, see the references cited in footnote 1. For an overall analysis of this political phenomenon, which has occurred periodically in American history, see Samuel P. Huntington, *American Politics: The Promise of Disharmony* (Cambridge, Mass.: The Belknap Press of Harvard University Press, 1981). Huntington's book represents one of the few scholarly efforts to analyse why the American public became more resentful toward all sources of authority, including the large corporation, during much of the 1960s and 1970s; he argues that since the 'Great Awakening', such 'crucial passion periods' have occurred in the United States approximately every sixty years. See Chap. VI, pp. 130–66.

16. For various perspectives on the political significance of this 'new class', see B. Bruce-Briggs, ed., *The New Class?* (New Brunswick, N.J.: Transaction Books, 1979).

17. These figures are from the Directory of Federal Regulatory Agencies, compiled by Ronald J. Penoyer Center for the Study of American Business, April 1982. For a summary view of the growth of federal regulation of business during this period, see Murray Weidenbaum, *Business Government and the Public* (Englewood Cliffs, N J.: Prentice-Hall, 1977), pp. 6–8; Theodore J. Lowi, 'Europeanization of America? From United States to United State', in Theodore J. Lowi and Alan Stone, eds., *Nationalizing Government* (Beverly Hills, Calif.: Sage Publications, 1978), p. 19. Between 1965 and 1970 as many federal consumer protection laws were enacted as had been adopted during the previous seventy-five years. See Weidenbaum, *Business, Government and the Public*, p. 35. Only a handful of these laws were initiated by business.

18. For statements of this position, see, for example, Marver Bernstein, *Regulating Business by Independent Commission* (Princeton, N.J.: Princeton University Press, 1955), and Gabriel Kolko, *Railroads and Regulation 1877–1916* (New York: W. W. Norton, 1965).

19. For a summary view of the pattern of conflict on social regulatory issues in Europe and the contrast with the United States, see David Vogel, 'The "New" Social Regulation in Historical and Comparative Perspectives', in Thomas N. McCraw, *Regulation in Perspective* (Division of Research, Graduate School of Business Administration, Harvard University, Boston, 1981), pp. 155–86.

20. For a discussion of the significant decline in the autonomy of regulatory officials that occurred during the 1960s and 1970s, see Eugene Bardach and Robert A. Kagen, *Going by the Book: Unreasonableness in Protective Regulation* (Philadelphia: Temple University Press, 1981).

21. For the political strategy of the public-interest movement, see David Vogel, 'The Public Interest Movement and the American Reform Tradition', *Political Science Quarterly*, xcv (1980–81), 607–28.

22. James Q. Wilson, 'The Politics of Regulation', in James Q. Wilson, ed., *The Politics of Regulation* (New York: Basic Books, 1980), p. 385.

23. See, for example, Juan Cameron, 'Nader's invaders are inside the gates', *Fortune* (October 1977), p. 254.

24. These figures are quoted in Steven Kelman, 'Regulation that works', *New Republic*, 23 November 1978, p. 18. Kelman argues that the benefits of regulation have well exceeded the costs. For a more critical view, see Murray Weidenbaum, *The Future of Business Regulation* (New York: Amacom, 1979).

25. See, for example, Bruce A. Ackerman and William T. Hassler, *Clean Coal, Dirty Air; or How the Clean Air Act Became a Multibillion Dollar Bail-Out for High-Sulphur Coal Producers and What Should Be Done About It* (New Haven and London: Yale University Press, 1981).

26. Steven Rattner, 'Productivity lag causes worry', *New York Times*, 8 May 1979, p. D2.

27. 'The profit famine', *Wall Street Journal*, 26 March 1979, p. 20.

28. For a discussion of the bureaucratic interdependence that has developed between corporate functions and government agencies, see Weidenbaum, *Business, Government and the Public*, pp. 285–89. For a description of the vastly increased enforcement powers available to regulatory officials. even at the inspectorate level, see Bardach and Kagen, *Going by the Book*.

29. Walter Guzzardi, 'Putting the cuffs on capitalism', *Fortune* (April 1975), p. 194.

30. These statistics are from Weidenbaum, *Business, Government and the Public*, p. 48.

31. Charles G. Burck, 'How G. M. turned itself around', *Fortune* (January 1978), p. 96.

32. A 1977 report of the Conference Board entitled *Action Plans for Public Affairs* noted: 'the petroleum industry, most business executives agree, is among the industries hardest hit by government regulation in recent years. After what one company executive terms the many 'boom' years when oil was 'riding high in Washington', there has now been a drastic drop in the credibility and the influence of the industry', p. 25.

33. For federal budgetary expenditures, see *Economic Report of the President, Transmitted to the Congress January 1979* (Washington, D.C.: USGPO, 1979), Table B-70, Federal Budgetary Receipts, Outlays, and Debt, Fiscal Years 1970–80, pp. 264–65.

34. For documentation on the extent to which the performance of the economy influences the re-election prospects of incumbents, see Edward

Tufte, *Political Control of the Economy* (Princeton, N.J.: Princeton University Press, 1980).

35. The auto industry was periodically able to postpone the enforcement of auto-emissions and fuel economy standards. See Lennart Lundquist, *The Hare and the Tortoise* (Ann Arbor: University of Michigan Press, 1980), Chap. 7. See below for the second example.

36. Not surprisingly, a concern with the lack of 'business credibility' became a major preoccupation of corporate executives. See, for example, Frederick Randall and Michael Duerr, *Private Enterprise Looking at Its Image* (New York: Conference Board, 1970).

37. The 1974–75 recession probably marked the nadir of business's political influence, coming as it did shortly after both the Arab oil embargo and the forced resignation of President Richard Nixon. For business reaction to these developments, see Silk and Vogel, *Ethics and Profits*, especially Chap. 2.

38. See, for example, L. Aspin, 'Shortage scenario: big oil's latest gimmick', *Nation*, 18 June 1973; and B. Hume, 'The case against big oil', *New York Times Magazine*, 9 December 1973, p. 40.

39. G. N. Wilson, *The Changing Role of Business in American Politics* (Political Studies Association Conference, Exeter, 1980). The following description and analysis of business's shift in political strategy during the 1970s closely parallels Wilson's argument.

40. According to a Conference Board survey, seventy-one of the government relations practitioners who reported an increase in their companies' political involvement said the strongest factor was the impact of recent government regulations and legislation (Phyllis S. McGrath, *Redefining Corporate–Federal Relations* [New York: Conference Board, 1979]).

41. McGrath, *Redefining Corporate–Federal Relations*, p. 2.

42. Ibid., p. 58. For a more detailed description of the role of corporate political affairs offices, see *Public Affairs Offices and Their Functions* (prepared by the Public Affairs Research Group, School of Management, Boston University, March 1981).

43. One management consultant estimates that 80 per cent of corporate planning is now concerned with how the world affects the company, and 20 per cent with what management wants; ten years ago these figures were reversed. See James K. Brown, *The Business of Issues: Coping with the Company's Environments* (Conference Board, 1979). For more on how corporations attempted to respond to the more hostile political environment of the 1970s, see 'Business Strategy for the 1980s', Staff Task Force on Corporate Social Performance in *Business and Society: Strategies for the 1980s* (US Department of Commerce, December 1980), pp. 1–45.

44. McGrath, *Redefining Corporate–Federal Relations*, p. 94.

45. Phyllis S. McGrath, *Managing Corporate External Relations: Changing Perspectives and Responses* (New York: Conference Board, 1976); and Robert L. Fegley, 'New breed of top executive takes charge', *Los Angeles Times*, 31 December 1976, Part IV, p. 6.

46. From a speech by Irving Shapiro quoted in Peter F. Drucker, 'Coping with those extra burdens', *Wall Street Journal*, 2 May 1979. This development

has led some firms to appoint two chief executives – one to deal with the public and the other to manage the business.

47. James W. Singer, 'Business and Government—A New "Quasi-Public Role," *National Journal*, 4:15 (1978), p. 596.

48. P. Vanderwicken, 'Irving Shapiro takes charge at DuPont', *Fortune* (January 1974), pp. 78–81+.

49. Louis M. Kohlmier, 'The big businessmen who have Jimmy Carter's ear', *New York Times*, 3 February 1978, Section 3, pp. 1, 11.

50. See, for example, 'Preparing for the TV appearance', *Business Week*, 14 September 1974, p. 167; and 'Grooming the executive for the spotlight', *Business Week*, 5 October 1974, pp. 57, 61.

51. McGrath, *Redefining Corporate–Federal Relations*, p. 48.

52. See Neil Ulman, 'Companies organize employees and holders into a political force', *Wall Street Journal*, 15 August 1978, pp. 1, 15.

53. The above figures are from Edwin M. Epstein, 'Business and Labor Under the Federal Election Campaign Act of 1971', in Michael Malbin, ed., *Parties, Interest Groups and Campaign Finance Laws* (Washington, D.C.: American Enterprise Institute for Public Policy Research, 1980), p. 117. For more on PACs, see Randall Rothenberg, 'The PACs go to market on the Hill', *Nation*, 18 November 1978, pp. 536–39, and Robert W. Merry, 'Firms' action groups are seen transforming the country's politics', *Wall Street Journal*, 11 September 1978, pp. 1, 31.

54. Silk and Vogel, *Ethics and Profits*, p. 178.

55. Quoted in the 'Business Roundtable (A)'–a case prepared by Thomas K. McGraw for class discussion at the Harvard Business School, 1979, p. 5. For more on the Roundtable, see Kim McQuaid, 'The Roundtable: Getting Results in Washington', *Harvard Business Review* (May–June 1981), pp. 114–23.

56. Thomas Ferguson and Joel Roberts, 'Labor law reform and its enemies', *Nation*, 6–13 January 1977, p. 20. Both General Electric and DuPont voted with the minority position, as reportedly did AT&T and General Motors.

57. According to *US News and World Report*, 'The business groups are co-operating with one another to a far greater degree than they did in the past, entering into informal coalitions to tackle one issue at a time and showing more willingness to compromise and come up with a unified position'; see also 'Now business shows its muscle in Washington', *US News and World Report*, 10 July 1978, p. 20.

58. Robert W. Merry and Albert R. Hunt, 'Business lobby gains more power as it rides anti-Government tide', *Wall Street Journal*, 17 May 1978, p. 15. More than a hundred organizations eventually collaborated to defeat this legislation, which was strongly supported by the building trade union. Common-situs picketing refers to the practice of picketing a worksite where employees of more than one employer are engaged in work. While the dispute is with one employer only, the intent and effect of the picketing is to shut down the entire job site, thus affecting employers who were not involved in the original labour dispute.

296   CHAPTER TEN

59. Theodore J. Lowi, 'American Business, Public Policy, Case-Studies and Political Theory', *World Politics*, xvi (1964), 677–715.

60. See, for example, Silk and Vogel, *Ethics and Profits*, Chap. 4, 'How Business Views Its Critics', and Louis Banks, 'Taking on the Hostile Media', *Harvard Business Review* (March–April 1978), 123–30.

61. See S. Prakash Sethi, *Advocacy Advertising and Large Corporations* (Lexington, Mass.: Lexington Books, 1977), for a full-scale study of this phenomenon. Sethi's data are updated in S. Prakash Sethi, 'Grass-roots Lobbying and the Corporation', *Business and Society Review* (Spring 1979), 8–14. For a discussion of Mobil's effort, see Randall Poe, 'Masters of the Advertorial', *Across the Board* (September 1980), 15–28. See also David Liff, Mary O'Conner and Clarke Bruno, *Corporate Advertising: The Business Response to Changing Public Attitudes* (Washington, D.C.: Investor Responsibility Research Center, October 1980).

62. William E. Simon, *A Time for Truth* (New York: McGraw-Hill, 1978), chaps 2 and 3. He writes: 'Business must cease the mindless subsidizing of colleges and universities whose departments of economics, government, politics and history are hostile to capitalism and whose faculties will not hear scholars whose views are otherwise', p. 231. Irving Kristol advocates a similar course in *Two Cheers for Capitalism* (New York: Basic Books, 1978). For a discussion of the growth in ties between intellectuals, universities and business in the late 1970s, see David Dickson and David Noble, 'By Force of Reason: The Politics of Science and Technology Policy', in Thomas Ferguson and Joel Rogers, eds., *The Hidden Election* (New York: Pantheon, 1981), pp. 260–312.

63. Ann Crittendon, 'The economic wind's blowing toward the Right—for now', *New York Times*, 16 July 1978, pp. 1, 9.

66. See John R. Lott, 'Economics educator', *Reason* (December 1978), p. 52; and Paul Van Slambrouch, 'A new kind of think tank', *San Francisco Business* (July 1976).

65. For a good summary of the lobbying efforts underlying each of these developments, see Philip Shabecoff, 'Big business on the offensive', *New York Times Magazine*, 9 December 1979, p. 134.

66. For a discussion of how business succeeded in this conflict, see Charles E. Walker and Mark Bloomfield, 'How the capital gains tax fight was won', *Wharton Magazine* (Winter 1979), pp. 34–40.

67. See, for example, the Special Issue of *Business Week*, devoted to 'The reindustrialization of America', 30 June 1980.

68. For the decline of public confidence in government, see Samuel Huntington, 'The Democratic Distemper', in *The American Commonwealth* (New York: Basic Books, 1976). He writes, 'Between 1969 and 1971 the proportion of the population having a great deal of confidence in the leadership in each of the major governmental institutions was cut in half', p. 17.

69. See, for example, Lester Thurow, *The Zero-Sum Society* (New York: Basic Books, 1980), and Ronald Mueller, *Revitalizing America: Politics for Prosperity* (New York: Simon and Schuster, 1980) Although their specific policy prescriptions clearly differed from those of business, their analysis of the

fundamental problems confronting the American economy was strikingly similar to that of more conservative analysts. For a broader analysis of this shift, see David Vogel, 'The Inadequacy of Contemporary Opposition to Business', *Daedalus* (Summer 1980), 47–58.

70. Isaac Balbus, 'The Concept of Interest in Pluralist and Marxist Theory', *Politics and Society*, 1(1970–71), p. 173.

Chapter Eleven

THE POWER OF BUSINESS IN CAPITALIST SOCIETIES: A COMPARATIVE PERSPECTIVE*

INTRODUCTION

The argument that business enjoys a dominant or privileged political position in capitalist polities owes much of its recent influence to Lindblom's *Politics and Markets*.[1] In the fifteen years since its publication, the majority of articles published by political scientists on the subject of the political power of business essentially echo Lindblom's position.[2] As David Menninger wrote in a 1985 newsletter of the American Political Science Association:

> While they may not reject outright the American formula of popular government and private enterprise that has prevailed thus far, political scientists are likely to judge the large corporation's concentration of resources and wealth to be an anomaly that upsets the balance between democracy and capitalism.[3]

Notwithstanding its grandiose subtitle—"The World's Political-Economic Systems"—Lindblom's analysis is primarily based on only one capitalist nation, namely, the United States. However, this shortcoming does not necessarily undermine the validity of his argument. For his analysis is, in most important respects, quite similar to those within the Marxist tradition which have generalized about the political influence of the bourgeoisie on the basis of data from more than one capitalist state.

This literature includes the writing of Marx himself, whose empirical research focused on Great Britain, France, and the United States. Ralph Miliband's *The State in Capitalist Society* primarily draws on evidence from Great Britain and the United States, but also examines patterns of business influence in other capitalist nations, including Italy, France, and Japan.[4] A more recent study of the political power of economic elites, *The Capitalist Class; An International Study* includes essays on business elites in seven countries.[5] All three

*Prepared for presentation at an international conference on "Government-Industry Relations in the 1990s: Comparisons with Japan," University of Exeter, May 20–22, 1992.

studies reach conclusions quite similar to the more theoretical work of the French Marxists, Louis Althusser and Nicos Poulantzas.[6] While there are differences among these writers, they share a belief in the stability or durability of business political power—both over time and in different capitalist societies. They argue that it is misleading to characterize business as an interest group or a pressure group. Rather, business constitutes a power elite, or a dominant, ruling, or hegemonic class. In Lindblom's phrase, its political position is "privileged"; in Marxist theory, states in capitalist societies exist to serve the interests of capital.

According to this perspective, there are three sources of business power: economic, ideological, and political. The most important source of business political influence is economic: politicians defer to the needs of business because of the critical connection between business activity and the public welfare. If their demands are not satisfied, investment will decline and the economy will stagnate.

According to Lindblom, this dimension of business power requires "no conspiracy theory of politics, no theory of common social origins uniting government and business officials, no crude allegation of a power elite established by clandestine forces."[7] For businessmen, "simply minding one's own business is the formulae for an extraordinary system for repressing change."[8] Miliband writes:

> If the national interest is in fact inextricably bound up with the fortunes of capitalist enterprise, apparent partiality toward it is not really partiality at all. On the contrary, in serving the interests of business and in helping capitalist enterprise to thrive, governments are really fulfilling their exalted role as guardians of the good of all.[9]

The second source of business power has to do with, in Gramsci's term, "ideological hegemony."[10] In capitalist societies, public attitudes and the climate of public opinion are supportive of the values of capitalist enterprise in general and the specific ideological and political preferences of the business community in particular. The ability of business to define the terms of public debate is reinforced by its ownership and control of the mass media, its advertising expenditures, its public relations campaigns, and its support of and influence over the educational system.

In sum, the interests of business are served "not by overt political action, but by the unstated and hence unquestioned assumption of certain beliefs about what is and what is not possible."[11] Poulantzas writes: "The dominance of this [capitalist] ideology is shown by the fact that the dominated classes live their conditions of political existence through the forms of dominant political discourse."[12]

The third basis of the political dominance of business is its political activity. Business enjoys disproportionate political influence because of its superior organizational and financial resources. The former lower the costs of political mobilization, while the latter enables companies to hire skilled lobbyists and lawyers and contribute generously to political candidates and parties. Business influence is further reinforced by the similarity in social backgrounds and outlooks of economic and political elites. As a result, according to Miliband,

> Business enters the [pluralist] competition on extremely favorable terms in comparison with labour or any other interest. . . . businessmen and their representatives normally have a rapport with ministers, civil servants and other members of the state which is very different from labour and its representatives.[13]

Equally important to this analysis, all three dimensions of business power are based on sources of influence not available to nonbusiness constituencies. Thus in a capitalist system, by definition, investment decisions are controlled by those who either own the means of production or who are appointed by those who do. Similarly, while other interest groups, classes, or social movements may seek to shape or change public attitudes, none of them rival business's capacity to shape and manipulate popular preferences and thus define the political agenda. Likewise, while nonbusiness constituencies may mobilize, they lack sufficient resources to compete with business for the attention and support of politicians. In sum, the sources of business political strength are either exclusively or disproportionately available to capitalists.

The most important alternative perspective is identified with pluralism. Pluralists contend that the economic, ideological, and political resources available to business to shape public policy do not provide any unique advantages.[14] They either do not automatically translate into political influence or they are counterbalanced by similar or equivalent resources available to other groups in society.

The pluralist position does not deny that business frequently exercises considerable political influence or that it is often highly organized. As Wyn Grant argues, "In economies organized on free enterprise, capitalist lines, it should not surprise us that business is one of the most important interests."[15] He adds: "Even the most primitive versions of pluralism did not pretend that all interests or potential interests in a society are able to exert an equal amount of influence on the decision-making process."[16]

Rather, pluralists contend that the scope and extent of business political influence varies considerably, both among capitalist societies as well as within them. Moreover, these variations are a vital and characteristic feature of democratic politics. In short, business political influence is contingent, rather than constant.

Unfortunately, there has been little systematic effort to describe or explain variations in the political influence of business. There are few comparative studies of business pressure-group activity; most students of business power typically focus on only one country, most often the United States or Britain.[17] Indeed, much of the literature on business political activity and influence is even narrower in scope. It frequently focuses on specific industries, policy-areas, or political subunits.[18] While there are a number of comparative studies of business organization, they have not attempted to compare the relative political influence of business in different countries.[19] This chapter represents an attempt to place business power in a cross-national context.

Because the sources and consequences of business influence are so complex, it is difficult to measure the political power of business in different capitalist nations. The following analysis compares the political influence of business *among* capitalist societies by examining the extent of its *variation within* capitalist societies. Accordingly, the more stable the political influence of business has been within a particular capitalist society, the greater it is. Correspondingly, business is least influential in those nations in which its political influence has been the least stable. (In principle, the political influence of business could be *both* stable and low. However, given the political importance of business in capitalist societies, this outcome is highly unlikely, particularly over a relatively long time period.)

The following analysis is based on five capitalist democracies: the United States, Great Britain, Japan, France, and Germany. The time frame is roughly thirty years, from the late 1950s or early 1960s through the early 1990s. After briefly tracing the political influence of business in each country, we will discuss the dynamics and dimensions of business influence in capitalist societies.

NATIONAL CASE STUDIES

The United States

The political influence of business in the United States has been relatively unstable during the last three decades.[20] American business was relatively influential throughout the 1950s and through the first half of the 1960s. Its influence declined from the mid-1960s through the mid-1970s, increased significantly from the mid-1970s through the early 1980s, and has declined somewhat over the last decade.

In the two decades following the Second World War, the prevailing ideological consensus, which business did not originate but which it helped reinforce, emphasized the importance of "limited government" and "states' rights."[21] Both of these norms effectively served to forestall a broader federal role in regulating business activity. At the same time, an alliance of powerful conservative Democrats and Republicans in the Congress exercised a virtual veto power over new domestic policy initiatives. The result was that business occupied a dominant position in American national politics during this period, even though most firms devoted relatively few resources to influencing federal policy.[22]

Beginning around the mid-1960s, a number of factors began to undermine the political power of business. First, the landslide victory of Lyndon Johnson in 1964 changed both the partisan and ideological composition of Congress: it swept into office a large number of liberal Democrats, many of whom subsequently assumed important leadership positions. Second, while relatively few of the domestic social programs associated with the Great Society directly affected business, their enactment signaled an erosion of the "legitimacy barrier" to increased federal intervention in all aspects of American society, including the economy. The federal government, whose role in American society had been regarded as a "necessary evil" since the end of the Second World War, was now seen as a constructive force for ameliorating the nation's various social problems.

Third, the degree of public trust in business peaked around 1965 and thereafter began a decline that persisted until the late 1970s. At the same time, public support for increased government regulation of a wide variety of dimensions of corporate social conduct, particularly in the areas of health, safety, and the environment, began to increase substantially. As a result, while national politicians had previously hesitated to challenge corporate prerogatives lest they be labeled "anti-business," now they began to compete among themselves to demonstrate their commitment to legislation designed to "keep the big boys honest."[23]

Nor was support for increased government regulation of corporate social conduct confined to Democratic Senators and President Johnson; in 1970, Republican President Richard Nixon supported the enactment of strong federal air pollution controls as well as the passage of federal occupational health and safety legislation in order to broaden his party's base of electoral support. Indeed, at the height of the expansion of social regulation that took place between 1969 and 1972, few politicians from either party were willing to defend publicly the economic interests of business.

A fourth development was the emergence of a new set of interest groups. While Olson's "logic" explains why diffuse interests have historically been underrepresented in American politics, a number of factors, including the emergence of political entrepreneurs such as Ralph Nader, sympathetic media coverage, the development of techniques of direct mail fund-raising, increased levels of education, and changes in American administrative law, enabled a significant segment of the American middle class to organize politically by the early 1970s.[24] A loose coalition of consumer and environmental organizations, often supported by trade unions, became an influential political and legal constituency for strengthening federal regulation of corporate social conduct. While their influence varied from issue to issue, the public interest movement represented an important source of countervailing power to business, one that had not existed a decade earlier.

During the first part of the 1970s, the public reputation and political influence of business was further undermined by a number of national and international developments. These included disclosures that a number of prominent corporations had made illegal contributions to the 1972 re-election campaign of Richard Nixon and had made substantial "payments" to a number of foreign governments in an effort to protect or advance their economic interests. The energy crisis that followed the Arab oil embargo of 1973 created substantial public hostility to the large integrated oil companies; major segments of the American public accused them of creating the oil shortage and then of taking unfair advantage of it.

Moreover, the "stagflation" that beset the American economy during the mid-1970s was initially blamed on mismanagement by the private sector, prompting calls for an expanded governmental role in directing corporate investment decisions. The nadir of business prestige and influence in the postwar period was reached during the first half of the 1970s.

Ironically, while business experienced many of its most important political reverses following the election of Republican Richard Nixon, its political fortunes began to improve markedly following the election of Democrat Jimmy Carter in 1976. Between 1977 and 1980, Congress defeated a trade-union proposal to reform the nation's labor laws, handed the consumer movement a major setback by voting not to establish a Consumer Protection Agency, restricted the authority of the Federal Trade Commission to regulate the marketing practices of a number of industries, deregulated oil prices, reduced price controls on natural gas, delayed the imposition of automotive emission standards, and reduced the capital gains tax.

These legislative victories were made possible by a number of factors, among the most important of which was an unprecedented increase in political activity on the part of business. As a response to both the political setbacks of the 1960s and the expansion of government regulation, beginning around 1970 the American business community began to take Washington seriously for the first time since the Second World War. Hundreds of large firms opened Washington offices, the size of corporate and trade association and public relations budgets increased substantially, and a number of new inter-industry organizations representing both large and small companies were established. The business community also became more skilled at grassroots organizing and coalition building.

At the same time, like the public interest movement earlier in the decade, business benefited from a change in public attitudes: the continued stagnation of the American economy had served to reduce the public enthusiasm for increased public expenditures and regulation and made voters more responsive to business complaints about "excessive" regulation and taxation.

In 1980, American politics changed as significantly as it had in 1964. Not only was a conservative Republican elected president by a wide margin, but the Republican Party captured control of the Senate for the first time in a quarter century. Early in 1981, a presidential assistant told a meeting of hundreds of corporate lobbyists in Washington, "Like the Confederacy, you have only won defensive victories. That leads to defeat. If you will march with us this time, you will win offensive victories."[25]

In its first year in office the Reagan Administration moved aggressively to deliver on this commitment. The Economic Recovery Act of 1981 significantly reduced tax rates for both corporations and wealthy individuals. The Administration attempted to reverse the direction of federal regulatory policy by appointing regulatory officials who were sympathetic to the concerns of business, cutting the staff and budgets of regulatory agencies and exercising close White House oversight of agency rule-making. As one CEO put it in the fall of 1981 after a meeting with Administration officials in Washington, "I almost feel like I'd died and gone to heaven."[26]

However, 1981 turned out to mark the apogee of business political influence. By the conclusion of its first term in office, the Reagan Administration had been forced to retreat from many of its most ambitious efforts to reverse the direction of American domestic policy. Corporate taxes were raised in 1982 and the two senior officials who had been appointed to reduce the burdens of environmental regulation on business were forced to resign. Nor was the Administration able to persuade Congress to repeal any of the scores of regulatory statutes enacted during the 1960s and 1970s. The 1986 tax reform bill raised taxes for a large number of corporations, and both the budgets and staffs of the nation's social regulatory agencies had resumed their upward trajectory by the time the Reagan Administration left office. On balance, the American environmental movement was better funded and organized and more influential at the end of the 1980s than it had been at the beginning of the decade.

Yet while business may well have been less politically influential during the 1980s than it had been during the 1940s and 1950s, it was certainly more powerful than it had been between the mid-1960s and the mid-1970s. The social prestige of business and businessmen improved dramatically during the 1980s: Lee Iacocca replaced Ralph Nader as one of the nation's most admired individuals, while the nation's brightest college graduates, who had previously shunned careers in the private sector as lacking any social purpose, now began to apply to business schools in record numbers. While relatively few regulations were repealed, the pace at which new controls over business were enacted did decline markedly. Most important, due in part to a number of administrative policies and decisions, organized labor was far less influential when Reagan left office than it had been at the onset of his presidency; by 1988, only 16% of American workers were union members, the lowest figure since the New Deal.[27]

The political influence of business eroded somewhat during the Bush Administration, particularly with respect to government regulation. Three important regulatory statutes were enacted: the Civil Rights Act of 1990, the Clean Air Act Amendments of 1991, and the Americans with Disability Act; the latter two imposed substantial additional costs on business. The annual costs of compliance with federal environmental regulation was $123 billion in 1991, up from $102 billion in 1988; these costs are projected to reach $171 billion by 2000.[28] More generally, while 40% fewer new rules were issued by federal regulatory agencies in 1988 than in 1980, the size of the Federal Register was 20% greater in 1991 than when Ronald Reagan left office.[29] Finally, the image of business was substantially tarnished by a large number of scandals involving individuals and institutions in the financial sector that surfaced at the end of the 1980s.

Great Britain

The nation in which the shifting political fortunes of business most closely resembles the United States is Great Britain. As in the United

States, the last three decades have been characterized by major shifts in the political influence of business. Business began to lose influence in the mid 1960s, suffered a major erosion of political power during the 1970s, and increased its influence during the 1980s.

Since British business has been a major financial supporter of the Conservative Party, while its most important political rival, the trade union movement, has been closely identified with the Labour Party, British elections provide a useful preliminary measure of changes in the relative political strength of business in Britain.

Following thirteen years of Conservative Governments, Harold Wilson became British Prime Minister in 1964. Labour held office through 1970, followed by four years of Conservative Party rule. The Heath Government, in turn, was forced out of office in 1974 due to its inability to cope with a strike by Britain's powerful mineworkers union. "During the period of the Heath administration, it became very apparent that there had been a fundamental shift in power toward the unions," many of which had also become more hostile to business.[30]

Labour held office between 1974 and 1979, but was unable to improve British labour relations, which remained among the worst in Europe; union wage settlements contributed to a significant increase in inflation while the winter of 1979–89 witnessed a major increase in strike activity. "In 1979 Britain hit the nadir of its postwar fortunes."[31] Growing public dissatisfaction with the performance of the British economy contributed to the election of Margaret Thatcher in 1979, ushering in more than fourteen years of Conservative Government.

One of the most important consequences of the Conservative governments of the 1980s was the reduction in power of the most important political adversary of British business, namely, the trade union movement. Thanks to the government's rigorous use of monetary policy to reduce inflation as well as the passage of new labor legislation, both the economic and political power of British unions declined. British unions lost a quarter of their membership during the 1980s and only a tenth as many worker-days were lost to strikes in 1990 as in 1979.[32]

Like the Reagan administration, the Thatcher government significantly reduced taxes in order to encourage investment and promote economic growth: the highest individual tax rate was cut in half, corporate tax rates were reduced by one-third, and a 15 percent surcharge on investment income was eliminated. Equally important, Thatcher embarked on a vigorous program of privatization: nearly two-thirds of the industrial assets owned by the state in 1979 were sold to private investors. By 1990, the number of shareholders in Britain exceeded the number of trade union members.

Nonetheless, in a number of important respects, relations between Thatcher and the business community were rather strained. In contrast to Reagan, Thatcher distrusted both capitalists and business organizations. Graham Wilson writes:

> Although for Thatcherism capitalism is good, capitalists in Britain are often lazy, incompetent. . . . Organizations representing capitalists . . . are dominated by business executives who are bureaucratically . . . minded. In Thatcher's view, business executives should be engaged in making or selling products, not attending government meetings.[33]

Moreover, Thatcher's program for economic recovery originated not in the business community, but was created by a faction within the Conservative Party. "A political strategy for business was evolved outside of the organization of business itself."[34] Not surprisingly, while the organized British business community was willing to accept the fact that, in the words of the Director-General of the Confederation of British Industry, "the shock of Thatcherism might be our last and only chance of survival," relations between the Confederation of British Industry, the main political organization of British industry, and the Thatcher government were less than ideal.[35] The Conservative government's tight monetary policy, coupled with its reluctance to aid firms in economic difficulty, imposed severe hardships on much of the private sector.

Germany

The political fortunes of business in Germany have been somewhat more stable than in the United States and Great Britain. In 1966, the coalition of the Christian Democratic Union (CDU) and the Christian Social Union (CSU) that had governed the FRG since its establishment in 1949 was forced to share power for the first time with the Social Democratic party (SPD). Following the general election of October 1969, Germany was governed by a coalition of the SPD and the Free Democratic Party (FDP) under the chancellorship of Willy Brandt, who was replaced by Helmut Schmidt in 1974. The SPD-FDP alliance remained in office until 1982, when the FDP withdrew from the coalition, paving the way for the formation of a CDU-FDP government led by Helmut Kohl, who has held the chancellorship since that time.

To the extent that the strength of the CDU represents a rough proxy for the political influence of German business and that of the

SPD as measure of the relative political strength of German trade unions, business did experience a relative loss in political influence between 1969 and 1982. However, it is probably more accurate to regard the chancellorship of Willy Brandt, who held office between 1969 and 1974, as the nadir of business's political influence in postwar Germany. Not only was Schmidt more conservative, but the electoral strength of the SPD began to steadily decline beginning with the general election held in October 1976.

But it is important to note that these changes in the electoral fortunes of Germany's major right and left of center political parties took place within the context of a substantial consensus regarding both economic and social policy. The German trade union movement has been more conservative than its counterparts in Great Britain while the German business community has accepted the economic role and political influence of the nation's trade unions to a greater extent than in both Great Britain and the United States. Indeed, German politics in the postwar period has been characterized by substantial cooperation between highly centralized business and labor associations.

However, this consensus has been effectively challenged by the growing political strength of German environmentalism, which has both questioned the values associated with Germany's "economic miracle," and challenged the investment decisions of a number of the nation's most important and powerful industries. As in the United States and Japan, public concern with environmental issues increased significantly in the Federal Republic during the late 1960s and early 1970s. In 1971, this heightened concern for environmental quality led to the establishment of a Cabinet Committee for Environmental Problems, responsible for coordinating the environmental policies of all federal ministries. Three years later, legislation was enacted allowing the federal government to establish uniform air pollution standards throughout the Federal Republic.

While interest in environmental issues diminished during the economic downturn of the mid 1970s, as the economy recovered "dissatisfaction with government environmental policy increased" once again.[36] "The late 1970s and the early 1980s were a golden period for environmental movements in the Federal Republic."[37] During the early 1980s more than fifteen hundred citizen organizations were concerned with environmental issues; their combined membership totaled nearly five million—more than double that of Germany's four major political parties combined—and their goals were supported by a majority of the German population. A 1982 survey reported that the level of public awareness of environmental issues was greater in Germany than in either Great Britain or the United States.[38]

In elections to the Bundestag held in 1983, the newly established Green Party, which had been formed from the merger of a number of local environmental organizations and parties, received 5.6% of the votes cast and twenty-seven parliamentary seats. Support for environmental regulation increased steadily throughout the 1980s. A poll taken in December 1986, one month after a major spill of chemicals from a Swiss plant into the Rhine River, indicated that for 52% of German voters the environment was now the most important issue, replacing unemployment."[39] In elections held the following year, 8.3% of the electorate cast their ballots for Green Party candidates, increasing the party's representation in the Bundestag to forty-two seats.

By the second half of the 1980s, environmental protection has ceased to be a partisan issue. The SDP acquired an increasingly "green" character. Equally important, the Government of Chancellor Helmut Kohl has made environmental quality one of its most important domestic and foreign policy priorities. The Federal Republic has embarked upon an ambitious and aggressive effort to reduce emissions of the pollutants that appear to be responsible for *Waldsterben*—"the dying of the forests"—both by enacting its own strict pollution controls and by pressuring the EC to tighten European standards. As of 1985, Germany was devoting a higher proportion of its GNP to pollution control than any nation in Europe.

France

The political power of business has remained relatively stable in France. The policies of the French Fifth Republic, established in 1958, were designed to promote the modernization of the French economy and the international competitiveness of French industry. French economic planning was based on an alliance between the managers of large companies and senior civil servants, from which farmers, small businessmen, and unions were effectively excluded. The latter have historically been relatively weak in France; a lower portion of French workers belong to unions than in any other major industrial nation—including the United States.

With the temporary exception of the events of May 1968, in which an alliance of students and workers challenged the Gaulist regime, the privileged position of French business was relatively unchallenged throughout the 1960s and 1970s. However, in 1981, Socialist François Mitterrand was elected President of France and a Socialist-Communist alliance also gained control of the French legislature.

At first glance, Mitterrand's decision to nationalize thirty-six private banks and eleven large industrial conglomerates would appear to represent a major political challenge to French business. In fact, however, this policy shift was more symbolic than substantive.[40] Not only did the French Treasury already effectively control the investment decisions of the major French banks, but most of the nationalized firms were functionally bankrupt. "The real winners from nationalizations were the stockholders, whose holdings in several companies that might have been considered bankrupt would have been worthless," had not the French government paid them thirty-five billion francs in compensation.[41]

The government's program to revitalize the French economy by increasing wages and welfare benefits resulted in a substantial increase in inflation, which in turn led to a decline in the value of the franc and subsequently to increased unemployment. Mitterrand responded by radically reversing French economic policy the following year: government expenditures were cut and priority was placed on reducing inflation.

French policies during the remainder of the 1980s were highly supportive of business, though the form of this support has shifted from state-led investment to a greater reliance on market forces, especially after the conservatives under Chirac captured control of the National Assembly in 1986. Equally important, the close and mutually supportive ties between business and government elites has remained essentially unchanged. Finally, French trade unions lost more than one-third of their membership during the 1980s and France's environmental movement has been less influential than that of any other major European country.

Japan

The nation in which the political influence of business has been most stable since the 1960s has been Japan. Japan is the only major capitalist democracy in which a conservative political party, the LDP, closely identified with the interests of business, has held office continuously during this period. Japanese economic and industrial policies have undergone a number of substantial changes in the course of the last three decades. But while there is considerable debate among scholars about the importance of the role played by Japan's government in that nation's postwar economic growth, there is little disagreement about the political importance of Japanese business throughout this period.

The Japanese business community is extremely well organized. The Federation of Economic Organizations (FEO), commonly referred to by its abbreviated Japanese name, the Keidanren, was established in August 1946 under the aegis of the government and the Occupation. The FEO consists of more than 100 major national trade associations and 750 large corporations. "It is the front office of the business community and is in effect a partner of the government."[42] In no other capitalist nation is business so extensively consulted on policy decisions that affect it: each of Keidanren's 20 standing committees, which cover every aspect of the national economy, enjoys close and continuous ties with the government bureaucracy, and the relevant Diet and Liberal Democratic Party (LDP) committees.

The business community's political influence is further enhanced by the unusually high costs of election campaigns in Japan: LDP politicians rely extensively on the financial support of business and particular firms; companies can and do use their contributions to individual candidates and LDP factions of the LDP to increase their access to policymakers. Retired government officials almost invariably move into the private sector—a practice known as *amakudari* or descent from heaven—which further strengthens ties between governmental and business elites.

By contrast, unions in Japan enjoy less political influence than in any western capitalist democracy. While union membership in Japan is relatively high—26.8% of the labor force, compared to 16.4% in the United States and 12% in France—Japan's unions are politically weak.[43] Japanese unions are company unions which tend to identify with interests of the companies for whom their members work. The political party with which they are most closely linked, namely, the Socialist Party, is not a serious contender for national office.

One scholar noted in 1968, "Business prestige, measured in terms of social acceptability, has never been higher."[44] While Japan, like the United States, has experienced a large number of political-business scandals during the last two decades, unlike in the United States, Japan's "money-soaked politics" have resulted in neither significant policy changes nor in campaign finance or electoral reforms.[45] Public cynicism toward politicians has recently increased, but to date this public mistrust has not weakened the political influence of business nor undermined the electoral strength of the LDP.

Consequently, much of Japanese politics has revolved around conflicts within the business community. Differences between large and small firms have tended to be muted due to the latter's dependence on and close ties with the former. By contrast, competitive rivalry between firms or groups of firms has often spilled over into the political process and have been a major source of the scandals which have implicated a number of prominent politicians. However, on issues in which there is a consensus within the business community, particularly among large firms, business preferences virtually always prevail—a fact that has been characteristic of no other capitalist democracy in the postwar period.

There is one important exception to this generalization.[46] It involves environmental policy and occurred during the beginning of the 1970s. While the physical quality of Japan's environment had deteriorated steadily throughout the 1950s and 1960s, those Japanese citizens who had been injured by toxic emissions were unable to challenge the government's pro-growth policies. This began to change toward the end of the 1960s. Almost overnight, the number of community groups concerned about pollution significantly increased: between 1969 and 1971 local governments received almost 75,000 pollution-related complaints, nearly double the number they had received two years earlier and quadruple the number they had received in 1966.

Disillusioned by the LDP's lack of responsiveness to their concerns, many citizens began to back Socialist Party candidates in local elections; a Socialist Party candidate was elected mayor of Tokyo in 1969. At about the same time, Japan's courts began to hear the suits filed against several major companies by groups of individuals who had contracted various diseases due to emissions from these firms. These suits, which graphically depicted the human price paid for Japan's rapid industrial growth, received extensive and sympathetic media attention and further increased public dissatisfaction with the LDP and Japanese business.

As a result of this accumulation of pressures, in 1970 a special session of the Japanese Parliament was convened. The "pollution Diet," as it came to be known, passed a total of fourteen pieces of environmental legislation. In addition to providing Japan with some of the world's strictest environmental controls, these statutes also established the world's first and only administrative system to compensate the victims of toxic substance pollution. As a result, corporate expenditures on pollution control increased significantly between 1970 and 1975. By 1975 Japanese industry was devoting a higher percentage of its total investment to pollution control than any other nation.

However, by the mid-1970s, public interest in environmental issues had begun to wane and the number of environmental organizations had declined significantly.[47] Most important, in sharp contrast to the situation in both the United States and Germany, the Japanese environmental movement was unable to establish a permanent national political presence; whatever political influence it retained operated primarily at the local level. Significantly, the political defeats experienced by business in the area of environmental policy neither reflected nor contributed to a more general erosion of business's political influence.

More recently, public interest in environmental issues has increased in Japan. In particular, strong opposition to nuclear power has emerged in a number of communities. There have also been a number of disputes over new commercial developments, particularly golf courses. A number of Japanese environmental laws, particularly with respect to nature and wildlife protection, have recently been strengthened. But compared to its counterparts in other capitalist nations, Japan's environmental movement remains relatively weak at the national level.

As a result, while pollution control remains an important priority for Japanese business—indeed, Japan continues to spend a relatively high proportion of its GNP on pollution control—since the mid-1970s the terms of environmental expenditures have been determined in much the same way as other aspects of Japanese public policy, that is, through a process of extensive negotiation between business and government from which other political constituencies are effectively excluded. In fact, far from undermining the competitiveness of Japanese industry, Japan's relatively strict regulatory requirements have contributed to the emergence of Japanese industry as a world leader in pollution-control technology.[48]

THE DYNAMICS OF BUSINESS POWER

The most obvious conclusion of our brief overview of changes in the relative political influence of business in five capitalist nations since the 1960s is that the political power of business is not uniform: it varies both within capitalist nations and among them. The political power of business was least stable in the United States and Great Britain, and most stable in Japan. Germany and France fall in between, with the former somewhat closer to the Anglo-American pattern and the latter more similar to Japan. Accordingly, during the last three decades, business has enjoyed the most influence in Japan, followed by France, Germany, Great Britain, and the United States, respectively.

In *Fluctuating Fortunes* I argued that there is no need to choose between the pluralist and elitist depictions of business power in America. Rather, the accuracy of each depends on which time period one is examining. Thus in the United States, the political position of business was "privileged" during the first half of the 1960s, while the balance of power between business and other interest groups is more accurately characterized as "pluralist" between the mid 1960s and the mid 1970s. We can apply this same approach to characterize the political power of business in different capitalist nations.

Business is neither accurately characterized as an interest group nor a privileged class or elite. Rather, the appropriateness of each term depends on the particular country one is describing. Thus Lindblom's depiction of business's "privileged" position does present a relatively accurate description of the role of business in Japan: the Japanese government has placed a high priority on promoting economic growth and a broad ideological consensus has identified the interests of business with the national interest. In addition, business is highly organized and its access to policymakers in the government's powerful bureaucracy is substantially greater than that of any nonbusiness constituency.

The political role of business in France also resembles the "power elite" model. As in Japan, French political and bureaucratic elites have placed a high priority on promoting economic growth by working closely with large corporations. This priority has in turn been both reflected and reinforced by an ideology that legitimates extensive government intervention in the economy and a political structure that limits the access of nonbusiness constituencies to the policy process. The French business community is not as highly organized as its counterpart in Japan—in part because "French culture is not . . . favorably disposed to interest groups."[49] However, as in Japan, French bureaucratic and industrial elites do constitute a relatively cohesive social unit.

While it would be accurate to describe both the French and Japanese business communities as "privileged," the former's dominance has been more contested. Both the events of "May 1968" and the election of François Mitterrand in 1981 demonstrated the strength of political forces committed to challenging business wealth and power. The impact of both these political challenges to business, fleeting though they were, in turn suggests another important difference between France and Japan. Unlike in postwar Japan, French political culture also includes an ideological strain that is hostile to capitalism. As a result, business is less hegemonic in France than in Japan.

In contrast to these two countries, it would be more appropriate to describe business as a pressure or interest group in both the United States and Great Britain. During the last three decades, policymakers in both these countries have pursued a wide range of policies, of which fostering rapid economic growth has been only one. Nor has business dominated the terms of public debate or political discourse; the trade union movement in Britain and the public interest movement in the United States have each articulated influential alternative visions of the appropriate relationship between business and government.

British business does possess two important advantages not enjoyed by its counterparts in the United States. First, it is much better organized; no organization in the United States approaches the CBI's ability to speak for the business community. Second, the British tradition of functional representation has provided trade associations and individual companies with automatic and in many cases, privileged access to the policy process. By contrast, the relations between particular government departments or agencies and business firms and trade associations in the United States is frequently armslength and adversarial.

On the other hand, during the 1970s British trade unions presented a far greater political and economic challenge to business than did the American public interest movement. Finally, in contrast to the strength of business values in American society, English culture contains an important strain that is hostile to the values of industrial development.[50]

While the political role of business in Germany is more difficult to classify in terms of the pluralist-elitist continuum, on balance German business is best understood as a pressure group, albeit an unusually well-organized one. "German capitalism has about it a quality of organization, concentration, and centralization."[51] However, the German trade union movement is also extremely well organized and powerful and its views are also regularly taken into account by policymakers; indeed, in many respects the organization of business and labor are mirror images of one another. And a political party closely identified with the trade union movement has periodically occupied national power. In addition to having a more powerful trade union movement than in any of the five countries surveyed in this chapter, the German environmental movement is the most influential in Europe.

A second important implication of this analysis is that the structural dimension of business power must be understood in dynamic rather than static terms. While it is certainly true that no democratic government can afford to be indifferent to the performance of the

economy, it is precisely when an economy is already growing relatively rapidly that the power business derives from its ability to control the rate of capital investment becomes less important. It is not
coincidental that the dramatic increase in government regulation in
the United States, the election of a Labour Government in Great
Britain, the electoral triumph of the SDP in the Federal Republic of
Germany, and the events of May 1968 in France all occurred during
the most prosperous decade of the twentieth century.

Likewise, public support for environmental regulation increased
in the United States, Japan, and Germany, and to a somewhat lesser
extent in Great Britain during the late 1960s and early 1970s—at
the tail end of nearly two decades of sustained and substantial economic expansion. And a resurgence of public support for environmental regulation took place in Germany, the United States, and
Britain during the second half of the 1980s, when all three economies were again growing relatively rapidly.

Conversely, the worldwide slowdown in growth rates during the
second half of the 1970s strengthened the political position of business in three, or possibly four, of the five countries. Thus within the
space of four years—1979 to 1982—Thatcher became prime minister of Britain, Reagan was elected president of the United States,
and the Christian Democrats were returned to power in Germany.
All three elections took place in the midst of a serious economic
downturn, and in each case the more conservative political party re-
gained power in large measure on its promise to improve economic
performance.

France represents a partial exception to this pattern: in 1981 the
Socialists took power for the first time in the history of the Fifth
Republic. Yet in response to a dramatic decline in the performance
of the French economy, French economic policy moved sharply to
the right for the remainder of the decade. Japan, however, is clearly
an anomaly: with the exception of a brief period during the late
1960s and early 1970s, high growth rates in Japan have not led to a
decline in the relative political influence of business.

The last three decades have thus witnessed an inverse relationship
between the performance of the economy and the political influence
of business in four of the five countries we have examined.

THE DIMENSIONS OF BUSINESS POWER

The third conclusion that emerges from our analysis is that most of
the factors that affect the relative political strength of business are
outside the control of business. We can examine this issue in more

detail by reviewing each of the three dimensions of business power identified by Lindblom et al.

One source of business power lies in its control over capital investment decisions. As we have already noted, the exercise of this power is contingent on the performance of the economy: it tends to diminish in importance when the economy is performing relatively well, and vice versa. However, managers and owners are hardly likely to deliberately slow down the economy or reduce their company's profits so they can increase their political influence. Moreover, business investment decisions are only one of a number of factors that affect economic performance.

A second dimension of business power is based on its ability to define the terms of public debate. However, capitalist nations differ significantly in the kinds of issues regarding the role of business that come before the political process. The relative influence of socialist ideology in France, social democracy in Great Britain and Germany, anti-industrial environmentalism in Germany, and eco-populism in the United States has each served to limit the ideological hegemony of capital: by challenging the identification of business with the public or national interest, they have opened the political agenda to a wider range of policy alternatives.

While each of these ideologies has important historical and cultural roots, their influence has varied over time. For example, the terms of public debate over the legitimacy of capitalism have been far different in postwar than in prewar Germany and Japan, while the influence of the radical left substantially diminished in both France and Britain during the 1980s. Similarly, environmentalism has become far more influential in both Germany and the United States since the early 1970s. Rather, our point is that there is relatively little business can do to affect either the emergence or intellectual appeal of antibusiness ideologies, though it can mobilize to limit their policy impact.

The same applies to pro-business ideologies. The American business community has benefited from the fact that the United States is the only capitalist nation in which the legitimacy of capitalism has never been the subject of public debate. Yet the lack of appeal of both socialism and fascism in America cannot be attributed to the ideological power of American business. Rather, it is due to a range of historical and cultural factors, each of which are unique to the United States and beyond the control of its economic elites.

Likewise, during the last three decades Japanese business has benefited from the absence of serious ideological debate regarding the role of the Japanese government in assisting the efforts of Japanese business to become internationally competitive. Yet while Japanese business has clearly benefited from this consensus, it hardly can be said to have been responsible for it. Rather, public agreement on these policy goals can be attributed to the circumstances surrounding Japan's military defeat in the 1940s and the discrediting of socialist ideology in Japan during the 1950s.

A third source of business power is political activity—the one factor that is within the control of business. The increase in the political influence of business in the United States during the 1970s was due in part to the decisions of a large number of companies, trade associations, and cross-industry organizations to become more politically active. And much of the political strength of business in both Japan and Germany can be attributed to their high degree of political organization.

But when examined from a cross-national perspective, the relationship between the degree of business political organization and business political influence is less clear. While British business is better organized and enjoys better access to policymakers than American firms and business associations, it has not been noticeably more influential. Likewise, while the French business community has enjoyed more influence than its counterpart in Germany, the latter is much better organized. Similarly, while both the British and American business communities are better organized than the French, the latter has been far more influential.

What matters is not so much the degree of business political organization, but rather its relationship to the political strength and access of nonbusiness forces. Accordingly, the reason why business is more powerful in France than in Germany is that the latter has faced better organized political opposition. Likewise, the decline in the relative influence of business in the United States during the second half of the 1960s was due to the gap between its political mobilization and that of the public interest movement. By contrast, American business was even less organized during the 1950s, and yet due to the absence of significant opposition, it enjoyed considerably more influence.

In addition, the relative stability in the political organization of business contrasts sharply with the relatively significant variations in business influence that we have described. Only in the United States has the business community become significantly more and better organized during the last three decades. By contrast, the level of business political activity has been relatively stable in France, Germany, and Britain during the postwar period. And yet the last three decades have witnessed important changes in the political influence of business in each country.

This analysis suggests that students of business power need to pay as much attention to the political organization and influence of non-business constituencies as they do to that of business. In each of the five nations we examined, the relative power of business has been significantly affected by the relative political influence of trade unions and middle-class-based environmental organizations. Indeed, the political strength exhibited by the latter in both Germany and the United States, and, more recently in France and Britain as well, suggests the emergence of a new social basis of opposition to business—one rooted in the politics of collective consumption and negative economic externalities.

Finally, while political organization and strength of nonbusiness groups play an important role in affecting the relative political influence of business, the impact of these groups is in turn affected by the degree to which a nation's political institutions are accessible to interest group pressures. "The defining characteristic of a political system is the power of the state in relation to its own society."[52] Strong states are able to define the terms of interest group competition, while weak states are permeated by interest group pressures.

Significantly, the relative ranking of business power in the five nations we have surveyed is identical to the ranking of state strength in the political economy literature. *State strength is highly correlated with business political power.*

It is not that strong states, such as France and Japan, necessarily favor business, while weak states, such as the United States and Britain, do not. Rather, this relationship helps illuminate the significance of the measure of business power proposed at the beginning of this chapter. Strong states are better able to control access to the political process; they make it much more difficult for nonbusiness interests to become politically effective. The result is greater political stability, and hence greater business power. Conversely, in weaker states, there is more opportunity for interest group activity, and hence business is less able to enjoy or maintain a privileged political position. In the final analysis the power of business is closely linked to the nature of specific national political-bureaucratic structures.

NOTES

1. Charles E. Lindblom, *Politics and Markets; The World's Political-Economic Systems* (New York: Basic Books, 1977).

2. David Vogel, "Political Science and the Study of Corporate Power; A Dissent from the New Conventional Wisdom," *British Journal of Political Science*, pp. 385–388.

3. David Menninger, "Business and Politics," *PS* XVIII (1985), p. 210.

4. Ralph Miliband, *The State in Capitalist Society: An Analysis of the Western System of Power* (New York: Basic Books, 1969).

5. *The Capitalist Class: An International Study*, edited by Tom Bottomore and Robert Brym (New York: New York University Press, 1989).

6. For a comprehensive review and analysis on Marxist writings on the state, see Bob Jessop, *State Theory: Putting Capitalist States In Their Place* (University Park, Pennsylvania: Pennsylvania State University Press, 1990).

7. Lindblom, op. cit., p. 175.

8. Charles Lindblom, "The Market As Prison," *Journal of Politics*, XLIV (1982), p. 326.

9. Miliband, op. cit., p.75.

10. A. Gramsci, *Selections from the Prison Notebooks* (London: Lawrence and Wishart, 1971).

11. Grant, op. cit., p. 14.

12. Quoted in A. G. Jordan and J. J. Richardson, *Government and Pressure Groups in Britain* (Oxford: Clarendon Press, 1987), p. 87.

13. Miliband, op. cit., p. 145.

14. For a critical overview of this literature, see Jordan and Richardson, op. cit., chapter 2. For critiques of Lindblom, see Jordan and Richardson, op. cit., chapter 4, and Vogel, op. cit., pp. 385–408.

15. Wyn Grant with Jane Sargent, *Business and Politics in Britain* (London: Macmillan, 1987), p. 27.

16. Ibid.

17. See, for example, Grant, op. cit., Jordon and Richardson, op. cit., and David Vogel, *Fluctuating Fortunes: The Political Power of Business in America* (New York: Basic Books, 1989). A notable exception is *Business and Politics: A Comparative Introduction*, by Graham Wilson (Chatham: Chatham House, 1985, 1990).

18. The most influential pluralist work, *Who Governs*, by Robert Dahl (New Haven: Yale University Press, 1961) examines political decision-making in one medium-sized city in the United States. For a more recent study of business political influence, which focuses on a particular policy, see *Hawke's Law; The Politics of Mining and Aboriginal Land Rights in Australia*, by Ronald T. Libby (Nedlands: University of Western Australia Press, 1989).

19. Andrew Shonfeld, *Modern Capitalism* (New York: Oxford University Press, 1965; *Between Power and Plenty*, Peter Katzenstein, ed. (Madison: University of Wisconsin Press, 1978); *Trends Toward Corporatist Intermediation*, Philippe Schmitter and Gerhard Lehmbruch, eds. (Beverly Hills: Sage Publications, 1979).

20. This section draws heavily from David Vogel, *Fluctuating Fortunes: The Political Power of Business in America* (New York: Basic Books, 1989).

21. See, for example, Francis X. Sutton et al., *The American Business Creed* (New York: Schocken Books, 1956); and Marvin Bernstein, "Political Ideas of Selected American Business Journals," *Public Opinion Quarterly* 17 (1953).

22. See, for example, Edwin Epstein, *The Corporation in American Politics* (Englewood Cliffs, N.J.: Prentice-Hall, 1969).

23. Michael Pertschuk, *Revolt Against Regulation* (Berkeley, Calif.: University of California Press, 1982), p. 25.

24. Mancur Olsen, *The Logic of Collective Action* (Cambridge: Harvard University Press, 1965).

25. Quoted in Sidney Blumenthal, *The Rise of the Counter-Establishment* (New York: Times Books, 1986), p. 85.

26. Edmund Pratt, Jr., "It Has Been an Exciting Beginning," *U.S. News and World Report*, November 2, 1981, p. 79.

27. "Struck Off," *Economist*, July 20, 1991, p. 85.

28. John Cushman, Jr., "Big Growth in Federal Regulation Despite Role of Quayle's Council," *New York Times*, December 24, 1991, p. 1; Daniel Seligman, "Here Come The Regs," *Fortune*, February 24, 1991, p. 114.

29. Ibid.

30. Alan Sked and Chris Cook, *Post-War Britain: A Political History* (Middlesex: Penguin Books, 1979), p. 330.

31. Spencer Warren, "The Lady's Not For Turning," *Policy Review*, spring 1992, p. 62.

32. Ibid., p. 64.

33. Wilson, op. cit., p. 83.

34. Grant, op. cit., p. 177.

35. Quoted in Grant, op. cit., p. 179.

36. J. R. Miller and L. Miller, "Principles of Environmental Economics and the Political Economy of West German Environmental Policy," *Environment and Planning*, vol. 6 (1988), p. 465.

37. William Paterson, "Environmental Politics," *Developments in West German Politics*, Gordon Smith, William Paterson, and Peter Merkl, eds. (Durham: Duke University Press, 1989), p. 270.

38. Hans Kessel, "Environmental Awareness in the Federal Republic of Germany, England and the United States," IIUB Discussion Paper, *WZB* 1984, p. 26.

39. Eric Sjogren, "Who Will Clean Up Europe's Pollution?" *Management Today*, January 1987, p. 19.

40. Stephen Cohen, Serge Halimi, and John Zysman, "Institutions, Politics and Industrial Policy in France" (Berkeley: BRIE Working Paper #4, January 1984).

41. Ibid., p. 25.

42. Chitoschi Yanaga, *Big Business in Japanese Politics* (New Haven: Yale University Press, 1968), p. 42.

43. "Struck Off," *Economist*, July 20, 1991, p. 85.

44. Ibid., p. 31.

45. The phrase is taken from an editorial in the *Japan Times*. "Public Mistrust Deepens," *Japan Times Weekly International Edition* March 9–15, 1992, p. 10.

46. This section is drawn from David Vogel, "Environmental Policy in Europe and Japan," in Norman Vig and Michael Kraft, eds., *Environmental Policy in the 1990s* (Washington, D.C.: Congressional Quarterly Press, 1990).

47. Toshio Hase, "Japan's Environmental Movement," in Thomas O'Rior-

dan and R. Kerry Turner, eds., *Progress in Resource Management and Environmental Planning*, vol. 2 (Chichester: John Wiley & Sons, 1980).

48. Neil Gross, "The Green Giant? It May Be Japan," *Business Week*, February 24, 1992, pp. 74–75.

49. Wilson, op. cit., p. 133.

50. Martin Weiner, *English Culture and the Decline of the Industrial Spirit, 1850–1980* (Cambridge: Cambridge University Press, 1981).

51. John Zysman, *Governments, Markets, and Growth* (Ithaca: Cornell University Press, 1983), p. 252.

52. See, for example, Stephen Krasner, "United States Commercial and Monetary Policy," in Peter Katzenstein, *Between Power and Plenty* (Madison: University of Wisconsin Press, 1978), p. 57.

Chapter Twelve

A CASE STUDY OF CLEAN AIR LEGISLATION, 1967–1981

THE PURPOSE of this chapter is to examine the relationship between corporate size and political power. Specifically, it seeks to analyze the ways in which the characteristics of a particular industry—its size, its degree of concentration, and its organizational links to other industries—affect its ability to influence the direction of public policy. The particular focus of this study is federal air pollution control legislation from the mid-1960s through the present.

There are, broadly speaking, two approaches toward measuring the relationship between industrial structure and political influence. One emphasizes the use of statistical methodology. Various quantitative measurements of corporate political participation and influence are established and then are correlated with indexes of industrial structure. If these relationships prove statistically significant, then, in the words of the best-known of such studies, "larger firm size does . . . seem to yield greater political power."[1] This research strategy does have a number of advantages: it not only makes it possible to synthesize a large amount of data, but it produces results that are capable of being both falsified and replicated. In fact, the results of several of these studies have tended to be relatively consistent. As Epstein summarizes them:

> Looking collectively at the studies discussed above in this section, their empirical analyses appear to allow for the following overarching hypothesis: the amount of political power generated by an industry is correlated at least in part to: the scope and intensity of the industry's political efforts (its "inputs"), which are in turn correlated to the politically valuable resources available to the industry (which in turn are related to the particular structural characteristics of the industry); the benefits expected by firms in the industry; and the incentives of the firms to organize for collective action.[2]

On the other hand, it is clear that these studies have by no means succeeded in resolving the problem that they address. As Epstein's review and critique of this literature concludes, they suffer from a number of important limitations. The most important is that correlativity does not by itself establish causality. Just because large firms are more active politically does not mean that firms are more politically active because they are large; the two in turn may be caused by a third factor. Moreover, there is no necessary relationship between political participation and political impact. The former simply documents a potential source of political influence; it does not necessarily mean that it has been employed effectively. A related difficulty with statistical studies of corporate participation and influence is that the selection of their data is limited by the nature of their methodology. They are confined to those manifestations of business political activity and power that lend themselves to expression in numerical terms. More fundamentally, this approach is incapable of providing us with an understanding of the actual mechanisms of corporate involvement in the policy process. As a result, much of both the drama and the substance of American politics is excluded from their purvue.

An alternative way of analyzing the basis of corporate political influence is the case study method. The efforts of a particular firm or group of firms in a particular industry to affect some public policy outcome is described in detail and an assessment is then offered of the extent to which they were successful in defining and achieving their objectives. This approach has the advantage of concreteness; it does allow us to trace and describe the actual dynamics of corporate political influence. Yet, it too has limitations. First, as Bartlett observes in his essay, "An Economic Theory of Political Power: Firm Size and Political Power," "It is not omnipotence that is at issue, but relative power."[3] Thus, the fact that a group of firms in a highly fragmented industry were able to achieve their political goals while a highly concentrated industrial sector suffered an important political defeat in itself demonstrates nothing about the political impact of corporate concentration; what may have been equally critical was the nature of the opposition that each confronted.

A more serious objection to the case study method lies in the representativeness of the issues analyzed. Clearly, specific political outcomes are contingent on a wide variety of factors, some structural and some dependent on circumstances peculiar to a particular controversy. Conclusions based on any one political outcome are thus inherently vulnerable to the criticism that the controversy analyzed or the time period in which it was resolved was somehow atypical. Unless the analyst has established some set of criteria that locates a particular conflict in the context of a broader analytical framework, the conclusions drawn from any case study, no matter how carefully documented, can be challenged.

The approach of this essay represents an attempt to synthesize elements of each of these approaches. Like the statistical analyses, it examines a fairly extensive amount of information about corporate political activity and its impact on public policy. But it does so not through the use of statistics but through a series of interrelated case studies. It is difficult to measure directly the political significance of corporate size, since relatively few important political disputes involve conflicts between individual firms. The most common units of political activity tend to be either a coalition of industries, an individual industry, or a subset of a particular industry. Although corporate size is by no means identical with corporate concentration, for the particular companies and industries examined in this study, virtually all of whom operate within national markets, the former does appear to represent a convenient surrogate for the latter: those industries that are more concentrated do tend to consist of relatively larger companies, while those industries that are highly fragmented tend to be composed of companies that rank fairly low on a national scale. My approach compares the relative political effectiveness of a series of industries—both over time and vis-à-vis each other. Since the degree of concentration (and consequently the average size of individual firms) varies considerably from industry to industry, we can begin to distinguish the ways in which an industry's structure affects both its political strategy and political effectiveness. My conclusions make no pretensions to be definitive; they are however based on a relatively novel and reasonably sophisticated way of assessing the political impact of corporate size.

There are a number of factors that make federal clean air legislation an appropriate issue-area to examine for the purposes of evaluating the political impact of the large corporation.

First, an examination of federal air pollution legislation makes it possible to trace the evolution of public policy over a considerable time period. Between 1967 and 1977, Congress enacted three major pieces of legislation in this area: the Clean Air Act Amendments of 1967, 1970, and 1977. (The most recent revision of the Clean Air Act was originally planned to be included in this study, but its enactment has been repeatedly delayed.) The political environment within which business functioned varied enormously over this turbulent decade, ranging from diffused support to widespread mistrust. In 1967, business in America enjoyed a relatively large degree of political influence, whereas from the late 1960s through the mid-1970s large corporations in America confronted the most severe set of challenges to their power and privileges since the 1930s. The Clean Air Act Amendments of 1967 and 1970 were enacted during a period of relative prosperity, while the 1977 amendments were debated amid substantial public anxiety over the performance of the economy. An analysis that focuses on political outcomes with respect to the same set of issues during a diversity of political and economic conditions is far more likely to capture the underlying factors affecting and shaping the political influence of industry than one that addresses an issue that was resolved within a relatively few years or within a constant political and economic environment.

A second distinctive feature of federal air pollution legislation is the sheer number and diversity of interest groups that have participated in its formulation. In addition to a substantial segment of the nation's business community, including the automobile industry, the pulp and paper industry, the utility industry, the oil industry, the coal industry, the steel industry, the chemical industry, the nonferrous smelter industry, railroads, automobile suppliers and dealers, and shopping center developers, much of the trade union movement, the entire environmental movement, and organizations representing state and local governments were also heavily involved in the debate over federal clean air policy. Indeed, the Clear Air Act Amendments of 1977 probably represent the most intensively lobbied piece of federal legislation since the Taft-Hartley Act.

Equally importantly, the industries that sought to shape federal clean air policy varied considerably among themselves in terms of their industrial structures.[4] The automobile and nonferrous smelting industry are both highly concentrated, consisting of a relatively small number of relatively large companies. The four largest companies involved in the primary smelting and refining of copper produced 75 percent of the value of industry shipments in 1970 and 87 percent in 1977, while the value of industry shipments accounted for by the four largest domestic motor vehicle manufacturers was approximately 80 percent throughout the 1960s and 1970s. The chemical, iron and steel, and petroleum refining industries are moderately concentrated: in 1972 the value of industry shipments accounted for by the four largest firms in these industries was 46.1 percent, 41.7 percent, and 31.0 percent, respectively. The average size of firms in the coal and utility industries tends to be somewhat smaller: between 1974 and 1977, the value of industry shipments accounted for by the four largest coal companies ranged from 21.3 percent to 18.0 percent, while the utility industry is also relatively decentralized. In 1977, there were also a number of extremely fragmented industries that played an active role in the legislative process, including auto dealers, automobile suppliers, automobile repair shops, and a host of firms involved in the development of shopping centers—including real estate development firms, construction companies, and retail outlets of varying sizes.

The industries concerned with federal clean air politics also vary considerably in terms of their degree of diversification. At one extreme is the coal industry. As of 1976, only 8 percent of the total domestic privately controlled reserves of coal were owned by independent coal producers; 38 percent were owned by diversified energy corporations, 20 percent by railroads, 6 percent by utilities, and 4 percent by steel or smelting concerns.[5] At the other end is the automobile industry, which enjoyed no organizational overlap with any other industry discussed in this study. Other industries such as chemicals, steel, and oil fall somewhere in the middle on this continuum. Thus by the mid-1970s both the oil industry and the steel industry owned considerable coal reserves, and the latter was also engaged in the production of chemicals. (Since Congress last legislated on clean air policy, the degree of organizational overlap among the major industries concerned with federal clean air legislation has increased substantially. A significant segment of the copper smelting industry is now controlled by oil companies; steel companies have diversified into both oil and chemicals; and a merger has taken place between the nation's largest chemical company and a major energy conglomerate. The political significance of these developments is beyond the scope of this study since it is impossible to assess their political impact until Congress has once again legislated in this area. At that point, however, we will have a clear vantage point from which to examine the political significance of conglomerate mergers.)

Thirdly, by any conceivable criteria, federal air pollution control policy constitutes an extremely important dimension of public policy. Aside from tax and defense policies, probably no single area of public policy has had a more profound impact on the domestic economy over the last two decades. Between 1973 and 1982, private sector expenditures to improve air quality totaled $127.9 billion, making "the Clean Air Act . . . one of the most costly pieces of regulatory legislation in history."[6] Moreover, for a significant number of industries and individual companies it has seriously affected—and at times threatened—their economic viability. Among the most frequently voiced criticisms of studies of corporate political power is that the controversies they examine are only of secondary importance to the nation's basic structure of business power.[7] But to the extent that any political conflict in which business has been a participant over the last generation deserves to be labeled "important," clean air legislation certainly falls into that category. It has simultaneously affected the distribution of benefits among particular firms and regions, the balance of power among particular industries and between various industries and other interest groups, as well as a number of core interests of the business system as a whole. It thus falls into all three of Lowi's policy arenas: it has redistributed wealth from the business community as a whole, affected the economic position of individual industries, and redistributed resources among the nation's business firms.[8]

This essay offers neither a history nor an evaluation of federal air pollution controls. Nor is it concerned with decisions undertaken by either the executive or judicial branches, save when these affected the legislative agenda. Rather its focus is more selective: its purpose is to describe and explain the effects of business and other interest groups on clean air legislation during the last fifteen years.

Throughout the 1960s, the federal government found itself under increasing pressure to become more actively involved in controlling air pollution. In 1963, Congress enacted its first comprehensive piece of legislation in the area of air pollution. The 1963 Clean Air Act, which became the basic federal air pollution law, represented a compromise between those who favored a more active federal role and those who wanted to maintain the primary role of the state governments in improving air quality.

For all the intense political conflict that surrounded it, the Clean Air Act of 1963 was a rather innocuous piece of legislation.[9] While its abatement-enforcement provisions did constitute an "opening wedge" for federal intervention—one that would be dramatically widened during the next decade—the procedures for federal enforcement of abatement orders were so complex and time-consuming as to make them virtually ineffective. Four years after the legislation was passed, the federal government had still not brought one legal faction to force compliance with a pollution abatement order; the main reliance for improving air quality still rested with the voluntary cooperation of industry with officials of local governmental units. The 1963 legislation thus neither threatened the financial interests of any industry nor brought about any discernible improvement in air quality. On the other hand, the act did increase federal research expenditures and helped encourage local authorities to establish their own regulatory bodies. By 1967, more than two-thirds of the states had established agencies responsible for air pollution, as compared with only seventeen six years earlier.

Both of these developments subsequently presented the coal industry with its first political challenge in the field of air pollution. In the fall of 1965, Mayor Lindsay of New York City announced his intention of banning coal from New York City on the grounds that its sulphur emissions threatened the health and safety of the city's residents. At hearings held on the mayor's proposal in March of 1966, the coal industry strongly challenged either the prohibition of the burning of coal or the burning of only low sulphur coal; the latter could not be produced by Appalachian-based companies, which at the time produced virtually all of the nation's coal. They contended that the limited availability of both low sulphur coal and residual fuel oil made the mayor's plan impractical. In addition to hearing testimony from the National Coal Association, the United Mine Workers, and the National Coal Policy Conference, the mayor received a letter from Senator Robert Byrd of West Virginia, an important coal-producing state. It urged him to conduct more research and to weigh carefully the costs of dispensing with high sulphur coal. In addition, the city's privately owned utility, Con Edison, fully backed the stance of the coal industry. New York City's elected officials backed down, and a considerably modified air pollution control ordinance was enacted that accepted stack gas removal as an effective alternative to the burning of low sulphur fuel.

The coal industry was equally successful in meeting a similar challenge from the federal government. In 1965, the Department of Health, Education and Welfare proposed emission standards for sulphur dioxide at federal installations. Faced with "repeated strong warnings of the adverse effects of proposed HEW institutions," from the coal industry, not only were the regulations postponed but government officials assured the industry that "regulations which are finally issued will be worked out in cooperation with the coal and oil industries as well as other interested parties."[10] However, two years later, HEW, attempting to carry out the provisions of the Clean Air Act of 1963 that required it to publish a series of studies on all major air pollutants, released a report entitled "Air Quality Criteria for Sulphur Oxides." Publication of the report was "vigorously opposed" by the coal industry, coal workers, and senators from coal-producing states.[11]

As one reporter put it, "The considerable power of the coal industry, under the virtuoso direction of coal lobbyist Joe Moody, was quickly mobilized to discredit the report's findings and delay its publication."[12] W. A. Boyle, president of the National Coal Policy Conference, argued that the control regulations proposed in the report would create "real danger of an electric power and fuel shortage in the future . . . [would] bar almost all coal in existing power plants and . . . prohibit the building of new coal plants."[13] In addition, Senator Jennings Randolph of West Virginia wrote a series of letters to HEW officials urging them that any determination of the health hazards posed by sulphur oxides be delayed until "technology was developed to control sulphur emissions from smoke stacks."[14] However, HEW proved unresponsive to the arguments of the industry and its supporters. Early in 1967 HEW both formally published its report and proposed relatively strict limits on sulphur content on coal burned at new federal installations. Moody interpreted HEW's actions as an indication that it "wants such low sulphur restrictions to become a nationwide standard for all fuel-burning facilities."[15] Subsequently, HEW announced regulations designed to control sulphur oxide emissions at 154 federal installations in New York City.

The conflict over the federal regulations limiting the burning of high sulphur coal then switched to Congress. Responding to an increase in public concern over air pollution—exacerbated by an air inversion in New York City in November of 1966 that was estimated to have caused the deaths of eighty people—President Johnson decided to make improvement in air quality a part of his Great Society program. In a special message to Congress entitled "Protecting Our National Heritage," the president called for "emission control levels . . . for those industries that contribute heavily to air pollution."[16] The administration introduced a bill that authorized the HEW secretary "to establish enforceable, uniform control levels for specific pollutants in various industries."[17] While virtually all stationary sources of pollution were decidedly unenthusiastic about the proposal of additional federal regulations—particularly if they included federal emission standards—for the coal industry, "New federal legislation in 1967 did have one possible advantage: . . . it offered the possibility of Congressional action to overturn HEW's standards on sulphur oxide emissions."[18]

The conflict over the enactment of the Clean Air Act of 1967 focused largely on the issue of federal emission standards. In the spring of 1967, hearings on the administration bill were held by the Subcommittee on Air and Water Pollution, chaired by Senator Muskie. While representatives of a wide variety of industries testified before the committee—including the pulp and paper industry, the steel industry, the oil industry, the mining industry, the utility industry, and the railroad industry—it was clear that the primary concern of the business community was with federal regulations that would restrict the use of high sulphur fuel, particularly coal. Thus, more representatives from individual coal companies appeared before the hearings than from any other type of corporation; similarly, the only union official to testify was W. A. Boyle of the United Mine Workers. The vast majority of those who were opposed to allowing the HEW secretary to set minimum national emission standards for industrial sources of pollution were either coal producers, important industrial consumers of coal, or trade associations whose members had subsidiaries that produced coal. The most important exception was the oil companies—with whom, at this point, coal producers had relatively few financial or organizational ties. However, on this issue, they had a common position: both were equally concerned about the federal government's recent effort to reduce sulphur oxide emissions since this pollutant is also produced by the burning of fuel oil.

The testimony of the "coal coalition" was both consistent and extremely well coordinated. The National Coal Policy Conference and the Edison Electric Institute, the latter representing the utility industry, played a critical role in coordinating industry testimony; individual industrial witnesses as well as Boyle of the United Mine Workers repeatedly endorsed each other's views. The legislative goals of the coal coalition—as well as the oil industry—were straightforward. They were willing to support legislation that encouraged the federal government to make additional efforts to control air pollution—including the spending of additional funds for research. However, they were opposed to national air standards and wanted the primary responsibility for enforcement to remain in the hands of the states. Most importantly, they insisted on the inclusion of three amendments offered by Senator Jennings Randolph, whose purpose was to require HEW to review its sulphur emission standards for federal installations.

In 1967, Senator Muskie's most critical contribution was to weaken significantly the bill proposed by the administration—a stance for which he was subsequently strongly criticized in the Nader task force report, *Vanishing Air*, published a few years later. Thus, while the administration favored national emission standards, Muskie instead urged the establishment of "national ambient air quality, applied as standards on a regional basis."[19] There exists some doubt as to whether Muskie accurately understood the significance of the distinction between these two approaches for dealing with air pollution; some evidence suggests that he may have viewed air quality standards as the more effective device for improving air quality. In any event, national emission standards certainly represented the more radical policy alternative—one for which significant public pressure would have been required to overcome both "industry opposition and legislative inertia."[20] In 1967, however, this pressure was simply not forthcoming. As one account of the 1967 legislation put it: "Pollution and environmental concerns, despite their recent vogue, simply do not impress most Americans as a problem of major concern to themselves or their country."[21] While six national conservationist and health groups did testify before Muskie's subcommittee, their efforts were uncoordinated and politically useless; the environmental movement had neither the manpower nor the technical capacity to participate seriously in the shaping of federal policy in such a complex area. In short, regardless of the personal preferences of Senator Muskie, emission standards were simply not politically feasible in 1967.

Shortly before the Air Quality Act was enacted into law, a spokesman for the National Coal Association summarized industry's lobbying efforts as follows:

> NCA and other groups in coal and oil industries set to work to convince Congress that whatever it did about controlling air pollution must be reasonable, practical, and economically feasible. . . . As a result of these activities and others, the coal industry and allies seem to be making some progress in the face of overzealous demands for instant clean air.[22]

In fact, not only did the act satisfy the preferences of all sources of stationary source pollution by its establishment of air quality regions rather than emissions standards, but it included a special provision that ordered HEW to reevaluate its sulphur oxide criteria. As one scholar concludes:

> In the view of industry and environmentalists alike, the 1967 Air Quality Act was coal's law, and *Coal Age* acknowledged the victory. As a result of "opposition" . . . mounted by coal . . . the final version . . . met most of the industry's objectives. The HEW's sulphur oxide criteria were modified and specific and detailed research . . . provided for.[23]

The coal industry began to confront federal regulation of air pollution during the very period when coal companies were increasing in size, many becoming subsidiaries of large and more diversified corporations. What effect did these developments have on the effectiveness of the coal industry through 1967? There is little evidence that these changes played a decisive role in the industry's 1967 legislative triumph. At first glance, it might appear that coal's organizational links with a number of other industries, such as oil, utility, and mining, would appear to have given it an important political advantage. Instead of just being able to influence representatives from districts or states in which there was substantial coal production, the industry now had access to the much larger number of representatives from states and districts in which companies that owned coal subsidiaries had facilities. But while it is true that the political efforts of the coal industry were certainly more sophisticated in the late 1960s than they would have been a decade or two earlier when the industry was more fragmented and independent, the political significance of this transformation is not readily apparent. In fact, the representatives from other states and regions supported the coal industry not because firms headquartered in their districts owned coal companies but because the interests of these companies and that of the coal producers coincided: neither wanted any restrictions on the burning of high sulphur coal. Thus, a particularly important ally of the coal industry was the utility industry. But like Con Edison in New York City, which did not own a coal company, utilities throughout the United States urged their representatives to back the demands of the coal industry not so much because of any organizational ties they might have had with coal companies but because they too had no desire to have their access to locally available reserves of high sulphur fuel restricted by the federal government. Such restrictions would only increase their costs.

Discussing the political significance of cross-ownership of coal reserves, an official of the National Coal Association stated:

> I make every effort to have representatives of coal companies owned by chemical, steel and utility firms on committees that deal with pollution problems, not because I can necessarily expect any help from these other industries, but because their perspectives are very useful to me. They give me a sense of what other industries are thinking. To the extent that we have common interests, it makes the job of coordination a bit easier.

A lobbyist for the utility industry made a similar observation:

> What matters is not so much the structure of any industry but the way in which a congressman defines his constituency. What ultimately matters is whether or not you can bring the interests of an industry down home to a congressman. Unless you can convince him that some particular policy is going to directly affect the plants located in his district, you have no particular leverage with him.

The staff member of an interindustry coordinating group noted:

> If the headquarters of a diversified company are in a congressman's district, he might be persuaded to care about what happens to a particular subsidiary, even if that subsidiary doesn't employ any of his constituents. But it has to constitute a very important part of the parent company's business. Otherwise you simply can't sell it on the grass-roots level. They won't give a damn.

Nor is there much evidence that the average size of either utility or coal firms affected the political outcome in 1967. As a utility industry lobbyist noted:

Perhaps it makes my job as an industry lobbyist a little easier to the extent that a company like American Electric Power has plants in six states. This means that there are a larger number of representatives that this one company can approach. But someone still has to visit all those congressmen one at a time. Nothing beats that one-on-one relationship. So even if concentration in the utility industry was significantly greater, it would still take just as many visits.

In essence, the legislative achievements of the coal industry in 1967 were due primarily to two factors. First, the industry confronted no effective political opposition. Not only was the environmental movement not well organized, nor environmental concerns particularly salient, but equally important, Eastern coal producers confronted no opposition from other firms or industries. In principle, low sulphur coal producers, located in the West, stood to gain an increased market share if the burning of high sulphur coal by utilities was restricted. But in 1967, Western coal reserves were relatively undeveloped. They did not have a distinctive voice within the National Coal Association, nor did any other industries have a stake in their development. Moreover, both the companies that produced and burned coal had identical and clearly defined interests; the "coal coalition," and in particular its two most important components, namely utilities and coal producers, was thus completely unified. In addition, the oil industry was concerned about possible restrictions on the burning of high sulphur fuel oil and was thus an important ally.

Secondly, both the utilities and the coal industry enjoyed considerable grass-roots political strength—though for rather different reasons. The political strength of the utilities was a function of their geographic dispersion: a significant number of congressional districts included the headquarters of a utility company. An official of the Edison Electric Institute, the trade association of the utility industry recalled:

> In the mid-1960s, the utility industry was an intimate and respected part of the local community. Rates were still going down. People found it easy to relate to their local power company. We thus didn't even need to mount a national political effort during the 1960s because we enjoyed so much local grass-roots support.

This strength was particularly strong in the South, were utilities were an integral part of the local business and community power structure. And given the relative importance of Southern representatives within Congress in 1967, the industry's strength at the grass-roots level was readily translated into congressional influence. The strength of the coal industry was a function not so much of their geographic dispersion as of their geographic concentration. The importance of the coal industry to the economies of the states in the Appalachian region in which it was located meant a number of representatives and senators readily identified with its welfare. Moreover, on this issue both coal operations and their employees, represented by the United Mine Workers, shared an identical interest. What made the industry's regional concentration particularly important was the pivotal position occupied by Senator Randolph of West Virginia. As chairman of the Senate Public Works Committee, of which Muskie's subcommittee was a part, he was in a uniquely favorable position to safeguard the jobs and profits of his constituents. None of the other members of the Public Works Committee, including Senator Muskie, chose to oppose his amendments, while Harley Staggers, the equally powerful chairman of the House Commerce Committee, represented a district from the coal-producing state of West Virginia. The active support of these two powerful congressmen considerably facilitated the industry's political effort in 1967.

THE CLEAN AIR ACT AMENDMENTS OF 1970

On December 31, 1970, President Nixon signed the 1970 Clean Air Act Amendments into law. This law represents one of the toughest environmental statutes ever approved by the U.S. government or indeed any other industrialized society.[24] The 1970 legislation represented a major political defeat for one of the nation's largest and most concentrated industries, namely the automobile industry, as well as the nation's largest chemical company, DuPont. It adversely affected the financial interests of a substantial segment of the nation's industrial structure, including the coal industry, the utility industry, the chemical industry, the steel industry, the pulp and paper industry, the oil industry, and the mining industry. The only segments of the business community clearly to benefit from the legislation were the independent manufacturers of pollution control systems, particularly the Englehard Minerals and Chemicals Corporation. How had such a major decline in the political effectiveness of so many companies and industries come about in so short a time span?

A critical factor was the change in the public attitudes toward business, particularly "big business," that occurred with striking rapidity in the late 1960s. While the climate and tone of social activism and social criticism during most of the 1960s was only indirectly concerned with issues that involved or affected business, beginning in the early 1960s a steady stream of abuses on the part of specific industries and companies had begun to transform public attitudes toward the private sector. By the middle of the decade, public opinion polls had begun to report an erosion of public confidence in the people who managed large companies. In 1967, John Kenneth Galbraith published his best-seller, *The New Industrial State*, which argued that big business and big government had become integral components of the same power structure, committed to the pursuit of goals inimical to those of the American public. By 1970, the issue of corporate accountability, with its explicit focus on the lack of adequate political and economic controls over the decisions of large corporations, had directly moved onto the political agenda, the subject of innumerable conferences, books, and reform proposals.[25]

This gradual and steady increase in public suspicion of big business had virtually no impact on federal clean air legislation in either 1963 or 1967. What made it politically relevant in 1970 was the sudden and dramatic increase in the public's interest in pollution control that took place between 1967 and 1970. As two students of the congressional process have noted,

> The Clean Air Act of 1970 was one result of a growing interest in controlling pollution of the nation's natural resources—air, water, and land. Indeed, by the late 1960s the concern about the environment expressed for years by scientists and conservationists had spread to the general public. . . .
>
> From the industrialized megalopolis along the Eastern seaboard from Boston to Washington, D.C., to the oil-blackened beaches of Santa Barbara, California, individual citizens were being affected and alarmed about the environmental emergency.[26]

Thus, while the *Christian Science Monitor* observed in 1967 that "national air-pollution control efforts seem caught up in a smog of political expediency thickened by public indifference," the *Monitor's* account of the beginning of congressional deliberations in 1970 advised its readers, "Mark the date: April 22. On that day, if the present indicators produce the expected snowballing effect, this nation will witness the largest expression of public concern in history over what is happening to the environment."[27]

The *Monitor's* prediction proved to be an accurate one. By any standards, April 22, 1970, "Earth Day," proved to be an extraordinary political event: literally hundreds of thousands of people from throughout the United States participated in a diverse array of activities designed to express their concern about the future of the environment. As Charles Jones argues,

[Earth Day] was important not only in stimulating national public interest in the environment, but also in uncovering and publicizing the widespread activities and accomplishments in many localities. For by April 22, 1970, enough had already occurred at state and local levels to indicate to public officials, including the president, that many people were supportive of stronger legislation at all levels.[28]

Clearly, "ecology" had become a part of the political lexicon. Senator Muskie's remarks on December 18, 1970, in support of the conference report for the Clean Air Amendments that "the country was facing an air pollution crisis [with] . . . the costs of air pollution . . . counted in death, disease, and disability" reflected not so much a change in objective conditions as in the public's heightened perception of pollution as a serious problem.[29]

This change in public attitudes was reflected in the increased number and size of the environmental organizations. The membership of the Sierra Club, one of the oldest and most prominent environmental organizations, increased from 15,000 to 85,000 during the 1960s. While many environmental groups found their participation in the political process limited by the restrictions placed by the Internal Revenue Service on lobbying by groups eligible to receive tax-deductible contributions, between 1969 and 1970, two environmental organizations were established with the express purpose of influencing public policy: Friends of the Earth, formed in 1969 by the former executive director of the Sierra Club, Earl Browder, and Environmental Action, which grew out of the organization that planned Earth Day. In sharp contrast to the situation in 1963 and 1967, when environmental lobbyists played a negligible role in the congressional process, Environmental Action was active in generating support for strong antipollution legislation: "[EA] helped form a coalition favoring a tough bill, worked with several House members in sponsoring amendments to the House-passed bill, coordinated letter-writing campaigns and visits to conferees, and issued press releases."[30]

There is no necessary reason why the public's increased concern with pollution control should have developed an antibusiness focus. Indeed, many corporations welcomed Earth Day, both as a way of redirecting student energies away from antiwar radicalism and as a way of demonstrating the need for all elements of society to work together to improve the environment; some even funded Earth Day activities. Public interest in the preservation of the environment also peaked about the same time throughout Europe, and yet the environmental laws and rules adopted by various European nations did not contain the kind of adversarial stance vis-à-vis industry that underlay the legislation enacted by the U.S. Congress in 1970. The distinctiveness of the political environment with respect to pollution control issues that confronted the American business community in the 1970s lies in the superimposition of an increase in public concern with pollution on a political culture already quite suspicious of the motives, integrity, and power of the managers of large corporations. Anticipating much of the political strategy of the environmental movement, Anthony Downs wrote in 1972,

> Much of the blame for pollution can be plausibly attributed to a small group of villains whose wealth and power make them excellent scapegoats. . . . Moreover, regarding air pollution, that small group actually has enough power to improve pollution seriously if it really seeks to do so. If the few leaders of the nation's top automobile manufacturing firms, power generating firms, and fuel supply firms could be persuaded to change their behavior significantly, a drastic improvement in the level of air pollution could be achieved in a relatively short time."[31]

Gladwin Hill, who covered the environment for the *New York Times* during most of the 1970s, noted a similar outlook in a piece he published in 1968. Describing the public perception of the cause of pollution, he found it dominated by the "economic giants of the steel industry, the power industry, the petroleum industry, the chemical industry, the pulp and paper industry, and many lesser enterprises."[32] Thus, while critics of the air pollution laws enacted in 1963 tended to focus on the need for a more aggressive federal stance vis-à-vis the states, the tone of public criticism of the effectiveness of the 1967 Air Quality Act was specifically directed at the intransigence of industry and its dominance of the political process.[33]

If big business in general was held to blame for pollution problems, then one industry in particular—the biggest, the most visible, and among the most concentrated—was subject to a particularly bad press: the automobile industry. Ever since GM's unsuccessful and highly embarrassing effort to intimidate Ralph Nader following the publication of his book-length exposé of auto safety efforts, the industry had been the focus of considerable "public mistrust."[34] Moreover, shortly before the debate over Clean Air Act amendments began, the automobile industry had signed a consent decree with the Department of Justice which "at least implied that the big three manufacturers had in fact illegally worked together to thwart air pollution control."[35] One scholar noted, "This incident unquestionably added to the public's impression of recalcitrance and bad faith on the part of the industry."[36] After noting that of the nation's total burden of air pollution—estimated by the U.S. Public Health Service at 133 million tons—85 million tons came almost entirely from motor vehicles, Gladwin Hill concluded,

> The extent to which the responsibility, if there is any such thing, for this automotive portion of the pollution laws rests upon the automobile industry, the petroleum industry, or motorists, could be argued in many ways. But in terms of political realities, rather than moral responsibility, growing public awareness of the automobile's big part in smog has tended to put the auto industry in the same uncomfortable position as if the car effluvia were coming out of the smokestacks in Detroit.[37]

During Earth Day, GM's headquarters in Manhattan was picketed by a local action group under the slogan, "GM Takes Your Breath Away," while at San Jose State College, students received considerable publicity by holding a wake for and burying a 1970 automobile. There was an additional factor at work: the state in which the public concern about air pollution was historically strongest, namely, California, was one in which the automobile industry had virtually no political influence.[38] From the perspective of the far more influential California-based utility and oil companies, having the state's pollution problems blamed on Detroit was an ideal way of deflecting public attention away from their own industrial practices. Likewise, the residents of New York City's metropolitan area, who were also particularly preoccupied about air pollution problems, had no direct stake in the economic health of the automobile industry.

Not surprisingly, the round of first hearings held to review progress under the 1967 legislation focused primarily on automobile pollution. In addition to the hearings held by the Subcommittee on Public Health and Welfare of the Interstate and Foreign Commerce Committee, Representative Leonard Farbstein of New York conducted a series of ad hoc hearings on automobile pollution in New York City. Attended by a number of members of the New York City congressional delegation, their purpose, according to Farbstein, was "to explore whether the industry is following this same course of avoiding responsibility with respect to cleaning up the dirty air we breathe, air polluted by the internal combustion engine."[39] Those testifying at the hearings included both Ralph Nader and representatives of the automobile manufacturers. The committee's report, signed by seventeen members of the New York and New Jersey Democratic delegations, concluded that the automobile was "predominantly responsible for air pollution" and recommended that strong measures be taken "to reduce and control emissions."[40]

Anxious to prevent the cause of pollution control from becoming identified with the Democratic party in general and Senator Muskie—then a front-runner for the 1972 Democratic presidential nomination—in particular, President Nixon's 1970 State of the Union message emphasized the importance of a prompt national response to the issue of environmental protection: According to the president, "Clean air, clean water, open spaces—these should once again be the birthright of every American. If we act now—they can be."[41] Reacting to substantial public criticism of the administration's record on pollution control, Nixon revealed his intention of proposing to Congress "the most comprehensive and costly program in this field in the nation's history."[42]

The president's legislative proposals, submitted to Congress on February 10, 1970, involved a substantial escalation of the federal government's role in air pollution control. They also went considerably beyond those proposed by Senator Muskie a few months earlier, thus enabling the president to emerge as the prime supporter of strong legislation. In addition to extending the 1967 Clean Air legislation for another three years, the administration's bill contained two important provisions: the first, focusing on pollution from stationary sources, gave the secretary of HEW the power to establish national air quality standards and to supervise their administration by the states. In addition, Nixon, as had Johnson before him, proposed that the federal government be authorized to establish and enforce national emission standards for stationary sources emissions determined to "contribute substantially to endangerment of the public health or welfare."[43] With respect to mobile source pollution, the administration recommended that HEW be given the power to establish emission standards for new vehicles and engines and to regulate fuel and fuel additives as well as to set standards for fuel composition. Bills either identical to or substantially similar to the administration's were immediately introduced in the House, cosponsored by nearly 130 representatives from both parties.

In sharp contrast to the situation that prevailed in 1967, industry's political response to the 1970 Clean Air Act Amendments was neither uniform nor vigorous. There was minimal effort at interindustry coordination, and the amount of lobbying pressure brought to bear upon the bill as it worked its way through the House was rather mild. There were three reasons for the lack of intensive industry opposition to the administration's proposals. First, corporations were responding to the change in the climate of public opinion that had occurred since 1967. As an official of one large industry association told a reporter, industry is "tired of being cast in the role of the heavy."[44] A historian of the coal industry similarly noted, "In deference to the intensity of public opinion, the coal coalition did not mount a frontal assault on the proposed amendments as they had in 1967."[45] Second, many industries were finding themselves under intense political pressure at the state level; particularly with a Republican in the White House, they had a strong incentive to prefer a more active federal role. As one administrative official put it, "Industry's opposition would be less than in the past because industrial representatives had 'come around to thinking that it's cheaper and better for us to have national emission standards than to fight all these battles locally.'"[46]

Third, industrial interests, those from both stationary and mobile sources, did not view the congressional arena as particularly critical. None of the bills debated by the House of Representatives included specific standards; these would be established at some future date by executive action. However, those industrial interests that would potentially be affected by either the ambient air or emission standards felt confident that they would enjoy substantial input into the setting of these requirements, particularly since the Nixon administration had recently established a National Industrial Pollution Control Council. The latter, formally attached to the Department of Commerce, consisted of "chief executives of major American industries and trade associations." It "provided a means for American industry abatement,"[47] assuring the business community that its concerns would be carefully considered before specific regulations were promulgated.

Even the automobile industry, which President Nixon had earlier singled out as the major source of air pollution, did not actively intervene in the deliberations of the House of Representatives. While its lobbyists did personally visit all members of the House Interstate and Foreign Commerce Committee, "its lobbying was not particularly intense."[48] Testifying before the Commerce subcommittee, Paul Chenea, a GM vice-president in charge of its research laboratories, stated, "General Motors endorses extension of the Clean Air Act and urges that its procedures be improved."[49] Likewise, DuPont, whose market for lead additives was potentially threatened by the authority over fuel composition now being given to HEW, confined its testimony to informing the assembled Representatives that it had "developed a device called an exhaust manifold thermal reactor," capable of "significantly reducing automotive emissions of hydrocarbons, carbon monoxide, and nitrogen, without requiring the removal of lead from gasoline."[50]

Spokesmen for the U.S. Chamber of Commerce, the major steel companies, the Manufacturing Chemists Association, and the Edison Electric Institute all publicly indicated their support for national air quality standards, while the American Mining Congress called for an independent study of the idea. The two trade associations that had played a particularly prominent role in the deliberations of Congress three years previously, namely the Edison Electric Institute and the National Coal Association, expressed their opposition to national air standards but indicated they would settle for "minimal ones."[51] Only the American Petroleum Institute, presumably reflecting the concerns of its smaller members concerned about possible restrictions on fuel additives, opposed the plan to establish national air quality standards. With the notable exception of DuPont, however, all industrial representatives who testified before the House subcommittee urged Congress to deny the federal government authority to establish emission standards.

The bill that was reported out by the House subcommittee and subsequently approved by the full House by an overwhelming margin included a provision authorizing the secretary of HEW to establish stationary source emission standards. It thus represented an important legislative defeat for a substantial segment of the American industrial community—including the steel, chemical, utilities, coal, oil refining, and mining industries—who would have preferred that the federal government confine its role to the setting of air quality standards. Nonetheless, while the bill was stronger than that favored by any interest group from the business community, most indicated that they could "live with it."

On the other hand, the House version differed from the administration bill in one important respect: over the strong opposition of the members from the New York and New Jersey congressional delegations, the committee significantly weakened the power of the secretary of HEW to control fuel standards. While Representative Farbstein of New York accused the House of "bend[ing] over backward to accommodate the auto and oil industries," in fact this provision reflected the efforts of one corporation and the congressman in whose district its headquarters were located.[52] The Ethyl Corporation, headquartered in the West Virginia district of Congressman David Satterfield, feared that any effort to regulate fuel composition would result in the banning of lead additives, a major source of earnings for the company. Because Satterfield was a member of the Subcommittee on Public Health and Welfare, he was able to exercise a significant influence over the language of the bill approved by the subcommittee. Jones writes: "What was less clear is why the committee, and subsequently the House, went along with the provision. Perhaps the principal reason was simply that this provision over others had a direct effect on a specific constituency with an aggressive spokesman."[53]

Even before the final vote by the full House, the Senate Public Works Subcommittee on Air and Water Pollution, under the chairmanship of Senator Muskie, had begun to conduct hearings. In contrast to the hearings conducted in 1967, these featured relatively little participation by industry: twenty-nine firms had testified in 1967, and only twelve either appeared or submitted statements in 1970. There was, however, substantially more representation on the part of interest groups favoring strong pollution control regulations than had been the case in 1967. Seven citizen action and professional groups, along with the AFL-CIO, testified in favor of strengthening the bill approved by the House.

It was following the formal hearings by Muskie's subcommittee, however, that the real drama of the 1970 Clean Air Act Amendments began to unfold. With the passage of the House bill, the Nixon administration had firmly established a preeminent position in the field of environmental protection. It had supported—over the objections of much of the industry—a significant strengthening and broadening of the federal government's regulatory authority with respect to what was literally the most visible dimension of pollution control. At about the same time that the Nixon administration had succeeded in identifying itself with the cause of environmental protection, Senator Muskie, the Democratic party's leading presidential contender, found himself challenged from another direction. In May of 1970, Ralph Nader's Study Group Report on Air Pollution, entitled *Vanishing Air*, was released. Along with a detailed description of industry's role in effectively preventing any serious effort to address the problem of air pollution, the report included a pointed attack on Senator Muskie's role in the shaping of federal pollution control policies:

> The Task Force . . . believes that Senator Muskie has failed the nation in the field of air pollution control legislation. . . . Muskie is . . . the chief architect of the disastrous Air Quality Act of 1967. That fact alone would warrant his being stripped of his title as "Mr. Pollution Control." But the senator's passivity since 1967 in the face of an ever worsening air pollution crisis compounds his earlier failure.[54]

The report added, "perhaps the senator should consider resigning his chairmanship of the subcommittee and leave the post to someone who can devote more time and energy to the task."[55] The report's criticisms of Muskie received widespread press coverage. While Muskie accused the report's authors of "distort[ing] the story of air pollution control legislation and my role in drafting it," there can be no question that it had its intended effect: Muskie was "put . . . in the position of having to do something extraordinary in order to recapture his leadership."[56]

Meeting in executive session, Muskie persuaded the other members of his subcommittee to endorse unanimously a bill significantly stronger than that approved by the House of Representatives. The subcommittee's chairman's principal innovation was to reduce substantially the amount of discretion available to the executive branch in enforcing clean air requirements. His revised bill included strict legislative deadlines for pollution abatement as well as for meeting stationary source emission standards. Its most controversial provision, however, was addressed to the problem of automotive emissions: the bill required that vehicular emissions of hydrocarbons and carbon monoxide be reduced by 90 percent by 1975, with a similar reduction in nitrogen oxide to take place a year later.

The subcommittee's report came as a total surprise to the industries affected by it. Neither the House nor the Senate hearings had given the business community any indication that such a significant escalation of the federal government's regulatory role was actually on the political agenda. An intense lobbying effort was immediately launched to weaken the bill before it was reported out by the full Senate Public Works Committee. A number of trade associations, including the National Lead Association, the American Petroleum Institute, the Manufacturing Chemists Association, the Automobile Manufacturers Association, and the Coal Policy Conference, as well as individual corporations including Standard Oil of Indiana, the Sun Oil Company, the National Steel Corporation, and the Union Carbide Corporation, either attempted to meet with members of the committee and subcommittee staffs or testified before the full committee. Not surprisingly, the four individual automobile manufacturers played the most active role. Between August 21 and September 17, General Motors, Ford, Chrysler, and American Motors launched a highly coordinated and intensive effort aimed at persuading the Senate Public Works Committee that, in the words of GM President Cole, "[We] do not have the technological capability to make 1975 production vehicles that would achieve emission levels the legislation requires."[57] The presidents of the three largest manufacturers along with the vice-president of American Motors, met with Senator Muskie on August 25, while each of the other fourteen members of the committee were "assigned" to one of the four companies in the industry. In addition, frequent strategy sessions were held among the companies' Washington representatives.

In spite of these efforts, the committee made no substantive changes in the subcommittee's stationary source requirements and only two changes in its rules affecting automotive emissions. By a ten to three vote the full committee voted to allow the Environmental Protection Agency the right to grant the auto industry a single one-year extension of the 1975 and 1976 deadlines. It also included a provision providing for judicial review of the secretary's decisions on extensions. The bill was then unanimously approved by the full committee.

Needless to say, the debate in the Senate focused primarily on the issue of the deadline for the reduction of automobile emissions. Muskie, the bill's floor manager, told his fellow senators, "Detroit has told the nation that Americans cannot live without the automobile. This legislation would tell Detroit that if this is the case, then they must make an automobile with which Americans can live."[58] Muskie publicly conceded that no hearings had been held on the issue of whether or not the automobile industry actually had the ability to meet the deadlines contained in the committee bill. He insisted that "the deadline is based not . . . on economic and technological feasibility, but on considerations of public health."[59] Senator Griffin of Detroit, after noting the importance of the automobile industry to the nation's economy, replied, "The bill holds a gun at the head of the American automobile industry in a very dangerous game of economic roulette."[60] After rejecting a number of amendments aimed at softening, though not eliminating, the 1975 deadline, the Senate approved the bill by a seventy-three to two vote.

Those interested in weakening the Senate bill then focused their attention on the House–Senate Conference Committee. The "conference was subjected to considerable pressure" on the part of industry, acting both indirectly through the administration, which strongly opposed the establishment of specific deadlines for both mobile and stationary source emissions, and directly through the various House conferees.[61] While both industry and the administration lobbied in favor of the House version, the role of the environmental movement was relatively passive: their lobbyists could only hope that Muskie would "hold the line" on behalf of the much stronger Senate version against the "heavy pressure from special interest groups."[62] After an unusually large number of extremely lengthy negotiations, agreement was finally reached on December 16. The bill finally adopted by the conference committee made relatively few concessions to either industry or the administration. With respect to automotive emissions, it agreed to grant the auto manufacturers an extra year in which to apply for an extension of the 1975 deadline and to limit automobile antipollution requirements to five years, or 50,000 miles, whichever came first, rather than the life of the car. It also agreed to some modification of the provisions governing warranties that were strongly desired by the independent manufacturers of auto parts.

The conference, however, ignored the requests of the oil industry and the manufacturers of lead additives for some modification of regulations affecting fuel composition: the government was granted the power to "control or prohibit fuels or fuel additives which harm public health or welfare or impair a device or system to control emissions."[63] It also retained a number of provisions with considerable potential for adversely affecting the interests of stationary sources of pollution. These included a requirement that the EPA promulgate national ambient air quality standards "for each air pollutant for which air quality criteria had been issued" based on "such criteria and allowing an adequate margin of safety . . . requisite to protect public health." (These became known as "primary air quality standards.")[64] The cumulative effect of various other provisions effectively established the preeminence of federal authority in air pollution control. The conference report was adopted by voice vote by both houses the day after it was formally issued and signed into law by President Nixon a few days later.

In analyzing the legislative outcome that took place in 1970, it is useful to distinguish between the defeat suffered by a large cross-section of American industry and that experienced by the automobile industry. The former was essentially a function of three factors. First, the opposition of companies to the 1970 amendments was weakened by the extent to which lobbying against a strong bill was dominated by large corporations. For their part, the automobile manufacturers made no attempt to mobilize or involve their independent dealers. Lobbying on the issue of fuel additives was led by the American Petroleum Institute. Neither the Independent Petroleum Association of America nor the National Petroleum Refiners Association, both of whose membership consisted of numerous small refiners who stood to be disporportionately hurt by restrictions on the use of leaded gasoline, played any role in the legislative deliberations. With the exception of the Ethyl Corporation, the companies who testified at both the House and Senate hearings tended to be relatively large. Thus, although the Senate committee explicitly indicated that it had determined that "existing sources of pollution either should meet the standards of the law or be closed down," it was obvious that none of the companies that represented stationary sources who testified at either set of hearings were themselves in danger of being forced out of business.[65]

The interests of those who were in such danger were, at best, represented only indirectly through the rather ineffectual lobbying efforts of the U.S. Chamber of Commerce and the National Association of Manufacturers. That Congress might conceivably have responded to the economic concerns of relatively smaller enterprises is suggested by the success of the Ethyl Corporation—in marked contrast to DuPont—in directly influencing the decision of a congressional committee. But Ethyl was unable to put together a coalition of firms with a similar stake in public policy affecting fuel composition. It counted on the influence of Congressman Satterfield, and when he failed to secure a place on the conference committee, it no longer had any meaningful political access.

Secondly, in sharp contrast to 1967, the interests of industry were divided. While the degree of interindustry conflict was considerably less than it would be in 1977—only Englehard Minerals, which stood to benefit from the production of catalytic converters, actually lobbied for strict regulations—the inability of industry to come up with a unified position certainly proved a political handicap. The most obvious division was between those companies concerned with stationary source pollution and those concerned with mobile emissions. Each pursued its political strategy completely independent of the others. Unlike in 1977, when the Business Roundtable was available at least to attempt to formulate a series of political positions that reflected the common interests of many larger companies, in 1970 the only interindustry organizations were the U.S. Chamber of Commerce and the National Association of Manufacturers; however, they confined their attention to the regulations affecting stationary sources. The National Industrial Pollution Control Council was in a position to represent the interests of a broad cross-section of major companies, but its status in the executive branch made it ill equipped to play a role in coordinating the lobbying efforts of business in Congress. Instead, business relied upon the lobbying activities of the administration.

What also made coordination more difficult was that differences also emerged among particular industries. Thus, while the Chamber "sponsored several meetings in its offices with representatives of companies and industry associations in an effort to develop common positions and legislative language,"[66] the industry that had spearheaded the fight against national emission standards in 1967, namely, the coal industry, declined to commit its resources in opposition to the conference report. Joseph Mullan, who had directed the successful lobbying effort of the National Coal Association three years earlier, was afraid that if there was no bill in 1970 his industry might confront an even tougher one the following year. Shortly before the conference agreement, he suggested, "if we were given our druthers right this minute, we'd just as soon see a clean air bill came out."[67] He added, somewhat inaccurately, that the coal industry would not actively work with other industrial groups to maintain the House version because, "When there was hell to pay on S.O2 (in 1967) nobody came to help us." Mullan predicted, equally inaccurately, "They're big boys—they can take care of themselves."

The attempt to impose restrictions on fuel composition was also facilitated by interindustry differences, in this case between the oil and automobile industries. Early in 1970, it had become clear to those companies with a financial stake in gasoline production that a move was underway in Congress to ban lead additives. At an emergency session of the National Petroleum Refiners Association, on April 15, 1970, more than 500 members crowded into the San Antonio Convention Center to hear speakers from DuPont, Ethyl, Mobil, and Union Oil of California assert that "there are various ways of meeting the probable standards [for automobile emissions] without a prohibition on the use of organic-lead antiknock additives—a ban that could have great impact on the chemical industry."[68] A few months later the Ethyl Corporation called a press conference in New York to "tell our story in an orderly way."[69]

However, even as the major factors of lead additives and segments of the refining industry were seeking to resist being "stampeded into a costly program to produce and market nonleaded gasoline," their position was being undercut from two directions. First, in April of 1970, two major oil companies, Shell and Atlantic Richfield, announced their intention of marketing unleaded regular gasoline as a third grade, by the fall of 1970, regardless of its cost. The *National Petroleum News* wrote in 1970:

> Seldom in oil industry history has such an important issue exploded so quickly. In the space of about a month, the industry found itself gearing up for a revolution that would affect every phase of its business. One by one companies stepped forward and said they were "prepared" to go unleaded—when in fact, some observers claimed, most weren't ready at all.[70]

More importantly, the automobile industry's future plans to reduce automobile emissions—unveiled even before Congress began to address itself seriously to the problem of automobile emissions—called for the use of either nonleaded or low-lead gasoline. It thus appeared that lead was likely to be banned anyway—by the marketplace if not by Congress. Peter Gammergard, the senior vice-president for environmental affairs at API, asked rhetorically: "How can we argue with Detroit? If I were running an oil company, and I got the word out of Detroit that their cars won't run on leaded gas, I'm going to make at least one grade of nonleaded gasoline."[71] Lawrence Blanchard, executive vice-president of Ethyl Corporation, was more bitter. He charged that General Motors "symbolically placed its sins in Ethyl's head."[72] A reporter for the *National Journal* summarized the whole dispute in the following terms: "With the automobile companies pointing to additives produced by the oil companies and the oil companies pointing to tailpipe emissions, each industry seemed to be trying to shift some blame to the other instead of working together against the bill."[73]

A third factor that weakened the overall influence of industry on the 1970 Clean Air Act Amendments was that the legislation that emerged from the Senate took business by surprise. The *National Journal* reported: "Senate action on the complex, one hundred-page bill was so swift that corporate interests had little opportunity to react before it was passed."[74] The director of air pollution control for the National Coal Association remarked, "The bill that came out of the Senate was not the bill that anybody had testified to."[75] When various staff members of Muskie's subcommittee met with industry representatives on August 21 to inform them of the committee's intention to report a bill requiring 90 percent reduction of various emissions by 1975, the meeting was, in the words of Leon Billings, "a little tense."[76] Industry representatives reported it was their first inkling that the 1970 amendments might contain the 90 percent provision. While environmentalists were equally surprised by the action of the Muskie subcommittee, their inability to mobilize sufficient resources to enter into the fray was not critical; all they required to triumph was for Muskie and the Senate conferees to hold firm.

Yet if one analyzes the impact of the 1970 amendments on business as a whole, it is clear that one industry suffered a far more substantial legislative defeat than all the rest. The only industry whose pollutants were actually mentioned by name in the statute and for whom percentage reductions in emission levels were specifically itemized was, of course, the automobile industry. Stationary sources of pollution had deadlines, but no numbers; the latter were left to be determined administratively. From one perspective, the size of the automobile companies did not appear to affect their political effectiveness; after all, the industry was just as concentrated throughout the 1950s and 1960s and yet it was able to resist successfully several congressional efforts to restrict automobile emissions below a level that the industry regarded as technically feasible.[77] But as our account of the political atmosphere surrounding the 1970 amendments suggests, the industry's degree of concentration appeared to have been a political factor in 1970: it made it far more vulnerable. Given a climate of public hostility against "big business," it is not surprising that the nation's biggest industry, dominated by the nation's largest industrial corporation, became singled out for particular congressional scrutiny.

Moreover, both the modesty and ineffectiveness of the major automobile companies' lobbying appear also to have been affected by the structure of their industry. Thus, in part because of the fear of antitrust action, GM had traditionally attempted to keep a very low profile: the world's largest industrial corporation actually had no Washington office until 1969. One Michigan congressman observed in 1970:

> GM probably has the worst lobby on Capitol Hill. It ranks at the bottom in terms of effectiveness. Its Washington operation is the most inept and ineffectual I've seen here.
>
> It's not the fault of the guys in the Washington office. It's just that management has this disdain for relations in Washington. . . . GM is constantly getting hit in the back of the head because they don't pay enough attention to Washington. They get more bad surprises than any other firm in Washington.[78]

Another added:

> They send a guy up here to talk to a committee chairman or a member, thinking that is the best way to do it. It isn't. A call from the district from someone you know who will be affected by a bill is far more effective.[79]

A congressional staff member voiced a similar observation: "GM's lobbying effort in 1970 was among the most inept I have ever seen. They had no idea how to relate to Congress." Clearly, as the largest and most visible part of the automobile industry, GM's negative reputation among congressmen and congressional staff clearly weakened the overall political position of the industry.

Finally, the automobile industry, far more than any other, appeared to suffer from a significant credibility gap. The industry's arguments as to the economic and technological problems associated with rapidly reducing automobile emissions were convincing to neither the general public nor its elected representatives. One of GM's lobbyists told the *National Journal* that "the atmosphere [in the Senate] was such that offering amendments appeared hopeless." He added, "We did nothing about the bill in the full Senate. I wouldn't think of asking anybody to vote against the bill."[80] The head of GM's lobby noted, "No matter how reasonable our arguments are, we always come out looking like we are against motherhood."[81] Leon Billings typified the industry's credibility problem, when he noted, "The industry's statement before this committee as to what they are capable of doing, and their performance in California in claiming that the state standards could not be met, have made us skeptical of what they say."[82]

THE 1977 CLEAN AIR ACT AMENDMENTS

On August 7, 1977, President Carter signed into law the Clean Air Act Amendments of 1977. The most aggressively lobbied and probably among the most complex pieces of legislation approved by Congress in at least a quarter of a century, the 1977 amendments represented the culmination of more than three years of extremely intense political struggle. By the mid-1970s, the enormous stakes involved in federal regulation of air pollution had become much more apparent than they were at the beginning of the decade. For the environmentalists and their allies, the legislative struggle over the revision of the 1970 act represented their most important political challenge since the reemergence of the environment as a political issue in the late 1960s. For the companies regulated under the provisions of the 1970 legislation, the 1977 amendments represented their first important opportunity to modify those particular aspects of the 1970 law, and its interpretation by the EPA and the courts, that they regarded as unreasonable.

Because of the complexity of the 1977 amendments, my analysis of them is organized by issue areas rather than chronologically. The first section will discuss the conflicts over the regulation of mobile pollution sources, including that of automobile emission standards, warranty provisions for pollution control equipment, and federal restrictions on automobile usage. The next part will analyze the disputes over the regulation of stationary sources of pollution, focusing specifically on three issues: the prevention of significant deterioration (commonly referred to as either PSD or NSD, no significant deterioration), the exemption for nonferrous smelters, and restrictions on the burning of high sulphur coal.

Mobile Pollution Sources

As in 1970, the most intense and extensive political conflict over the Clean Air Act Amendments of 1977 revolved around the issue of automobile emission standards. A series of postponements—two granted by the Environmental Protection Agency and one extended by Congress as a response to the Arab oil embargo of 1973—had given the automobile manufacturers until the 1978 model year to meet the emission standards specified by the Clean Air Act of 1970. While the cars produced by the mid-1970s emitted significantly fewer pollutants than those manufactured at the beginning of the decade, as early as 1975 the automobile manufacturers became convinced that they lacked the technology to meet the 1978 deadline—particularly its nitrogen oxide standards. As Dr. Fred Bowditch, GM's senior executive responsible for emissions control, noted, "Anything is possible in the technical community given enough time and money. What we are saying is that we don't know how to do it right now."[83] As a result, unless Congress approved legislation that either delayed or reduced the emission standards it had established in 1970, the industry would find itself unable to begin production in 1977 of its cars for the 1978 model year.

Following a lengthy series of markup sessions, on February 5, 1976, the Senate Public Works Committee granted the automobile industry an initial if modest concession. Respondong to the public's heightened interest in fuel economy following the 1973 OPEC price increase, the committee voted in favor of postponing the final auto emissions standards for carbon monoxide and hydrocarbons until 1979—while relaxing the final standard for nitrogen oxides altogether. Although Senator Muskie had opposed this provision when it had previously come before his subcommittee, he nonetheless indicated his general support for the legislation, regarding it as a reasonable compromise. However, in order to encourage the industry to continue to endeavor to upgrade its technology, the bill also required the major manufactures—excluding American Motors and some small importers—to meet all three standards on at least 10 percent of their total output. After rejecting several amendments designed either to strengthen or to weaken the auto emission standards, the bill was approved by the Senate by a vote of seventy-eight to thirteen.

Dissatisfied with this compromise, the automobile industry decided to focus its lobbying efforts on the House of Representatives. Even after the House Interstate and Foreign Commerce Committee had voted to extend the final emission standards beyond those agreed to by the Senate, the industry launched a major effort to further amend the bill when it reached the floor of the House. Congressman John Dingell of Michigan, whose district is not only a major producer of automobiles but also includes the corporate headquarters of the Ford Motor Company, and James Broyhill of North

Carolina offered a floor amendment. It would not only have post-poned the final emission standards until 1982 but, equally impor-tant, would have eliminated the nitrogen oxide standard from the statute entirely, leaving it to be determined by the EPA. Dingell ar-gued that his amendment would "save fuel, reduce consumer costs, promote economic recovery, and reduct unemployment in the auto-mobile and related supplier/service industries."[84] One of his support-ers, Marvin Esch, also of Michigan, contended, "[It] is designed to give predictability to the automobile industry, and quite frankly, that means jobs."[85] The Dingell-Broyhill amendment which, according to one reporter, "gave the industry virtually everything it wanted," passed the House by a vote of 224 to 169.[86] The automobile industry thus had its first important legislative victory on the issue of air pol-lution in nearly a decade.

The industry's victory on the House floor, however, proved short-lived. The Senate conferees refused to compromise on the issue of automobile emissions deadlines, and the bill reported out of the House–Senate conference committee more closely reflected the Sen-ate version. Now faced with the prospect of a relatively stringent bill, the industry reversed its call for the urgent reform of clean air regu-lations and announced that it preferred no bill to the one approved by the conference committee. Thanks to a filibuster on an unrelated issue, Congress adjourned without approving new clean air legisla-tion. The industry's lobbyists were pleased with the outcome. For what they had done was to raise the stakes significantly: now unless Congress acted shortly after its return to revise or delay the require-ments of the 1970 act, Detroit would be forced to stop producing automobiles in the fall of 1977, an eventuality that Congress pre-sumably would be unwilling to countenance. Muskie was under-standably bitter. Pointing to a Senate gallery filled with lobbyists, he warned: "If they think they can come back in the early months of next year and get a quick fix from the Senate to make them legal, they better take a lot of long careful thoughts about it."[87] Equally defiant, the president of General Motors declared to a wire service reporter: "They can close down the plants. They can get someone in jail—maybe me. But we're going to make [1978] cars to 1977 stan-dards."[88]

When Congress returned in 1977, the pattern of conflict appeared to repeat itself. Once again Dingell and Broyhill offered an amend-ment to the bill on the floor of the House of Representatives, only now their amendment included a provision eliminating the original statutory standards for both carbon monoxide and nitrogen oxide. Following an extremely close vote in which the House defeated a compromise offered by the Carter administration, the Dingell–Broyhill amendment was adopted, 255 to 139. And again, the automobile industry was rebuffed in the Senate. While a compromise measure, approved on June 9, both gave the industry until 1980 to meet federal emission standards and somewhat reduced the original nitrogen oxide requirement, it represented a setback for the automobile manufacturers in two important respects. First, it required the industry to reduce nitrogen oxide emissions two years earlier than it would have preferred, and second, it maintained the original emission standards for carbon monoxide. After a prolonged and exhausting series of meetings between the House and Senate conferees—the final session lasted until after two in the morning—a compromise was reached. The final bill was closer to the Senate than the House version, but the Senate conferees were considerably more conciliatory than they had been in 1976. Their most important concession was to accept a smaller reduction in two out of the three major automobile pollutants for cars produced for the 1980 model year than was specified in the Senate version of the bill. The conference report was adopted by voice votes of both Houses two months later.

The automobile industry thus secured a major legislative victory in 1977: they won sufficient modifications in the 1970 statute to enable them to continue producing "legal" automobiles for the next five years. The extent of their impact on the 1977 amendments is particularly striking when it is contrasted to both their role in the shaping of federal air pollution legislation in 1970 as well as to the setbacks experienced by most other major industries in 1977 law. In terms of both these comparisons, the lobbying efforts of the automobile industry in 1977 must be judged extremely effective. A comparison of the success of the automobile industry with that of other major business lobbying groups in 1977 must await a discussion of the other provisions of the 1977 Clean Air Act amendments. For now it is instructive to compare the performance of the industry in 1970 and 1977. Why did it do so much better in 1977?

The explanation has little to do with the effectiveness of the lobbying efforts of the automobile companies themselves. Although it is certainly true that the automobile companies, like many large American corporations, substantially upgraded the size and budget of their Washington offices between 1970 and 1977, these changes appear to have had little political impact. The industry still faced a serious credibility problem. As Bernard Asbell wrote in 1976, "The auto lobby's biggest problem is that virtually nobody on the [Senate] Environmental Pollution Subcommittee believes them."[89] Muskie continued to view the automobile companies as "stonewalling" while his principal staff assistant, Leon Billings, characterized General Motors as "arrogant."[90] Senator James A. McClure, a conservative Republican senator from Idaho, informed one reporter in the midst of the debate over the 1977 amendments,

> The thing that impressed me is that the auto company reps stationed here are so inept. The low-level staff people they send in from Detroit to work with our staff people are very competent. They're not lobbyists but technical people.
>
> Occasionally the company hierarchies—their presidents and vice-presidents—fly in to see us, and they start reinventing the wheel. They want to tell us from the beginning what their problem is. It's a terribly wasteful exercise. They sound like they've never heard of the problem before, like they've just memorized somebody's briefing, and they assume we've never heard of it before.[91]

Nor can the changes in the public policy concerning automobile emission between 1970 and 1977 be ascribed to changes in the climate of public opinion. It is true that passage of the Energy Supply and Environmental Coordination Act of 1974, which delayed the achievement of motor vehicle emission standards by two years, was a direct response to the "energy crisis" that had materialized so suddenly in the fall of 1973. But notwithstanding the rhetoric of the Carter administration, the sense of public urgency over the need to reduce energy consumption appears to have substantially diminished by the time Congress began seriously considering amendments to the 1970 Clean Air Act. To be sure, as Senator Domenici put it, the "sunny legislative atmosphere" that surrounded the passage of the 1970 legislation had, thanks to the combination of 9 percent unemployment and double-digit inflation, become "decidedly gloomier" by 1975.[92] But the fact is that, on balance, the 1977 amendments maintained relatively strict pollution control requirements for most industrial sources of pollution; the overall burdens it placed on industry as a whole were, if anything, more severe than they had been in 1970.

Rather, the key to the relative responsiveness of the Congress to the arguments of the automobile manufacturers was the alliances they were able to form with other interest groups. In a sense, the automobile industry in 1977, like the coal industry a decade earlier, was able to mobilize a broad coalition of powerful interest groups whose interests in weakening auto emission standards either were identical with or complemented their own. However, unlike in the case of the "coal coalition" of 1967, the "automobile coalition" of

1977 did not consist of businesses that were actually parts of the automobile industry itself.

The most important reason for the increased political effectiveness of the automobile industry was that in 1977, unlike in 1970, the manufacturers had the full support of the United Automobile Workers. As Billings put it, "The auto companies never got to first base in persuading Congress to relax auto emission standard until they got the support of the UAW on the issue of jobs. The UAW has got a credibility up here that the auto companies don't."[93] Another supporter of strict pollution controls asked rhetorically, "What are you going to do when you have Henry Ford and Leonard Woodcock on the same side?"[94] According to *Congressional Quarterly*, "Virtually all observers of the battle agreed that a union—the United Auto Workers—was the key group in the clean air lobbying fight."[95] A lobbyist from another industry recalled: "The auto companies' success in 1977 was due to one key factor: they employ so many God-damned people."

In 1970, the UAW and six major conservation groups had publicly called for the "creation of air pollution guidelines so harsh that they would banish the internal combustion engine from the automobile within five years,"[96] while the AFL-CIO had publicly opposed industry efforts to weaken the Muskie bill. However, in 1974 the UAW began to shift its position. After commissioning an independent technical study designed to sort out the conflicting contentions of Muskie and their employers, the union announced its support for a five-year pause in emission standards—provided that the industry continued to work to develop the technology that would eventually allow clean air goals to be met.

> The proposal was significant for what it was saying to the American people—that the powerful UAW, in the forefront among unions on most environmental issues, felt industry deserved a break if it would only show strong good faith in moving toward the ultimate goals of the Clean Air Act.[97]

In spite of the fact that Leonard Woodcock, a strong supporter of Carter, had been nominated by the administration to be the U.S. envoy to the People's Republic of China about the same time that Congress was moving toward final passage of the 1977 amendments. Woodcock made it clear that, on this issue, he strongly dissented from the position of the administration. He told a reporter on May 25, "I sent word to the White House that if this position was a problem for them, then to forget about my being an envoy. . . . There was no question of my changing my position."[98]

In contrast to 1970, when the UAW's support for the Clean Air Act had been relatively perfunctory, their opposition to strict automobile emission standards in 1977 was extremely aggressive. It was Woodcock and the UAW staff experts who originally sat down with Congressman Dingell to develop the specific provisions of the Dingell–Broyhill amendment; the automobile manufacturers, each of whom had earlier publicly advocated even weaker standards, eventually supported Dingell–Broyhill because, in the words of UAW lobbyist Howard Paster, "The companies had nowhere else to go."[99] Imitating political tactics that public interest groups had earlier employed so successfully, the UAW, working through its headquarters in Detroit, communicated its position on emission standards to forty Community Action Program councils. These councils in turn contacted every one of the union's 1.5 million members urging them either to write to or personally contact their senators and representatives. Booklets were distributed to union members with the message: "Congress must be told *quickly* that your job is at stake. . . . Tell Congress you are supporting [the Dingell–Broyhill amendments] because your future depends on protecting air quality without disrupting jobs."[100] In addition, Paster personally contacted large numbers of people on the Commerce Committee, and during the week of May 23, ten union officials from throughout the country spent two days personally lobbying on Capitol Hill.

The automobile companies also received considerable support from two groups of small businessmen whose economic interests paralleled their own. Senator Peter Domenici of New Mexico, a member of the Senate Environment and Public Works Committee, after describing the entire conflict as "a bloody two-year brawl,"[101] observed,

The toughest vote I have made in the U.S. Senate was on the issue of auto standards. For years, despite their importance to the economy, the automakers had been comparatively easy for the Congress to handle because their base of operations was in Detroit, Michigan, and Michigan has only two senators. There are 98 other ones. The mathematics was relatively easy. Since 1970, however, automakers have begun to diversify plant sites. They now are scattered throughout the country. Yet again, the math does not make them winners. . . .

But by 1975, the automakers had figured something out: Every state in the country has automobile dealers and these dealers have employees. Every state in the country has gasoline stations and they have employees. Every state in the country has automobile parts stores and they have employees. In fact, large segments of each state's economy are based on the health, care, and feeding of the automobile. Most importantly, the more rural a state (and thus previously the more immune their representatives to Detroit's pleas), the more they relied on the automobile in their local economy. Accordingly, the auto industry mounted a massive grass-roots campaign.

It realized that most representatives will meet with groups of concerned constituents. And that it is very, very tough, in fact painful, for an elected representative to have to tell so many people no.[102]

Two trade associations developed a particularly close working relationship with the UAW and the automobile manufacturers. One was the National Automobile Dealers Association. One of the largest and oldest trade associations, by the mid-1970s it had 2,000 members and eight full-time Washington lobbyists. Although, like the UAW, the interests of its members and those of the auto manufacturers were frequently in conflict, on this issue they were identical: both were opposed to any public policy that threatened to reduce the volume of automobile sales. Not at all active in the deliberations over the 1970 amendments—in part because of the lack of advance warning of congressional intentions—they were well prepared when the Clean Air Act came up for renewal in 1976. In both 1976 and 1977, NADA sent separate letters to each of its 21,000 dealer members, urging them to make personal contact with their representatives in Washington. This strategy appeared to work quite effectively. As one of their lawyers put it:

Dealers are very effective lobbyists. They are important members of the local community. They serve on hospital boards, lead charity drives. Many are active in local politics and know their congressman by his first name. They tend to be outgoing, friendly. They're salesmen. So it's not surprising that they do a good job.[103]

Asbell comments:

The corridors of the House office buildings were as alive with local franchise dealers as if new models were being shown there. In a congressional district, an auto dealer is often a community leader and quite likely to be among a congressman's leading campaign contributors. A congressman from Kentucky, and who couldn't care less about the concern of the Detroit Economic Club, heeds the songs of his local Dodge Boys.[104]

Asked to account for the unexpected passage of the Dingell–Broyhill amendment during 1976, a lobbyist for the Friends of the Earth summarized his side's defeat in one word, "Dealers."[105]

The second trade association to join the ad hoc "auto coalition" was the Automobile Service Industry Association, an organization representing the 7,000 firms that manufactured and distributed automobile parts. In 1970, Congress had included in the Clean Air Act a provision requiring that automobile manufacturers guarantee the performance of pollution control systems on new cars for five years or 50,000 miles. The EPA had never implemented this part of the statute because of its failure to develop an adequate "in-use" test. But by the mid-1970s it had begun to draft regulations in anticipation of such a test. Independent part stations, repair shops, and parts dealers feared that the enforcement of this provision would seriously hurt their business, since the auto manufacturers—in order to protect themselves from legal liability—would henceforth require that the servicing and replacement of auto emissions parts be done exclusively by their dealers. Richard Turner, a lobbyist in the law firm of Courtney and McCamant, which represented ASIA, feared that the maintenance of this provision would wipe out the after-market parts industry.

While the warranty issue was regarded by many as a side issue, in 1976 ASIA, working essentially alone, waged an "intense lobbying campaign."[106] A Senate aide recalled that the service industry had "brought in gas station operations from every corner of the senator's state," while a House staff member estimated that 40 percent of the mail received by Congress on the Clean Air Act in 1976 concerned warranties.[107] On the floor of the Senate, an amendment was offered by Senator Lloyd Bentsen of Texas that would have reduced the warranty period to eighteen months or 18,000 miles. Bentsen argued that maintaining the original warranty requirement would "sharply restrict the car owner's service options; freeze tens of thousands of small, independent parts manufacturers, distributors, and service stations out of routine auto service work; and result in only a further concentration within the automobile industry."[108] Muskie opposed the amendment, contending that the longer warranty period was necessary to "make the manufacturer stick to his commitment" on pollution controls.[109] Bentsen's amendment failed by an extremely close vote: forty-five to fifty-one. However, immediately following its defeat, the Senate unanimously agreed to a compromise proposal by Senator Baker that "assured car owners that they could have maintenance and repair work done by anyone—including independent garages—without losing their warranty rights."[110] Like the car manufacturers, ASIA found the House considerably more sympathetic. Responding to fears that an extended warranty period would allow the major auto companies to monopolize the replacement parts and service business, the House voted to reduce the warranty term to eighteen months or 18,000 miles. Unlike the car manufacturers, however, ASIA emerged from the 1976 conference negotiations with its victory in the House of Representatives largely intact: the Senate conferees agreed to delay the enforcement of the original warranty until after the next three model years—unless overruled by the Congress. The legislation adopted by the conference committee also directed the FTC to undertake a study of the longer warranty's effect on competition.

Following the annulment of their 1976 legislative victory by the Senate filibuster, ASIA decided to cooperate more closely with the automobile manufacturers in 1977. Thus, the Dingell–Broyhill amendment offered on the floor of the House in 1977 included a provision on car warranties that met the needs of both the automobile manufacturers and the after-market parts dealers and suppliers. In addition to reducing the warranty period to eighteen months or 18,000 miles, it required the manufacturers to replace properly maintained, emission-related parts only if the owner could prove that they were defective at the time the car was sold. It also eliminated a provision from the bill reported by the House Commerce Committee that would have required the EPA to conduct production-line tests of new models. To demonstrate support for his amendment, Broyhill placed in the *Congressional Record* a list of more than one hundred business associations who supported his position on car warranties. A Senate committee staff member noted, "ASIA waged a very powerful big grass-roots effort. They had had a task force in every district. Overall, they were both very skillful and very effective." Both the Motor Vehicle Manufacturers Association and ASIA worked together to promote passage of the Dingell–Broyhill amendment. Turner, ASIA's lobbyist recalled, "In 1976, I fought alone. In 1977 . . . many of our interests were similar. They brought some votes to me that I wouldn't have had, and I brought some votes to them they certainly wouldn't have had."[111] As a House staff committee member closely involved in the deliberations over the 1976–1977 amendments put it, "The auto dealers and suppliers made a big difference in 1977. They helped a hell of a lot."

ASIA did less well in the Senate, where the provisions they favored were viewed as anticonsumer. The final version of the 1977 amendments to the Clean Air Act was closer to the House than to the Senate version: the automobile companies were required to guarantee that emission standards would be met for twenty-four months or 24,000 miles, with a limited performance warranty in effect thereafter. While these provisions met the industry's most vociferous objections, ASIA nonetheless was disappointed by the final legislative outcome. One congressional aide put it, "Given what they were up against, they probably did as well as they could have." On balance, they appeared to have been more successful in assisting the automobile manufacturers than in achieving their own specific legislative objectives.

What do the different political experiences of the automobile industry in 1970 and 1977 reveal about the impact of the large corporation on the political process? Most obviously, the industry's degree of concentration cannot be directly correlated with its political effectiveness: the size of the average firm in the industry did not change significantly between 1970 and 1977. Yet at the same time there is an important sense in which its domination by a relatively few, unusually large firms was politically relevant. Its concentration made it both a tempting target for those strongly committed to improving air quality in 1970 and an obstacle for those who wanted to maintain this commitment in 1977. Given a situation in which a relatively large number of individuals are employed by a relatively few companies, it becomes extremely difficult for the government to enact public policies whose effect would be to force any one of them out of business. Thus, Leon Billings noted in January 1977,

> Right now the Congress has only a "nuclear" deterrent—the power to block car sales altogether—which Detroit knows we can't use. As a result we have a situation in which Detroit is challenging the credibility of the Congress as an institution. Firms like General Motors and suppliers like United States Steel are so big they think they are above Congress and can force it to change. So far, they've been right.[112]

Analyzing the problem of regulating an industry composed of only a few, relatively large companies in *The Public Interest*, Lawrence White described what he termed "the fewness problem" in somewhat more academic terms:

> There are only four domestic automobile manufacturers, three of which are among the largest seven manufacturing companies in the nation. (A large truck manufacturer, International Harvester, also comes under the law due to its manufacture of large station wagons). If one meat packer out of 2,500 had to close down because it could not meet government sanitation standards, few outside a handful of workers and owners would be affected. But if one or more of the four automobile firms . . . were required to shut down, the structural consequences for the industry, and the employment consequences for the economy as a whole, would be quite serious indeed.[113]

There is considerable evidence to support White's contention. For example, several firms in the steel foundry industry, consisting of a large number of relatively small companies, were actually driven out of business by the 1970 Clean Air Act. Yet this industry secured absolutely no relief in 1977. On the other hand, precisely because the automobile industry was already dominated by a relatively few, large companies, Congress was extremely reluctant to mandate the enforcement of any regulations that would have had the effect of reducing the degree of competition still further. Thus the Senate, without any objection from Senator Muskie, overwhelmingly approved an amendment to the 1977 legislation that established a temporary delayed compliance schedule for automobile manufacturers producing less than 300,000 cars annually that were dependent on emission technology produced by other manufacturers. Its purpose was explicitly designed to help American Motors. In addition, a provision of the 1977 legislation specifically reduced standards on lead levels in gasoline produced by small refineries, thus enabling them to maintain their competitive position vis-à-vis the larger integrated oil companies.

On the other hand, one of the most politically successful industries in 1977 had a market structure that could not contrast more sharply to that of either the automobile or oil industry: these were the group of firms involved in the construction and operation of shopping centers. Their objective was to make certain that as great a share as possible of the burden of meeting national air quality standards took place via the reduction of automobile emissions rather than through restrictions on land use and automobile usage. Accordingly, they wanted automobile emission standards to be maintained as strictly as possible, lest the federal government mandate restrictions on automobile use. As early as 1974, when Congress began reevaluating auto emission standards in light of the sudden increase in energy prices, spokesmen for the National Realty Committee, an organization of several hundred developers, realtors, and investors, told a congressional subcommittee that "delays granted the auto industry would cripple the nation's air clean-up effort."[114] Their concern was echoed by the National League of Cities, the U.S. Conference of Mayors, and the National Association of Realtors. When Congressman Paul Rogers of Florida, the floor manager of the Clean Air Act amendments in the House, presented a list of companies and trade associations that opposed the adoption of the Dingell–Broyhill amendment reducing automobile emission standards, virtually every one of them had an important financial interest in maintaining the existing pattern of urban land use, with its extensive reliance on automobile transportation. His list included the American Retail Federation, the Building Owners and Managers Association, the International Council of Shopping Centers, and major retailers such as J. C. Penney, Montgomery Ward, and Sears, Roebuck and Company. As a lobbyist for the International Council of Shopping Centers noted in 1975, "Clean Air is a piece of dynamite. Every time something is done to make life easier for the car manufacturers, the dynamite gets bigger."[115]

However, regardless of what decision Congress ultimately made on automobile emissions, the "shopping center coalition" had a more specific and pressing concern: to prevent the EPA from enforcing the section of the 1970 act dealing with land use and transportation controls in a way that required local governments to place restrictions on parking in urban areas. Responding to the public uproar over its effort to reduce the pollution levels in urban areas by way of transportation controls, between 1970 and 1975, Congress voted on three occasions to postpone the implementation of parking regulations by the EPA. As Congress began the long process of revising the 1970 Clean Air Act, the future authority of the EPA to restrict local development projects that created "indirect sources" of pollution emerged as a critical issue in its own right; indeed, the resentment of state and local governments at the EPA's effort to require them to enforce transportation control plans was among the earliest sources of pressure on Congress to revise the 1970 legislation.

The interests of the "shopping center coalition" in Washington were represented by a trade association, the International Council of Shopping Centers. By the mid-1970s, ICSC consisted of approximately 10,000 companies. Primarily an organization of commercial real-estate developers, its members included a variety of both large and small companies with an economic stake in the growth of shopping centers, such as construction companies, retailers, investors, and purchasers. All told, it represented a majority of the 32,000 shopping centers in the United States. ICSC not only mobilized its own members but coordinated its lobbying efforts with the building trade unions, home builders, realtors, and major retailers. Thus, most of their political constituency consisted of relatively small firms and organizations. But in the words of one of their chief lobbyists and strategists, "They are very active locally. Developers deal with local governments all the time. Retail groups also have a tradition of political involvement, as do construction trade unions."

The challenge for ICSC was to bring this tradition of local political involvement to focus on the federal government—an arena with which they had relatively little political experience or expertise.

Their strategy was to form an alliance with those congressmen who favored the strict regulation of auto emissions. In return for helping "get the automobile industry," the shopping center coalition sought their support for an amendment restricting the EPA's veto power over local development projects. As their lobbyist put it,

> Congressman Rogers supported our amendment in order to keep the heat on the automobile industry, while our lobbyists helped Rogers take on the automobile industry. Once we had reached an agreement with Rogers, the environmentalists were neutralized. Since they were relatively weak in the House, they could not afford to do anything that might antagonize Rogers.

The coalition also sought to capitalize on the widespread resentment against the automobile companies' relatively slow progress in reducing auto emissions. Their lobbyist continued: "The more car emission control deadlines were extended, the more EPA turned to regulate us. This created considerable sympathy. After all, our shopping centers didn't cause pollution, cars did. We were willing to do our share of reducing pollution, but no more."

How did the industry's relatively fragmented structure affect their lobbying strategy? A lawyer from the firm that spearheaded their political efforts in 1977 observed:

> Our problem would have been easier if we had fewer, bigger companies, but the trade associations play some of that coordinating role. Perhaps we got a bit more sympathy because we were smaller. In my opinion the most effective trade associations are those that are democratic in structure rather than dominated by a few companies.

He added:

> The biggest problem that faces an industry made up of lots of fairly small firms is in identifying its political interests. A larger company can more easily calculate the cost of regulation. But a more scattered business can't calculate as easily how much a particular regulation will cost them. It is much harder for them to figure out whether or not it pays to fight. It's harder to get smaller guys to appreciate their self-interest. But that's where a firm like mine [a Washington law firm] can play a useful role.

While the Senate strictly limited but still maintained the EPA's authority to oppose land use controls on local authorities, the House explicitly ruled out controls on parking as a transportation control strategy. The bill that emerged out of the conference committee adopted most features of the House version: strict limits were placed on the EPA's authority to require consent permits for major "indirect sources" of auto pollution—such as shopping centers, apartment complexes, sports stadiums, and airports. The Clean Air Act Amendments as finally approved satisfied virtually all of ICSC's objectives: The EPA was prohibited from requiring indirect sources review programs, except with respect to certain federally funded projects.

For relatively fragmented industries, political organization is clearly a necessary condition for effective participation in the legislative process. In contrast to both ASIA and the shopping center coalition, the steel foundry industry was able to exert no influence whatsoever on the 1977 amendments. As a lobbyist for the NAM put it, "The steel foundry industry got wiped out because it was not politically organized. It consisted of lots of small firms, who no one cared about. They never knew what hit them. They simply weren't well enough organized to cut a deal."

Yet political mobilization is not equivalent to political influence: both ASIA and shopping center developers were extremely well organized, and yet the latter proved more politically effective than the former. Moreover, both were supported by extremely broad political coalitions. Why did one do so much better than the other? One critical factor has to do with the nature of the opposition each confronted. No one actually lobbied against the shopping center coalition: the environmentalists were neutralized by Rogers, while the automobile manufacturers obviously had other priorities. By contrast, the environmental coalition strongly opposed the interests of ASIA; they regarded a reduction in the warranty provision as a way of "getting Detroit off the hook." Some of the consumer organizations opposed ASIA for a different reason: they wanted a strict warranty provision to help protect the interests of consumers. Secondly, the arguments of the shopping center developers struck many congressmen as more persuasive than those of ASIA: the interests of the former were perceived as reflecting the interests of a large number of ordinary urban motorists, while the latter was viewed as a typical trade association interested only in protecting the economic interests of its membership.

Stationary Source Pollution

The automobile industry was the major legislative "loser" in 1970, while stationary pollution sources emerged, at least from the legislative process itself, relatively unscathed. In 1977, the situation was reversed: stationary sources of pollution were, on the whole, far less successful in achieving their legislative objectives than were those companies that contributed to pollution, either directly or indirectly, from mobile sources. In 1977, it was the steel, chemical, utilities, and oil companies that achieved relatively few of their political objectives in the area of air pollution control. Indeed, if the general purpose of the 1977 amendments was to weaken or modify some of the excessively harsh standards promulgated seven years earlier, then for these industries the legislation approved in 1977 represented a significant step "backward" in several critical respects. They emerged in 1977 with stronger regulations than they had in Congress's third revision of the Clean Air Act. Summarizing the 1977 amendments, one lawyer remarked,

> The new statute places Detroit on an oily pedestal, while inexorably demanding high ransom from utilities, steel mills, energy developers, and other stationary sources. I can only suggest that a lot of lobbyists for stationary sources interests should be swelling the unemployment roles after the thorough drubbing they suffered in Congress this year.[116]

The issue on which stationary pollution sources suffered a particularly important legislative setback in 1977 involved the "nonsignificant deterioration" of air quality. Commonly referred to either as "nondegration" PSD or NSD, the question before the national legislature was relatively straightforward: to what extent, if any, should the federal government allow the quality of air in those areas whose level of pollution was below that mandated by the 1970 Clean Air Act to deteriorate as a result of industrial expansion? While the 1970 legislation did not include any explicit reference to "nonsignificant deterioration," the legislative history of the 1970 act did indicate the intent of Congress to prevent the deterioration of relatively clean air as well as to improve the quality of already polluted air. Thus, the Senate report accompanying the 1970 legislation stated, "The Secretary [HEW] should not approve any implementation plan which does not provide . . . for the continued maintenance of . . . areas where current air pollution levels are already equal to, or better than the air quality goals." Moreover, the act did include in section 101 the phrase "protect and enhance," lifted verbatim from the 1967 legislation.[117]

While stationary sources of air pollution were far from pleased with the 1970 legislation, they did not regard any of its provisions as particularly threatening. The actual text of the law did not hint at any change in the letter or spirit of federal policy toward industrial development in clean air areas. Equally importantly, unlike with respect to mobile pollution sources, Congress did not specify any actual numbers with respect to either primary, secondary, or new source performance standards; it delegated that task to the EPA. This meant that industry, acting in part through the National Industrial Pollution Control Council, would be able to influence the federal government's interpretation and enforcement of those regulations and rules that were critical to it. In fact, business's confidence was not misplaced: when in June 1971 the EPA sought to issue guidelines for the implementation of state air quality standards that included a nonsignificant deterioration provision, the Department of Commerce, responding to substantial pressures from the NIPCC, convinced the Office of Management and Budget to force the EPA to "drastically weaken" them.[118]

What the business community had not anticipated was the critical role that the courts would play in the interpretation of the 1970 legislation. Following the EPA's decision, the agency was promptly sued by the Sierra Club. The latter won, and in 1973 the Supreme Court affirmed a lower court ruling that enjoined William Ruckelshaus from approving state control programs that did not provide controls for the maintenance of clean air. The following year, the EPA officially promulgated regulations implementing PSD: the nation's areas were divided into three classes, according to how much deterioration would be considered "significant." Thus, regions falling into class I would be allowed virtually no deterioration of air quality; while regions falling within the other two classes would be allowed progressively more. Both the decision of the Court and the EPA's effort to enforce it created an uproar within the nation's industrial community. The National Coal Association claimed that PSD "will stop the construction of any new fossil fuel power plants in most of the United States [and] . . . wash out any prospect of producing synthetic natural gas or petroleum."[119] The American Petroleum Institute, acting on behalf of nine of its largest members, filed suit to stop the EPA from implementing NSD. It argued, "EPA's significant deterioration regulations could virtually destroy this country's goal of energy self-sufficiency, aggravate the already overcrowded and polluted conditions of our urban centers, and deprive our rural and economically depressed regions of any opportunity for economic growth."[120]

The most bitter opponent of PSD was the electric utility industry, whose members' plans to construct large-scale coal-fired plants at or near coal mines in the West would be effectively disrupted. The Electric Utility Industry Clean Air Act Coordinating Committee calculated that PSD might add as much as $15 billion to their already considerable capital requirements, estimated at $54 billion, for complying with other clean air regulations.[121] At congressional hearings held shortly after the EPA issued its guidelines, representatives of coal, electric utilities, paper, steel, chemicals, and oil all strongly urged Congress to review the Clean Air Act of 1970. As one observer put it, "By 1974, the NSD concept had become the most controversial aspect of public environmental policy."[122]

As Congress began the long process of rewriting the 1970 Clean Air Act in 1975, it was clear that preventing the EPA from implementing its PSD regulations would be the major legislative priority of much of the nation's industrial community. Attempting to coordinate industry's effort was a loose coalition, the "Washington Coordinating Committee." It included individual firms, a wide array of industrial trade associations, the U.S. Chamber of Commerce, the National Association of Manufacturers, and the Business Roundtable. Following a strategy similar to that employed by the auto manufacturers, the committee strongly encouraged local businessmen to communicate their views to their representatives. Stan Hulett, the chairman of the committee and an official of the American Paper Institute, told *Congressional Quarterly*, "We don't plan any mass marches on Washington, but we are trying to mobilize support."[123] The U.S. Chamber of Commerce, in addition to waging an aggressive lobbying campaign—it sent each member of the House and Senate committees considering the legislation a map showing areas that could be cut off from development—also organized a grass-roots effort. Seeking to refute the accusation by environmentalists that the Chamber's effort was oriented to the interests of the large oil and utility companies, Gary Knight, associate direction of the Chamber's energy and environment program, affirmed that "85 percent of the organization's member-firms have less than twenty-five employees. These are *people* that are concerned, and congressmen read their mail."[124]

The focus of business's lobbying effort was to secure support for an amendment by Senator Moss of Utah that would have postponed the EPA's new policy on nondeterioration by one year, pending a study of its economic and energy impacts. While the Moss amendment went nowhere near as far as the utility industry would have wanted, its lobbyists supported it as "a practical matter." Moss's motivation was straightforward: because of the national parks that existed within its borders, much of Utah fell into class I—the most stringent classification. PSD thus threatened to interfere with the state's effort to encourage energy development, thus depriving its citizens of prospective employment opportunities and additional tax revenues. However, his amendment was defeated in the Senate by a more than two to one margin; in fact, the bill approved by the Senate contained PSD regulations that were actually more stringent than the EPA's existing rules. The regulations approved by the House were only marginally less severe than those approved by the Senate. Carl Bagge, president of the National Coal Association, stated in a trade association publication:

> Congress has turned a deaf ear on all of the administration's pleas. What is more, both the Senate and House subcommittees have added insult to injury by writing a hazy environmental slogan into their bills. It's called nonsignificant deterioration, and it has already caused the coal and electric utility industries more harm than any other single interpretation of the Clean Air Act.[125]

The bill approved by the conference committee meeting in 1976 accepted the Senate version of PSD as part of a compromise by which the Senate agreed to the House's request for an extension of automobile emissions. While the automobile industry, at least initially, was willing to accept the conference committee bill, the two senators from Utah were alarmed by a map published by the American Petroleum Institute that showed huge sections of their state closed to energy development. They successfully filibustered against the bill when it came up near the end of the congressional session. Senator Gary Hart of Colorado, a strong supporter of strict air pollution control standards, was bitter. He told his colleagues in the Senate, "What this [the killing of the Clean Air Act] suggests to me is that a few companies in a handful of industries still can control the Senate of the United States. It's as simple as that."[126] Senator Jake Garn of Utah replied: "I must say to my colleague from Colorado, our neighboring state, I resent the continuing implications that somehow big business lobbies are running this Senate. Nobody has talked to me from industry. I am trying to protect my state."[127]

In 1977, those seeking to restrict the implementation of PSD focused their attention on the House of Representatives. An amendment was offered on the floor of the House by Representative John Breaux of Louisiana that would have permitted the state governor to let the allowable increases for emissions of sulphur dioxide and particulates in class I and II areas to be exceeded 5 percent of the time, or eighteen days a year. Strongly opposed by the environmentalists and House Committee Chairman Rogers, the amendment was nevertheless adopted by a vote of 237 to 172. As in the case of auto emissions, the Senate proved less responsive to the arguments of industry. An amendment offered by Senator Stevens of Alaska, roughly similar to the Breaux amendment adopted by the House, was defeated by a vote of 61 to 33. Other efforts on the part of Western senators to modify PSD requirements on the Senate floor were equally unsuccessful. The PSD provisions in the bill reported out of the conference committee proved far closer to the Senate version. In a limited concession to the House, the conferees approved language that allowed the twenty-four-hour maximum standard for sulphur dioxide emissions to be violated up to eighteen days a year, but only in class I areas and only after public hearings. No exemption was provided for particulates. This variance would allow construction of the Intermountain Power Project in southeastern Utah (the Breaux amendment)—only nine miles from the Capital Reef National Monument—but did nothing to facilitate industrial development in class II or III areas. William Megonnell, environmental advisor for the National Association of Electric Companies, told *Industry Week*, "We got half a loaf." The more general industry reaction was, "It could have been worse."[128] On the other hand, the National Clean Air Coalition and the EPA were both extremely pleased with the final outcome.

Why was such a broad cross-section of the nation's industrial business community so unsuccessful in changing the direction of a public policy that was so important to it? The most obvious factor altering the balance of power between stationary sources of pollution and environmentalists between 1967 and 1970, on the one hand, and 1977, on the other, was the significant increase in political importance of the latter. The setbacks experienced by the automobile industry in 1970 reflected not so much the political strength of the environmental movement—which had yet to emerge as an organized political force—as the eagerness of various politicians to capitalize on the sudden increase in public enthusiasm for environmental protection. For a variety of reasons that have already been explored, the automobile industry had the misfortune of getting caught up in the rivalry between Muskie and Nixon to outdo each other in dramatizing the extent of their commitment to pollution control. By 1977, however, the environmental movement was important enought to assert its own priorities and powerful enough to exert considerable influence on the legislative process. Because of its historic concern with the preservation of wilderness areas, PSD emerged as one of its most important political priorities: it represented a way of limiting the ability of industry to expand in the one region of the country that had yet to experience the pollution associated with industrial development and with whose pristine state its members most closely identified, namely, the West.

As early as 1973, environmentalists had begun to organize a coordinated lobbying effort to resist industry efforts to weaken the 1970 amendments. By November 1973, a Clean Air Coalition had been formally organized. Operating out of the offices of the Urban Environment Conference Center, the coalition eventually included two major trade unions, the United Steelworkers and the Oil, Chemical and Atomic Workers, all the major environmental organizations, including the Sierra Club, the Friends of the Earth, Environmental Action, and the National Audubon Society, as well as the American Public Health Association, the League of Women Voters, and Common Cause. The total membership of these groups was in excess of one million people. Although the coalition operated on a rather low budget—roughly between $20,000 and $30,000 per year—it was also able to draw upon the resources of its constituent organizations, many of which included substantial numbers of people who strongly supported its legislative objectives. In addition to working through already well-established organizations, the coalition developed a field organization consisting of several hundred environmental activists who could be counted upon to contact their representatives on relatively short notice. Rafe Pomerance, a member of the staff at Friends of the Earth who organized and directed the coalition, noted,

> Lobbying is a reflection of organized power, not unorganized power, and that's the weakness of it. Those with the greatest economic resources can win. . . . But there are [215] million people who breathe auto emissions and are concerned about air. . . . We must bring the issue before the American people and make them aware of what's going on and what we think about it.[129]

Yet the relative increase in political sophistication and organization of the environmental movement and its supporters between 1970 and 1977 is only part of the explanation for the inability of industry to persuade Congress to modify PSD requirements substantially. After all, the National Clean Air Coalition was only marginally less concerned about the issue of automobile emissions, yet the automobile industry was able to reduce the severity of the regulations that affected it. How can we account for this contrast in the political influence of mobile and stationary sources of air pollution in 1977?

Clearly, the relative concentration levels of these industries was not decisive: the relationship between industrial structure of the oil, chemical, steel, and utility industries and that of the automobile industry did not change between 1970 and 1977. Instead, what was most decisive was their respective ability to broaden their political base of support. In this context, the role of organized labor was particularly critical. While the automobile manufacturers had the wholehearted support of the United Automobile Workers in 1977, the other two unions that represented large numbers of employees of stationary sources of pollution, namely the Oil, Chemical and Atomic Workers Union and the United Steelworkers, sided with the environmentalists in 1977. A historian of environmental politics noted:

> Especially valuable to the defense of the 1970 Act was the support of groups which, although not integral parts of the Clean Air Coalition, worked in cooperation with it. While the Oil, Chemical and Atomic Workers Union was a coalition member, having formed close ties with environmentalists on the common ground of protecting workers from pollutants in industry, other unions were not. Yet during the debate over the Clean Air Act, organized labor threw its weight in defense of the act and against weakening it, save for the major exception of postponing the automobile standards . . . they . . . refused to judge on the basic principles of the Clean Air Act.

Samuel Hays added: "Even more surprising was the degree to which labor supported the principle of prevention of significant deterioration, not itself a work place issue."[130]

Moreover, even if these unions had been persuaded that strict air pollution controls threatened the employment of their members, there is no reason to believe that they would have supported challenges in the statute that would have benefited stationary pollution sources as a whole any more than the UAW put any effort into opposing PSD. What each most likely would have done would have been to seek to secure an exemption for the particular industry or industries in which their members were employed. Thus, only those industries whose employers were heavily unionized would have been in a position to benefit from the potential support of organized labor even if it had been forthcoming. In reality, this meant only one industry: steel. The others—utilities, chemicals, oil—were handicapped not only in that they employed relatively few people, but also in that only a relatively small proportion of their employees were unionized. As one oil company lobbyist put it: "You know what killed us in 1977? Too damn few of our employees belong to trade unions. When it comes to fighting pollution controls, you got to really envy the auto companies, the way they can get the UAW to go to bat for them." Another added, "The problem with the political effort of the petroleum industry in 1977 was a simple one. Unlike the auto companies, we couldn't get a coalition of smaller businesses and unions together."

There was also another set of factors at work. Steel, utilities, chemicals, and oil each suffered from a particular handicap in making a case for more flexible air pollution controls. In the case of steel, the industry suffered, in the words of one of its lobbyists, from a "negative image." To a large extent the reputation of each industry in Congress is shaped by the conduct or attitude of its largest member firm. In the case of the steel industry, U.S. Steel was regarded by many in Congress as among the most obstinate corporations when it came to complying with pollution controls. Indeed, the industry as a whole appeared to have made remarkably little progress in complying with the 1970 amendments. Hays writes,

> A critical aspect of the give-and-take of political struggle in the evolution of the 1977 amendments was the role of the steel industry. This was one of the major industrial groups which remained to comply with the 1970 act. Its slow progress was emphasized by a rather dramatic session which took place at hearings conducted on revision of the 1970 act by the House Subcommittee on Health and the Environment, chaired by Representative Paul Rogers of Florida. At the meeting were representatives of the American Iron and Steel Institute, in the person of corporation leaders of the largest steel firms in the nation. Representative Rogers asked each one, in turn, about the progress made by his firm in meeting clean air requirements. Were any sources in compliance? Each replied that, in fact, none were. The expression of shock from Representative Rogers was repeated on later occasions; the episode was described in the Report of the House Committee and continued to play an important role in the somewhat negative attitudes toward the steel industry which persisted in Congress during enactment of the amendments.[131]

Moreover, steel plants tended to be located in heavily populated areas in which environmental groups were frequently very active. These organizations were strongly opposed to making the regulations affecting this industry more flexible.

The utility industry had suffered a considerable erosion of local support since the 1973 OPEC price hike. The steady increase in utility rates that took place throughout the country during most of the decade not only alienated the industry from the general public; equally important, they created considerable antagonism on the part of other companies. Accounting for the industry's lack of political effectiveness in 1977, a former EPA official explained, "Many industry lobbyists were privately delighted by any adversity that confronted the utilities. They reasoned that if environmental regulations prevented the utilities from building so many new power plants, the costs on which their rates were based might be lower." A Senate staff member added, "There was a decided lack of sympathy for dirty Eastern utility companies. Other companies blamed these bastards for the severity of the air pollution control legislation to begin with."

For environmentalists, utilities made an ideal target for a somewhat different reason; not only were they responsible for a major proportion of sulphur dioxide emissions, but their regulated status meant they could pass on any additional costs to their consumers. Finally, the vulnerability of the oil and chemical industries to strict air pollution control standards in 1977 was in large measure due to their relative prosperity. One official from a major chemical company recalled, "A congressional staff person kept asking me, 'What are you guys complaing about? You make lots of money. Why not spend more of it on controlling pollution?'"

As far as PSD is specifically concerned, the inability of the business community to have any substantive impact on this provision was due to another set of factors. While many industries would clearly have been better off if PSD requirements were relaxed, in fact the beneficiaries of such a modification were by no means evenly distributed either among these industries or even within them. Most obviously the auto industry, in the words of a utility lobbyist, "couldn't give a dman about PSD." In addition, the steel industry, with its production heavily concentrated in already heavily polluted (i.e., nonattainment) areas of the country (primarily the Northeast) and with little interest in expanding into pristine regions, stood to gain virtually nothing from a change in the regulations affecting PSD. Its primary preoccupation was with those portions of the Clean Air Act affecting compliance deadlines; as a consequence, its commitment to the campaign to weaken PSD was all but nonexistent.

But even companies in industries such as chemicals, utilities, mining, and oil refining, whose corporate plans did call for substantial new investments in class I and II regions, found themselves confronted with a political handicap. For the net effect of weakening PSD requirements would be to encourage the flow of investment from relatively polluted regions, located predominantly in the Northeast, to relatively unpolluted areas, located disproportionately in the West. Such a shift in the locus of investment might well be in the economic interests of many of the companies in these industries, but it was certainly not in the interests of the residents of the communities in which their investments were already located. For them, strict PSD regulations were essential if companies were to be prevented from shifting capital and jobs from the "Frostbelt" to the "Sunbelt" in order to reduce air pollution. These industries were thus unable to appeal to the representatives in whose districts their facilities were located to support their position on PSD for the simple reason that the interests of these communities and that of the corporations themselves were quite distinct. By contrast, the environmentalists were able to form an enormous affective alliance with congressmen from industrialized regions: both had a common interest in preventing increased air pollution in regions whose air quality already exceeded national standards. For a similar reason both the U.S. Conference of Mayors and the National League of Cities endorsed strong PSD requirements. They argued:

> The health of the economies of urban-industrial regions is dependent upon industrial continuation and growth. It is in the best economic interest of these regions that sources remain in them and utilize emission controls necessary. . . . The requirement of no significant deterioration prevents rural regions from allowing lenient emission controls that are so much less expensive that an industry will have a financial incentive to relocate. . . . No significant deterioration removes the possibility of economic coercion between competing regions.[132]

Thus, from one perspective, the fact that these industries were dominated by relatively large companies constituted an important political handicap: unlike in the case of the auto dealers, or shopping center developers, who were closely identified with the prosperity of the particular communities from which they derived their profits, the firms in these industries had a national—if not international—orientation; the interests of each company as a whole were by no means similar to those of the communities in which it currently had facilities. On the contrary, in the case of PSD, they could be said to be diametrically opposed. Not surprisingly, congressional voting on PSD took place largely on regional lines. As one congressional staffer put it, "Frostbelt senators were more than happy to gang up on PSD to screw the Sunbelt."

There were, however, two industries that were able adequately to defend their interests with respect to the provisions in the 1977 amendments governing pollution from stationary sources. Section 119 of the Clean Air Act allows qualifying nonferrous smelters to receive nonferrous smelter orders; these orders permit smelters to meet ambient air standards through the use of either continuous or intermittent controls through January 1, 1978. This meant that copper smelters would not be required to install scrubbers to reduce their sulphur dioxide emissions; instead they had the option of employing either tall stacks or plant shutdowns during adverse weather conditions. Although the EPA has done everything possible to avoid implementing this provision—in fact, through 1981, not one bona fide NSO was actually granted—the copper smelter industry did accomplish what no other stationary pollution source was able to achieve in 1977: an explicit recognition of the financial obstacles it faced in complying with the emission requirements established by the EPA under the 1970 Clean Air Act. What accounts for its unique achievement?

There can be no doubt that the industry did have a compelling economic case for some sort of regulatory relief.[133] During the 1970s the industry's pollution control expenditures averaged nearly 18 percent of its capital expenditures—compared with 5.5 percent for all businesses; the majority of these expenditures were to control sulfur dioxide emissions. Between 1970 and 1978, the copper smelting industry spent approximately $1.1 billion on air pollution controls—more than sixteen times original government estimates. For the period 1971 through 1979, FTC data indicated that companies in the nonferrous smelting industry averaged a return on stockholders' equity of 9.6 percent compared with 13.3 percent for all manufacturing firms. Furthermore, the industry existed in an extremely competitive world market, one in which its competitive positions had been steadily eroding. Between 1972 and 1977 U.S. smelter production declined at an annual rate of 4.5 percent. As a result, the ratio of imports to domestic copper production rose from 8.8 percent in 1973 to 20.7 percent in 1977. While the industry had made substantial progress in reducing air pollution following the 1970 legislation, its emission of sulphur dioxide still remained substantially in excess of that allowed by the EPA. It was obvious that the likely consequence of requiring the industry to meet national ambient air standards in the manner required by the EPA under the 1970 legislation would be a substantial reduction in domestic smelting capacity—followed by an increase in imports.

Yet these facts, compelling as they might appear, cannot be themselves accountable for the inclusion of section 119 in the 1977 Clean Air Act. For as the industry's own position paper on the subject makes clear, virtually all applied with equal force to the steel industry. It too had been confronted with a low growth rate, low profits, a declining share of world output, and considerable pollution control expenditures. And yet an attempt to secure it a special exemption in the 1977 legislation was unsuccessful. Moreover, both industries are roughly equally geographically concentrated—steel in the Northeast and copper smelting in the West. Nor can the amount of workers employed in the two industries explain this variance, for the obvious reason that the steel industry employes far more people than does the smelting industry.

In this case, the difference in concentration levels between the two industries may have been a factor. The primary copper industry is heavily concentrated; in 1977 the four largest companies accounted for 87 percent of the value of industry shipments. By contrast, in 1977, the four largest companies in the steel industry accounted for only 45 percent of the value of industry shipments; not until the twenty largest companies are included does the steel industry account for the same value of industry shipments as the four largest primary smelters and refiners of copper.[134] As in the case of autos, the relatively small number and large size of the companies involved in the industry made their plans for regulatory relief more persuasive; the economic consequences of not addressing an industry's problems appear far more visible when it consists of a relatively few, relatively large firms. Moreover, in the case of copper smelters, Congress could provide an exemption for an entire industry and yet benefit only a handful of firms.

A second explanation has to do with the role of their respective trade unions. Although smelter workers are members of the United Steelworkers Union—which opposed any special treatment for the steel industry—the locals who represented the employees of the smelting industry broke with the position of the national union: they strongly supported the copper smelter industry's efforts to secure special treatment. The importance of organized labor's position was underlined four years later, when Congress enacted legislation that specifically gave the steel industry additional time to meet federal air pollution standards. Critical to this shift in the industry's political fortunes with respect to federal pollution policies was a reversal of the position of the United Steelworkers Union. Concerned about increasing unemployment in the steel industry and having recently closely cooperated with management on the issue of steel imports, the USW strongly supported the steel industry's request for regulatory relief. The 1981 legislation was enacted with virtually no opposition, though lobbyists from many other industries that felt equally hardpressed by the 1977 Clean Air Act Amendments would have preferred that the steel industry work with them to secure a more general reform of clean air regulations.

Third, the environmentalists were much less concerned about emissions from smelters than they were about the air pollution produced by steel mills for the simple reason that smelters were generally located in relatively unpopulated areas. In contrast, environmental organizations drew much of their political strength from those urban residents who were most directly affected by emissions from steel mills. Finally, the smelters also had the good fortune to have Senator Domenici on both the Senate committee and the conference committee. Representing New Mexico, a state with an important smelting industry, Senator Domenici was able to use his considerable influence to represent this industry's interests effectively. Unlike the representatives from steel-producing districts, Domenici was not subject to any conflicting pressures from his constituents on this issue. In fact, a deal was worked out: in exchange for Domenici's support on PSD, the environmentalists agreed not to oppose a special exemption for smelters.

The second industrial segment to secure a special provision in the 1977 Clean Air Act that safeguarded its economic interests were the producers of Eastern coal. The production of coal does not by itself create air pollution; substantial pollutants are, however, emitted by coal when it is burned by utilities. Section 111 of the 1970 Clean Air Act provided that all new plants of the same type had to meet uniform emission standards. Known as New Source Performance Standards, NSPS were to be established by the EPA so as to provide the "best system of emission reduction which (taking into account the costs of achieving such reduction) the administration determines has been adequately demonstrated."[135] The ambiguous language of the legislation left the EPA with a choice: it could allow newly constructed coal-fired utilities to reduce sulphur dioxide emissions either by installing scrubbers or by burning coal with reduced sulphur content. The latter policy was strongly favored both by utilities—who distrusted scrubbers—and by the owners of Western coal reserves, where low sulphur coal deposits were located. The adoption of this pollution control strategy, however, threatened the economic interests of Eastern coal producers, whose coal tended to be relatively high in sulphur content. Responding in part to pressures from environmentalists, who strongly favored the use of scrubbers as a means of reducing air pollution and were reluctant to antagonize the congressmen from coal-producing states, the EPA chose to require all utilities to install scrubbers. The utility industry was outraged by this decision, and the nation's largest utility, American Electric Power, waged a highly visible crusade against it. The stage was now set for Congress to address the issue.[136]

The fight over universal scrubbing was among the most intense inter-industry conflicts that Congress confronted in 1977. In favor of allowing utilities the option of reducing sulphur emissions by burning low sulphur coal was the entire utility industry as well as Western railroads and Western coal producers; the latter were owned in large measure by both oil companies and railroads. Supporting a universal scrubber requirement were, in addition to the producers of Eastern coal—most of whom were also owned by firms in other industries—a coalition of trade unions, environmentalists, and Eastern railroads. The support of the United Mine Workers, as well as the United Steelworkers and the AFL-CIO, for a mandatory scrubbing requirement was due to the fact that Eastern coal producers, including those owned by steel and utility companies, were heavily unionized. By contrast, Western coal was largely produced by nonunionized workers. The environmentalists in turn opposed allowing Eastern utilities to burn low sulphur coal shipped from the West in order to prevent the Western regions of the country from being destroyed by strip mining.

The National Coal Association, faced with a strong difference of opinion among its membership, took no position. Clearly the coal coalition, notwithstanding all the extensive organizational links that had developed between coal producers and other large industries throughout the 1970s, had fallen into disarray. In fact, while the interests of Western coal subsidiaries and those of their parent companies were identical, in the East they clearly were frequently opposed: steel and utility companies who owned Eastern coal reserves bitterly opposed mandatory scrubbing requirements, while their subsidiaries favored them.

The outcome of this legislative struggle favored Eastern coal producers or, more specifically, the producers of medium sulphur coal. The most crucial vote took place on the floor of the Senate. Senator Metzenbaum of Ohio offered an amendment, cosponsored by three senators from the coal-producing states of West Virginia, Indiana, and Pennsylvania, that would have allowed the president or the EPA to prevent utilities and other large coal users from going outside their regions to purchase coal that was locally available—provided the importation of coal from another state would produce "significant local or regional economic disruption or unemployment."[137] (According to Metzenbaum, nineteen Ohio utilities intended to comply with air quality standards by switching from Ohio coal to low sulphur Western coal). Among the organizations officially supporting Metzenbaum's proposal were the National Clean Air Coalition, the Environmental Policy Center, the Sierra Club, the United Mine Workers of America, the AFL-CIO, the United Transportation Union, the United Steelworkers of America, and the Consolidated Rail Corporation. Senator Domenici criticized the amendment as "economic Balkanization that did not belong in the Clean Air Act."[138] It was also opposed by Senator Muskie. The amendment was adopted by a forty-three to forty-two vote, with the Senate dividing largely along regional lines: Eastern and Southern senators supported Metzenbaum's amendment; Western senators opposed it. A subsequent amendment by Senator Domenici, approved by voice vote, modified the Metzenbaum amendment to require that the cost to consumers be figured in any decision to mandate the use of particular kinds of coal.

The regional distribution of coal usage was never explicitly debated on the floor of the House of Representatives. The House committee, however, did report out a bill that contained a provision whose effect was roughly similar to that of the Metzenbaum amendment. Unlike the 1970 legislation, which directed the EPA to set performance standards that reflected "the degree of emission limitation achievable through the application of the best system of emission reduction," the version of section 111 approved by the House of Representatives in 1977 required a standard that "reflects the degree of emission reduction achievable through the application of the best technological system of continuous emission reduction."[139] This phrase itself is somewhat ambiguous; however, the intention of the House staff members who drafted it was clearly to require all utilities to install stack-gas scrubbers.

Under intensive pressure to report out a bill, and faced with strong differences of opinion over PSD and auto emission standards, the House–Senate conference committee was unable to devote much attention to the coal scrubber controversy. In any event, proscrubber forces enjoyed a number of advantages. First, they had the unequivocal support of Senator Randolph of West Virginia. Senator Domenici of New Mexico, on the other hand, who opposed the mandatory scrubber requirement, cared less strongly about it: he was more preoccupied with the conflict over PSD, an issue of far greater importance to the economy of his state. Likewise, the coalition of industrial interests, who favored allowing Eastern utilities to burn Western coal, namely, the utilities, the Western railroads, and the corporations that owned substantial Western coal reserves, were unable to give the issue their undivided attention; they too were far more concerned with weakening the PSD requirement. By contrast, the Eastern coal companies, both those that were independently owned and those that were subsidiaries of firms in other industries, faced no such distractions. They were fighting for the very survival of their industry. And in this objective, they enjoyed, as they had in 1967, the strong support of the representatives of those states with significant reserves of high and medium sulphur coal.

However, what was most important in tipping the balance of influence in Congress was that Eastern coal producers enjoyed the support of two powerful nonindustry constituencies: the environmental lobby, and organized labor, particularly the United Mine Workers. It was this "clean coal/dirty air" coalition, dubbed an "unholy alliance" by one environmentalist, that ultimately triumphed in the national legislature.[140] While, as Bruce Ackerman and William Hassler point out, both the text of the 1977 act and its legislative history are somewhat muddled, the legislation can be appropriately viewed as a victory for the interests of Eastern coal producers—though one that would subsequently be refought within the executive branch.

What effect did the relative size of Eastern and Western coal producers have on this outcome? It does not appear to have made any difference. In fact, the ownership of Western coal reserves is far more concentrated than is Eastern coal: there are nearly ten times as many coal companies in West Virginia as there are in Montana, Wyoming, Colorado, New Mexico, Arizona, and Utah combined.[141] Of far greater significance was the relative importance of Eastern coal production to the economies of the states in which they were located.

Conclusion

Four sets of factors appear to be most critical in accounting for the relative influence of various companies on federal clean air legislation between 1967 and 1977. The political impact of companies in a particular industry is affected by the pattern of opposition and support from other interest groups, how well their lobbying effort is organized, the perceived merits of their position, and the geographic distribution of their production.

Probably the most important factor influencing the ability of various companies to achieve their legislative goals was the relationship between their objectives and those of other interest groups, both business and nonbusiness. Obviously the less opposition a group of companies faces, the more likely they are to achieve their political aims. Alternately, the broader a coalition it can form to support its policy goals, the more likely it is to achieve them. The preceding pages provide numerous illustrations of this generalization. Coal producers accomplished their legislative objectives in 1967 both because of the support they received from other industries and because they faced no effective political opposition. Most industries did less well in 1970 than in 1967, in part because in 1970 they had less support from each other and faced more organized environmental opposition. The contrast in the political effectiveness of the automobile manufacturers between 1970 and 1977 is largely attributable to the fact that in 1970 they struggled alone, while in 1977 they enjoyed the support of two other trade associations as well as the

United Auto Workers. The success of shopping centers developers in 1977 is largely a testimony to the broad coalition they were able to put together in support of their objectives—a coalition that included not only other commercial interests but also organized labor and various organizations representing local governments. It was also abetted by the fact that it was not directly opposed by either the environmental movement or the automobile manufacturers. Similarly, in 1977, Eastern coal producers clearly benefited from the support of both the United Automobile Workers and the environmental movement. Copper smelters triumphed in 1977 both because they had an important ally—namely, various locals of the United Steelworkers—and because no one, including the environmentalists, actively opposed them. The other stationary pollution sources in 1977 faced two sets of handicaps. Not only did the companies in each industry receive no support from other interest groups—indeed, these industries tended to offer relatively little assistance to each other—but they were also faced with strong opposition from both the environmental movement and organized labor. The success of the companies in the steel industry in convincing Congress to give them more time to comply with environmental standards in 1981, although beyond the scope of this study, is likewise clearly attributable to the role of other interest groups. Both the environmentalists and the United Steelworkers, who had opposed a similar extension in 1977, reversed their position four years later.

The importance of political alliances in shaping political outcomes was particularly apparent in 1977. The relative political impact of the companies in each industry in 1977 can be attributed almost completely to the role played by organized labor: whenever labor supported the companies in a particular industry, the latter attained a significant share of their objectives. On the other hand, when labor was either neutral or supported the environmentalist position, business did less well. By contrast, the environmentalists, like industry, triumphed only when organized labor did not oppose them. (This occurred only once, in the struggle over automobile emission standards; on every other legislative conflict in 1977, environmentalists and organized labor were allies). This does not mean, of course, that in 1977 organized labor was the most politically powerful interest group in Washington: in fact, the trade union movement was notably unsuccessful in advancing its own legislative agenda. What it does suggest is the danger of generalizing about the political influence of any interest group: in the world of congressional politics, what is critical is the relative power of the coalition one is able to mobilize on any given issue. As the experience of ASIA in 1977 demonstrates, an interest group may be unable to achieve its own legislative goals, yet still constitute a critical component of a broader coalition.

To what extent does the average size of firms in a particular industry affect the nature of the coalitions they are able to organize? There does not appear to be any consistent relationship between the two. In 1977, the three most effective coalitions were organized by firms in industries with dramatically different degrees of concentration, namely, the automobile industry, Eastern coal producers, and shopping center developers. Moreover, the inability of companies in the steel industry, the oil industry, utilities, and the chemical industry to form effective alliances with other interest groups does not appear to be related to their size. Nor does diversification appear to be an important factor in affecting the ability of a given industry to enter into alliances. Neither the automobile firms nor the copper smelters were handicapped in 1977 by their emphasis on one particular product line; the producers of relatively high sulphur coal triumphed in spite of their industry's organizational links with other industrial sectors, not because of them. On the other hand, the far more closely integrated producers of Western coal were less successful.

A second set of factors affecting the political influence of a group of companies is their degree of political organization and sophistication. There is nothing automatic about business access to government; like any interest group, business must first actively communicate its positions on various issues to elected officials and their staffs. The success of both the coal coalition in 1967 and Eastern coal producers a decade later were in part a reflection of the sophistication of their lobbying efforts. One factor underlying the improvement in the political fortunes of the automobile companies between 1970 and 1977 was that they were largely caught unprepared in 1970; however, seven years later they were well organized for a major legislative struggle. The major industrial stationary sources of pollution fared relatively poorly on the PSD issue in 1977, in part because they were not prepared for the degree of political opposition to their efforts to weaken PSD requirements. (Just as the automobile industry learned from its experiences in 1970, so are the other major industries who suffered a legislative setback in 1977 seeking to benefit from their experiences: for nearly three years they have been preparing for the forthcoming congressional revision of the 1977 amendments.) The contrast in the political impact of shopping center developers and the steel foundry industry in 1977 is largely a function of their respective degrees of political organization: the former were able to establish an effective Washington presence; the latter were not. Similarly, whatever political impact was achieved by both automobile dealers and the manufacturers and servicers of automobile parts was due to the fact that they had well-established, politically experienced trade associations.

How does the size of firms in an industry affect their ability to bring their resources to bear on the policy process? Companies in concentrated industries do appear to enjoy an important advantage: firms in these industries are more readily able to perceive their political interests and can more easily communicate with each other. To the extent that firms in more concentrated industries are often relatively larger, this advantage is reinforced: larger firms are more able to monitor political developments, analyze and document the impacts of various public policies, and support a Washington office than are smaller firms. While this does not automatically translate into political power, it certainly constitutes a necessary condition for its exercise. On the other hand, while an industry comprised of large firms may find it easier to influence government, corporate concentration is by no means essential to this process. Firms in highly fragmented industries certainly can and do enjoy access and organize extremely sophisticated lobbying efforts, though the amount of effort involved is likely to be considerably greater than for firms in more concentrated industries. On occasion, organized labor can provide firms in a relatively fragmented industry with some of the advantages of larger size. Moreover, as the experience of the automobile industry in 1970 suggests, large size is not equivalent to political sophistication.

A third set of factors affecting the political influence of companies in a given industry has to do with the perceived merits of their arguments. The political climate in general and an industry's or company's reputation among legislators and the staff of congressional committees have important political consequences. The dramatic decline in the ability of both coal and the automobile companies to shape federal air pollution policy between 1967 and 1970 cannot be understood without reference to the change in the climate of public opinion with respect to pollution control and industry's responsibility and capacity to ameliorate it. Likewise in 1977 the automobile companies benefited from the increase in public awareness of the technical and economic obstacles to reducing control emissions to the levels specified in the 1970 statute. The ability of companies in the steel industry to delay the enforcement of pollution controls in 1981 was significantly affected by a notable shift in the public's perception of its economic difficulties—a development dramatized by the closing of a major facility in Youngstown, Ohio. Similarly, the steel company's inability to secure legislative redress in 1977 was in part due to its poor reputation among environmentalists and congressional policy makers. The manufacturers and suppliers of automotive parts clearly suffered from the perception of many legislators that their legislative goals were "anticonsumer."

On the other hand, both the copper smelter companies and the shopping center developers benefited in 1977 from substantial congressional sympathy for their positions—a perception that was to some extent independent of either their political organization or the alliances they formed. Much of the conflict over coal scrubbing in 1977 took place on an ideological level: the environmentalists succeeded in part because they were able to make the installation of scrubbers into a symbol of a commitment to air pollution control. Many congressmen also appear to have been persuaded by the argument that the government's pollution control policies should not preclude the use of a significant segment of the nation's coal reserves. Alternatively, the opposition of the utility companies to scrubbers was widely perceived as demonstrating their unwillingness to reduce the amount of pollution they generated. Most dramatically, the ability of organized labor to play such an important role in the legislative outcome in 1977 was largely due to the fact that its position on environmental issues enjoyed far more credibility than that of industry: Congress was far more prepared to respond to labor's concerns about employment than it was to industry's arguments about profits.

The structure of an industry does influence the ways in which its positions are perceived by Congress, but this relationship is by no means a clear one. On one hand, it is true that, on balance, smaller firms and firms in more competitive industries enjoy more congressional sympathy than do larger firms and firms in more concentrated industries. The fact that Congress specifically exempted both smaller automobile manufacturers and smaller oil refineries from various regulations affecting their larger competitors clearly illustrates this. Similarly, the automobile dealers found Congress more responsive to their concerns about the loss of sales stemming from automotive emission standards than did the larger, more concentrated manufacturers. Moreover, the perceived identification of the companies in the automobile, steel, oil, chemical, and utility industries as "big business" weakened their influence on Congress: as large and thus presumably affluent companies, they were regarded as readily capable of absorbing any additional expenditures. As virtually the very symbol of "big business," the automobile companies undoubtedly suffered from a particular handicap in 1970.

But while there may be more sympathy in Congress for relatively small firms in relatively fragmented industries, there is also relatively more awareness in Congress of the need to maintain the prosperity of the larger, more concentrated sectors of the business community. When a concentrated industry's economic viability actually appears to be threatened—as was the case with respect to the automobile industry and copper smelters in 1977 and the steel industry four years later—then Congress appears relatively likely to grant it the relief it needs to survive. In this context it is significant that few firms in relatively concentrated industries and no large companies have actually been driven out of business by federal air pollution requirements. This has not been the experience of smaller firms and firms in more fragmented industries, a disproportionate number of whom have suffered rather severe consequences as a result of air pollution regulations.

A final set of factors that appears to influence a firm's political power in Washington is the geographic distribution of its economic activity. The more a company or industry is an important factor in the economy of either a state or a congressional district, the more likely it is to find a particular congressman or senator responsive to its arguments. And if that particular representative occupies a strategic position in the congressional power structure, that company's or industry's influence is enhanced still further. We have seen how companies in the automobile industry, the copper smelter industry, and most importantly, Eastern coal producers benefited enormously from the extent to which various senators and representatives identified with their interests because of the importance of firms in these industries to their constituents. On the other hand, the very dispersion of shopping center developers and automobile dealers also worked to their political advantage: they constituted relatively influential segments of the economies of an extremely large number of legislative districts.

In a sense, geographical dispersion appears to involve a certain tradeoff: the more a company is concentrated in a particular political unit, the more likely its representative in Washington will play a leadership role in defending its interests. But this also means that it will enjoy proportionately less access to other representatives in whose districts it has no facilities. Having facilities in many political units increases the number of representatives to whom one has access, but this dilution of a company's geographic concentration also decreases the likelihood that any one representative will assume a major personal responsibility for safeguarding its interests. Finally, geographical distribution appears only indirectly related to corporate size. While a large firm whose facilities are geographically concentrated is obviously likely to be of considerable importance to the economy of a particular political unit or units, a large firm whose facilities are geographically dispersed may enjoy no such advantage. On the other hand, a group of smaller companies whose operations are geographically contiguous are likely to enjoy considerable influence with their representatives.

On balance, among the most important factors underlying the relative lack of political effectiveness of business as a whole in 1977 was its lack of unity. In sharp contrast to 1967, when the business community was confronted with a relatively small number of issues that affected a relatively large number of companies, the issues involved in the 1977 legislation were both more complex and more numerous. However, in 1977 the business community did enjoy one potential political advantage that it did not have either in 1967 or 1970: the Business Roundtable, formed in 1972, now existed as a vehicle to coordinate the lobbying strategy of a significant cross-section of the nation's largest corporations. The Roundtable did take a formal position on a number of the most controversial issues that Congress confronted in 1977—including auto emission standards and PSD—but it had virtually no political impact. One can fully account for all the legislative outcomes in 1977 without any reference to its role. The explanation is a simple one: the positions of different companies in different industries were simply too disparate. No company or industry was willing to subordinate the achievement of its particular legislative goals in order to benefit other segments of the business community. As a result, the environmentalists and their congressional supporters were able to pursue a divide and conquer strategy: by giving particular industries what they wanted, they were effectively able to "neutralize" them.

A cross-industry coalition such as the Roundtable is likely to be most effective on issues whose impact is relatively sweeping and indivisible. Thus, the very specificity of the 1977 Clean Air Act Amendments served to promote business disunity. Whether the Business Roundtable—or, for that matter, any coalition of firms in different industries—will be able to cooperate to increase the overall political effectiveness of the business community when the Clean Air Act is again revised by Congress remains, at this juncture, problematic: it is one thing for companies in different industries to agree on a common set of legislative objectives but quite another for them to resist the temptation to agree to a compromise that particularly benefits them—regardless of its impact on the economy as a whole.

There is another development that could conceivably affect the political effectiveness of particular companies when Congress again considers the fate of the Clean Air Act. Since 1977, a number of highly publicized mergers have occurred between relatively larger firms in substantially different industries. Will the influence of these larger, more diversified companies be greater than the sum of their component parts? More specifically, will they facilitate the task of interindustry coordination and cooperation? On one hand, they will certainly make the management of these companies more aware of the impact of air pollution regulations on a wider segment of industry as a whole. But at the same time, these mergers may contribute only marginally to the search for an interindustry consensus. Different industries will continue to have differing priorities, only instead of negotiations taking place between firms in different industries, they will now take place between the divisions of an individual firm. The more diversified a company, the more difficult and time-consuming will be its effort to define its corporate interest with respect to clean air legislation. It is certainly true that a diversified firm may find it easier to force each of its subsidiaries to adopt a similar position than would be the case were their divisions managed separately. But the political impact of such a strategy is unclear: a subsidiary that is forced to subordinate its interests to that of the company as a whole not only is likely to suffer a loss of credibility within its trade association but may not be in a position to use whatever political influence it possesses to benefit its parent company. Why should a representative with a copper smelter in his district care about restrictions on oil refinery construction? (Ironically, in the case of copper smelters, now owned almost wholly by energy companies, their larger size may actually work against them: they will find it more difficult to argue against strict pollution control requirements on the grounds of financial hardships.) In fact, many of the diversified companies interviewed for this study indicated that in the event of intracorporate differences, their strategy would be to turn each subsidiary "loose," letting it do its best to protect its own interests, even if they differed from that of other units within the firm. (This is what apparently occurred with respect to the conflict over the mandatory installation of coal scrubbers). Other firms indicated their intention of enforcing a more disciplined stance.

In sum, the size of the firms has important political consequences. By itself, however, it does not directly translate into political power; there are numerous other factors involved that are equally important. While this study has focused on federal clean air legislation, there is no reason to believe that these conclusions would not also be valid for many other kinds of legislative conflicts.

NOTES

1. Lester Salamon and John J. Siegfried, "Economic Power and Political Influence: The Impact of Industry Structure on Public Policy," *American Political Science Review* (1977), 71:1042.

2. Edwin M. Epstein, "Firm Size and Structure, Market Power and Busi-

ness Political Influence: A Review of the Literature," in John J. Siegfried, ed., *The Economics of Firm Size, Market Structure and Social Performance* (Washington, D.C.: Federal Trade Commission, 1980), p. 252.

3. Randall Bartlett, "An Economic Theory of Political Power: Firm Size and Political Power," in Siegfried, ed., *Economics of Firm Size, Market Structure and Social Performance*, p. 298.

4. Department of Commerce, Bureau of the Census, *Census of Manufacturers* (Washington, D.C.: Government Printing Office, 1977).

5. Richard H. K. Vietor, *Environmental Politics and the Coal Coalition* (College Station: Texas A&M Press, 1980), p. 20.

6. These statistics are from the Council on Environmental Quality, quoted in Murray L. Weidenbaum, *Business, Government and the Public* (Englewood Cliffs, N.J.: Prentice-Hall, 1977), p. 78. The quotation is from Kenneth Chilton and Ronald Penoyer, "Making the Clean Air Act More Cost-Effective," Working Paper (St. Louis: Center for the Study of American Business, September 1981).

7. See, for example, Charles Lindbloom, "Commentary," in Siegfried, ed., *Economics of Firm Size, Market Structure and Social Performance*, pp. 319–24.

8. Theodore Lowi, "American Business, Public Policy, Case Studies—Political Theory," *World Politics* (July 1964), 16:667–715.

9. For an extremely comprehensive account of the political conflict surrounding the approval of this legislation, see Randall B. Ripley, "Congress and Clean Air," pp. 175–200, in David Paulsen and Robert Denhardt, eds., *Pollution and Public Policy* (New York: Dodd, Mead, 1970). See also J. Clarence Davies III and Barbara S. Davies, *The Politics of Pollution*, 2d ed. (Indianapolis: Bobbs-Merrill, 1975), pp. 44–48; and Charles D. Jones, *Clean Air: The Policies and Politics of Pollution Control* (Pittsburgh: University of Pittsburgh, Press, 1975), chap. 3.

10. Vietor, p. 140.

11. "Congress Strengthens Air Pollution Control Powers," *1967 Congressional Quarterly Almanac* (Washington, D.C.: Congressional Quarterly Services, 1967), p. 878.

12. Douglas Ross and Harold Wolman, "Congress and Pollution: The Gentlemen's Agreement," *Washington Monthly* (September 1970), 2:18.

13. *1967 Congressional Quarterly Almanac*, p. 878.

14. Ross and Wolman, p. 18.

15. Vietor, p. 142.

16. Jones, p. 79.

17. *1967 Congressional Quarterly Almanac*, p. 878.

18. Vietor, p. 142.

19. Ibid., p. 144.

20. Ibid.

21. Ross and Wolman, p. 20.

22. Vietor, p. 144.

23. Ibid., p. 149.

24. For an analysis that places the 1970 Clean Air Amendments in perspective, see Lennart Lundquist, *The Hare and the Tortoise: Clean Air Policies in*

the United States and Sweden (Ann Arbor: University of Michigan Press, 1980). For more on the significance of the 1970 legislation, see Jones, pp. 175–210; and Helen Ingrams, "The Political Rationality of Innovation: The Clean Air Act Amendments of 1970," pp. 12–56, in Ann Friedlander, ed., *Approaches to Controlling Air Pollution* (Cambridge: MIT Press, 1978).

25. For an overview of these developments, see David Vogel, *Lobbying the Corporation* (New York: Basic Books, 1978).

26. Norman J. Ornstein and Shirley Elder, *Interest Groups, Lobbying and Policymaking* (Washington, D.C.: Congressional Quarterly Services, 1978), p. 160.

27. Quoted in Jones, p. 145. For more on the political impact of "Earth Days," See James Wagner, "Washington Pressure: Environmental Teach-In," *National Journal*, February 21, 1970, pp. 408–11.

28. Jones, p. 146.

29. Ibid., p. 175.

30. Richard Corrigan, "Environment Report: Muskie Plays Dominant Role in Writing Tough New Air Pollution Law," *National Journal*, January 2, 1971, p. 29.

31. Anthony Downs, "Up and Down with Ecology: The Issue-Attention Cycle," *Public Interest* (Summer 1972): 27.

32. Gladwin Hill, "The Politics of Air Pollution: Public Interest and Pressure Groups," *Arizona Law Review* (Summer 1968), 10:41.

33. See, for example, John Esposito, *Vanishing Air* (New York: Grossman, 1970), esp. chaps. 4, 5.

34. Davies and Davies, p. 53.

35. Ibid.

36. Henry D. Jacoby and John D. Steinbruner, "The Context of Current Policy Discussions," in Henry D. Jacoby et al., eds., *Cleaning the Air* (Cambridge, Mass.: Balinger, 1973), pp. 10–11.

37. Hill, p. 42.

38. For an overall account of the efforts of both the state of California and the federal government to regulate motor vehicle air pollution, see James H. Krier and Edmond Ursin, *Pollution and Policy: A Case Essay on California and Federal Experience with Motor Vehicle Air Pollution, 1940–1975* (Berkeley: University of California Press, 1977). See also Edwin S. Mills and Lawrence J. White, "Government Policies Toward Automotive Emissions Control," Friedlander, ed., *Controlling Air Pollution*, pp. 348–418.

39. Jones, p. 178.

40. Ibid.

41. Ibid., p. 179.

42. "Pollution: Will Man Succeed in Destroying Himself?" Congressional Quarterly, January 30, 1970, p. 279.

43. Jones, p. 180.

44. Richard Corrigan, "HEW: Air Pollution Control," *National Journal*, May 9, 1970, p. 969.

45. Vietor, pp. 157–58.

46. Jones, p. 180.

47. Henry Steck, "Why Does Industry Always Get What It Wants?" *Environmental Action*, July 24, 1971, pp. 3–11. For more on NIPC, see idem, "Private Influence on Environmental Policy: The Case of the National Industrial Pollution Council," *Environmental Law* (1975), 5:241–81; and Richard H. K. Vietor, "The NIRCC: The Advisory Council Approach," *Journal Of Contemporary Business* (1979), 8:57–70.

48. Frank V. Fowlkes, "Washington Pressures: GM Gets Little Mileage from Compact, Low-Powered Lobby," *National Journal*, November 14, 1970, p. 2498.

49. "Clean Air Bill Cleared with Auto Emission Deadline," *1970 Congressional Quarterly Almanac* (Washington, D.C.: Congressional Quarterly Services, 1970), p. 478.

50. Ibid.

51. Vietor, "Advisory Council Approach," p. 158.

52. *1970 Congressional Quarterly Almanac*, p. 478.

52. Jones, p. 188.

54. Quoted in ibid., p. 192.

55. Ibid.

56. Ibid.

57. Fowlkes, p. 2511.

58. *1970 Congressional Quarterly Almanac*, p. 482.

59. Jones, p. 201.

60. *1970 Congressional Quarterly Almanac*, p. 483.

61. Jones, p. 207.

62. Corrigan, p. 30. The second quotation is from Jones, p. 196.

63. *1970 Congressional Quarterly Almanac*, p. 485.

64. Ibid.

65. Jones, p. 198.

66. Corrigan, p. 32.

67. Ibid.

68. "They're Not Giving up on Leaded 'Gas,'" *Chemical Week*, April 15, 1972, p. 58.

69. James Beizer, "Getting the Lead out Isn't Answer, Ethyl Says," *Iron Age*, August 15, 1970, p. 70.

70. "What Anti-Lead Uproar Means," *National Petroleum News* (April 1970): 47.

71. Corrigan, p. 32.

72. Beizer, p. 70.

73. Corrigan, p. 37.

74. Ibid., p. 26.

75. Ibid., p. 3.

76. Fowlkes, p. 2509.

77. See Krier and Ursin for a more detailed account of these conflicts, which began in the mid-1950s.

78. Fowlkes, p. 2504.

79. Ibid.

80. Ibid., p. 2511.

81. Ibid., p. 2498.

82. Ibid., p. 2507.

83. Jean Briggs, "Detroit and Congress: Eyeball to Eyeball," *Forbes*, February 15, 1977, p. 34.

84. *1976 Congressional Quarterly Almanac*, p. 137.

85. Ibid., p. 140.

86. Bernard Asbell, "The Outlawing of Next Year's Cars," *New York Times Magazine*, November 21, 1976, p. 86.

87. Ibid., p. 83.

88. Ibid.

89. Ibid.

90. Ibid.

91. Bernard Asbell, *The Senate Nobody Knows* (Baltimore: Johns Hopkins University Press, 1978), p. 197.

92. Pete Domenici, "Clean Air Act Amendments of 1977," *Natural Resources Journal* (July 1979), 19:476, 477.

93. Ornstein and Elder, p. 172.

94. Mercer Cross and Barry Hager, "Auto Workers, Manufacturers and Dealers Unite to Dilute Car Pollution Standards on Clean Air Bill," *Congressional Quarterly*, May 28, 1977, p. 1024.

95. *1977 Congressional Quarterly Almanac*, p. 636.

96. Jerry Hultin, "Unions, the Environment and Corporate Social Responsibility," *Yale Review of Law and Social Action* (Fall 1972), 3:51.

97. Ornstein and Elder, p. 172.

98. Ibid., p. 173.

99. Ibid., p. 181.

100. Ibid., p. 182.

101. Domenici, p. 478.

102. Ibid.

103. Ornstein and Elder, pp. 170–71.

104. Asbell, p. 86.

105. Ibid.

106. Al Gordon, "Environmentalists, Auto Makers, UAW Lobby . . . on Auto Emissions, Warranty Requirements," *Congressional Quarterly*, May 1, 1976, p. 1037.

107. Ibid.

108. *1977 Congressional Quarterly Almanac*, p. 131.

109. Ibid., p. 134.

110. Ibid.

111. Ornstein and Elder, p. 171.

112. J. Dicken Kirschten, "It's Washington Taking on Detroit in the Auto Pollution Game," *National Journal*, January 1, 1977.

113. Lawrence White, "The Auto Pollution Muddle," *Public Interest* (Summer 1973), 32:103.

114. *1976 Congressional Quarterly Almanac*, p. 140.

115. Arthur Mageda, "Environment Report: New Clean Air Provisions Respond to Local Complaints," *National Journal*, November 22, 1975, p.

1590. See also "The EPA's New Rules Hit City Planners," *Business Week*, December 7, 1974, p. 112.

116. Frank B. Friedman, "Oil and Air Do Not Mix: The Clean Air Act Amendments of 1977," *Institute on Oil and Gas Laws and Taxation* (1978), 29:333.

117. Richard H. K. Vietor, "The Evolution of Public Environmental Policy: The Case of No Significant Deterioration," *Environmental Review* (Winter 1979), 4:8.

118. Ibid., p. 11.

119. Ibid., p. 10.

120. Richard Vietor, "PSD: The Politics of Air Pollution" (Case distributed by the Intercollegiate Case Clearing House, 9-380-095 Rev., February 1980), p. 9.

121. Ibid., p. 10.

122. Vietor, "Evolution of Public Environmental Policy," p. 13.

123. Gordon, p. 1035.

124. Ibid.

125. Vietor, "PSD: The Politics of Air Pollution," p. 13.

126. Asbell, p. 446.

127. Ibid.

128. John Sheridan, "Clean Air Compromise," *Industry Week*, August 15, 1977, p. 17.

129. Ornstein and Elder, pp. 166–68.

130. Samuel Hays, "Clean Air: From the 1970 Act to the 1977 Amendments," *Duquesne Law Review* (1978–1979): 17:62.

131. Ibid., p. 63.

132. Vietor, "PSD: The Politics of Air Pollution," p. 11.

133. The statistics in this paragraph are from American Mining Congress, "Clean Air Act Issue Paper: Facts Relevant to the Copper Industry," Working Paper, March 2, 1981.

134. Department of Commerce, Bureau of the Census, *Census of Manufacturers* (Washington, D.C.: Government Printing Office, 1977).

135. Bruce A. Ackerman and William T. Hassler, *Clean Coal, Dirty Air* (New Haven: Yale University Press, 1981), p. 11.

136. See "Donald Cook Takes on the Environmentalists," *Business Week*, October 26, 1974, pp. 66–67.

137. Dick Kirschten, "Coal War in the East: Putting a Wall Around Ohio," *National Journal*, January 13, 1979, p. 50.

138. *1977 Congressional Quarterly Almanac*, p. 63.

139. Ackerman and Hassler, p. 29.

140, Kirschten, p. 51.

141. Department of Commerce, Bureau of the Census, *Census of Mineral Industries* (Washington, D.C.: Government Printing Office, 1977).

APPENDIX

INDIVIDUALS INTERVIEWED

John Adams, Huntin & Williams

C. B. Arrington, Jr., Atlantic Richfield

Richard Ayres, Natural Resources Defense Council

Robert Baum, Edison Electric Institute

Katherine Bennett, Crown Zellerbach, Washington Office

Bruce Beyaert, Chevron, San Francisco

Leon Billings, Former Staff, Senate Committee

David Branard, American Mining Congress

Virginia Burdick, Journalist, Government Research Corporation, *National Journal*

Frank Chapman, Atlantic Richfield

Jeffrey Conley, E. Bruce Harrison Company, Staff, NEDA-CAP

Philip Cummings, Senate Committee, Minority Staff

Jerry Dodson, Staff, Waxman House Subcommittee

Esther Foer, Environmental Industry Council

F. B. Friedman, Atlantic Richfield

Albert Fry, Business Roundtable, Air Quality Project

Peter Fury, California Council on Economics and Environmental Quality, San Francisco

Ivan Gillman, Chevron, San Francisco

Stanley Greenfield, formally at EPA

Mark Griffiths, Office of Environmental Affairs, National Association of Manufacturers

David Hawkins, Natural Resources Defense Council

John Klocko, DuPont, Washington Office

R. W. Kreitzen, Manager, Environmental Affairs, Chevron, San Francisco

Bobby Lamb, American Petroleum Institute

David Litvin, Kennicott, Washington Office

Fred Maeder, Attorney, Winston & Strawn

Earl Mallic, U.S. Steel, Washington Office

Joseph Mullan, National Coal Association

A. F. Pope, Atlantic Richfield

Carl Pope, Sierra Club, San Francisco

Charles Powers, Former Lobbyist, Cummins Engine

J. R. Radle, Atlantic Richfield

Dan Rathburn, American Petroleum Institute

Paul Rogers, Former Congressman

Jeff Schwartz, Former Majority Staff, House Committee

Philip Shabacoff, *New York Times*, Washington Office
D. M. Smith, Atlantic Richfield, Formerly at EPA
Martin Smith, Staff, Minority, House Committee
Andy Van Horn, Teknekron, San Francisco
Murray Weidenbaum, Chairman, Council of Economic Advisors
Earle Young, American Iron and Steel Institute

INDEX

DAVID VOGEL is Professor of Business and Public Policy at the Haas School of Business, University of California, Berkeley.